HANDBOOK OF PRESCHOOL SPECIAL EDUCATION

Allen A. Mori, Ph.D.
Associate Professor
Department of Special Education
University of Nevada, Las Vegas
Las Vegas, Nevada

and

Jane Ellsworth Olive, M.A., M.Ed.
President
Newborn Education and Development, Inc.
Las Vegas, Nevada

AN ASPEN PUBLICATION®
Aspen Systems Corporation
Rockville, Maryland
London
1980

Library of Congress Cataloging in Publication Data

Mori, Allen A.
Handbook of preschool special education.

Bibliography: p. 503.
Includes index.
1. Education, Preschool.   2. Ability—Testing.
3. Child development—Evaluation.   4. Perceptual-
motor learning.   I. Olive, Jane Ellsworth, joint
author.   II. Title.
LB1140.2.M66   371.9   80-14199
ISBN: 0-89443-276-1

Library of Congress Catalog Card Number: 80-14199
ISBN: 0-89443-276-1

Printed in the United States of America

1 2 3 4 5

Table of Contents

Preface

The field of special education, and particularly the provision of early intervention to infants and toddlers with special needs, is emerging as a national priority. There is a sense of urgency in this effort for it is now recognized that intervention must begin in the earliest weeks and months of life if these children are to reach their utmost levels of ability. This text is an attempt to fill certain gaps in the available literature concerning this subject. Our work with parents, professionals, paraprofessionals, and children has demonstrated the need to combine materials on general developmental theory and assessment with pragmatic methods of preparing practitioners and parents to become effective teachers of these special infants and toddlers.

To assist in this effort, Part I presents suggestions for the development and implementation of intervention programs. We have included suggestions for a paraprofessional training program and comments that may be useful to more effective and expeditious resolution of parental grief. A major portion of this section of the text deals with the basic principles of teaching, including behavior modification, a positive environment for maximizing learning, the use of imitation, games, manipulation, and an explanation of the importance of the discovery method of teaching. Further training on the maximal use of the human sensory system, developmental theory, the importance of gross and fine motor skill activities, and in the enrichment of language stimulation for the child is provided. The importance of independence, self-esteem, and self-help skills is stressed in this training section. Included are enrichment activities toward the foundations of academic learning for the benefit of those children who are able to conceptualize and maximize their intellectual achievements and a glossary of terms for the convenience of those who are not professional educators.

Part II is a compilation of lesson plan activities that are based upon major developmental goals in five important areas of growth: reflex/gross motor, perceptual/fine motor, sensory/cognitive, language, and personal/ social/self-help. Within each of these lesson plans are goals and specific objectives, suggested teaching activities, instructional materials for use, language cues, and comments that may prove helpful to the trainer.

We have come to recognize that busy people need to learn teaching principles and plan lessons quickly and well. Thus we have chosen a simple, concise "look-and-do" approach to the pragmatic sections of this book. We have included Skinnerian type drills to expedite the adult learning process. We appreciate the fact that practitioners must be able to quickly find the teaching materials that relate to the developmental goals they are currently implementing. Therefore, we have numerically coordinated the assessment checklist and developmental goals with the appropriate lesson plans.

These lessons and the teaching methods suggested are applicable to all children. Each device may be adapted and modified for the individual child's needs. Flexibility in use has been perceived as one of the criteria for the development of these materials.

It is our sincere hope that the reader of this text will feel optimistic about taking on the awesome task of teaching the young child with special needs. Those who overcome the discouragements involved and their own emotional resistance will discover gratifying associations. They will become more sensitive to the needs and feelings of others; they will discover methods of teaching and influencing the learning of those they work with; and they will become more appreciative of the miracle of life and human growth and development.

Allen A. Mori, Ph.D.
and
Jane Ellsworth Olive, M.A., M.Ed.
September 1980

Acknowledgments

Many people have directly and indirectly contributed to the completion of this textbook. The pioneering efforts of people like Montessori, B. L. White, W. S. Stoner, J. Beck, S. and T. Engelmann, Alice Hayden, Valentine Dmitriev, Verna Hart, Louise Phillips, S. Bluma, D.E. Shearer, M. Shearer, A. Frohman, J. Hilliard, A.D. Quick, A.A. Campbell, and others too numerous to mention have influenced the direction of this work. We owe special thanks to the parents and special children with whom we have worked for many years. The adults have given us a realistic perception of the needs and capabilities of human beings who must cope with difficult and complex problems. Each child has demonstrated to us that every human being can make a loving contribution to the lives of others.

The senior author would be remiss in not acknowledging his wife Barbara Mori. To her I owe unlimited appreciation for her love, support, constant encouragement, and patience throughout the many years it took to complete this book. My daughter Kirsten Lynn Mori was a continual source of learning about the miracle of human development. The joy and love she gave me was a steady source of needed inspiration.

The coauthor wishes to thank Elmo and Charlotte Rowberry Ellsworth, who have contributed to this effort for decades. Grateful thanks are extended to them, to my children, and the friends who have expressed confidence in me and in this work.

Special thanks are extended to Karen Bloomdahl, who spent countless hours typing and retyping this manuscript, to Liz Ream, who provided us with so many thoughtful suggestions and enthusiastic support, and to John Pendleton for his steadfast encouragement and consideration.

An Overview of Early Intervention for Youngsters with Special Needs

Special educators are rapidly entering an era of exciting promise regarding early intervention services to preschool handicapped children. More recently they have discovered the need to extend this intervention to infants and toddlers. Certainly if special educators are to embark upon such an awesome venture, it will be necessary to employ effective planning prior to any implementation in order to maximize the impact of our resources. The first part of this text has been written for professionals, paraprofessionals, and parents who have an interest in developing, designing, implementing, or participating in programs for handicapped infants and toddlers. Chapter 1 presents an extensive discussion of the rationale for early intervention along with an in-depth presentation of principles of child growth and development in the areas of reflex/gross motor, perceptual/fine motor, sensory/cognitive, language, and personal/social/self-help. In addition, this chapter presents the rationale for dividing the first three years of life into five developmental phases.

Chapter 2 provides a detailed analysis of assessment, including an overview of the various standardized instruments that can be used to gather information about a child's performance. The second part of this chapter is devoted to an explanation of the use of the direct data-based system that we have designed to be used with the teaching materials presented in Part II.

Chapter 3 focuses on the steps that must be taken to plan early intervention programs. Included as topics in this chapter are approaches for involving parents in the program, a training program for paraprofessionals, and two special sections written specifically for the helping practitioner and the parent of a handicapped preschooler.

The final chapter in Part I considers the important principles of teaching methodology. This chapter adopts a "Skinnerian" approach to self-learning and self-teaching that will be extremely valuable to the inservice practitioner, the parent, or the preservice student.

Chapter 1

Early Intervention and the Development of the Young Child

EARLY INTERVENTION: A PERSPECTIVE

Early intervention, the delivery of special educational services to young handicapped children, is a relatively new phenomenon. Since the early 1960s there has been an increasing appreciation for the special needs and special problems that children with handicaps have during their early years. Certainly much emphasis has been placed upon the first few years of life as a critical period and time for great learning to take place.

During the late 1950s and early 1960s, pioneer efforts (Kirk, 1958; Hunt, 1961; Bloom, 1964) gave birth to the notion that external experiential and environmental factors could greatly influence and enhance the course of a child's development. In 1965 the national Head Start Program created a new public focus on the importance of early education. As Caldwell (1973) noted, regardless of the problems and limitations, Head Start was a milestone in preschool education. For the first time large numbers of young children were exposed to mass screening programs that had the potential for identifying and perhaps remediating problems at an early age. Further, the program focused upon the needs of the total child and set about to remediate deficiencies whether they were medical, educational, or nutritional (Caldwell, 1973).

The motivation and support for early intervention with young handicapped children may be largely traced to three events. Tjossem (1976) noted that these factors or events were as follows:

1. the notion of plasticity of the central nervous system during infancy and the toddler years
2. animal research indicating the beneficial effects of early stimulation upon the developing organism

3. evaluations of various experimental intervention programs provided during the first three years of life.

Plasticity of the Central Nervous System

In describing various research data in the new field of neurobiology, Lipton (1976) concluded that the environment in which an infant lives after birth determines the extent to which potentialities will be reached as well as the exact form they will take. For example, the hereditary aspects of the central nervous system create the possibility for the development of a language, but environmental factors determine the number of words learned and the language the child will speak. Further, Lipton (1976) noted the implications of this research for early intervention:

1. Heredity and environment will always interact because the plasticity of the central nervous system is genetically assured.
2. Learning is not merely an accumulation of isolated factors, but actually an elaboration and differentiation of already existent behavioral possibilities.
3. Critical learning periods exist, thus facilitating maximal learning.
4. The individual's ability to learn is largely influenced by those environmental contingencies which the child assimilates into existing cognitive structures.

Animal Research on the Effects of Early Stimulation

Denenberg (1969) has noted that 20 years of research with rats has suggested that the way in which the animal is handled in infancy has profound and far-reaching effects on the behavioral responses of the adult rat. In describing deprivation studies with dogs, Thompson and Heron (1954) discovered that those terriers raised in isolation showed significant problems in responding to various tasks.

While the various studies of deprivation with primates have yielded mixed results, it appears that chimpanzees raised in human homes are capable of complex responses far beyond the capabilities of chimpanzees raised in laboratories or in nature (Hayes, 1951). One fact remains largely indisputable—early experiences have a profound impact upon the development of young chimpanzees. Clearly, when various environmental variables are manipulated, critical developmental milestones can be accelerated or retarded.

The overall evaluation of the results of animal research tends to support the critical importance of stimulating experiences during early infancy.

While direct applications to human development must be tendered with some caution, it appears that stimulation to human infants during the time when complex neural patterns are being formed is extremely important.

Intervention during the Early Years of Life

Two early studies (Skeels & Dye, 1939; Kirk, 1958) provided empirical evidence that allowed early intervention to move from the theoretical, buttressed by animal research, to the practical. In the Skeels and Dye (1939) study, a group of young orphans was taken to an institution for the mentally retarded and given enriching experiences by retarded adolescent girls. A similar, and somewhat less "deprived," control group was not moved to different surroundings. After an experimental period of one and one-half years, the experimental group had an average IQ gain of 28 points. After two and one-half years, the control group showed a loss of 26 points on an IQ measure. After 30 years the groups were examined again and the results remained startlingly in favor of the original enriched children. This adult group had achieved total independence and self-support with educational achievement that far surpassed the control group.

In 1958, Kirk reported the results of a study in which groups of retarded children three to six years of age were provided enriched preschool educational experiences versus a group of retarded youngsters who did not receive these experiences. After a period of several years had elapsed, 70 percent of youngsters receiving the special preschool educational program showed IQ gains that ranged from 10 to 30 points. In contrast, the control group showed a decline in IQ scores with the differences being statistically significant. Kirk (1958) was able to further demonstrate that the gains were sustained for a number of years subsequent to the preschool experience.

In 1969 the first of a group of projects, which were to become known as the First Chance Network, was funded by the Bureau of Education for the Handicapped. Now nearly 200 projects are operating throughout the United States for the purpose of demonstrating service delivery models to handicapped preschoolers and their parents. Young children served by these projects have a much greater chance of entering regular education programs rather than special education programs once they reach school age (DeWeerd, 1977). Further, in evaluating the gains made by a random sample of children in First Chance projects, the Battelle Center concluded that many of the children gained one and one-half to two times more than would have been expected had they not received any project experiences.

In reviewing the results of 40 longitudinal intervention programs for high risk and handicapped young children, Steadman (1977) summarized the results as follows:

1. The manner in which the child is raised and the environment he is reared in have the major impact on how he will develop.
2. Factors such as race and sex do not appear to be related to the child's ability to experience gains from intervention programs.
3. The family's methods of establishing social roles support the notion that early family environment (parental language styles, attitudes toward achievement, parental involvement, and concern for the child) has a significant impact on the child's development before he becomes two years old.
4. In situations where families are so disorganized that they cannot supply a supportive environment, an intensive external supportive environment may contribute to the youngster's development.
5. The effects of a stimulating or depriving environment appear to be most powerful in the early years of childhood when most rapid growth and development take place. The primary focus of the child during these early years is the home. Thus intervention programs with the home focus or programs with a one-to-one teacher–child ratio appear to be the most effective in stimulating developmental gains.
6. Evidence supports the notion that parental involvement greatly strengthens early intervention programs.
7. Due to lack of appropriate controls, it is possible to describe program intervention conditions that lead to success in only general terms.
8. The socioeconomic status and entry level IQ of the child are not certain predictors of the child's ability to profit from an intervention program.
9. There is strong evidence that intervention during the first two years of life will be more effective than intervention efforts begun at later years.
10. A child's social and intellectual development during the period from four to six years can be greatly enhanced by an organized intervention program.
11. The effects of intervention programs last only during the time the child is in the program. Effects tend to be sustained longer when the child is in home-based as opposed to school-based programs.
12. Follow-up studies of children in intervention programs generally show that the initial gains are no longer measurable. It is often not possible to cite the reasons for this failure to sustain early gains.
13. One of the major determinants of program success is the quality and motivation of the professional staff.

It appears that in spite of methodological flaws, lack of variable control, lack of appropriate instruments, narrow program focus, small sample sizes, and the possible effects of continuous measurement (Hawthorne effect), children in successful early intervention programs make gains that would not occur in the absence of these programs.

Much remains to be done including work on nutrition and prevention of birth defects or other handicaps, child identification and assessment (DeWeerd, 1977). Further, as Steadman (1977, p. 12) noted, it is critical that research be conducted "in the field with carefully described curriculum components and the best child variable control possible, within bounds of natural groupings of children," to further validate and document the effects of early intervention.

THE DEVELOPMENT OF THE YOUNG CHILD

Significant developmental influences begin at the exact moment of conception. During the first few days after conception, the fetus receives its nourishment from the woman's body. In the early stages, the first two months prenatally, the fetus grows from the head to the tail (known as cephalo-caudal development) and from the inside towards the outside (known as proximo-distal development). During the gestation period, the fetus undergoes development that includes differentiation and integration of the body's internal organs and the growth of the fetus in height and weight. Also during this prenatal period, various factors may have a detrimental effect upon the developing fetus. Included among these factors are inadequate nutrition, radiation, drugs, toxins and other pollutants, infections, and maternal stress.

Prenatal Development

Inappropriate nutrition during the fetal period will cause lasting damage to the development of the central nervous system. During the first trimester when major brain growth occurs, fetal malnutrition results in both reduced numbers of brain cells and insufficient brain cell growth. This malnutrition may be caused by poor maternal diet or insufficient nutrition as well as placental insufficiency. Placental insufficiency may be caused by closely spaced pregnancies as well as too frequent pregnancies in addition to maternal nutritional deficiencies.

In addition to the problems nutritional deficiencies may cause the developing fetus, radiation poses a serious hazard. Radiation, whether it comes from overdosage from a typical X-ray or exposure to dosages of atomic radiation, has been proven to cause serious deformities in both physical and mental development.

Drugs, whether those prescribed by a physician or those of the illegal street type, present serious hazards to the fetus. Without belaboring the point, sufficient evidence exists to substantiate the deleterious effects of heroin, LSD, and even marijuana. The problem of maternal drug use was tragically brought under public scrutiny by the thalidomide disaster of over 20 years ago. Thalidomide was thought to be a nonharmful tranquilizing agent until many women using the drug produced grossly deformed children. Other "drugs" such as tobacco and alcohol have been proven to produce premature and low birth weight babies.

Toxins and other pollutants may pose serious hazards to the unborn child. Various industrial chemicals, insecticides, cleaning agents, and airborne toxins all have the potential of retarding fetal brain development. Additionally, possible relationships exist between exposure to these chemicals and the incidence of low birth weight babies.

Maternal exposure to rubella, hepatitis, syphilis, toxoplasmosis, and other infections may cause serious damage to the central nervous system of the fetus. Further, such infections have caused serious physical deformities as well, including cardiac, pulmonary, auditory, and visual problems.

Maternal stress is another factor that may affect fetal growth and development. Pregnant women who are highly anxious, resent the pregnancy, do not want the child, or have serious personal or marital problems may unknowingly create problems for their unborn child. These stresses may result in birth complications or frequent illness in the child in later years.

Problems in Development during the Perinatal Period

The perinatal period, or the actual birth process, can be complicated by many factors. Included among these factors are a breech or transverse presentation, extremely prolonged labor, low birth weight, prematurity, and anoxia. The latter three are both serious and common enough to merit further explanation.

Low birth weight, while often a combined factor with prematurity, can also occur in full-term babies whose weight is less than expected. Low birth weight may be associated with later intellectual and/or behavioral problems, as well as genetic disorders. Therefore, low birth weight poses a serious threat to the child in spite of recent advances in neonatal intensive care.

Premature babies are those who have a gestational period of less than 38 weeks and/or a birth weight of less than 2,500 grams (5.5 pounds). Factors related to the birth of premature babies include maternal health and prenatal status, the socioeconomic status of the mother, and the mother's usage of tobacco. Often premature infants present difficult problems of development. Because they may have problems breathing, swallowing, and maintaining a stable body temperature, premature babies are often placed in incubators to control their temperature and assist with breathing and feeding. Due to the myriad problems of prematurity, premature babies are often at risk for later learning and/or behavioral problems.

The third problem associated with the perinatal period is and may be described as oxygen deprivation and, if prolonged, w   . in serious and irreversible damage to the brain. Depending upon the length of time the brain is deprived of oxygen, the damage to the brain can result in cerebral palsy, mental retardation, speech and language handicaps, learning disabilities, and behavioral disorders. The two most common causes of anoxia are the interference of the blood flow through the umbilical cord because it is twisted or wrapped around the child and severe maternal hemorrhaging that also decreases blood flow.

Development during Infancy and Early Childhood

The first few months of life are considered a period of time that infants spend adjusting to their new environment. During this time, infants possess a number of sensorimotor reflexive behaviors that: allow them to lift their heads off the mattress when in the prone (on the stomach) position; startle if they hear a loud noise or are moved swiftly through space; curl their toes if the souls of their feet are touched; locate and then suck an object placed near their lips; and blink their eye if the eyelid is touched.

Between four and six weeks of age, infants begin to exert more influence on their world. The four-to six-week-old infants will regard objects and briefly follow them, regard an adult's face, begin to regard their hands, hold their fist in their mouth, and tightly grasp objects placed in their hands.

By the time infants reach four to six months, they will be able to roll over, hold their heads steady, laugh, smile, discriminate strangers, and often sit with support. Between eight months and 18 months, the children's sensorimotor abilities become extensive. Children will usually crawl at eight months, stand and hold on to furniture at 10 months, and walk between 12 and 15 months. The children will also be able to locate sounds well and by 15 months will have a vocabulary of four to eight words. During this time, infants will also show interest in cause and effect and develop a high level of curiosity and exploratory behavior.

From two to three years of age, the toddler will show an interest in social peer interaction, an increase in awareness, make great use of small sentences and engage in conversations, have a great deal of curiosity and interest, anticipate consequences, and deal with abstractions.

The course of typical development through infancy and into the toddler period can be adversely affected by a number of factors. Surprisingly, one of the major factors resulting in handicapping conditions in the birth to three population is accidents. Accidents involving poisoning, falls, and injuries to the head may result in brain damage and subsequent mental retardation.

Disease and infections, particularly those resulting in high fever, can have a harmful effect on the child. Respiratory infections, meningitis, encephalitis, rubella, measles, chicken pox, and the like may all result in permanent damage to the child.

Malnutrition and other forms of deprivation or abuse may have serious ramifications for development. In combination, these factors may result in physical, intellectual, and emotional handicaps that greatly retard normal development. Children who are raised in a nonstimulating environment rarely do well in the areas of intellectual and social skill development. Burton White (1975) notes that the period from eight months to three years is a period of great importance in a child's life. If adults wait until a child is two years old to begin a program of educational development, it may already be too late.

Finally, various conditions may likewise be present at birth and greatly affect early development both quantitatively and qualitatively. This would include chromosomal abnormalities like Down's Syndrome resulting in mental retardation, cerebral palsy resulting in physical and/or intellectual handicaps, otosclerosis resulting in hearing loss, and congenital cataracts that may result in visual impairments. For youngsters in this category (that is, the handicap is readily recognized in the first year of life) early intervention is crucial. Since development occurs along a continuum of relatively predictable events, it is important to remember that handicaps may cause serious deviations from this normal pattern. Thus far this chapter has presented an overview of normal development along with various influences or factors that may affect the child's growth. The focus has been upon normal growth and development and the ways in which the expected developmental pattern could be interrupted by genetic or environmental factors. The remaining sections of this chapter will examine the five important areas of development along with the key phases within these areas. The five major areas are: (1) reflex/gross motor, (2) perceptual/fine motor, (3) sensory/cognitive, (4) language, and (5) personal/social/self-help.

Reflex/Gross Motor Development

As indicated previously, development follows the cephalo-caudal and proximo-distal principles. Cephalo-caudal (head to tail) development can be observed in newborn infants who display much rotary head movement in the supine position. However, the dominating head movement is rotation to one side causing the tonic neck reflex (t-n-r) movement of the arms. At approximately four months of age, infants will assume a spontaneous midposition placement of their heads with rather symmetrical arm positioning. By about six months of age the t-n-r disappears, and infants are capable of turning their heads without the associated movement of the arms. While exceptions do exist, body and motor skill development occurs downward beginning with the neck, then following with arms, chest, back, and legs.

The proximo-distal principle of development suggests that development occurs from the body's midpoint out to the body's extremities. As will be discussed in detail later in this section, early arm movements are gross and undifferentiated shoulder movements with further growth and development bringing movements of the elbow, then the wrist, and finally the fine finger movements.

Also at six months of age, children begin to lift their heads, and one month later will have sufficient muscular development to hold their heads erect and steady. By the seventh month the nonhandicapped child will achieve independent head lift from a supine position, certainly suggestive that an independent sitting position is imminent. Abnormal patterns of motor development in head control may be noted in the child of six to seven months whose head is held unsteadily or pushed backward or away from the body midline.

Following both cephalo-caudal and proximo-distal principles, head and neck development are followed by development of the arms and hands. Nonhandicapped infants will exhibit their first attempts at reaching for suspended objects within their reach around four months. These early reaching attempts are characterized by lack of coordination and direction as the children are likely to end up with their hand(s) in their mouth rather than on the offered object.

Usually within one month of these early reaching attempts, children are able to perform more coordinated, smoother, and better directed arm approaches to objects. These improved movements are bilateral (two-handed) and do not become one-handed until children are approximately seven months of age.

As this development unfolds, body posture and locomotion are determined by the degree of development of the trunk (chest and back) and the legs. Remember that children do not develop any specific motor skill in total isolation, simply adding new skills like building blocks in a tower. Rather motor skill development occurs along a continuum with related skills developing simultaneously and eventually becoming fully integrated, merged, and coordinated as a skill. Such is the case with posture and locomotion. Once again, the cephalo-caudal principle owns that children begin with head control, then progress to sitting, crawling, creeping, standing, cruising, walking with support, and, finally, independent walking.

While supported sitting may occur in infants as young as four months, it isn't until children are between six and seven months that they can sit briefly on a firm surface without support or assistance. Observation of children of this age sitting reveals a sitting posture characterized by a broad, somewhat diamond-shaped "base" with the knees resting on the surface and the back bent forward for appropriate balance. In this position, children are not truly sitting independently since the hands are braced on the floor for support and thus not usable for exploration or play. From eight to nine months infants begin to develop the skills to maintain forward balance. The arms will come off the floor, the back will become more erect, and the sitting base will become substantially smaller or narrower. Then by nine to ten months, children develop sufficient balance to sit and "scoot" around regardless of leg-base position. In this posture, children's arms and hands are completely free to engage in exploration or play. The children can move about using only their legs; they rarely lose this balance that would result in falling backward from this position.

From the sitting position many children will proceed through a stage of development called crawling (i.e., dragging the body along a surface with the stomach touching the surface using movements of the arms and legs). Early developmental skills preceding actual crawling include various arm, chest, and leg movements or postural adjustments in the prone position. These movements begin at two months with head lifting and continue through six months when children roll from supine to prone and are able to remove their arms from beneath their chest.

At seven to eight months infants will usually exhibit their first coordinated movements aimed at locomotion. At this time the symmetric movement of arms and legs gives children the appearance of swimming. This position is not effective for movement, however, and soon gives way to an alternating and coordinated flexing and extending of the arms and legs and results in an ability to crawl.

The crawling movement generally lasts only a few weeks. By nine months, infants elevate the trunk and are able to assume the more upright creeping position. Early movements in this position reflect a rocking motion as the infants attempt to master the necessary alternating movements and balance required to creep successfully. Nonhandicapped infants of ten months are usually able to master creeping along with the integration of movement from the prone position smoothly into a sitting position and back into a creeping position. At this point infants are capable of movement almost anywhere in their environment.

At this particular point (ten months) infants can assume a totally erect or standing posture. Previous development that allows infants to achieve this posture includes reflexive neonatal stepping responses, leg extension and some weight bearing at three to three and one-half months, and almost total weight bearing and active running when held firmly around the chest at seven to eight months. By nine months infants can stand at their crib rail or at a low table without leaning their chest against the support item. By ten months infants can achieve the standing position and the sitting position in a coordinated fashion.

By 12 to 13 months infants have developed the ability to walk forward when both their hands are held. Additionally they will be able to cruise around their crib, playpen, or other furniture. Cruising is the locomotive movement in which infants walk sideways, moving one leg out, then bringing the other leg in toward the first leg. At the same time youngsters make these leg movements, they move their hands along the object. Within the space of a few weeks, infants will "walk" by taking a few forward steps into the arms of a waiting parent.

From this point, although an "average" age would be about 15 months, the infant achieves truly independent walking. Independent walking is characterized by the infants' getting to their feet unaided and toddling about in a rigid, wide stance. As youngsters grow and have the opportunity to practice walking, a smoother and more coordinated walk replaces the rigid, wide stance.

Perceptual/Fine Motor Development

Perception, or the interpretation of data gathered by our senses, is greatly related to cognitive development in human beings. Perception and fine motor skill development are seen as meriting separate categorization since it is through the development of these areas that children will master the intellectual demands of their world. It will be through the perceptual and fine motor processes that children become gatherers of information about their environment. Later children will integrate, rearrange, recall, and employ information in such a fashion as to indicate advanced cognitive development.

Early visual perception begins with fixations on large, moving, and distinctive objects brought directly into the infants' line of vision. By two months of age, infants will be able to focus clearly on objects at distances of about one-half to one foot. At this age, infants will show a particular interest in black and white faces or forms. By four months of age nonhandicapped infants can focus their eyes on all objects at all distances. Also at this age, infants have developed visual convergence (the ability to look at an object with both eyes), and by four months will be able to follow objects 180 degrees across their line of vision. Progressively infants will, at four to eight months, attend to objects dropped from their sight. By the time infants reach 10 to 15 months of age, they will pay attention to visual attributes of objects, begin to perceive roundness, identify forms, and associate the visual experience of objects with representations of those objects. Finally, by the time children are three years of age, they will have a well-developed visual memory and be able to copy or reproduce by drawing objects presented visually upon request.

Auditory perception during the neonatal period can be detected by the cessation or reduction of activity that occurs when a bell is rung or a rattle is shaken near infants' heads. By the sixth or seventh week, infants will appear to be interested in the sounds around them and by three months of age will be interested in listening to the sounds they can make with their mouths. At about six months of age infants will be able to localize the source of sound by turning their heads appropriately. Also during this time and well into the eighth month, infants will show an increasing interest in the sounds of their world. Further interest develops in listening to self-produced sounds; and eventually at eight to nine months, infants will respond selectively to a number of common words. White (1975) noted that the first spoken words of babies with English as a major spoken language are mama, dada, bye-bye, and baby.

Further perceptual/fine motor skill development occurring in early developmental periods includes the development of grasping and releasing skills. Infants do not possess the first prerequisite for grasping, the open hand, until about three months of age. At five months of age, infants will have developed sufficiently to demonstrate prehension or the integration of visual perceptual (eye-hand skills) with approach to the object, grasping it, and retaining it. The grasp of infants of six months moves from the palm or whole-hand grasp, to radial (off center with thumb opposition) at seven months of age, and then to a more adult pattern of finger usage around eight months of age. At this time, infants begin to acquire more specialized finger usage although hands are still used like paws to "rake" objects toward the infants. By ten months most infants will develop what is called the inferior pincer grasp. That is, while infants can use their index finger and thumb to pluck a small object from a surface, the arm must be braced against the surface for major support. The inferior pincer becomes a neat pincer grasp at twelve months when infants are capable of deftly plucking a small object from a surface using only their fingertips without arm support.

Release, a more mature task than the grasp, appears around ten months of age. It can be observed when infants place an object such as a cube on a surface and then deftly remove their hand from the object. From 10 to 12 months infants will be able to release objects correctly into containers (cubes into a cup). At 15 months skills are sufficiently integrated to allow infants to place a small pellet into a narrow top bottle and construct a tower of two, one-inch cubes. By 18 months, a tower of three cubes becomes a possibility along with the ability to throw a ball from a standing position.

Sensory/Cognitive Development

In many ways, the area of cognitive development in the period from birth to three years of age is a subtle blend of other major developmental areas. For cognitive development to occur, infants and toddlers must be able to perceive, recognize, organize, categorize, and understand. For many this definition implies an ability to interpret, adapt, and act in one's environmental setting.

No discussion of the cognitive development of young children is complete without mention of the brilliant work and theories of Jean Piaget. Piaget described four broad areas of cognitive growth spanning birth to adulthood. For the purposes of this text, the discussion shall focus only on those areas that pertain to children age three and younger. Piaget theorized that the mind contains a number of structures that he referred to as *schema*. At birth an infant's schema or *brain plans* consist of innate automatic reflexes and a few crude explorations performed by the mouth, hands, and eyes. For example, newborns will suck anything put to their mouths; then in only a short time infants begin to differentiate between milk-producing and nonmilk-producing stimuli, generally rejecting the latter. Additional schema become a part of the human mind as infants continue to explore the environment, thus collecting brain plans much as an aspiring chef would begin forming a card file of gourmet recipes. As the quantity of data increases the individual continues to differentiate, forming new associations and generalizations, creating a cycle of intellectual refinement. This process of accumulating new schema through perceptions to form concepts is called assimilation.

To illustrate this learning process picture a child with his parents walking through a pet store. As the child approaches a cage with a monkey inside he says, "Mommy, see doggy." In this case, if the child is serious, he sifted through his memory file and came up with the schema that fit the object. The closest he found was one that had four legs, brown hair and a tail, and was about the same size as a dog. Of course, the response was logical but incorrect. Such an experience enables children to add new things (monkeys) or see old things in new ways by adding features to the present schema. As Wadsworth (1971) explained, the assimilation process theoretically does not change the development of the schema but does change its growth, which can be compared to a balloon. As more air is added (assimilation growth) schema are broadened, but the balloon doesn't change its shape (development). Since schema do change—adult schema are different from children's—another process must take place. Piaget calls this process accommodation.

There are many times that children are introduced to a new stimulus but find it impossible to assimilate this new data into their present schemata; therefore, they can do one of two things—create a new schema or change the existing schema so it will fit. Either of the choices are forms of accommodation and result in a change in or development of schemata. Once children have used a method of accommodation, the new stimulus can be assimilated. In this growing process the final product is always assimilation (Wadsworth, 1971).

The coaction of these two processes adds a two-dimensional characteristic to mental development. Assimilation (the addition of new features) provides a quantitative change as accommodation (the subtraction of features or creation of a new schema) imposes a qualitative change. The balance between these two processes is called equilibrium.

Piaget identifies four broad growth periods in which assimilation and accommodation will take place: (1) sensorimotor, (2) preoperational thought, (3) concrete operations, and (4) formal operations.

The first period of sensorimotor development (birth to two years old) is marked by six separate stages. The infants' behaviors in stage one (0 to one month) are reflexive in nature as evidenced by grasping, sucking, crying, and gross arm movements. At this point all stimuli are assimilated, producing a reflex schema that has no differentiation. In stage two (one to four months) the reflexive behaviors present in stage one begin to be modified. Selectivity can be observed and infants begin to differentiate between milk-producing and nonmilk-producing things. Some additional behaviors include habitual thumb sucking (hand-mouth coordination) and following objects with the eyes (eye coordination). By stage three (four to eight months) infants' behavior becomes less egocentric as they become increasingly aware of objects within the immediate environment, grasping and manipulating them. Reproductive assimilation also appears as infants intentionally try to grasp objects that are interesting to them. As the end of the first year draws near, the first clear pattern of intellectual behavior emerges in the fourth stage (eight to twelve months). Now infants begin to use two or more concepts, thoughts, or acts to evoke a different response. Wadsworth (1971, p. 48) states that "children can be seen to set aside one object (means) to get to another object (end). A pillow is moved out of the way to reach a toy."

At the time of stage five (12–18 months) a higher level of cognitive thought develops through utilization of new schemata to solve new problems. Previous to this stage the infants' only means to solving problems was through the application of old schemata. Now, the infants' ingenuity is elaborated as experimentation through trial and error creates new means to solving daily problems. In stage six (18–24 months) sensorimotor experimentations are replaced by cognitive representation. Where toddlers formerly solved problems by manipulating objects through trial and error, they now "think" or invent a solution to elementary motor problems. Piaget (1952) observed this occurrence:

> At 1:10 (27) Lucienne tries to kneel before a stool, but, by leaning against it pushes it further away. She then raises herself up, takes it and places it against the sofa. When it is firmly set there, she leans against it and kneels without difficulty (p. 338).

The termination of the sensorimotor period is not the end of toddlers' sensorimotor development; however, from this point forward, conceptual development will take place primarily through conceptual-symbolic means, not by motor activity. The development of language, higher cognitive operations, and behavioral changes are the major attainments as toddlers enter the preoperational period.

During the preoperational period (2–7 years) toddlers and young children make a transition from direct sensorimotor actions to representative symbolic behaviors. No longer are toddlers required to physically manipulate objects, as objects and events now possess labels acquired from a rapidly developing language.

Language, the major developmental aspect of this period, begins with one-word sentences called holophrases, expanding by age four to an understanding of spoken language and the use of grammatical rules.

The acquisition of language, although recognized by Piaget as extremely important to intellectual development, is not imperative. Research studies involving blind and deaf children illustrate that, despite an omission of verbal language, children can develop logical thought patterns through the same sequential stages as nonhandicapped children (Piaget & Inhelder, 1969). The difference occurs in the length of time taken to reach each stage. Language, Piaget maintains, is a facilitator of intellectual life and/or logical thought, but not an essential prerequisite.

In the acquisition of intellectual behavior, Piaget identifies sensorimotor operations as the most influential factor in language development. Piaget stated that language development is the facilitation of cognitive development (Wadsworth, 1971).

A second aspect of this period is the acquisition of socialization behaviors, which is the interaction between people and exchange of thoughts. In the early stages of the preoperational period, the toddlers' language is egocentric (self-directed). The holophrases or even multiword sentences that they chatter in the presence of others are only a means of talking to themselves. It is not until children reach six or seven years that a true interchange of ideas (socialization) begins to take place.

Children in the preoperational stage, although quite advanced when compared to the sensorimotor stage, face many limitations. First of all, they remain egocentric in thinking as they believe that everyone views the world as they do. This behavior remains until age six or seven, at which time they begin to see their views as differing from their peers. Such egocentric behavior will not appear again until adolescence, when many new cognitive structures have been acquired.

A second limiting aspect of this period is called transformation—the ability to view an object or event from a number of perspectives as it changes states.

Centration, which occurs over the majority of this period, is a third limiting factor. This element allows children to focus their attention on only the most salient perceptual characteristic of an object or event instead of other cognitive aspects. Centration will continue until age six or seven when children's cognitions attain a level that is proportional to their thought perceptions.

A fourth and final obstacle characteristic of this period is reversibility. Preoperational children who are cognizant of their own thought processes can recognize similarities and commonalities between objects, yet they have not discovered that through their own manipulation they can disarrange objects to systematize, order, and relate them. The ability to reverse operations is something the child has not experienced before. In the sensorimotor period infants' actions were irreversible; therefore, children who are now using concrete representations find it just as difficult to perform activities employing reversibility.

Even though the four obstacles or characteristics of the preoperational period make thought concrete, rigid, and slow, the process is essential to further cognitive development. The processes of assimilation and accommodation are building the children's schemata to a level that will soon have little or no resemblance to that of the earlier periods.

While other theories of cognitive development exist, Piaget and his colleagues have carefully documented the occurrence of these cognitive milestones. Further, Piaget recognized the actual need for learning to relate to external situations. Thus, interaction with other human beings, experiences within the environment, and maintenance of equilibrium are critical factors influencing the acquisition of learning.

Language Development

The development of language in young children is truly a remarkable event. From undifferentiated crying during the neonatal period, infants progress in an amazingly short period of time to the acquisition of sophisticated and complex adult speech. During the first few weeks, neonates cry randomly regardless of the stimulus. Once infants realize that crying is related to the appearance of food, then alarm crying becomes established. Further vocalizations are evident when infants receive pleasure from listening to their own sound production or coos to show contentment to their parents. By the fourth month of life, infants will make gurgling and other baby sounds as well as shriek with delight over toys or other stimuli.

Also at four months of age, infants are likely to be able to identify their mother's voice through its sound qualities. White (1975) cited research that indicated that four-to-five-month-old babies could identify their mother's voices from among other voices. Further, mother's voice is capable of provoking smiles and attention by the infant.

By eight months of age, certain words will have meaning for infants. Common among the first words understood are bottle, the baby's name, mama, dada, bye-bye, juice, cookie, and so on. Immediately after the primary acquisition of these common words (around nine or ten months) infants will respond to simple commands with understanding. Included among these simple commands are "wave bye-bye" and "kiss me."

Somewhere around 12 to 15 months, infants will speak their first words. Much earlier than this infants were making specific vocalizations referred to as babbling and lalling. Babbling is often considered a universal phase for all infants in which the total possible range of speech sounds are attempted. Lalling is much more dependent upon the spoken language infants hear and refers to the stage when infants reduce sound utterances to those that are heard. Babies' first words often include dada or mama since these or their reasonable facsimiles are the ones most likely to be reinforced. From this point on to the 24-month range, toddlers undergo rapid language development. During this period toddlers' receptive (words understood) vocabulary is likely to contain several hundred words.

Spoken language will explode at the two-year level. The toddlers' vocabulary will expand from about 200 words at age two to about 900 to 1,000 words at age three. Also during this period toddlers will begin to string together two-and three-word sentences. These sentences, while largely telegraphic, will contain pronouns or nouns and verbs—therefore, being functionally complete sentences. By the third year of life children are quite capable of understanding much of the language used for ordinary conversation by even adults. From this point on, language emerges rapidly so that by age four, most children have mastered the basic syntax of their language.

Personal/Social/Self-Help Skill Development

White (1975) contended that all children have, during the first two years of life, a need to establish a bond with a loving adult figure. In this process, children become socialized so that by age two a personal/social style has been acquired.

During the first seven months of life, White (1975) suggests that a primary social goal is to encourage the development of a sense of trust. Natural responses to an infant's normal discomforts will allow the infant to develop a strong sense of being cared for and loved. Throughout this period and well into the remainder of the first year of life, infants experience rapid shifts in mood states. Infants can shift from pleasant and cooing one moment to screaming and highly distressed behavior the next.

Around four months of age infants will exhibit a high degree of positive social behavior including emergence of the true social smile. At this point infants will seem euphorically happy and will often laugh or giggle. These factors would seem to indicate a state of enjoyment and contentment.

Members of infants' families will be able to evoke much visible joy including smiles and cooing with infants of six months of age. Shortly after this time, however, or about eight months of age, a phenomenon referred to as stranger anxiety may occur. That is, people outside the family are regarded with fear rather than the broad social smile. At this point infants narrow their range of preferred human company.

From one to two years of age, infants undergo some interesting social changes so much so that by age two, most children are firmly established social beings (White, 1975). The path the youngster follows in becoming a social being can be greatly facilitated if parents allow infants to explore their world and satisfy their natural curiosity in an "accident proofed" environment. Second, infants' natural orientation toward their mothers or other primary caretakers will intensify. This orientation and relationship will allow them to learn the limits of their world, that is, if they can climb the stairs, touch the vase, whether verbal threats have physical back-ups, and so on. During this period infants learn the answers to literally thousands of social questions.

By age two, toddlers can become fairly well adjusted and fun-to-be-with social beings. This is particularly true when parents assist children to become independent and more directed at people other than mother and father. Two-year-olds are also more capable of ranges of emotional behaviors and less apt to be subject to rapid shifts in mood states.

Between two and three years of age, White (1975) notes that children will develop an interest in peer interaction. As more activities become available outside the home, children have a less intense need to focus upon their families. Children become more capable of controlling their emotions and far more likely to engage in certain social activities (White, 1975):

1. getting and holding the attention of adults
2. using adults as resources to help do jobs the child has determined are too difficult
3. expressing affection and moderate annoyance to adults
4. leading and following peers
5. expressing affection and mild annoyance to peers
6. competing with peers
7. showing pride in personal accomplishment
8. engaging in make-believe activities.

Self-help skills are developing simultaneously with personal/social skills. The earliest self-help skills to emerge are those associated with eating. By about six months of age infants will feed themselves a cracker or cookie. At 12 months of age infants will finger feed themselves all or part of a meal. At this point other self-help skills in dressing, toileting, other eating, and grooming begin to develop and emerge in sequential order. Also at 12 months infants will fuss to be changed after a bowel movement, will remain dry after a nap, and will remove small articles of clothing.

The 15-month infants will use a spoon with some spilling, indicate wet pants, and begin to develop bowel control. From this point until toddlers reach two years of age, the following skills will emerge: drinking from a cup, does not turn spoon in mouth, dry at night if taken up once, removing coat or dress, and unzipping zippers. From two to three years of age toddlers can be taught independent toileting skills, unbuttoning buttons, improved eating skills, and washing and drying hands.

In summary, these five important areas of development represent different aspects of growth. As behaviors develop, they assume certain general characteristic patterns that may be observed. While these sequences of development follow fairly predictable chronological age levels, great variance can occur because of genetic disorders, injury, disease, or other factors. While development cannot be measured precisely, these central tendencies allow special educators to determine approximately how far below expected developmental milestones a delayed child is falling.

THE DEVELOPMENTAL PHASES

The curriculum materials presented in Part II are divided into five developmental phases. The literature on child development describes numerous stages (Knobloch & Pasamanick, 1974), phases (White, 1975), or periods (Piaget, 1952) of development that children progress through during the first three years of life.

Knobloch and Pasamanick (1974) noted that a child's development proceeds stage by stage in a predictable sequence. Each stage the child passes through represents a significant change in degree or level of maturity. The key periods represent integrative periods and major shifts in focus and in the various centers of organization. Knobloch and Pasamanick (1974) cited the key ages as follows: one month, four months, seven months, ten months, one year, 18 months, two years, and three years.

White (1975) described seven developmental phases that children pass through from birth to three years of age. Various phases have special qualities that set them apart from other periods. As children pass from one phase to another, certain behaviors disappear and others emerge. In some cases behaviors developing in a parallel fashion become integrated and coordinated as one unitary skill. White's (1975) phases and corresponding ages are as follows:

Phase   I   birth to six weeks
Phase   II   six weeks to three and one-half months
Phase III   three and one-half to five and one-half months
Phase IV   five and one-half to eight months
Phase   V   eight to fourteen months
Phase VI   fourteen months to two years of age
Phase VII   two to three years of age.

Piaget's (1952) various periods have been previously described and their corresponding age ranges listed. Piaget also viewed these periods as distinct, with uniqueness of behavioral responses delineated by each period.

A thorough review of the literature in child development combined with our many years of experience observing young children develop has led us to distinguish five distinct developmental phases. Each phase represents a distinguishable period of growth and development in which various quantitative and qualitative integrative behaviors occur and become refined. With movement from one phase to the next, major shifts occur in focus on the centers of neuromotor, social, and linguistic behaviors. Children in one phase are quite different both to the degree they can perform skills (qualitatively) and in the number and types of observable skills they can perform (quantitatively). However, since normal child development is variable, the phases must reflect this variability. The phases must not be viewed as fixed or rigid, but rather as flexible periods of development within which children reach the various levels at their own unique rate of development.

As can be seen from the following phases and corresponding age levels, beginning–ending ages tend to be ranges rather than specific time periods so that users of this curriculum will recognize child growth rate variability and not become trapped by hard and fast ages:

Phase   I   birth to between 16 to 20 weeks
Phase II   16 to 20 weeks to between 32 and 36 weeks
Phase III   32 to 36 weeks to between 15 and 18 months
Phase IV   15 to 18 months to between 21 and 24 months
Phase V   21 to 24 months to three years.

SUMMARY

This chapter has presented a rather detailed argument for providing early intervention to handicapped preschoolers. Intensive coverage has been provided of normal child development for a better understanding of the nature and scope of the learning problems of handicapped children. Development from birth to three years of age was discussed by describing significant milestones in reflex/gross motor, perceptual/fine motor, sensory/cognitive, language, and personal/social/self-help skills. Finally, a rationale for viewing the first three years of life as unfolding in five distinct phases of development was provided.

Chapter 2

Assessing Child Performance

If educators are ever to achieve a national goal of providing services to all children with special needs, then they must be prepared to engage in the cooperative process of identification, screening, assessment, and finally intervention. Many checklists, inventories, instruments, and devices have been developed and are currently being used by specialists in many disciplines. This chapter will provide an overview of identification and screening, discuss some different strategies for assessment, and provide an in-depth discussion of a direct data-based assessment system that will provide the information necessary to utilize the teaching materials provided in Part II.

IDENTIFICATION

Identification is the first step in the process and may be defined as establishing an awareness that a problem exists (Hayden & Edgar, 1977). Rapid advancements in medical technology now allow identification to take place prenatally, through infancy, and in early childhood. The people involved in identification include parents, obstetricians, pediatricians, nurses, public health professionals, and day care workers.

For conditions present at birth, identification may occur in the first five minutes of life. Down's Syndrome, microcephaly, cleft palate, severe brain damage, and some physical handicaps are often diagnosed by the obstetrician or the pediatrician. Problems that occur during the first few days of life such as seizures, absent corneal reflexes, or rapid head growth are indicators of a child who is at risk. Often professionals employ instruments like the Apgar Scale (Apgar, 1965) that measures heart rate, breathing, muscle tone, color, and reflex irritability or the Brazelton Neonatal Assessment Scale

(Brazelton, 1973) that identifies central nervous system anomalies to predict abnormalities in neonates.

Later, parents and other professionals may detect serious developmental lags or other problems that serve as an impetus for further assessment. Because many subtle developmental problems may go undetected for long periods of time, it is critical to introduce formal procedures community wide to reduce the time span for determining that a handicap exists. Screening is one means of reducing the time.

SCREENING

Hayden and Edgar (1977) defined screening as the testing of large numbers of children in order to identify those individuals who are most likely to be handicapped. Screening does not have as its purpose labeling or even intervention; it is simply an essential first step or early warning signal that a problem *may* exist. Many of the early screening tests and scales were limited to assessing only one or two factors in the total range of development. Further, they required considerable time and training to administer and interpret properly, thus limiting their usefulness as primary screening devices (Meier, 1976).

Meier (1976) described five screening instruments that were multifactorial and thus could be employed in primary or secondary screening programs. These tests include:

- *Rapid Developmental Screening Checklist* (Giannini, Amler, Chused, Cohen, deLeo, Gallerzzo, Greenspan, Kaessler, Haas, Michall-Smith, O'Hare, Swallow, Taft, Winick, & Goodman, 1972). This checklist consists of 40 items covering the ages of one month to five years of age. It is designed to be used by a physician or nurse (Meier, 1976).
- *Guide to Normal Milestones of Development* (Haynes, 1967). Designed initially for use by nurses, this device consists of wheel and disc apparatus with basic reflexes on the top disc and key developmental ages listed on the bottom disc. As the wheel turns, symbols appear on the bottom disc indicating the presence, absence, emergence, or inhibition at that particular developmental stage (Haynes, 1967).
- *Developmental Screening Inventory* (Knobloch, Pasamanick, & Sherard, 1966). This instrument is divided into 21 four-week periods covering nearly 18 months of age. Each four-week period is divided into five major areas: adaptive, gross motor, fine motor, language, and personal-social (Meier, 1976).

- *Boyd Developmental Progress Scale* (Boyd, 1974). This scale consists of 150 items in developmental areas related to adaptive behavior and activities of daily life. Included in this scale are parent interview items, but the instrument may be given by professionals from any of the disciplines working with young children.
- *Denver Developmental Screening Test* (Frankenburg, Dodds, & Fandal, 1970). The Denver Developmental Screening Test (DDST) may be the most widely used developmental screening instrument today. It has been subjected to extensive reliability and validity studies (Frankenburg, Camp, VanNatta, & Demersseman, 1971). The DDST covers the period from birth to six years of age and consists of 105 task items in four major areas: personal-social, fine motor-adaptive, language, and gross motor. With training, the test can be administered by paraprofessionals.

In spite of the advances of certain screening devices and attempts to improve validity and reliability, there remains the nagging problem of large numbers of false positives (children identified as handicapped where no handicap exists) and false negatives (children who are really handicapped but screening identifies them as having no handicaps) (Hayden & Edgar, 1977).

Kakalik, Brewer, Dougharty, Fleischauer, Genensky, & Wallen (1974) described at least six problems with the current screening strategies:

1. Many children who are handicapped are not detected.
2. Many children are identified inappropriately.
3. Many of the children who are identified are labeled, which serves to further stigmatize them.
4. Even if a child is identified as potentially handicapped, follow-up services are inadequate.
5. Currently there remains a lack of trained personnel to work with these children.
6. Technology has not been sufficiently created or utilized in the effort to provide intervention services to identified children.

Meier (1976) has called for a comprehensive screening program employing a battery of instruments to improve predictive validity. In spite of these acknowledged problems, less-than-adequate screening is far better than no screening effort at all. Early detection remains the only hope many handicapped preschoolers have as it at least allows professionals a better chance to provide needed services.

ASSESSMENT

Assessment may be defined as "the collection of information for the purpose of making decisions; the kind of information gathered depends upon the decisions to be made" (Kazdin, 1978, p. 269). Hayden and Edgar (1977, p. 73) referred to the assessment process as the "complete and exhaustive pinpointing of an individual's skills and deficits." Thus professionals have a specific, intensive, and exhaustive data collection process that allows them to profile children's individual strengths and weaknesses so that they apply "appropriate prevention and intervention measures" (Fallen & McGovern, 1978, p. 43).

The most appropriate type of assessment involves a transdisciplinary approach—the collaborative and cooperative interaction of professionals from the fields of medicine, allied health, psychology, and education. The purpose of this transdisciplinary assessment approach is the gathering of extensive information about the child from each discipline's point of view and the careful integration of this information into a complete profile of the child's needs.

Since the focus of this text is educational assessment and intervention, assessment from the medical and health care fields will be touched upon only briefly. According to Fallen and McGovern (1978) the medical assessment consists of a medical history and a physical examination. The medical history consists of basic information on the prenatal period and postnatal development, as well as any birth complications. A developmental history (the recording of key milestones, such as when the child sat up) will also be included in the history.

The physical examination serves to provide a picture of the child from a medical perspective as well as to detect various abnormalities (Fallen & McGovern, 1978). Besides the pediatrician or general practitioner who conducts this examination, other specialists and professionals in the allied health areas may be called upon to provide input in the assessment process. Included in this group would be the following:

1. otologist—a medical doctor specializing in hearing problems
2. ophthalmologist—a medical doctor specializing in visual problems
3. neurologist—a medical doctor specializing in problems of the central nervous system
4. orthopedic surgeon—a medical doctor specializing in problems of bones, muscles, and joints
5. psychiatrist—a medical doctor specializing in emotional or psychological disorders
6. dentist—for detecting problems with teeth that may cause speech impairments or pose health hazards

7. audiologist—a professional who is trained to determine the nature and extent of hearing losses
8. optometrist—a professional who is trained to prescribe corrective lenses
9. physical therapist or occupational therapist—a professional who is trained to carry out prescribed interventions in the motor area
10. psychologist—a professional who is trained to determine cognitive and socioemotional functioning
11. speech/language therapist—a professional trained to perform speech and language evaluations
12. nutritionist—a professional who is trained in determining nutritional needs or inadequacies
13. psychiatric social worker—a professional who is trained in social work and may provide family social data.

EDUCATIONAL ASSESSMENT

For children from birth to two years of age, many assessment instruments designed to lead to intervention are largely sensorimotor in nature. While certain tests may purport to be infant tests of intelligence, their accuracy in assessing and more importantly predicting intelligence is at best highly questionable. Only in those cases where severe retardation is detected do the infant tests have acceptable predictive validity. For children of normal or even near normal intelligence, the two most popular infant tests, the Bayley Scales of Infant Development (Bayley, 1969) and the Cattell Infant Intelligence Scale (Cattell, 1940) do not have satisfactory predictive validity (Erickson, Johnson, & Campbell, 1970).

In spite of these drawbacks, assessment devices for infants and for the two-to three-year-olds will be described:

- *Bayley Scales of Infant Development* (Bayley, 1969)—consists of both a mental and motor scale of over 200 items covering the period from birth to 30 months.
- *Cattell Infant Intelligence Scale* (Cattell, 1940)—this test yields a mental age score which may be converted to an IQ.

At two years of age, the somewhat greater measurability of children's intelligence allows both more accurate assessment and prediction of later intelligence with more accuracy (Fallen & McGovern, 1978). Intelligence tests for preschoolers include some of the following:

- *McCarthy Scales of Children's Abilities* (McCarthy, 1973)—One of the best preschool intelligence tests, the McCarthy covers the ages two and one-half to eight and one-half. This test yields a general cognitive index with scores for verbal, quantitative, perceptual, memory, and motor.
- *Pictorial Test of Intelligence* (French, 1964)—This test can be used to assess the intellectual ability of children three to eight years of age even if they are nonverbal.
- *Stanford-Binet Intelligence Scale* (Terman & Merrill, 1960)—The Binet can be used for age ranges of two to adult and yields a mental age for the two to 18 group from which the IQ can be determined.
- *Wechsler Preschool and Primary Scale of Intelligence* (Wechsler, 1967)—This test, which may be used for four- to six-year-olds, has two major sections, verbal and performance. Subtest scores can be useful in pinpointing specific problems.

Various preschool programs or First Chance Network projects have devised their own assessment packages. Often these packages are tied into curricular formats that allow the user to go from the assessment to a series of curriculum training procedures that help the child to acquire a defined skill. Others are merely general diagnostic instruments from which a planned program must be designed. Some of the more widely used packages or instruments are as follows:

- *Developmental Indicators for the Assessment of Learning* (DIAL) (Mardell & Goldenberg, 1975)—While mainly a screening instrument, the DIAL is useful for pinpointing the learning problems of children from two and one-half to five and one-half years of age.
- *Developmental Potential of Preschool Children* (Haeussermann, 1958)—This test, designed for children two to six years of age, evaluates functioning in the intellectual, sensory, and emotional areas.
- *Learning Accomplishment Profile* (LAP)—Developed by Anne Sanford and her associates (1973, 1974) at the Chapel Hill Training Outreach Project, the LAP assesses learning difficulties in the areas of gross motor skills, fine motor skills, social skills, self-help skills, cognitive skills, and language. The LAP is a total package that has coordinated curricular materials to assist teachers in designing appropriate individual educational programs.
- *Portage Project*—Originally developed by David Shearer and his associates (see now Bluma, Shearer, Frohman, & Hilliard, 1976), the Portage Project provides a sequenced developmental checklist and a set of curriculum cards. The checklist covers the period from birth to five

years of age and has 450 separate behaviors sequenced in the areas of language, self-help, motor, social, and cognitive development.

• *Project MEMPHIS*—Quick and Campbell (1976) developed this three-part program that includes a developmental scale covering five developmental areas of personal-social skills, fine motor skills, gross motor skills, language skills, and perceptual-cognitive skills. The assessment is linked to a comprehensive curriculum that provides specific behavioral objectives and presents skills in small sequential steps.

THE CRITERION-REFERENCED APPROACH TO ASSESSMENT

The remainder of this text will focus upon a criterion-referenced, curricular-based assessment approach employing a sequenced developmental checklist. The checklist corresponds to a curriculum with individual specific objectives with task-analyzed skill sequences. Prior to the discussion of this developmental checklist and curriculum materials, an overview of this type of assessment will be presented.

The task-analytical approach has as a basic premise that task failure is related to the student's inability to master certain subtasks within a major task. According to Mori and Masters (in press), the task-analytical approach uses criterion-referenced tests that contain validated skill sequences. The major focus then becomes what the student is able or not able to do with educational intervention and planning directly related to a specific sequence of subtasks (Mori & Masters, in press).

The criterion-referenced test is designed to assist teachers in determining students' skill levels (Howell, Kaplan, & O'Connell, 1979). The model has a great deal of utility because evaluation is directly related to intervention.

The criterion-referenced test, which is central to the task-analytical model, has all items at the same or nearly the same level of difficulty. It is designed to discriminate between mastery and nonmastery of specific behavioral objectives. The criterion-referenced test does not actually yield a score, but a profile of skills the child has mastered and those that remain to be acquired. The items that are part of the assessment instrument reflect the standing of the child with respect to the curriculum. Thus children are not compared to other children, but their performance is gauged to instructional needs so that a teacher can plan intervention strategies that account for the child's present mastery level and potential for mastering specific skills (Fallen & McGovern, 1978).

Informal Assessment

One final form of assessment that is often a useful supplement to formal standardized and criterion-referenced assessment is informal assessment. It is often conducted by employing several observation techniques including anecdotal records, behavior measurements, inventories, rating scales, and individualized observation (Fallen & McGovern, 1978). By systematically observing the performance of young children, professionals and even trained parents may note areas where children are deficient in skill acquisition.

Pasanella and Volkmor (1977) discussed the advantages of using observation:

1. Behavior is observed in naturalistic settings and helps to alleviate the artificial nature of assessments that occurs in clinics or test centers.
2. The focus of the observer is the child's actual behavior.
3. Educational effectiveness is enhanced by observation since there is an on-going monitoring of intervention strategies.
4. The child's behavior is observed in the context of the environment, thus making it more likely that factors contributing to the handicap will be discovered.
5. The experienced observer may employ the results of the observation and judgment to plan an effective educational program.

One observation technique employed for many years in education is the anecdotal record. In the anecdotal record the teacher or day care worker records impressions of the child's natural performance over an extended period of time. By systematically observing and then recording the child's specific behaviors that occur excessively, that occur rather than appropriate behaviors, or interfere with the acquisition of appropriate skills, the teacher or other observer is able to determine patterns of behavior and thus provide a far more precise assessment of a child (Hayden & Edgar, 1977; Fallen & McGovern, 1978).

Measurements of behavior is another observation technique that may be employed with young children. This technique includes such things as frequency recording, duration, and time sampling, and provides baseline data about a child's performance (Fallen & McGovern, 1978). These techniques will be discussed further later in this chapter.

A third technique of observation employs inventories and rating scales. These scales such as the *Developmental Checklist for 3-, 4-, and 5-year olds* (Frost & Kissinger, 1976), the *Preschool Evaluation Form* (Pasanella & Volkmor, 1977), and the *Preschool Profile, Model Preschool Center for Handicapped Children* (Lynch, Rieke, Soltman, Hardman, & O'Conor,

1974) allow personnel to assess a child's performance quickly, informally, and efficiently (Fallen & McGovern, 1978; Hayden & Edgar, 1977). Personnel using inventories must exercise caution in interpreting the information gained from their use so as to avoid further labeling or stigmatization. Further, observations with these devices should occur over a lengthy time span to assure more consistency and reliability of the results.

The final method discussed by Fallen and McGovern (1978) was the individual observation methods. The authors described this method as a combination of techniques that a teacher or day care professional finds useful and informative. Included among these are teacher-constructed checklists, interviews with parents, medical personnel including school nurses, social workers, and so on. Further, home visitations yield useful information about the child's home environment that supports the individual's behavior.

In the remaining sections of this chapter the authors will present the assessment instruments they have developed to be used with the curricular materials. These assessment devices were developed and field tested by the authors during their work with handicapped infants and toddlers.

THE DEVELOPMENTAL CHECKLIST

Parents and educators can plan a highly individualized program of intervention for any child by using the two assessment tools explained in this chapter. The first tool is the Developmental Checklist. The checklist is merely a list of skills typically learned by children between birth and three years. The skills are listed in all five areas of development: reflex/gross motor (RM); perceptual/fine motor (PFM); sensory/cognitive (SC); language (L); and personal/social/self-help (P/S/SH). The skills are then broken down into the five phases of development, explained in Chapter 1. The phases are marked with Roman numerals as I, II, III, IV, and V. Phase I corresponds to the skills ranging from birth to 4 months; Phase II, 4 to 8 months; Phase III, 8 to 15-18 months; Phase IV, 15-18 to 24 months; Phase V, 24 to 36 months. The skill itself is given an Arabic numeral and a description. (See examples on page 34.)

Using the Developmental Checklist

The checklist is based upon actual observation of the child and must be filled in by the parents as well as the educator. Once parents have become familiar with the checklist, they can do it themselves as they find it simple, quick, and quite interesting to follow the development of their child. The child may be evaluated on a weekly or monthly basis depending upon the individual child's rate of progress. This system of charting a child's progress makes possible rapid identification of problem areas and areas of strength.

Examples:

	Area of Development	Phase	Skill	Description
RM II 7	Reflex/Motor	II	7	Bears some weight on legs.
PFM I 2	Perceptual/Fine Motor	I	2	Follows horizontal movement or light to midline.
SC V 5	Sensory/Cognitive	V	5	Builds tower of 6–7 cubes.
L IV 5	Language	IV	5	Names one picture.
P/S/SH III 2	Personal/Social/Self-Help	III	2	Plays peek-a-boo.

The checklist (see Exhibit 2-1) is used in the following manner:

1. Write the child's name in the upper right-hand corner in the space provided. If the copy is to be retained for permanent records, it is well to so indicate for office use. (Copies should be made in triplicate, one set for the office records, one for the educator, and one set for the permanent records of the parents.)
2. Observe the child for a few minutes and ask the parents questions about the child's general abilities, which will give the interviewer (or parents if they are filling it in) the opportunity to decide on the approximate phase of development to begin marking.
3. Notice that the columns under the child's name are to be filled in by going downward in a straight line.
4. At the top of the column, mark the date in the darkened area.
5. Read the skills list and mark in the space provided to the right of the skill. Use the code given in the upper left-hand corner of the paper. This code provides a flexible rating system that is most helpful in planning the child's program.
   0 = Never (The child has performed it once accidentally or has never been seen to perform the skill.)
   1 = Occasionally (The child has made a recognizable, deliberate, and successful attempt to perform the skill on one or two occasions.)
   2 = Frequently (The child performs the skill up to ten times within a period of five days.)
   3 = Mastery (The child performs the skill commonly and is successful 85 percent of the time.)
6. As long as children receive 2s and 3s on the evaluation, they are in the area of mastered skills. No work is required in these areas. When the

examiner begins to check a number of 0 or 1, the areas of weakness have been identified and training can begin on these skills.

7. It is often unnecessary to go any further on the checklist and may be a waste of time. However, some children have special difficulties that hinder their progress on some skills in a phase but not in all. In such a case go on further down the checklist just to be sure all the child's accomplishments are marked.

8. List the skills first marked with 0 or 1. Agree on those skills that would be appropriate for the child to learn. Parents and educators should plan this individualized program together.

9. Explanations of the skill may be found in the curriculum section of this manual. The activities are encoded with the same numeration for skill development, phase, and number as used in the checklist. For example, RM II 7 (Bears some weight on legs) is also RM II 7 in the Reflex/gross motor section, Phase II, number 7 in the curriculum. The process of correlating the checklist skills and the curriculum activities becomes quite easy after a little practice. This helps parents move along with the child's program when educators are unavailable to help.

10. Check the curriculum in this manual for suggestions on language cues and activities.

11. Break the skill down to its simplest parts by listing every movement and body part involved in the activity. List the parts of the skill the child can perform and those areas that he has yet to master. Devise activities to strengthen those areas of weakness, choose "key" words or "cues," then combine for the total skill.

12. Once the child's level of development has been established, turn to Chapter 4. This chapter describes basic practices of education that are vitally important for children in each of the five developmental phases. The appropriate teaching techniques should be learned well, reviewed, and applied daily. Think through how each of these teaching principles can be applied to the skills being worked on as well as to the general household living pattern.

13. On successive evaluations, begin the evaluation by checking only those items previously marked 0 and go on. In other words, there is no need to reevaluate items already marked 3 and most times items marked 2.

14. Remember: The child is not in competition with any other human being. Find the child's strengths (coded 2 and 3), then help the child grow stronger by working on the first skills marked sequentially with a 1 or 0.

15. The Developmental Checklists are shown in Exhibits 2-8 through 2-12 of this manual and may be copied for your use.

Exhibit 2-1 Reflex/Gross Motor Skills

REFLEX–MOTOR SKILLS   NAME_____   Birthdate_____

CODE	0 = Never 2 = Frequently 1 = Occasionally 3 = Mastery	*Denotes skill repeated in other sections of Developmental Checklist #Denotes self-help skills

			Date	9/7/79	10/7/79	11/9/79				
PHASE I										
RM II	12	Held standing, bears weight and bounces		4						
RM II	13	Rolls from back to stomach, from stomach to back		3	4					
RM II	14	Sits alone momentarily, leaning forward on hands		2	4					
RM II	15	Lifts head on back		2	3	4				
RM II	16	Sits alone for a short while		0	2	3				
RM II	17	Can support entire weight on legs when held		0	2	4				
RM II	18	Attempts belly crawl using hands and feet		1	2	4				

The same developmental checklists are of great value to parents and educators as they make possible quick and easy evaluation of the child's on-going progress. They are flexible, employ a simple evaluative code, and may be used to help plan an appropriate program of early intervention. When used in combination with the worksheets (see Exhibits 2-2 through 2-7), simple but accurate data may be taken to document the child's progress and refine the parent and educator's teaching skills.

THE WORKSHEETS

The worksheets record the actual working efforts on the child's program. They help parents and educators take data on their own teaching efforts. They are valuable because they help the adults keep honest track of the time and work they actually do. They help evaluate the child's progress too. The worksheets make all this data keeping possible in four ways by: (1) noting the Rate of Observed Activity (ROA); (2) Timed Activity (TA); (3) Numbered Activity (#A); and (4) Programmed Activities (PA).

Rate of Observed Activity (ROA)

A child's efforts at a particular skill can be counted and recorded on the worksheet before actual training begins. They can also be counted and recorded to note progress during the training period and again for data proving the skill is mastered. For example, if a parent and educator wanted to know how often a baby tended to lift its head while in a prone position, they would:

1. fill in the Activity space with RM I 14
2. write in the date
3. mark in the time they will start (4:10 P.M.)
4. circle (ROA) in the little squares under Activity Rate-Response Data
5. put a check (✓) in one of the squares under Activity Rate-Response Data each time the baby's head raised during a timed period of five minutes. In Exhibit 2-2 the baby's head was lifted one time (✓).
6. stop counting the head lifts at the end of five minutes, and mark the time (4:15 P.M.) under time finished (F)
7. note the total time (5m) 5 minutes
8. comment on extenuating circumstances in Comments (tired and on medication at the time)

Exhibit 2-2 Sample Worksheet—ROA

Activity	Date	Time	Total Time	Activity Rates-Response Data										Comments
1 RMI 14	2 9/7	³S 4:10 F 4:15	7 5 m	4 ROA		✓							⁸	Tired and on medication

After a two-week period for training, rechart the ROA on RM I 14. The worksheet might indicate the child now lifts the head six times in a five-minute period. (See Exhibit 2-3.)

Exhibit 2-3 Sample Worksheet—ROA after Two Weeks of Training

Activity	Date	Time	Total Time	Activity Rates-Response Data									Comments
RMI 14	9/21	S 3:15 F 3:20	5 m	ROA	✓	✓	✓	✓	✓	✓			Great work!

Observing the rate of activity (ROA) is helpful for proving a child's progress in a skill. There are some forms of work for the child that have nothing to do with the child's skill. Rather, the parents and educators may wish to see how much time they are really spending on a particular activity.

Timed Activity (TA)

When it is very important to be sure certain work is done on a daily basis and for a certain amount of time each day, it is wise to chart for timed activity. This is particularly true when the child's program includes daily physical stimulation or exercise.

For example, should parents and educators wish to keep track of the time spent (see Exhibit 2-4) in physical stimulation (SC I 1) they would:

1. fill in the Activity space with SC I 1
2. write in the date
3. leave Time blank
4. circle (TA) in the little squares under Activity Rate-Response Data
5. put the minutes (m) spent on physical stimulation each time it is done during the day. In this case, the baby was "stimmed" twice for three minutes each (3m), once for five minutes (5m), and once for one minute (1m)
6. Mark the total time spent, in this case twelve minutes (12m), on that date
7. comment in this case that massage and tactile stimulation were stressed with fabric samples.

Exhibit 2-4 Sample Worksheet—TA

Activity	Date	Time	Total Time	Activity Rates-Response Data											Comments
1 SCI 1	2 9/11	S ─3─ F	6 12 m	4	TA	5 3 m	3 m	5 m	1 m						7 Massage & Tactile Stimulation

Timed Activities are marked when it is necessary to be sure a definite amount of time is spent working on certain activities in a child's program. TA is typically marked for activities like physical stimulation and for exercises prescribed by doctors or physical therapists. On occasion it is necessary to keep track of the number of times an activity is done rather than the total time spent on it.

Numbered Activity (NA)

Numbered Activities (NA) are charted when a skill must be performed a certain number of times each day. For example, parents may be asked to play games with a baby in such a way that the baby's hands touch at midline (in the center of the chest) one hundred times a day. This would be a numbered activity. The parents could break the activity into ten groups of ten and perform them at various times of the day. On the worksheet (see Exhibit 2-5) they would:

1. fill in the Activity space with PFM I 15
2. write in the date
3. leave Time blank
4. circle (NA) in the little squares under Activity Rate-Response Data
5. mark 10 in the appropriate activity rate square each time a set of ten is done during the day. In this case the parents did seven sets of ten or touched the baby's hands together at midline seventy times on 9/12
6. write (70) in the total time slot for the number of midline touches accomplished on that date
7. comment in this case that the child was sick and slept most of the day making 100 attempts impossible.

Exhibit 2-5 Sample Worksheet—NA

Activity	Date	Time	Total Time		Activity Rates-Response Data									Comments
1 PFMI 15	2 9/13	S _3_ F	6 70 x	4 #A	5 10	10	10	10	10	10	10			7 Baby sick, Slept most of day.

Over a period of time, it is possible to be sure exactly how many attempts to work on a certain skill are being made. Sometimes the actual training in a skill must be charted to improve the teaching techniques. In this case, actual training for the child's mastery of the skill would be marked as PA, Programmed Activity.

Programmed Activity (PA)

As the actual training of a skill takes place, that programmed learning may be charted on the worksheets simply. A *cue* (common word) must be chosen and rewards or reinforcers (marked as /) available to quickly reward the child when the skill is performed.

The actual steps of programming an activity are these:

1. Cue the child (give the command).
2. If the child does not obey, mark 0 in one of the squares in the Activity Rate-Response Data section of the worksheet.
3. Give the command or cue and help the child perform the skill (mark it 1), then *immediately* reward the child and mark a / behind the 1 (1/) indicating that the child's movement through the skill was reinforced.
4. Repeat Steps 2 and 3 as required.

5. When the child responds to the cue and does the skill without help (shaping), mark 2 in the square and immediately reward the child, adding a / behind the 2 (2/) showing the behavior was reinforced.

A programmed activity would be marked on the worksheet as any other skill. For example, when teaching the child to touch hands together in midline, the cue or command could be "touch together;" then, with the reward close at hand (possibly a little fruit juice) the teacher would fill out the form (see Exhibit 2-6):

1. fill in the Activity space with PFM I 15
2. write in the date
3. circle (PA) in the little square under Activity Rate-Response Data
4. mark in beginning time (2:20)
5. mark 0, 1/ or 2/ for each attempt to teach and reinforce the child following the cue "touch together." Have fun! In this case, 9 attempts were made. There was no response and no reward three times; the baby was "shaped," moved through the skill, and reinforced four times and actually did it twice and was rewarded (/) each time
6. note the time the activity finished (2:25 P.M.)
7. write in the total time spent (5 minutes—5m)
8. no comments necessary

Given the worksheet, most training and observational needs may be recorded to keep accurate information on the child's abilities. The actual time or number of activities involved in the baby's daily program is also available for evaluation. Finally, the programming or training techniques used to teach the child are also recorded.

Exhibit 2-6 Sample Worksheet—PA

Activity	Date	Time	Total Time	Activity Rates-Response Data												Comments
1 PFMI 15	2 9/15	⁴S 2:20 ⁶F 2:25	7 5 m	3	PA	0	1/	1/	0	1/	2/	0	1/	2/		8

SUMMARY

The need for assessment is recognized throughout the field of early childhood intervention for handicapped children. It is useful to the parents and those who train all young children, especially when based upon on-going observation. The Development Checklist is based upon observation and is

Exhibit 2-7 Example of Worksheet

WORKSHEET

Name _____

Activity	Date	Time		Total	Activity Rates — Response Data	Comments
		S				
		F				
		S				
		F				
		S				
		F				
		S				
		F				
		S				
		F				
		S				
		F				
		S				
		F				
		S				
		F				
		S				
		F				
		S				
		F				

Exhibit 2-8 Developmental Checklist—Reflex/Gross Motor

NAME_____ Birthdate_____

CODE			
0 = Never 2 = Frequently 1 = Occasionally 3 = Mastery	*Denotes skill repeated in other sections of Developmental Checklist #Denotes self-help skills		

		Date							
PHASE I									
RM I	1	Sucking reflex							
RM I	2	Palmar grasp							
RM I	3	Asymmetrical tonic neck reflex							
RM I	4	Symmetrical tonic neck reflex							
RM I	5	Tonic labyrinthine reflex							
RM I	6	Positive Support Reflex							
RM I	7	Segmental Rolling							
RM I	8	Moro reflex--startle response							
RM I	9	Galant reflex							
RM I	10	Reaching reflex							
RM I	11	Walking reflex							
RM I	12	Relaxes for touch and massage							
RM I	13	GENERAL EXERCISE PROCEDURE							
RM I	14	Lifts head prone							
RM I	15	Pushes adult hand with feet							
RM I	16	Marked head lag when pulled to sitting position							
RM I	17	Prone, head up 45							
RM I	18	Holds head erect for a few seconds							
RM I	19	Landau reflex--head comes up from ventral suspension							
RM I	20	Prone, head up 90							
RM I	21	Prone, chest up with arm support							
RM I	22	Some head lift on back							
RM I	23	Rolls side to back							
RM I	24	Sits with support, head steady							
RM I	25	Rolls over stomach to back							
RM I	26	Hands engage at midline							
PHASE II									
RM II	1	Pulls to sit, no head lag							
RM II	2	Lifts head and chest, weight on hands, legs extended (prone)							

useful in planning an individualized program for any child who functions developmentally between the ages of birth and three years. The worksheets help gather data toward assessment of the child's progress in that program and also help those teaching the child keep track of their own efforts and teaching techniques.

Exhibit 2-8 continued

NAME_____ Birthdate_____

CODE	0 = Never 2 = Frequently 1 = Occasionally 3 = Mastery	*Denotes skill repeated in other sections of Developmental Checklist #Denotes self-help skills

		Date									
PHASE II (cont'd)											
RM II	3	Rolls from back to side									
RM II	4	Turns head fully, sitting in chair									
RM II	5	Sits in high chair with support									
RM II	6	Body balance while held extended									
RM II	7	Bears some weight on legs									
RM II	8	Rolls back to stomach									
RM II	9	Toe play									
RM II	10	First crawling reaction, draws up knees, pushes on hands									
RM II	11	Parachute reaction									
RM II	12	Held standing, bears weight and bounces									
RM II	13	Rolls back to stomach, stomach to back									
RM II	14	Sits alone momentarily, leaning forward on hands									
RM II	15	Lifts head on back									
RM II	16	Sits alone momentarily									
RM II	17	Briefly supports entire weight on legs when held									
RM II	18	Attempts belly crawl using hands and feet									
RM II	19	Protective reaction, sitting balance suddenly disturbed laterally									
RM II	20	Body righting reflex									
PHASE III											
RM III	1	Sits indefinitely, good coordination									
RM III	2	Up on knees, belly crawl									
RM III	3	Gets to and from sitting independently									

The Developmental Checklists (Exhibits 2-8 through 2-12) for each developmental phase and sample worksheet (Exhibit 2-7) are shown on the following pages. Copies of these forms may be made without fear of penalty by copyright laws.

Exhibit 2-8 continued

NAME_____Birthdate_____

CODE			Date								
	0 = Never 2 = Frequently 1 = Occasionally 3 = Mastery	*Denotes skill repeated in other sections of Developmental Checklist #Denotes self-help skill									

PHASE III (cont'd)

RM III	4	Pulls to stand									
RM III	5	Sits well in chair									
RM III	6	Creeps or hitches									
RM III	7	Protective reaction, sitting balance disturbed backwards									
RM III	8	Can stand holding on to furniture									
RM III	9	Beginning of hip rotation, leads with hips when turning									
RM III	10	Cruises sideways holding on									
RM III	11	Walks two hands held									
RM III	12	Walks forward--one hand held									
RM III	13	Stands alone									
RM III	14	Walks alone									
RM III	15	Creeps upstairs									
RM III	16	Lowers self from standing to sitting with support									
RM III	17	Supports weight on entire sole surface and walks									
RM III	18	Kneels alone with balance									
RM III	19	Stoops and recovers									
RM III	20	Walks pushing large wheel toy									
RM III	21	Stands self up supported									

PHASE IV

RM IV	1	Stoops to pick up object without losing balance									
RM IV	2	Sits in low chair									
RM IV	3	Walks about well with immature gait									
RM IV	4	Walks fast or runs stiffly									
RM IV	5	Walks up stairs--one hand held									
RM IV	6	Walks carrying toy									
RM IV	7	Pulls/pushes toy when walking									
RM IV	8	Climbs stairs with rail									
RM IV	9	Creeps backwards down stairs									

Exhibit 2-8 continued

NAME_____Birthdate_____

CODE	0 = Never 2 = Frequently 1 = Occasionally 3 = Mastery	*Denotes skill repeated in other sections of Developmental Checklist #Denotes self-help skill

		Date								

PHASE IV (cont'd)

RM IV	10	Walks as adult, no longer stiff legged									
RM IV	11	Effort to jump off objects									
RM IV	12	Effort to run									
RM IV	13	Pushes chair about, climbs on it									
RM IV	14	Walks backward									
RM IV	15	Kicks large ball (demo)									
RM IV	16	Squats in play									
RM IV	17	Throws ball overhand									

PHASE V

RM V	1	Runs well (rarely falls)									
RM V	2	Climbs and stands on chair									
RM V	3	Walks up and down stairs without help--two feet per step									
RM V	4	Kicks ball forward									
RM V	5	Walks on tiptoes									
RM V	6	Jumps down with both feet									
RM V	7	Can carry breakable object									
RM V	8	Walks a balance beam									

Exhibit 2-9 Developmental Checklist—Perceptual/Fine Motor Goals

NAME_____Birthdate_____

CODE		
0 = Never 3 = Frequently	*Denotes skill repeated in other sections of Developmental Checklist	
1 = Occasionally 4 = Mastery	#Denotes self-help skill	

Date

PHASE I

PFM I	1	Eye contact
PFM I	2	Follows horizontal movement or light to midline
PFM I	3	Cries or startles in response to loud noises
*PFM I	4	Diminuation of activity for loud or unusual noises
*PFM I	5	Shows interest in black/white forms
*PFM I	6	Follows past midline
PFM I	7	Retains toy briefly
*PFM I	8	Responds to human voice by attending, stopping, or changing activity
PFM I	9	Holds toy one minute
*PFM I	10	Follows object 180°
PFM I	11	Glares at toys in hand
PFM I	12	Hand regard
PFM I	13	Disappearance of palmar reflex
PFM I	14	Grasps rattle (thumb participates)
PFM I	15	Hands engage at midline
PFM I	16	Hand play
PFM I	17	Mouths objects
*PFM I	18	Looks with intent at objects in hand
PFM I	19	Pays particular attention to tones of voices
*PFM I	20	Begins to localize sound laterally

PHASE II

PFM II	1	Reaches for object
PFM II	2	Grasps only large objects
PFM II	3	Approaches objects with two hands

Exhibit 2-9 continued

NAME_____ Birthdate_____

CODE		
0 = Never 2 = Frequently 1 = Occasionally 3 = Mastery	*Denotes skill repeated in other sections of Developmental Checklist #Denotes self-help skills	

			Date								
PHASE II (cont'd)											
*PFM II	4	Attends to objects dropped from sight									
*PFM II	5	Uses hands to affect objects (reach, grasp, splash, bang)									
PFM II	6	Scoops to grasp objects									
*PFM II	7	Resecures dropped object									
*PFM II	8	Fixates where object disappears									
PFM II	9	Transfer objects from hand to hand									
PFM II	10	Approaches objects with one hand									
PFM II	11	Sits, takes two toys									
PFM II	12	Definitely shakes rattle									
*PFM II	13	Looks for fallen objects									
*PFM II	14	Finds partially hidden objects									
*PFM II	15	Localizes sound well									
PHASE III											
*PFM III	1	Responds to "no" and name									
*PFM III	2	May use one object to move another									
PFM III	3	Drops one of two toys to take a third offered									
PFM III	4	"Rakes" radially and attains objects									
PFM III	5	Uses one object to affect another									
PFM III	6	Manipulates string or small object									
PFM III	7	Pincer grasp used, thumb and forefinger									
*PFM III	8	Uncovers hidden toy									
*PFM III	9	Explores and probes the holes and grooves in toys									
PFM III	10	Begins to deliberately release objects									

Exhibit 2-9 continued

NAME_____ Birthdate_____

CODE	0 = Never 2 = Frequently 1 = Occasionally 3 = Mastery	*Denotes skill repeated in other sections of Developmental Checklist #Denotes self-help skills

		Date								

PHASE III (cont'd)

PFM III 11	Attends to detail										
*PFM III 12	Removes objects from container										
PFM III 13	Reaches for image of toy in mirror										
PFM III 14	Tears paper										
PFM III 15	Neat pincer grasp										
*PFM III 16	Places objects in container										
PFM III 17	Palmar grasps crayon--dots imitatively										
PFM III 18	Imitates sound of toys										
*PFM III 19	Perceives roundness										
PFM III 20	Easy release										
*PFM III 21	Begins imitative scribbling										
PFM III 22	Book--pats pictures										
*PFM III 23	Builds tower with two cubes										
PFM III 24	Fills box or cup with toys										
PFM III 25	Plays appropriately with nesting cups										
PFM III 26	Assists turning book pages										
PFM III 27	Toys thrown in play										
*PFM III 28	Enjoys looking out window at moving cars and trees										
PFM III 29	Works with form boards										

PHASE IV

PFM IV 1	Two objects held in one hand										
*PFM IV 2	Builds tower with three or four cubes										
*PFM IV 3	Turns two or three book pages together										
PFM IV 4	Imitates adult activities										
*PFM IV 5	Spontaneously scribbles										
*PFM IV 6	Builds tower with five or six cubes										
*PFM IV 7	Imitates pushing train of cubes										
PFM IV 8	Stacks rings on peg										

Exhibit 2-9 continued

NAME_____Birthdate_____

CODE	0 = Never 2 = Frequently 1 = Occasionally 3 = Mastery	*Denotes skill repeated in other sections of Developmental Checklist #Denotes self-help skills

	Date								

PHASE V

PFM V	1	Fits toys together								
PFM V	2	Preference for handedness								
PFM V	3	Unscrews lids								
PFM V	4	Turns doorknob back								
*PFM V	5	Turns book pages one at a time								
*PFM V	6	Recalls events of previous day								
*PFM V	7	Listens to stories								
*PFM V	8	Increased visual memory span-- looks for missing toys								
*PFM V	9	Builds tower of six to seven cubes								
*PFM V	10	Imitates vertical stroke								
*PFM V	11	Imitates circular stroke								
PFM V	12	Works with pegboard materials								
*PFM V	13	Builds tower of eight cubes								
*PFM V	14	Builds tower of nine to ten cubes								
*PFM V	15	Imitates bridge								
*PFM V	16	Imitates cross								
PFM V	17	Works with puzzles								

Exhibit 2-10 Developmental Checklist—Sensory/Cognitive Skills

NAME_____ Birthdate_____

CODE	0 = Never 2 = Frequently 1 = Occasionally 3 = Mastery	*Denotes skill repeated in other sections of Developmental Checklist #Denotes self-help skills

			Date								
PHASE I											
SC I	1	Responds to physical stimulation									
SC I	2	Attends to certain sounds or sensory stimulations									
*SC I	3	Shows interest in black/white forms									
*SC I	4	Follows past midline									
*SC I	5	Responds to human voice by attending, stopping, or changing activity									
*SC I	6	Follows object 180°									
*SC I	7	Attends to adult mouth									
SC I	8	Visual interest begins									
SC I	9	Beginning of memorization of patterns									
*SC I	10	Looks with intent at object in hand									
*SC I	11	Begins to localize sounds laterally									
PHASE II											
SC II	1	Object permanence begins									
SC II	2	Turns head toward speaking voice									
*SC II	3	Attends to objects dropped from sight									
*SC II	4	Fixates where object disappears									
SC II	5	Talks and gestures to objects									
*SC II	6	Uses hands to affect objects (reach, grasp, splash, bang)									
*SC II	7	Resecures dropped object									
*SC II	8	Looks for fallen objects									
*SC II	9	Finds partially hidden objects									
*SC II	10	Localizes sound well									
SC II	11	Retains objects in hands									
SC II	12	Attempts to acquire objects to self									

Exhibit 2-10 continued

NAME_____Birthdate_____

CODE	0 = Never 2 = Frequently 1 = Occasionally 3 = Mastery	*Denotes skill repeated in other sections of Developmental Checklist #Denotes self-help skills								

			Date							
PHASE III										
*SC III	1	Uses one object to affect another								
SC III	2	Manipulation with forefinger and thumb to affect objects								
SC III	3	Symbolic meaning begins (gesture, language, and object identification)								
SC III	4	Begins to match two objects								
*SC III	5	Uncovers hidden toy								
SC III	6	Beginning of symbolic meaning (pictures)								
SC III	7	Overpermanence of objects								
SC III	8	Beginning indication of causality								
*SC III	9	Responds to "no"								
*SC III	10	Responds to name								
*SC III	11	Explores and probes holes and grooves in toys								
*SC III	12	Removes objects from container								
SC III	13	Sequential play								
*SC III	14	Places objects in container								
*SC III	15	Scribbling imitatively with crayon								
SC III	16	Begins other imitative behaviors								
*SC III	17	Perceives roundness								
SC III	18	Regards pictures in book								
SC III	19	Overpermanence or objects disappears								
SC III	20	Space perception								
SC III	21	Begins process of trial and error								
SC III	22	Causality established								
SC III	23	Comprehends a few objects by name								
*SC III	24	Builds tower with two cubes								
SC III	25	Fills box or cup with toys								
*SC III	26	Enjoys looking out window at moving cars, trees, etc.								

Exhibit 2-10 continued

NAME_____ Birthdate_____

CODE	0 = Never 2 = Frequently 1 = Occasionally 3 = Mastery	*Denotes skill repeated in other sections of Developmental Checklist #Denotes self-help skills

			Date								
PHASE IV											
*SC IV	1	Scribbles spontaneously									
*SC IV	2	Builds tower with three or four cubes									
*SC IV	3	Turns two or three book pages together									
*SC IV	4	Builds tower with five or six cubes									
*SC IV	5	Imitates pushing train of cubes									
SC IV	6	Formulates negative judgment									
SC IV	7	Object permanence									
SC IV	8	Says "no" with reason									
SC IV	9	Growth in object identification									
PHASE V											
SC V	1	Understands spatial concepts									
SC V	2	Answers "What do you do with ____?"									
*SC V	3	Imitates vertical stroke									
*SC V	4	Imitates circular stroke									
*SC V	5	Builds tower of six to seven cubes									
*SC V	6	Increased serial memory span-- looks for missing toys									
*SC V	7	Recalls events of previous day									
*SC V	8	Listens to stories									
SC V	9	Points to big and little									
*SC V	10	Turns book pages one at a time									
*SC V	11	Builds tower of eight cubes									
*SC V	12	Builds tower of nine to ten cubes									
*SC V	13	Imitates bridge									
*SC V	14	Imitates cross									
SC V	15	Finds book by name									
·SC V	16	Recognizes ten shapes									
SC V	17	Recognizes eleven colors									
SC V	18	Recognizes numbers zero - ten									
SC V	19	Recognizes phonetic symbols									
SC V	20	Matches smells									

Exhibit 2-10 continued

NAME_____ Birthdate_____

CODE	0 = Never　　　2 = Frequently 1 = Occasionally　3 = Mastery	*Denotes skill repeated in other sections of Developmental Checklist #Denotes self-help skills

	Date								
PHASE V (cont'd)									
SC V　21　Matches sounds									
SC V　22　Matches textures									
SC V　23　Counts to ten									
SC V　24　Names phonetic symbols									
SC V　25　Recognizes one or more printed words									
SC V　26　Sorts by big/little, color, shape, or texture									
SC V　27　Participates in Unit Activities									

Exhibit 2-11 Developmental Checklist—Language Goals

NAME_____ Birthdate_____

CODE				
0 = Never 2 = Frequently 1 = Occasionally 3 = Mastery	*Denotes skill repeated in other sections of Developmental Checklist #Denotes self-help skills			

			Date								
PHASE I											
L I	1	Reflex vocalizations									
L I	2	Throaty noises									
L I	3	Indicates bodily discomfort by change in pitch									
*L I	4	Diminuation of activity for loud or unusual sounds									
L I	5	Babbling and cooing efforts begin									
L I	6	Repetition of sounds for stimulation and pleasure									
L I	7	Facial and/or vocal change of expression when spoken to									
L I	8	Laughs and squeals									
L I	9	Differentiated crying									
L I	10	Attends to adult mouth									
L I	11	Babbling, cooing, chuckling									
L I	12	Makes responsive sounds when spoken to									
L I	13	Recognize familar human voice									
L I	14	Localizes sounds									
L I	15	Responds with laughter									
L I	16	Babbles several sounds in one breath									
L I	17	Attends to language enrichment activities									
PHASE II											
L II	1	Turns head toward speaking voice									
L II	2	High squeal									
L II	3	Vocal play									
L II	4	Imitates cough									
L II	5	Imitates protrusion of tongue									
L II	6	Combines sounds as ma and da									
L II	7	Gestures and babbles to objects									
L II	8	Cries with mum-mum-mum									
L II	9	Listens to self									
L II	10	Makes serial vowel sounds									
L II	11	Single syllable da, ma									

Exhibit 2-11 continued

NAME_____ Birthdate_____

CODE	0 = Never 2 = Frequently 1 = Occasionally 3 = Mastery	*Denotes skill repeated in other sections of Developmental Checklist #Denotes self-help skills								

	Date								
PHASE II (cont'd)									
L II 12 Gums objects									
L II 13 Tongue play									
PHASE III									
L III 1 Nonspecific dada, mama									
L III 2 Imitates sounds									
L III 3 Responds to "bye-bye" and "no"									
L III 4 Responds to own name									
L III 5 Combines syllables									
L III 6 Vocabulary of one or two words									
L III 7 Variations in volume									
L III 8 Waves bye-bye									
L III 9 Symbolic use of voice tone									
L III 10 "Mama," "dada" spoken with meaning									
L III 11 One word besides mama and dada									
L III 12 Carefully listens to words									
L III 13 Understands whole words and phrases									
L III 14 Responds consistently to name									
L III 15 Two other words besides mama and dada									
L III 16 Comprehends "give it to me" with gesture									
L III 17 Imitates sounds and words									
L III 18 Understands gestures									
L III 19 Follows one step directions									
L III 20 Comprehends a few objects by name									
L III 21 Vocalizes three - four words									
L III 22 Communication by gesture									
L III 23 Indicates needs by pointing or vocalizing									
L III 24 Uses "jargon"									
PHASE IV									
L IV 1 Understands some commands									
L IV 2 Understands simple questions									

Exhibit 2-11 continued

NAME_____ Birthdate_____

CODE	0 = Never 2 = Frequently 1 = Occasionally 3 = Mastery	*Denotes skill repeated in other sections of Developmental Checklist #Denotes self-help skills

		Date							
PHASE IV (cont'd)									
L IV	3	Ten word vocabulary							
L IV	4	Identifies five named objects by pointing							
L IV	5	Names one picture							
L IV	6	Recognizes pictures without naming							
L IV	7	Pulls for communication							
L IV	8	Imitates animal and toy sounds							
L IV	9	Vocabulary of twenty words							
L IV	10	Spontaneous combinations of two or three words							
PHASE V									
L V	1	Points to one named body part							
L V	2	Recognizes 120 - 275 words							
L V	3	Points to ten pictures							
L V	4	Uses two-word sentences							
L V	5	Names eight pictures							
L V	6	Uses some prepositions, pronouns, and adjectives							
L V	7	Vocabulary of 20 - 300 words							
L V	8	Identifies uses of many objects (Show me the one you wear, eat, drink from)							
L V	9	Talks about feelings and activities							
L V	10	Speech with pointing							
L V	11	Uses three-word sentences							
L V	12	Uses I, me, mine, and you							
L V	13	Comprehends time words							
L V	14	Uses plurals							
L V	15	Questions begin							
L V	16	Uses compound and complex sentences							
L V	17	Acts out "in," "on," "run," "walk"							
L V	18	Knows first and last name							

Exhibit 2-12 Developmental Checklist—Personal/Social/Self-Help Goals

NAME_____ Birthdate_____

CODE	0 = Never 2 = Frequently 1 = Occasionally 3 = Mastery	*Denotes skill repeated in other sections of Developmental Checklist #Denotes self-help skills							

			Date							
PHASE I										
P/S/SH I	1	Regards face--activity diminishes								
P/S/SH I	2	Quiets when picked up								
P/S/SH I	3	Eye contact								
P/S/SH I	4	Emotional response to distress								
P/S/SH I	5	Smiles responsively to mother								
P/S/SH I	6	Recognizes mother (visually)								
P/S/SH I	7	Follows moving person (visually)								
P/S/SH I	8	Responds emotionally to delight								
P/S/SH I	9	Squeals with pleasure								
P/S/SH I	10	Hand regard								
P/S/SH I	11	Smile at mirror image								
P/S/SH I	12	May sober at sight of strangers								
P/S/SH I	13	Enjoys evening play with father								
P/S/SH I	14	Spontaneous social smile								
P/S/SH I	15	Hand play								
P/S/SH I	16	Cries if adult stops playing with him								
P/S/SH I	17	Laughs out loud, smiles, sobers								
#P/S/SH I	18	Anticipates on sight of food								
PHASE II										
P/S/SH II	1	Cries when ignored by adult								
P/S/SH II	2	Cries when left by adult								
P/S/SH II	3	Stretches arm to be taken								
P/S/SH II	4	Emotional response appropriate to specific situations								
#P/S/SH II	5	Feeding, pats bottle								

Exhibit 2-12 continued

NAME_____ Birthdate_____

CODE	0 = Never 2 = Frequently 1 = Occasionally 3 = Mastery	*Denotes skill repeated in other sections of Developmental Checklist #Denotes self-help skills								

			Date								
PHASE II (cont'd)											
P/S/SH II	6	Plays with foot									
P/S/SH II	7	Discriminates strangers									
P/S/SH II	8	Smiles and vocalizes at mirror image									
P/S/SH II	9	Responds with fear to loss of support or to sudden loud noises									
#P/S/SH II	10	Holds bottle									
#P/S/SH II	11	Strained food taken well									
P/S/SH II	12	Begins showing fear of strangers									
P/S/SH II	13	Pats image of self in mirror									
P/S/SH II	14	Goes to familiar person for companionship									
P/S/SH II	15	Unhappiness is specifically fear or disgust, etc.									
P/S/SH II	16	Happiness is specifically elation or affection									
P/S/SH II	17	Amuses self briefly									
#P/S/SH II	18	Feeds self cookie									
#P/S/SH II	19	Chews food									
P/S/SH II	20	Pulls toy away from adult									
P/S/SH II	21	Reaches persistently for toys									
PHASE III											
P/S/SH III	1	Works for toy out of reach									
P/S/SH III	2	Plays peek-a-boo									
P/S/SH III	3	Responds to own name									
P/S/SH III	4	Responds to pickup gesture with understanding									
#P/S/SH III	5	Feeds self bottle--puts in and removes from mouth									
P/S/SH III	6	Strong anxiety regarding strangers									
#P/S/SH III	7	Remains dry one to two hours									

Exhibit 2-12 continued

NAME_____ Birthdate_____

CODE	0 = Never 2 = Frequently 1 = Occasionally 3 = Mastery	*Denotes skill repeated in other sections of Developmental Checklist #Denotes self-help skills

		Date								
PHASE III (con'd)										
P/S/SH III 8	Able to play alone for about an hour--but prefers company									
#P/S/SH III 9	Accepts new solid food									
#P/S/SH III 10	Finger feeds									
#P/S/SH III 11	Eats mashed foods									
P/S/SH III 12	Waves bye-bye responsively									
P/S/SH III 13	Plays pat-a-cake responsively									
P/S/SH III 14	Offers toys to adult, but does not want to give them up									
P/S/SH III 15	Enjoys dropping toys from playpen or chair to be retrieved by adult									
P/S/SH III 16	Increased affection and interest in family group									
P/S/SH III 17	Releases object to another upon request									
P/S/SH III 18	Distinguishes between you and me									
P/S/SH III 19	Shows fear, affection, anger, jealousy, sympathy, and anxiety									
#P/S/SH III 20	Dry after nap									
#P/S/SH III 21	Fusses until changed									
#P/S/SH III 22	Begins to coope ate in dressing									
P/S/SH III 23	Manipulates string or small object									
P/S/SH III 24	Shows shoe, eye, nose, etc responsively									
P/S/SH III 25	Hugs and shows affection toward doll or teddy bear									
P/S/SH III 26	Plays near other children									
P/S/SH III 27	Varies behavior according to emotional reaction of others									

Exhibit 2-12 continued

NAME_____ Birthdate_____

CODE	0 = Never 2 = Frequently 1 = Occasionally 3 = Mastery	*Denotes skill repeated in other sections of Developmental Checklist #Denotes self-help skills							

	Date								
PHASE III (cont'd)									
P/S/SH III 28 Indicates wants without crying									
P/S/SH III 29 Attempts to play ball with adult									
#P/S/SH III 30 Holds spoon and puts into dish									
#P/S/SH III 31 Grasps cup with fingers, but likely to tip cup too quickly									
#P/S/SH III 32 Indicates wet pants, but not toilet needs									
#P/S/SH III 33 Tries to put on clothes									
#P/S/SH III 34 Extends arm or leg cooperatively when being dressed									
PHASE IV									
P/S/SH IV 1 Imitates observed activities									
P/S/SH IV 2 Pulls a toy									
P/S/SH IV 3 Short attention span									
P/S/SH IV 4 Negativism--opposes most request									
#P/S/SH IV 5 Tries to put on shoes									
#P/S/SH IV 6 Can take off small items of clothing									
#P/S/SH IV 7 Can unzip zippers									
#P/S/SH IV 8 Fills spoon, but spills much while attempting to feed self									
#P/S/SH IV 9 Spoon turns in mouth									
#P/S/SH IV 10 Cup lifted to mouth, drinks well									
#P/S/SH IV 11 Hands empty cup to adult									
#P/S/SH IV 12 Holds glass with both hands									
#P/S/SH IV 13 Bowel and bladder may be regulated in daytime									
P/S/SH IV 14 Identifies parts of own body									

Exhibit 2-12 continued

NAME_____Birthdate_____

CODE	0 = Never 2 = Frequently 1 = Occasionally 3 = Mastery	*Denotes skill repeated in other sections of Developmental Checklist #Denotes self-help skills

	Date								
PHASE IV (cont'd)									
#P/S/SH IV 15 Eating and drinking skills well established									
#P/S/SH IV 16 Asks for food, toilet, and drink by gesture or word									
PHASE V									
P/S/SH V 1 Helps in house in simple tasks									
P/S/SH V 2 Plays toy telephone, "reads" newspaper									
P/S/SH V 3 Curious and busy									
P/S/SH V 4 Uses me, you, I, mine									
P/S/SH V 5 Calls self by name									
P/S/SH V 6 Temper tantrums									
P/S/SH V 7 Has mother-baby relationship with dolls									
P/S/SH V 8 Self-centered play									
P/S/SH V 9 Separates readily from mother when well handled									
#P/S/SH V 10 Needs help in feeding, no longer turns spoon before it reaches the mouth									
#P/S/SH V 11 Drinks holding small glass one-handed									
#P/S/SH V 12 Pulls on simple clothes									
#P/S/SH V 13 Removes unlaced shoes									
#P/S/SH V 14 Removes coat									
#P/S/SH V 15 Often dry during naps									
#P/S/SH V 16 Verbalizes or signs toilet needs consistently									
P/S/SH V 17 Notices different facial expressions									
P/S/SH V 18 Possessive with toys									
P/S/SH V 19 Insists on same routine									
P/S/SH V 20 Helps put things away									
P/S/SH V 21 Pushes toy--good steering									
P/S/SH V 22 Beginning efforts toward cooperative play									
#P/S/SH V 23 Self-feeds with little spilling									

Exhibit 2-12 continued

NAME_____ Birthdate_____

CODE	0 = Never 2 = Frequently 1 = Occasionally 3 = Mastery	*Denotes skill repeated in other sections of Developmental Checklist #Denotes self-help skills

	Date							
PHASE V (cont'd)								
#P/S/SH V 24 Attempts to button and unbutton								
#P/S/SH V 25 Puts on untied shoes--often on wrong feet								
#P/S/SH V 26 Tries to brush teeth								
#P/S/SH V 27 Washes and dries hands								
#P/S/SH V 28 Dry at night if taken up at least once								

Planning Early Intervention Programs: Preparing Parents and Paraprofessionals To Become Infant Educators

STRATEGIES FOR PROGRAM PLANNING AND IMPLEMENTATION

When planning intervention programs on behalf of handicapped infants, many professional educators are in general agreement on the importance of being guided by developmental guidelines and accurate assessment whenever possible. Educators also recognize that a number of complex logistics are involved in providing effective services to the families of such children. Those logistics often include the training of paraprofessionals to further extend the services of the program. Effective training of parents as educators of their own children is also mandatory because parents and home environment comprise the dominant factors in any child's life. Indeed, parents very nearly require sufficient training to enable them to qualify as paraprofessionals themselves. Thus, this chapter includes suggestions for the components of an effective intervention program and an outline of a training program for parents and paraprofessionals.

Planning for Early Childhood Intervention Programs

Planning early intervention programs for young handicapped children involves three areas of concern. The first is the initial feasibility planning research. The second deals with the structures involved in the delivery of services. The third is the theory and structure required for the educational program itself.

When considering such a program, many factors must be researched and analyzed for effective decision-making processes. These endeavors include:

1. researching various types of programs
2. deciding upon the area to be served

3. establishing the needs of the area
4. estimating the number of children that can be helped
5. determining the qualifying conditions of the children for participation
6. determining the program model
7. staffing requirements
8. housing requirements
9. material requirements
10. financial requirements.

Delivery of service falls into four areas of concern. First, is the need for administrators and those who test and evaluate the children as well as plan the children's programs. Second, actual service to the children should be provided in the home, in the center, or in a preschool setting. Third, supportive services for parents and parent involvement should be provided. Finally, service to the community should be offered by means of dissemination of information on the program's advantages and contributions; parent, student, and paraprofessional training; and inservice training for other professionals.

In a program that includes a heavy reliance upon parent participation and paraprofessional involvement, it is recommended that the actual program for the children have a practical orientation. If there are children with a variety of handicapping conditions, the program should be very flexible. As educational levels of parents will vary, the materials should be clearly outlined and simply stated. They should have a "look and do" approach. There must be a heavy emphasis upon the development of language. A simple method of data gathering and ongoing evaluation should be included. Principles of good education may be taught as basic procedures that are applicable in many learning situations. Finally, the program itself should be founded upon basic developmental theory and provide training to parents and paraprofessionals in basic and fundamental teaching techniques. Those techniques may themselves be multidisciplinary as they are only tools for helping children.

The underlying foundation of the program may be goals or normal behaviors outlined in a developmental sequence. Activities may be devised to help children in areas of reflex and gross motor development, perceptual fine motor development, sensory cognitive growth, language, and, finally, personal/social/ self-help skills. These areas of emphasis may be divided into phases of development from birth through early childhood and often including the period of ages three to six. Flexibility must be an integral part of any program because no child's condition or progress is identical to another child's.

Areas of education and teaching techniques should include environmental enrichment, physical stimulation, fine and gross motor activities, developmentally appropriate criteria, language stimulation, suggestions toward an emotionally healthy climate in the home, management procedures, manipulation of concrete objects and symbols of abstractions, games, and, finally, "unit" activities to include knowledge of objects, the world, colors, numerical concepts and numbers, and reading skills for those who are able to learn them during the preschool years. These may be taught in the home as well as in groups in a preschool setting. Again, a multidisciplinary approach should be used that includes developmental elements, motoric and neurophysical involvement, Montessori tools and procedures, as well as the principles of behavior modification.

The use of these teaching devices should be based upon accurate evaluation of the child's needs. Such evaluation is ideally the result of an intervention program that includes a transdisciplinary approach to assessment and programming for the child. Such programming is most likely to meet the needs of the individual child and family.

A Transdisciplinary Approach to Assessment and Programming

The need for transdisciplinary approaches to providing intervention on behalf of children with problems and their families is becoming more and more evident. This clarification of need results from a growing awareness of the entire child and a more wholistic approach to care and training toward normalized life functioning, as the child is an entity unto himself. The child's progress and well-being are vitally affected by the family and home environment. This environment includes the community at large.

No one discipline is, at the present time, equipped to deal with this enormous gestalt. As indicated in Chapter 2, physicians diagnose and treat within a medical model that deals with the physical care and healing of the body. This alone includes a monumental body of information and techniques to be mastered. Physical therapists, occupational therapists, and speech therapists also work within a physical model, but with theories and techniques known only to their areas of endeavor. Educators are trained to teach skills and concepts necessary for effective functioning in the culture. Psychologists and counselors seek to "heal" the mind and enable people to cope with life stress factors. Occasionally, children have problems that demand the expertise of specialists like neurosurgeons or heart surgeons. Finally, no program can be effected without those who are able to administrate and see to the delivery of services.

As a result, a transdisciplinary approach to intervention on behalf of handicapped preschool children must include members of many disciplines. The physicians, educators, therapists, special consultants, counselors, and administrators all come to the child's aid with areas of strength. They also come with limits to their expertise. Thus, an attitude of mutual respect and appreciation is necessary to effectually cooperate on behalf of the child. That effort must be directed toward five areas of concern—diagnosis, programming, education, ongoing reassessment and reevaluation, and parent involvement.

Establishing transdisciplinary cooperation in order to deal with those five areas of need is not without problems. Indeed, members of such a team will be called upon to deal with many problems beginning with the rigorous demands of scheduling group meetings. As there has been a lack of training in all disciplines toward this technique of serving the public, there currently exists a lack of communication among most individuals involved in such an approach. Hopefully, those professionals will gradually become aware of the strengths and limitations of each field. Given time and mutual respect, effective diagnosis, programming, and outstanding services to families will result.

Diagnosis

The initial diagnosis may be made by those having input to the specific problems of the child under consideration. The basic staff would consist of the physician, educator, administrator, and parent counselor. Physical and speech therapists as well as consultants would be called in as deemed appropriate.

The logistics involved in such a gathering may be formidable. Scheduling for many busy people is most difficult. Time must be regularly allotted for group assessment following either group or individual evaluations. Those evaluations are most effectively done when video taped and later reviewed together. Questions and parental answers should be taken once if possible and reviewed before being asked again and again by each member of the team. Diagnosis should be as immediate as possible so that valuable time will not be lost on behalf of either the child or the parents. Obviously, the administrator's managerial skills are vital. Finally, it is not enough merely to evaluate the child. Team members should give input into the desired program if it is to be as effective as possible.

Diagnosis of handicapping conditions is most effective for intervention when made shortly after the birth of an infant. As noted in Chapter 2, some handicapping conditions may be identified before birth. Counselors and educators may begin training parents in advance of the birth and a most successful program may result. Some birth defects are often physically apparent. For this reason, the more severe handicaps can be treated with immediate intervention programs. However, mild and moderate handicapping conditions generally do not become apparent until children are older or enter school. Children in *high risk* categories such as low birth weight or premature babies should be periodically evaluated on tests such as those discussed in Chapter 2. Their developmental progress should be noted and carefully observed. Additional handicapping conditions may occur to preschoolers as a result of accidents and illness. Here again, transdisciplinary medical diagnosis and therapeutic involvement should be used as well as educational diagnosis to implement continued development. In each case, rapid servicing of the children and their families is highly desirable.

Reevaluation

The transdisciplinary team must be prepared to give ongoing input into the children's programs, as change is a fundamental of life. The initial crisis situation will not reveal all the elements of the children's situations. Family coping skills, disease, vacations, deaths in the family, despair, and financial problems will affect family participation. The children's personalities, health, and stages of growth will also require input for successful programming.

Child Programming

The children's programs should be based upon their individual needs, strengths, and weaknesses. Following birth, the program is best initiated immediately. If a child is in the hospital, parents may be trained with dolls or with the infant or child whenever possible. Parental contact is vital to establish bonding between the newborn and the parents as well as to expedite an effective program. Basics in physical stimulation often provide a simple, good beginning. Educators and therapists should help as often as necessary (daily or twice weekly) until the parents are able to assume more of the program. Thereafter, once a week or once a month may prove sufficient.

Parent Services

Counseling members of the transdisciplinary team should ideally initiate supportive services for the parents with crisis counseling techniques (Parad, 1975). Educators may help by teaching parents the rudiments of infant care and by demonstrating the simplest procedures in the child's program. They may also provide volunteer training for friends and relatives of the family. Parents of children with similar handicapping conditions may lend support to the family as models and as individuals with some understanding of the family's crisis. Educators may gradually present appropriate written materials to the family and encourage participation in parent groups when it becomes appropriate for the family. Counselors and educators may be called upon to assist the family in gaining financial help as well as acquiring an understanding of bureaucratic problems to be encountered.

As members of the transdisciplinary team expedite the child's program, parents may be expected to gradually become more involved with the total intervention project. Parental involvement occurs where good diagnosis, reevaluation, child programming, and parent services have been of great help to the family in crisis.

APPROACHES TO PARENT INVOLVEMENT

A child's problems are not the child's alone nor can the child solve those problems alone. The problems will affect all those who live with the child. The adult reactions in turn affect the progress of the child in matters of eventual adjustment to the problem, social, mental, and emotional growth, and, eventually, the degree of participation the child may achieve in society. Therefore, it is most desirable to encourage parents to participate actively in their child's intervention program.

Several purposes are served by involving parents in their child's intervention program. The parent–child relationship can be greatly improved. Intervention is far more effective when parents understand and meet the child's needs. Parents are benefited by the exchange of information with professionals and others who have undergone similar experiences. Finally, parents may benefit the program itself by becoming advocates in the community for stronger programs.

Indeed, parents have taken many active roles in numerous intervention programs throughout the country. They have worked as administrators and participated on advisory councils and as parent group leaders. Parents have disseminated information and advocated the cause of such programs through public relations activities and legislative activities. They have served as volunteers to programs and as models for other parents. In many instances, parents have given much time and support by counseling parents whose children have similar problems. Parents have recruited additional children in need of programs. They have served as the primary teachers of their own children, developing curriculum and original teaching devices. They have learned the skills of data gathering, recording, assessing, and evaluating. Indeed, they have become paraprofessionals in every sense of the word. Many parents have gone back to school for further training and have reentered the field as professionals. Their personal experience and expertise have made their contributions most valuable.

Frequently, professionals become disappointed in parent participation in formalized groups. Parents frequently resist participation because they are not yet ready to listen to other's problems. They feel their needs are being met by the teacher, and they do not realize the benefits that sharing may afford. Scheduling, vacations, illness, and general reluctance to attend any meetings add to the absenteeism at structured gatherings. Furthermore, it is inappropriate to involve grieving parents in such groups until they have had sufficient time to adjust to their new situation.

The initial introduction of parents to the intervention program is critical. The program must not be made to seem overwhelming. Parents must be convinced that the program can meet their needs and the needs of the child. When they perceive their first efforts as successful, parents become much more hopeful and open to the work of the program. It is also wise to stress the abilities rather than the problems of the child. Parents are soon able to participate in planning their child's program with the aid of educators and therapists.

Thus, a successful program of parent involvement should recognize the need to provide counseling and supportive services and open avenues of access to other community services. It should also provide inservice training and individual as well as group programs for parent involvement. In order to succeed in this phase of programming, educators must be able to truly perceive the needs of the child and the family. They must set reasonable and attainable goals that can be achieved through practical planning. Finally, the program must be realistically scheduled, allowing for practical investments of time, emotional involvement, and temperament. Educators are well advised to remember that the parents did not originally choose to participate in this field of endeavor. A certain reluctance to fill in endless forms and data sheets is to be expected. Parents chose other professions, and they are rarely dedicated to the cause of educational research. On the other hand, more and more parents are refusing to be intimidated by professionals and hope to participate in all decisions affecting their child. They expect to read all reports and attain copies of their child's files. They want realistic suggestions for managing the child as their problems are ongoing and few pat solutions exist. Parents resent "final" diagnoses and labeling, although they may find no diagnosis equally frustrating. They need to be continually helped to look for the good in their child and their situation.

Programs that meet those needs will be most effective in intervening on behalf of children with problems. Further suggestions for dealing with the needs of parents and children are included in the following section on paraprofessional training.

PLANNING PARAPROFESSIONAL TRAINING PROGRAMS

Paraprofessionals are of great importance to intervention programs that strive to meet the needs of increasing numbers of families whose children are born with problems. Paraprofessionals serve as a bridge between those assessing children and planning programs for them and the families to be served. They are, in a sense, extensions of those professionals—extensions that make possible serving increasing numbers of families.

Paraprofessionals extend services between professionals and families by going to urban or rural homes or by working as additional staff members at program centers. Paraprofessionals experience the satisfactions and frustrations of actually implementing programs. For this reason, it is important that they be included as valuable members of the professional team. In order to qualify as team members, they require common sense, as well as solid training in basic teaching techniques and theory. Although they are not expected to have the expertise of professionals, they must have sufficient understanding to carry out the prescribed programs. Their training program should be founded first upon a realistic understanding of local needs and logistics.

The design for a comprehensive training program for paraprofessionals in the field of early childhood intervention must be developed within four areas of concern. First, the need for such a program must be established and the structure involved well organized. Second, there must be processes that permit constructive exchange of information among professionals designing the infant intervention program, the paraprofessional, and the parents and children being served. Third, the goals of the program must be outlined and the teaching designed to meet that end. Finally, the structure of the actual training sessions must have a flexible format in order to be taught under a variety of circumstances. A description of those four areas of concern is given herein with specific suggestions for the training program.

Need and Logistics

Any assessment of need for a paraprofessional training program and the logistics of establishing such a program must begin with research. That research must include study into the effective strengths as well as weaknesses of other such programs. Research must also be done to establish the need for such a program in the area to be served.

The area of service involved as well as the needs of the population requirements will also affect planning for the program. The logistics include decisions on the following questions:

1. How many children need to be served?
2. What are their handicapping conditions?
3. Where are they located?
4. Who is available to reach them?

5. How many individuals are required to provide paraprofessional services?
6. How can they be reached for training?
7. Where can the training be given?
8. When can it be scheduled?
9. What are the staffing requirements for delivery of training?
10. What materials will be required to provide the training?
11. What costs will be involved in the training program?
12. What will be the administrative expenditures?
13. What standards shall be required to qualify those serving as paraprofessionals?

The Role and Qualifications of the Paraprofessional

The program must establish a chain of service procedures that will permit an efficient exchange of information among (1) the professionals testing and planning programs for individual children, (2) the paraprofessional, and (3) the child and the family. The following diagram illustrates a possible program of interaction.

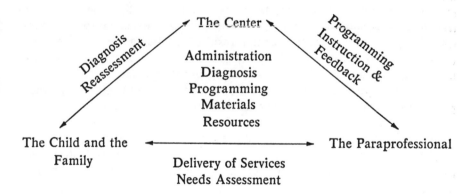

The center suggested in the diagram may be expected to house the administrators, program designers, data collectors, and, occasionally, members of the transdisciplinary team. Facilities for the storage and preparation of teaching materials should also allow for ease of access to reference materials. Meeting rooms for transdisciplinary team members, inservice training, and parent groups are recommended. Demonstration rooms, testing rooms, and preschool facilities may be incorporated at the center depending upon the structure of the program.

The paraprofessional may be expected to work at the center or travel to the greater community. This individual implements the programs of the professional teams. The paraprofessional may also be expected to work closely with other educators and various therapists throughout the region.

While delivering program services to children and their families, the paraprofessional must remain alert to ongoing needs assessment as children and families' situations frequently undergo changes. Plans may need to be altered due to illness, financial setbacks, and discouragement. There will also be times of progress to report to the center. For this reason, weekly or biweekly meetings should be held with the paraprofessional as a time of sharing and reevaluating program developments. In addition, the paraprofessional should encourage parents to bring the child back to the center for regular retesting and reassessment.

In fact, the paraprofessional must "sell" the family on the child's program and be able to support the family's every good effort. Such responsibility requires certain qualities in the character of a paraprofessional. Hopefully, those individuals chosen to work as paraprofessionals will be highly dependable, trustworthy, and self-motivated. They should be truly convinced of the desirability of early intervention programs and enthusiastically able to present or "sell" the many facets of the program to the parents. It is most helpful if the paraprofessional is by disposition basically patient, compassionate, understanding, firm, stubborn, and optimistic. Paraprofessionals should also enjoy the confidence that results from being well prepared, well informed, and well trained. Parents, professionals, and children alike will demand these qualities from those serving in this capacity.

In order to provide paraprofessionals with sufficient strength to meet these demands, a training program should be based upon realistic recognition of the rigors of the work. Hopefully, professionals experienced in on-the-floor work with children and parents will prepare such a training program. This will certainly facilitate reasonable goals and provide quality instructional service. It is hoped the following program will help implement that instruction.

The Training Program

It is suggested that a strong training program will incorporate the following goals:

1. Training will qualify the paraprofessional to work in center-based, home, or preschool designed programs.
2. Training will provide the paraprofessional with a strong, practical, and experiential orientation. This training will help the paraprofessional ac-

quire appropriate teaching skills and the confidence necessary to successfully help children and their families.

3. Training will provide opportunities to develop counseling and "selling" skills.
4. The paraprofessional will gain a solid understanding of the principles of intervention programming. As no two situations will be totally alike, the paraprofessional will be able to apply those principles in a variety of problem areas.
5. Data keeping, record keeping, and evaluation procedures will be well taught enabling the paraprofessional to perform and teach this part of the program without overwhelming difficulty.
6. The paraprofessional will understand the operation of the total program, personnel, and the bounds of the paraprofessional's area of concern.

The Format

A training program follows in outline form that is based upon ten instructional periods. Each session is complete in itself. Each may be given in a three-or preferably six-hour period. The total program may be delivered in one to two weeks or on successive weekends. It is imperative that those periods of instruction include practice on materials with dolls or children. Questions and discussion times are vital in each session. Testing that is designed to reinforce the learning of vital concepts should be included. Thus, time management by instructors is of great importance.

The instructors must be experienced staff members who have worked "on the floor" with children and parents. They should be prepared to call in experts in the fields of physical, speech, and occupational therapy. Professional counselors and parents who have been in previous programs might well augment the training.

Physical materials for use in this training program should include prepared audio-visual tapes, handouts, outlines of the lectures and concepts to be learned, testing papers, Skinnerian training papers, a training manual, dolls, physical therapy equipment, basic teaching toys and materials, the film *The Miracle Worker*, and children when or if possible. Books and reference materials pertinent to the training program should also be available.

Additional Suggestions for Successful Implementation of the Training Program

Books and reference materials and handouts might wisely be read before the actual training begins if it is to be given in a short, intensive period of time. Should the training sessions be offered on weekends or intermittently, the reading could precede the appropriate session, which will help the paraprofessional begin to think in terms of the skills to be acquired.

It is also helpful to train paraprofessionals to really "think" in terms of applying the principles to be taught. Since no two children or families will be alike, techniques and principles must be well understood. Skinnerian worksheets (called "teaching tests" in this manual) similar to those included in the teaching section of this manual might advisably be included in the training program.

It is also helpful to teach paraprofessionals to think by leading discussions and asking questions that require them to use (1) memory skills, (2) skills of translating situations from one example to another, (3) comparing and contrasting skills, (4) problem-solving questions to strengthen thinking on "how" and "why" situations, (5) reasoning skills, (6) problems of synthesis ("How would you have done this?"), and (7) evaluative thinking skills that help the student recognize what is good and valid rather than faulty in technique and theory (more information on these teaching methods may be found in Norris M. Saunders' *Classroom Questions: What Kinds*, New York: Harper and Row, 1966).

Many of these teaching techniques, principles, theories, and materials might well be adapted to parent training programs. Certainly some of the training sessions should be attended by parents when deemed appropriate. Items starred (*) in the following outline are discussed in greater depth in various places in the manual. Please check the index for page numbers.

Session I. The Program and Intervention Theory
  I. The theory of *normalization* (see Wolfensberger, 1972). Point out the importance of early intervention as implementation of this theory. Use as a means of gaining parental support.
  II. Purpose of intervention programs, goals, and background
  III. Basic developmental theory and handouts*
  IV. Structure of the sponsoring program
      A. The center
      B. The transdisciplinary team and the transdisciplinary approach to assessment and planning*
      C. The role of the paraprofessional*
      D. Work in the field, the center, the preschool, the home
  V. Introduction to program materials
      A. Reference materials and books
      B. Training manual and handouts
      C. Parent handbook
      D. Developmental checklists*

E. Worksheets*
F. Curriculum*
G. Other assessment tools being used in the program
VI. Discussion and teaching-tests
Session II. The Child
I. More detailed work on developmental theory*
II. Basic information on common handicapping conditions
A. Blindness
B. Cerebral palsy
C. Down's Syndrome
D. Hearing loss
E. Hydrocephalus
F. Mental retardation
G. Spina bifida
H. Others depending upon needs of the particular program

Note: Each child's condition is unlike any other's. Flexibility is demanded. Paraprofessionals must note small changes in the child's condition and report to professionals for further instruction.
III. Passive techniques for intervention
A. Enriching the environment*
B. Physical stimulation*
C. General language program*
D. General gross and fine motor program*
IV. Discussion, practice of intervention techniques and teaching-tests
Session III. Practitioners Serving Families
I. Counseling
A. The process of grief (Kübler-Ross model)*
1. denial
2. anger
3. bargaining
4. depression
5. acceptance
B. Crisis counseling (Parad, 1975; Lazarus, 1966)
II. Attitudes
A. General principles of listening, caring, not judging, providing appropriate help
B. Know your limitations and when to refer to more highly trained personnel
III. Coping with your own feelings
A. Burning out
B. Alternate programs and professionals

      C. Kaufman's questions (*To Love Is To Be Happy With*)
      D. Recognizing your own fears
      E. Understanding your own griefs
  IV. Discussion, practice, and teaching-tests
Session IV. Implementing Programs
    I. Programs involve the family
      A. General conditions
        1. financial concerns
        2. illness
        3. malnutrition
        4. siblings, inlaws, and friends
      B. Family coping skills, based upon
        1. values
        2. role perceptions
        3. communications systems
  II. Initiating an intervention program
      A. Relating the infant's program to the family's lifestyle
      B. Easing in gently
      C. Selling the program
      D. Periods of rest
      E. Involving parents in programming
  III. Problems that delay child's progress
      A. The family
        1. illness
        2. divorce
        3. vacations and holidays
        4. financial problems
        5. despair
        6. relatives
      B. The child
        1. illness and seizures
        2. fussing
        3. periods of frustration
        4. finding good reinforcers
  IV. Good manners
      A. Guest and friend
      B. Smoking
      C. Scheduling and being on time
      D. Casual yet professional
      E. Accepting
      F. Plan for immediate success

    V. Parent-community involvement
        A. Teaching
            1. curriculum development
            2. assessment-evaluation
            3. data gathering
            4. volunteer staff
        B. Administrating
        C. Locating children in need of programs
        D. Modeling and counseling other families
        E. Public relations
            1. fund raising
            2. legislating
            3. disseminating information
        F. Parent groups*
   VI. Discussion, practice, and teaching-tests
Session V. Teaching Techniques
    I. Behavior modification techniques*
        A. Reinforcement and motivation
        B. Reinforcing behaviors
        C. Eliminating behaviors
        D. Teaching new behaviors
   II. Task analysis or LIVING SKILLS PROCEDURES*
  III. Teaching tips
        A. Go slowly
        B. Simplify, simplify
        C. Allow for reaction time
        D. The use of cues
   IV. The general family atmosphere*
        A. Training rather than disciplining
        B. Overprotecting
        C. Balance
        D. Keeping a positive attitude
    V. Discussion, practice, teaching-tests
Session VI. Language
It is suggested that a speech therapist specializing in work with young
children teach this session.
    I. Basic principles of language development
   II. Basic language program*
  III. Common speech difficulties and coping suggestions (Connelly)
        A. Articulation
        B. Delayed speech

    C. Hearing disorders

    D. Stuttering

    E. Voice disorders

  IV. Discussion, practice and teaching-tests

Session VII. Physical Disabilities and Appropriate Care

It is suggested that a physical therapist specializing in work with young children teach this session.

    I. Basic information on common physical disabilities

      A. Types of cerebral palsy

      B. Seizures

      C. Hydrocephalus

      D. Spina bifida

      E. Paralysis

      F. Other conditions depending upon program needs

   II. Basic techniques of physical therapy

      A. Range of motion exercises and CAUTIONS!

      B. Handling children with problems (Finnie)

  III. Use of basic PT equipment—adaptations for home and preschools

  IV. Necessity of PT prescriptions

      Paraprofessionals to know their limitations!

   V. Discussion, practice, teaching-tests

Session VIII. Laying Foundations for Academics

As this manual deals with no one handicapping condition and as many children with certain handicaps are quite capable of learning academic materials, basic suggestions for such cognitive programs are included here and in the tools for teachers' section of this manual. Those paraprofessionals being trained through a preschool program may expect to have this session expanded to meet program needs.

    I. Cognitive development, ages 0–6

   II. Review teaching principles*

      A. Imitation*

      B. Discovery*

      C. Games*

      D. Manipulation*

      E. Review behavior modification techniques*

  III. Unit activities

      A. The concept*

      B. Suggested materials*

  IV. Appropriate concepts to be taught

      A. Colors*

      B. Shapes*

    C. Numbers*
    D. Numerical concepts*
    E. Reading readiness*
  V. General enrichment
    A. Stories*
    B. Choosing children's books*
    C. Caldecott awards*
    D. Songs and music
    E. Fingerplays
    F. Art activities
  VI. Personal/social development
  VII. Discussion, practice, teaching-tests

Session IX. Practicum and Inspiration

  I. Review of past sessions
    A. Review of demonstrations
    B. Discussion
    C. Questions and answers
    D. Review of teaching-tests
    E. Buzz group sessions
  II. Film: *The Miracle Worker* (VA/16, United Artists Corporation, 729 7th Avenue, New York, N.Y. 10019, (212) 575–4715, cost @ $120.)
    A. Analysis of film
      1. child's position
      2. parents' position
      3. siblings' position
      4. teacher's position
    B. Compare to modern paraprofessional's position
    C. Compare Sullivan's teaching techniques to "modern" methods
    D. Alternate solutions
    E. Application to situations of local program
  III. Discussion, teaching-tests

Session X. Wrapping It Up

  I. General discussion and review of Session IX teaching-test materials
  II. Final examination
    A. Based upon total program
    B. To be reviewed prior to exam for purposes of teaching and clarification
    C. The exam
    D. Correction of exam for purposes of teaching and clarification
  III. Certification

THE ROLE OF THE HELPING PRACTITIONER

A certain sensitivity to the feelings, messages, and needs of others is required of those who would participate in early childhood intervention programs. Ostensibly, such programs are designed to intervene on behalf of the child. In practice, the feelings and needs of the family have such great bearing upon the success of the work that helpers must also be well trained in crisis and family counseling techniques. That training is most effective when it provides practice for those who would counsel others to understand and gain command of their own feelings when under stress. It is well that practitioners have acquired the skills of an educator, a counselor, and general social worker as they work with people who are living through very trying situations.

Indeed, those who bear and raise handicapped children are experiencing an event considered a "tragedy" in United States society. Their frustrations and disappointments are intense and their emotional adjustments follow the pattern of grieving noted among those who have just suffered the death of a loved one or those who may be facing their own imminent death.

Those stages of adjustment are particularly well described in Dr. Elizabeth Kübler-Ross's book, *On Death and Dying*. Her method of questioning patients in order to help them clarify and resolve their own feelings is most helpful; the careful choice of words, genuine sensitivity, and effectiveness are worthy of note. Her model for the process of grief is clear, and applicable to families whose children are born with problems. It is recommended that this process be well studied by those in the helping services. To this end it is suggested that practitioners review the section of this chapter in Mori and Olive entitled "Parenting a Child with Special Needs."

It may also be useful to understand the basic principles of "crisis counseling" as taught by Parad (1975) and Lazarus (1966). It is believed that important changes in family living are occasioned by crisis. The family's values, concepts of role, and communication systems may suffer drastic alteration. Crisis counseling and intervention involves an intensive six-week period of counseling and problem-solving supports immediately following the event that precipitated the crisis. It can be a most helpful method of providing supportive services for families in distress.

Certain principles of caring for others are useful when providing quality counseling, whether during the period immediately following the crisis or during the long years of programming that may follow. Good counselors must be good listeners. They listen with acceptance rather than shock and judgment. They *ask* how the other person *feels* about a situation. They know that in order to effect change, they must do it with a loving heart. Counselors become adept at watching "body language" and hearing what is *really* being said. They are able to accept the fact that those they serve may turn upon them in anger due to stress and disappointment. Dr. Kübler-Ross (1969) notes that

> If we tolerate their anger, whether it is directed at us, the deceased (in this case the child) or at God, we are helping them take a great step towards acceptance without guilt. If we blame them for daring to ventilate such socially poorly tolerated thoughts, we are blameworthy for prolonging their grief, shame and guilt which often results in physical and emotional ill health (p. 180).

Effective counselors try to get in touch with a person's pain and get it out of the heart and into reality where it can be handled. On the other hand, counselors do not flood people suffering denial with reality. They introduce facets of the problem gradually because human beings adapt one step at a time. Practitioners accept the children and the parents as they are and guide them through programs based upon many immediate and small successes.

Practitioners, whether functioning as educators or counselors, sometimes reach a point where they cannot solve all a child's or family's problems. They should recognize their own limitations and refer clients to more highly trained professionals or recommend other programs. If conflict arises they may suggest another practitioner, which is not unusual.

Nor is it unusual for them to begin to feel burned out. Burning out is an occupational hazard. Practitioners may become too involved with the care of their families and exhaust themselves. It is wise to research, think on the child's program, teach it to the parents, love them, weep with them, laugh with them, and go home and leave the work at work. It is also wise for the intervention program administrators to organize the schedule in such a way that there will be periodic vacations or rest periods throughout the year.

Those who work "on the floor" with kids and their parents might also prepare themselves for the profession by seriously analyzing their own system of fears. All people fear poverty, criticism, failure, loss of love, ill health and mutilation, and death. When they worry, feel guilty, angry, or jealous, one of these fears is making them uncomfortable. This uneasy worrying can severely tax peoples' energies and the effectiveness of their work. Barry Kaufman (1977) suggests four questions that are most helpful when people probe into their feelings to gain an understanding of their fears. Those questions are:

What are you unhappy about?

Why are you unhappy about that?

Why do you believe that or do you believe that?

What are you afraid would happen if you weren't unhappy about that?
(p. 43)

These questions may be asked and then answered on paper when the person
is alone. It is also helpful to ask these questions in a conversation. Again,
care must be taken that there is no inflection of criticism in the questioner's
tone of voice. As people gain understanding of their own feelings and as they
learn to express their own fears, they are better able to understand those who
are also enduring the process of grief.

The Kübler-Ross model describes periods of denial and isolation, anger,
bargaining, depression, and acceptance as stages in that process. Practitioners who seriously study her model will soon recognize they too follow a
similar pattern of suffering when they have experienced a great sense of loss.
Once familiar with that pattern, people who would counsel families in crisis
will become far more understanding and more effective as helpers.

The family not only must be assisted through the process of grief, but also
may require help with problems of general living. Financial concerns may
become paramount factors in the family's adjustments. Good training in
available community services are vital in this regard. Some members of the
family may suffer illness and malnutrition. Again, practitioners will feel most
competent when well informed on the availability of community services and
the process involved in their implementation.

Siblings may either help or add to the problems of families in a state of
crisis. The number of children in a family as well as the temperaments of
those children will have great bearing upon the energy and time a parent may
be able to expend upon a child with special needs. However, handicapped
children frequently have a great desire to be like and play with their brothers
and sisters. This desire can become a highly motivating factor in the child's
successful growth and development. In this case, practitioners are well advised to include siblings in the training program and listen to them for helpful suggestions.

Grandparents, aunts and uncles, as well as family friends may also become
important considerations in intervention programs. Their support is in-
valuable. They frequently provide respite for the parents and often become
involved in the training program itself. They may also become advocates in
community efforts to gain legislative funding for special education programs.
They may have tremendous effect upon the family's "coping" skills as they
influence value systems, role perceptions, and family communication
systems.

These three patterns are already a part of every family's system of functioning. Just as all individuals have different ways of reacting to stress,
families have evolved different patterns of coping. There are strengths and

weaknesses in every family. Crisis may unify one family and cause the collapse of another. Knowing practitioners become sensitive to the family's emotional climate as they begin the intervention program.

On the first several visits the practitioners should become well acquainted with the family's values, patterns of living, and perceptions of roles rather than only assessing the child's problems, that is, they should (1) look for the strengths of the family and the child, (2) learn what family members enjoy, dislike, and feel about their lives, and (3) learn how they feel about the effect of their child's birth upon their lives. This knowledge will provide a vital foundation for good rapport and a successful ongoing program.

If various facets of the infant's needs are shown to relate to family interests, more enthusiastic participation can result. It is most important not to bombard the family with intensive training, theory, and group meetings until the process of grief is somewhat ameliorated. However, simple exercises, physical stimulation, and games involving immediate reward can be taught as a part of the daily bathing and diapering routine. The program should begin so gently that all involved quickly come to feel confident and successful. It is well to approach individuals and families much as one runs along side a moving train before jumping on board. Body language, posture, and voice inflection all give valuable clues as to a parent's feelings at the moment. They may lead to an understanding of a family's overall value system.

Practitioners need to recognize a family's value system as a means of "selling" or interesting a family in the intervention program. Everyone who wishes to influence another person must be able to use fundamental methods of persuasion. People will not try something new until their resistance is softened, their interest has been captured, and they begin to want what is being offered. Once they see the value of what is offered, the practitioner has only to get them to truly commit themselves to the program. The practitioner may have to give them new information or additional reasons to desire the recommended program. They may need many opportunities to reconsider until they decide to fully participate in the intervention program.

New information is often given by demonstrating or modeling the teaching techniques involved in the baby's program. The demonstration should be simple, thorough, and explicit. It should involve the parent and allow for practice and success! Parents need to be rewarded for improvements, but perfection need not be required. If the baby is ill or fussy, the demonstration can often be given using a doll for practice. As the parents see progress, no matter how small, they will become more involved in the actual program.

Parents' desire to participate in the program will continually be affected by a variety of circumstances. The babies themselves frequently become ill, fussy, and occasionally have seizures. They have periods of growth and development that cause them to become frustrated and irritable as when they are on the brink of walking. It may also be difficult to find good reinforcers for severely retarded infants. Certainly despair and lack of motivation on the parents' part will slow progress—so also will family illness, separations and divorce, visitors, holidays, and vacations. Indeed, there may be periods such as the Christmas season when nearly all these factors become so intertwined that it is best just to declare a ten-day holiday from the intervention program itself. Certainly less guilt will result. Parents and educators both may regard the new start as most beneficial.

Occasional rests from the program are beneficial; it is also helpful to involve the parents in planning the program. Few parents are able to handle more than five goal plans at a time, especially if data keeping is required. Parents may be encouraged to work out the developmental checklists and then, as they recognize appropriate goals, be allowed to choose the ones they feel most able to cope with. Eventually, they will try more and more of them as their confidence grows.

With the growth of confidence, parents and families will begin to accept the practitioner not only as a "professional" guest in the home, but also as a friend. There is a fine line between maintaining an image as a professional (which increases the parent's confidence in the program) without causing families to find the practitioner cold and austere (in which case they will always be defensive and unable or unlikely to permit the full implementation of the program). That line may be found as families sense genuine caring for them and their child.

Despite all the caring for the families, certain good manners are to be expected. Smoking may not be at all appreciated in some homes. It is not considered professional to smoke while visiting families. It is also considerate to be on time, which may prove difficult if there is a particularly important circumstance in one home that delays the next visit. This problem may be handled by explaining to parents that the practitioner may be expected within fifteen minutes on either side of the set appointment. Most parents are quite understanding when the problem is explained to them.

Practitioners will be most welcome in homes where they are perceived as casual yet professional, caring, interested, and accepting. Their support may not only help families through the grieving period, but also lead some family members to contribute to community services on behalf of the handicapped. Although parent groups are often not as fully attended as professionals might wish, individual parents frequently become involved as staff members in the child's educational program. They may contribute to curriculum development, materials development, assessment, evaluation, and data processing. They may help with administration, "child-find," fund raising, legislation, and the public dissemination of information. They frequently become fine counselors and models for other families with handicapped children. They may even become professional practitioners, thereby enriching society through their sensitivity and expertise.

PARENTING A CHILD WITH SPECIAL NEEDS

In the United States, people are uncomfortable admitting that they have fears. Yet, all emotional suffering is based upon fear of one sort or another; and, as everyone experiences suffering, so everyone is subject to the battle against fear—all emotional suffering is basically fear. Threat, anxiety, worry, guilt, anger, neurosis, psychosis, and addiction are all words that describe degrees of fear. The word *anger* may not immediately appear to be based upon fear, but consider the old term "fight or flight." When people feel threatened or afraid, they react by feeling angry (fight) or depressed and try to avoid dealing with the issue (flight).

It may take some thought and some time to really become aware that negative, unhappy feelings are feelings of fear. Yet this is true. Fears seem to fall into several categories. As people analyze their feelings, they realize they are afraid of poverty, criticism and failure, loss of love, poor health and mutilation, old age, and death.

When people are in a crisis and feel confused and frightened yet know they have a responsibility to fulfill, it is very helpful to know just what they fear and exactly why it is bothering them. The family of an infant with severe emotional problems developed a series of questions that are most helpful when people must understand their true problem in order to deal with it. Those questions are

What are you unhappy about?

Why are you unhappy about that?

Why do you believe that or do you really believe that?

What are you afraid would happen if you weren't unhappy about that? (Kaufman, 1977, p. 43).

Remember, people's lives enter into situations, and they have learned to think of these situations or happenings as being either good or bad. People's feelings about an event immediately follow their opinion as to whether the situation is good or bad. This opinion is affected by both training and previous life experiences.

People can better understand their interpretation of whether or not a situation is good or bad in several ways. If they have a calm, loving friend, they can discuss the fear-provoking situation. The friend can ask the questions just listed, and they can think and discuss the values and feelings they hold concerning the situation. People can also sit down alone with paper and pencil, ask themselves the questions, and write out their beliefs and feelings. After a while, they will perceive the cause of their fears quite quickly and can handle the entire process alone in their minds.

As a result, people feel better able to resolve the turmoil they feel within them. Sometimes, they are even able to laugh at themselves as they repeat the same fear pattern again and again.

What has this to do with helping a handicapped baby? Very simply, very importantly, the baby's greatest hope for survival and improvement is the rapid response and intervention of the most important people in a child's life—the parents. Training programs are most effective when begun immediately after the discovery of the problem. Yet that discovery precipitates a terrible crisis for the family. No one is really prepared for this crisis. Crisis provokes fear and a process of grieving. Everyone must work through that process of grief. The sooner families work through their necessary but preoccupying grief, the sooner the child can be helped.

Grief is affected by a sense of loss and many types of fear. The fears of criticism, poverty, illness, mutilation, and even death are involved to one degree or another when a child is born handicapped. Parents also feel a fear of failure. They believe they know how to raise a normal child. They are able to identify with the usual problems of raising children because they experienced childhood. Yet they have no idea of where to begin when their child has problems they perceive as "terrible." The situation is very threatening because they feel helpless; they are forced to once again realize that they are not omnipotent; this situation will not just go away. They are disappointed, stunned, and angry. They grieve. Grieving is a normal human experience. It seems to go through a series of stages (Kübler-Ross, 1969). Although those stages generally follow one another, grieving people's feelings may swing back and forth between them on any given day. Sometimes they get stuck on one stage. Then they need to discuss their feelings with someone they trust and work them out so they can go on with their lives.

At first, when people are hurt or grieve, they usually try to deny the problem. They think that if they don't look, it may go away. They feel like they are in shock—in a daze. They don't really hear or understand all that is being said to them. This stage of *denial* gives them time to get ready to fight their battle. It acts as a buffer against reality. They hear themselves thinking and saying, "No, not me. It can't be true." "No, not my child. There has been a mistake!" "Let's look for other doctors." "This is just unbelievable." It is particularly unbelievable if their baby looks physically normal.

Yet even while people cannot accept their "terrible" situation, they are called upon to make many important decisions. They need to learn how to teach the baby in appropriate ways. They must find appropriate care and make important financial arrangements. They don't feel ready for "parent groups" because they have yet to perceive themselves as belonging to such a group. They have not had the sort of preparation for loss that comes with physical illness. They would help their child and their spouses, but they can hardly help themselves.

They also feel terribly isolated from others. Other people do not quite know what to say to them and fear saying something thoughtless. The parents sense other people's discomfort and grow more inward in their suffering and denial. Sometimes their loved ones tell other people not to discuss their sorrow with them so they won't be reminded. While there are moments when parents don't want to be reminded, sometimes they desperately need to talk and cry out their pain. Then it helps to call friends and say, "I need to talk. Will you just listen and not judge or advise? Just let me talk."

At some point in time the parents allow that there is a problem and it is not going away. They will return to feelings of denial from time to time, but they really begin to feel *anger.* Now they are no longer in flight from their fears—they are furious with those involved in the situation, and look around to place the blame. "Whose fault is this?" (Probably no one's) "Why did the doctor say that?" "What an insensitive thing for the nurse or social worker to say!" "Why did God let this happen to us?"

Indeed, their anger with God (however they conceive the creative force of the universe) may be extreme. They may curse the name of deity, cry out against God; indeed, they may deny God altogether. This anger is often coupled with or results in feelings of guilt. Perhaps people fear that they are being punished, and this is why the child has such problems. Perhaps they think God will punish them in the future for hating Him now. But these guilts are not in keeping with a deity who proclaims principles of faith, hope, love, patience, and forgiving. People torture themselves needlessly with such thoughts. They need to find a way to express these guilt fears because they will not go away as long as people hold them inside themselves! If they cannot speak of their anger at God, they can write out their feelings on paper, answer the four questions listed previously, and then burn the paper or crumple it, tear it, kick it, and throw it away. They must also find harmless ways of expressing their resentment toward those individuals who will never understand this disappointment and who will go on raising children without their child's problems. Although some of those others may be able to help them, they do not necessarily want help even though they sense they could use it.

At this point, parents may begin to go into a new stage of grief. They may *bargain* in the hope they will be able to solve the problem. They make promises to God and themselves that if they do such and such, maybe the problem will go away. They may shop for wiser doctors and social workers. They may really get into the child's educational program. They may make tremendous sacrifices. The child may show improvement during this period of intense care and work, but the realities of the situation finally convince them of the years of effort ahead.

As a result of those realities, parents often become very *depressed*. They sense such loss—loss of the child they hoped for and loved, loss of their fantasies of family fun and honor, loss of money, loss of time, even loss of a sense of worth. They are overwhelmed by the challenges ahead. They are afraid they cannot meet all the child's needs. They fear failure, criticism, loss of esteem in the eyes of others. They fear poverty as the costs of care are so great. They even feel guilty because they fear they can no longer fulfill all the social activities they enjoyed before. They also may feel guilty because they resent the tremendous disturbance the child has created in their living patterns. Again, they must express these feelings to someone who will understand and not judge them. They may write them out until they feel resolved to the situation.

When parents have been warned the baby may die, they hesitate to really permit themselves to love the child for fear of further hurt and loss. Yet they feel guilty because they sense this child needs their love in order to live. This is particularly true when the baby is hospitalized, and parents cannot perform the acts of caring that "bond" or build a relationship between parents and their child. If the child has severe problems, parents may feel guilty because they think it might be better if the child did die. They may also hate themselves because they are ashamed of the child's appearance. These are feelings experienced by thousands of people under these same circumstances. There is no reason for them to hate themselves for those feelings. There is every reason to find someone who is understanding and express those feelings, cry about them, and work them out of their systems as quickly as possible.

It is important for parents to discuss the situation with their other children. Young children particularly tend to believe they may have caused the problem. This is because they may not have wanted a new baby in the family. They may also have suddenly become aware of death and illness. They may feel very confused and frightened. Parents can let the children express their ideas and concepts while they "play dolls." Sometimes it is pretty rough. Parents must not scold them or judge them for their anger any more than they want to be judged. Parents can comfort and console them and assure them of their worth once they understand their feelings.

Eventually parents will resolve themselves to a happier stage of accept-ance. They will accept themselves, their limitations, their child, and their child's limitations. The gifts in the situation will become more obvious to them. They will recall those who loved them and stood by just in case they could help. They will feel their own growth in patience, compassion, and wisdom. They will thrill to the miracle of life. They will know the simple beauty of love in these children. Their children will have helped them become ready to receive the greatest gifts of this existence.

How then can these children be helped? Every child is different, yet every child requires love and attention. Every child requires physical stimulation or withdrawal from active participation in life may result, especially for men-tally retarded youngsters. Every child needs to do things independently and feel some sense of control. Every child needs to move as much as possible. Every child needs to find ways to communicate, no matter how primitive that communication may seem. Every child needs training.

So then, no matter how great the parents' denial, anger, bargaining, and depression, they must begin to meet their child's needs. The following chapters will provide an understanding of training and teaching methods as well as possible activities for helping any child according to individual need. Parents can read these chapters, discuss, think, and practice the ideas therein. They can do a little each day to help the babies develop. They must do something toward the child's program each day or their procrastination will result in increased guilt and depression. That is a risk they cannot af-ford; for although their pain is great, their gifts are coming as surely as they relinquish their grief and enter into the work ahead.

ATTITUDES THAT HELP

People can greatly reduce their suffering just by controlling the thoughts they permit their minds to dwell upon. For example, worry about "what others will think" can increase the parents' pain—so also can worry about all the years ahead and the possible problems. It would be far wiser to utterly vanquish such ideas and, every time they occur, substitute concepts of just planning for the hour or day or even the week, looking forward to those things they enjoy while actually implementing their child's present program. If parents keep up the basic pattern of family living, if they all continue to love, support, and enjoy each other, everyone will be happy and their special babies will be able to blossom to their utmost in a happy family environment.

Parents will also be wise to cultivate friendships among people who do not weaken them with pity and hopeless remarks. Rather, they are wise to spend time with those who are supportive of them and their efforts on behalf of their children, because their work with the children must begin as soon as possible after the problems are identified. The work must be based upon daily, consistent programming. Parents can ill afford the setbacks of depression. Many facets of the program can be integrated into daily activities. For example, parents can do physical stimulation for the baby while watching TV with the family. They can do exercises and physical stimulation while waiting in doctors' offices if they carry a little set of "stimming" materials with them.

It is also helpful to spend waiting moments by thinking very positively of the child's future progress. They can review the goals they have set with professional educators and, shutting their eyes, visualize the baby accomplishing those goals. As parents gain hope, they will find themselves getting more and more ideas that will be productive and help them meet the goals they have set.

In all this they must remember to remain confident and hopeful of improvement. They must try. They must not give up quickly. It takes months for children to adjust to life and quite some time before anyone really knows how well the child will progress. Parents must give the child every chance by following the programs they plan for them with the professionals whose jobs are to help them and their children.

Parents can rest assured that they are doing their best for their special children as they minimize the effects of grief in their lives and implement the programs, teaching techniques, and activities suggested by those who would help them and their children. In time parents may find their horizons widening to the community at large. Many parents of special children have become very active in fund raising, legislative efforts, and in programs to educate the public. They have become involved in child-find programs and acted as counselors and models for others who have handicapped children. Parents have become very involved in their children's educational programs and have sometimes gone on in the field as educators and administrators.

All these activities may prove to be very worthwhile and rewarding by-products of a most challenging situation. The great rewards will include a gradually growing awareness of the worth of each individual, the miracle of human growth and life, and the loving that people contribute to their world no matter how "special" their circumstances may be.

SUMMARY

This chapter presented a detailed discussion of the steps to follow in order to design, plan, and implement an early intervention program for handicapped infants and toddlers. The transdisciplinary approach to evaluation, planning, and programming was defined and discussed. A rather extensive discussion of parental involvement, planning training for paraprofessionals, an outline of ten sessions that could be used to provide training for paraprofessionals, a discussion of the role of the helping practitioner, and finally, a section that addressed the parent of a child with special needs were provided.

Chapter 4

Mastering Teaching Techniques

All people are teachers. Everyone teaches something to someone whenever two or more people meet. A great *quantity* of the time in people's lives is spent teaching. When those they love and influence have problems, they must learn to teach with such *quality* that the time they spend may become more productive and valuable. The materials included in this chapter are designed to teach principles of learning and teaching in such a way that parents and paraprofessionals may improve the quality of their teaching efforts. (This chapter is designed only as a teaching tool for nonprofessionals. Those who are professionals may wish to become familiar with this chapter only in order to answer the questions that may arise.)

An understanding of basic principles is of great benefit to all who would help young children with special needs. A principle, once understood, may be applied in any specific situation. No two children are alike, despite similar handicapping conditions. For this reason, the training portion of this manual is divided into sections that are designed to develop an understanding of related principles. Each basic principle or teaching tool is simply stated. Examples are then given of the principle as applied to young children with problems. The children represent five different developmental levels of functioning. One child is severely retarded and physically disabled. One child is deaf, another is blind. A Down's child is included as is a bright child whose physical condition restricts him to bed care.

This practical application of principles to a variety of situations is accomplished by presenting a series of statements in three-part frames. A problem is contained in each statement and shown between parentheses. The problem may be a choice between (is/is not) or (does/does not) (see Exhibit 4-1), or a single (_____) (see Exhibit 4-2) or multiple (____ ____) (see Exhibit 4-3) word answer. The frames also include a blank space for the practitioner's response. To the left of that space, still within the frame, is the correct italicized answer in a sentence that reiterates an aspect of the basic teaching principle, which allows for immediate reinforcement and correction for the learner. A piece of colored construction paper or an index card may be cut to expose the blank space yet cover the correct answer. The paper or card may then be moved slowly down the page as the statements and answers are completed.

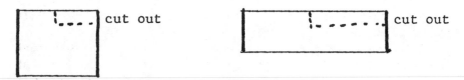

Exhibit 4-1 Example Exercise of Verb Choice

Repetition has always been used to teach information. Repetition (is/is not) used by adults and children to gain many skills as well.	
Repetition _is_ used to teach information and gain skills.	Answer Space

Exhibit 4-2 Example Exercise of Single Word Completion

Tommy is learning to roll. He rolls again and again. This (_____) or practice will help him be able to roll well in a few months.	
Repetition or practice must be continued over a period of time in order to learn a skill.	

Exhibit 4-3 Example Exercise of Multiple Word Completion

Sam found a new truck in the gift package. His hands went over the truck again and again. He repeatedly felt the truck in order to (_____ _____) about this object.	
Children repeatedly explore objects in order to _gain information_ about them.	

Review sections include spaces for correct answers and additional applications of the principle. The purpose of these drills is to help those who teach special children gain an applicable understanding of basic teaching techniques and principles. That understanding is strengthened by thinking and through the use or involvement of the hand in the learning process. Answering questions strengthens learning as thinking and writing are required. Reading with understanding is also helped by marking the text. Answers to questions, underlining important concepts, jotting comments in the margins, and drawing diagrams and pictures have long been methods used by students to turn books into tools for understanding.

Hopefully this manual and curriculum will become such a used and useful text. A book is not sacred. It is a tool for learning. It is the authors' hope that this book will be used and reused, marked, answered, diagrammed, and replaced on the shelf battered and dog-eared. In that case, it will have served its purpose—being a useful tool for those who would intervene on behalf of children with special needs. Throughout this textbook reference is made to five general materials:

1. Education in Infancy
2. General Education Program for Ages One to Six
3. Thoughts on Discipline
4. Practical Life Skills
5. Academics in Infancy

To avoid repetition or duplication, we shall credit the author initially and only once and then allow the reader to be aware of the source: J. E. Olive. Newborn Education and Development, Inc. Reprinted by permission of the author.

DEVELOPING ATTITUDES THAT PROMOTE LEARNING

Growth and Change Take Time (Patience)

Instant gratification is the byword of modern society. When people want light, they turn a switch. When they want entertainment, they turn a knob. People's expectations of instant gratification make it difficult for them as they rear children. The development of a human from a child to an adult requires decades of time. Parents must think horizontally of reaching their goals, in months and years rather than moments and days.

When they think in terms of months and years, they become more patient. As they are more patient, they feel less frustration and find more pleasure in their work with children. The children sense their parents' increased satisfaction, and they respond by being happier and more motivated to learn and please because they sense parental acceptance.

People cannot love happily until they accept others the way they are. Once they accept them, they can help them grow and change without the pressures of their secret fears. When people work out of fear, their feelings tend to be angry and resentful. Those they would help sense this underlying hostility through tone of voice, body language, and facial expressions. When people list all the good they can find in a situation—all that they can love and enjoy, and when they memorize and focus on this fact of the situation, they become more accepting, hopeful, and possibly enthusiastic. When enthusiasm is combined with patience and appropriate goal planning, people will be more likely to succeed in their efforts.

When adults remember the principle of *patience,* they become more flexible and less stressed in setting goals for the children. They set their goals realistically, basing those goals on the child's immediate and specific needs. Each child is different. Each child functions differently from any other child although two children may be in the same general phase of development. People who work with the children enjoy them without comparing them to others, working one day and one goal at a time.

Creating a Happy Atmosphere

People learn with confidence when they feel liked and loved. They are easier to live with when they like themselves and feel liked by others. Babies are loved by their families; but once the baby poses many problems, the emotional atmosphere in the home begins to change.

This change frequently takes place once a baby begins to creep and disrupt everything in the home. If parents constantly feel angry and show it, the child will become discouraged and unhappy, which often leads to annoying attention-getting behaviors such as screaming, whining, or pestering. Occasionally, the child will refuse to respond to any parental requests. At other times the child may break other people's favorite objects, or the child may become so discouraged that withdrawal results. The child may refuse to attempt anything due to fear of failure. If this happens, a happier atmosphere for learning can be created using the following suggestions:

1. List what the child can do well. Memorize the list. Review it daily.
2. List what you like about the child. Memorize the list. Review it daily.
3. Be hopeful. Believe growth and change will come.
4. Visualize the child's reaching the next realistic goals. Do this daily.

5. Be firm with the child, but feel love so you can show what is to be done in a kindly way.
6. Be happy. Focus on the aspects of life that you like. Continue the activities you enjoyed before the child's birth. Happiness and love change people.

Suggestions for Training Constructively

Parents can enjoy a much happier atmosphere in the home when they know constructive or loving ways to teach and train little children. Constructive ideas give them better alternatives than spanking and screaming. It is more constructive to think of *training* a child than *disciplining* that child. Training gives a sense of the time involved in learning. The TRAINING PROCEDURE outlines the process involved in good training practices.

1. List all the difficulties noticed in the child's behavior.
2. Choose the most troublesome, which becomes the goal or behavior to be changed.
3. Plan to eliminate the problem.
   a. Write the specific desired behavior in a brief sentence.
      Example: The children shut the door quietly.
   b. Choose cues for training. Make them short and direct. Use them every time you train.
      Example: "Quiet door."
      Use the same tone of voice consistently.
   c. Choose appropriate rewards and punishment.
      Example: STP PROCEDURE—Reward with smiles, touching, pleasure.
   d. Set a goal date for accomplishing the behavior.
      Example: The children will shut the door quietly 85 percent of the time in four weeks.
   e. Allow daily time to work on goal.
      Example: 15 minutes daily games and practice quietly shutting doors; 1 minute "stand-bys" three times a day for reinforcement.
   f. Devise games and activities to teach desired behavior.
      Examples: Tape record the children making "quiet door" sounds. Reward each time the sound is not loud on the recording.
4. Train intensely and regularly.
5. Be consistent.
6. Be patient. Immediately reward small improvements and ignore uncooperative behaviors.
7. As the desired behavior is established, reward intermittently.

The TRAINING PROCEDURE is good for teaching or eliminating specific behaviors. It is also necessary to have a number of approaches to dealing with behavioral problems constructively, but not as a part of a training program. The following suggestions may be helpful in keeping the home atmosphere cheerful when young children are present.

1. When a child is crying or behaving inappropriately, *distract* the child by drawing attention to other objects or activities.
2. When children fight or become destructive, don't scream. Change the activities. Get them to move around, sing or march, stretch or dance. Their play will improve. Fighting children are afraid. Both need comfort. Have the offending child sit down a minute or two after being comforted. It takes several minutes to scold. It takes several minutes to join in happily with a new physical activity.
3. Sitting in a chair for 30 seconds may be perceived as punishment if you present the child with a very serious face and vocal tone.
4. Children like to race a kitchen timer when getting ready for bed or picking up toys. Start it with one minute periods of time. Increase the work and time as the child matures.
5. Pull numbers out of boxes or hats to decide who will be first. Children will not perceive favoritism as the numbers have the final say!
6. Devise family signal systems, warning taps or whistles.
7. Use charts for children who like stars for rewards.
8. Speak firmly. Mothers often ask, plead, apologize, and finally scold, spank, or scream. It is best to speak firmly once when giving a command. If the child hears but does not obey, shape (show) the desired behavior. Train children to obey. This takes time, but the attitude of training is constructive.
9. Use puppets to train the children or show disappointment in inappropriate behaviors.
10. Restrain a child from hitting or inappropriate touching and explain in three words or less—"Hands down. That hurts." "Hands down. That's hot."
11. Immediately shape (show) the appropriate behavior.
12. Judge the behavior. The child is not "bad." The behavior was a mistake.
13. Distinguish between feelings and actions. Help the child express feelings. If the child does not have language, try to express the feelings for the child as you perceive them. "Your face looks angry." "I can tell you are hurt." Discuss the feelings so they can be worked out and resolved.

14. Use the WORD COMMAND PROCEDURE to teach the commands wait, come, go, quickly, no-no, stop, and signals like a snap of the fingers. The WORD COMMAND PROCEDURE is used to condition young children to certain commands. Always speak the command in one tone of voice. Teach the command as a game and repeat the game many, many times until the child responds automatically to the command and before it is needed in a crisis. Reward with STP for obedience. Keep the game fun! This procedure is a part of the overall TRAINING PROCEDURE.
15. When children misbehave, remove them from the activity. Ignore the sulking or crying that may follow.
16. Teach and play with the child frequently through the day. Children love being played with, and they enjoy the company. Children pay more attention to those who remain interesting rather than those they "shut out" as being punitive only.

The Principle

Given an atmosphere of happiness, children learn better and parents find more satisfaction in child rearing. Parents make progress when they allow time for an attainable goal. They can enjoy any situation if they continually focus on the pleasing factors in their lives. They suffer as much as they dwell upon the thoughts that give them pain. There are two ways to handle the problems all children present. Adults can be threatened and angry, or can enjoy what is beautiful while devising training programs and constructive methods for solving the problems. It all works better when adults remember to be patient, loving, and reasonably happy.

MOTIVATION TO LEARN AND THE TRAINING OF HUMAN BEINGS

People do what they want to do. They do the things that reward them with something they want or enjoy. As little children, everything aroused their interest because they loved the sensation of learning. They enjoyed the sensations of looking, hearing, touching, smelling, and tasting. Everything that came to them through their bodily senses seemed new and exciting. Learning to move their bodies was rewarding in itself. And so they practiced running, looking, touching, and speaking just for the pure joy of it. They repeated activities that rewarded these sensations until they became very good at knowing what their bodies could do. Then as they watched other people, they

Exhibit 4-4 Exercise I

1.	Hazel's mother is trying to get her to respond to sound toys. She does like bells, but has been slow to respond to the others. Her mother keeps trying because she set a goal of three months for Hazel to respond to sound toys. This (is/is not) an example of patience.
Setting realistic goals and sticking to them in spite of setbacks is an example of patience.	
2.	Susan's mother is helping her to improve her walking skills. Every day they practice this skill in gamelike activities. So often Susan will not be able to do the skill exactly, yet her mother just shows her the correct way and keeps on trying. Because Susan's mother is (_____), she will be less likely to become frustrated.
Being patient helps people feel less frustrated.	
3.	Sam's father is anxious to have him start walking better. He tries to make Sam "practice" scooting along the couch even though Sam does not want to do it. When Sam starts to cry, his father becomes frustrated and stops working with him. Sam's father (is/is not) being patient with him. Later on he will feel less frustrated and want to work with Sam again.
Becoming angry or frustrated and stopping an activity is not an example of patience.	
4.	Hazel's mother has found that just being patient helps her feel better about working with Hazel. She feels Hazel senses this and responds by being (_____) and easier to teach.
Children are usually happier when the people who teach them are patient.	
5.	Paul's father is trying to teach him to recognize shapes. First he gives him several plastic circles and stars to play with. Paul does not want to play with these shapes, so his father switches to a shape mobile that Paul's uncle made. Paul likes this mobile and wants to play with it. Paul's father's flexibility in switching to a new activity is an example of how being (_____) helps children to grow and learn.

Exhibit 4-4 continued

Having the flexibility to change their activities or goals makes people much more <u>patient</u> and happy.	
6. At times children will cry or throw temper tantrums because they want their parents' attention. Parents who are discouraged or depressed sometimes shut their children out. But, if they decide they will list what the child can do well, it may help them become more (_____) and accepting of the child.	
Creating a <u>happy</u> atmosphere will help parents to promote the child's learning.	
7. To maximize learning, it is essential to create an atmosphere that supports learning. Being optimistic and focusing upon the child's strengths will help adults be (_____) and establish the most appropriate atmosphere.	
Looking at the strengths instead of dwelling on weaknesses will make people <u>happy</u>.	
8. Adults' work with children who have special needs requires them to be firm. They need to show children how to do things in a kindly fashion. They (can/cannot) be firm and also feel love for a child.	
Firmness is an important trait when working with young children. Firmness <u>can</u> exist with happiness and love.	
9. Hazel occasionally becomes a difficult baby to live with, as she cries, fusses, and sleeps for short periods of time. Her parents try to accept this and focus on her strong points. They do this by listing what she can do well and also what they (_____) about Hazel.	
To help create a happy atmosphere parents can list children's strengths and the things they <u>like</u> about them.	

Exhibit 4-4 continued

10.	Tommy's parents used to get very angry at his behavior and often resorted to screaming at him or spanking him. The paraprofessional who comes to their home to help teach them to work with Tommy suggested more (____) things they could do.
	Using strategies other than spanking or screaming is more constructive and helping to the child.
11.	Sam's parents want to prepare him to walk without bumping into objects if possible in a few weeks. They have set this goal, chosen "hands up" and "listen" as cues, and play games to teach Sam these commands. They (are/are not) using the TRAINING PROCEDURE.
	They are using the TRAINING PROCEDURE to prepare Sam for walking hazards.
12.	Sam's parents (do/do not) say "hands up" and "listen" in the same tone of voice each time they use the TRAINING PROCEDURE.
	Sam's parents do use the same tone of voice whenever they cue while training Sam.
13.	Sam's parents try to play the "hands up" or "listen" games on a (_____) basis as they are training him over a definite period of time.
	They play the games daily while training specific skills.
14.	Susan was watching two neighbor children play with a large set of blocks. Not understanding how to play cooperatively, she walked over and destroyed the walls of the block fort. The children were angry. Susan's mother (did/did not) distract them by calling them to go outside and play ball with her for a few moments. When they came back in, she gave a few of the blocks to Susan while the older children continued their play.

Exhibit 4-4 continued

Distraction can be used to change the atmosphere when children quarrel. Susan's mother <u>did</u> distract the children from their quarrel by changing the activity. She can teach Susan to play alongside when they start the game again as the emotional climate will be more positive.	

15.	Paul and his cousin were playing together on the floor. Paul could not reach a toy he wanted. His cousin was playing with the toy and teased him by keeping it just out of reach. Paul's mother came over with a funny poem. She (_____) the boys from the teasing. When feelings were calm, she asked Paul's cousin to play, not tease.
	Paul's mother <u>distracted</u> them from the negative way the play was going. By giving some constructive attention, the situation improved.

16.	Sam bumped into a toy car on the floor as he cruised alongside the coffee table. He picked up the car and began banging it on the coffee table. His father came over and (_____) a desired behavior by showing him how to move the car on the floor.
	Sam's father <u>shaped</u> a desired behavior.

17.	Sam and mother sat at the kitchen table while mother cut up the salad ingredients. His small hands found the knife, and he picked it up to put it in his mouth. Mother said, "Hands down, Sam, that will hurt." She removed the knife from his hands and placed his hands in his lap. Mother was (___ ___ ___ ___) to teach Sam the meaning of "hands down."
	<u>Shaping a desired behavior</u> is an effective tool to teach a simple command.

18.	Paul was playing with his toy cars on the bed. A few of them rolled off onto the floor, and Paul became angry because he couldn't get them. He picked up the rest of the cars and threw them around the room. Mother came in and picked up all the cars from the floor and took them out of the room with her. When Paul played inappropriately with the toys, Mother would quietly (_____) the activity from him.

Exhibit 4-4 continued

When children misbehave, <u>remove</u> them from the activity, or remove the activity from them. Scolding is not necessary. Teach the proper behavior when feelings have calmed down.	

19.	Susan and her sister were playing with crayons and paper. Susan's sister wanted her to imitate making lines with the crayon, but all Susan wanted to do was scribble. Her sister began to get frustrated until she realized that it was Susan's (personality/behavior) that she didn't like.

Susan's sister judged the <u>behavior</u> and accepted Susan.	

20.	Hazel was often fussy. It was hard to distract her because of her physical problems. Her mother was feeling frustrated and angry much of the time and was not feeling happy about the child. She made a list of all of Hazel's attractive features. She also made a list of all the cute expressions Hazel made. She then realized it was Hazel's fussing behavior she (liked/disliked), not Hazel.

Hazel's mother <u>disliked</u> the fussing behavior, not Hazel.	

21.	Hazel's mother gathered a few sound toys Hazel liked and left them nearby the child. The toys rang when Hazel moved, and she seemed less fussy. Hazel's mother (did/did not) try to eliminate the behavior that annoyed her.

Hazel's mother <u>did</u> try to modify or eliminate the behavior that bothered her.	

wanted to do the things they did. So great was their zest to learn and so rewarding the effort itself that they tried and tried, practicing again and again until the skills they wanted were theirs.

Increase and Maintain Behaviors

Obviously then, people learn what they want to learn; they do what they want to do. They continue doing the things that continue to satisfy them.

This tremendous factor of motivation may be stifled when a child is born with problems. Parents must influence these children to make a greater effort to learn. If these children are to make this effort, parents must show them that something they desire or enjoy will quickly result, which is called *positive reinforcement* or reward.

People may also influence others to maintain or increase behavior by showing them that the threat or presence of something they don't want or fear will be removed if they perform as they wish. This is called *negative reinforcement*. For example, when a parent picks up a crying baby and the crying stops, both receive reinforcement for that behavior. The baby is positively reinforced and now feels crying may well result in being picked up. The parent is negatively reinforced because the awful crying noise has stopped. Both are satisfied by the result of the behavior.

People perceive many things as rewards or reinforcers. *Primary reinforcers* are basic to survival. They include food and water. Little children show particular interest in food and favorite drinks, which may be nicely used as a reinforcement in training programs. Simply feed the child the normal quantities of food eaten at a meal throughout the morning. Use the food as a series of rewards rather than feeding the child all at one time.

Little children enjoy many of the sensations they receive through their bodies. Some children will work hard to make a bell ring; others love to make lights turn on. Some children make tremendous efforts just to handle or manipulate a favorite toy.

Primary reinforcements can be combined with social contact, and the two will become associated as something good in the child's mind. These are called *secondary reinforcements*. Social rewards are smiles, touches, laughter, and praise. The STP PROCEDURE referred to in the curriculum is simply rewarding with smiles, touches, and praise. Being rocked and played with is also socially rewarding. Enthusiasm is socially rewarding, as is feeling accepted and appreciated.

Primary and secondary reinforcements tend to generalize or be applied to many different situations as time passes. Young children often make mistakes as they generalize behaviors that are appropriate in one situation but inappropriate in another.

Decreasing Behaviors

When a behavior does not result in something people like or want, they tend to stop that behavior. When adults want a child to stop certain behaviors, they must find out what is rewarding the behavior *anywhere* in the environment. Then they must eliminate or interfere with that satisfying factor.

Often people pay attention to behaviors they don't like in others. It is this very attention that is strengthening or increasing the behavior. Adults should consistently *ignore* that behavior and keep the child busy doing things that are satisfying, but interfere with the undesirable behavior. Ignoring displeasing behavior is hard to do consistently; but, when well planned and continued over a period of time, it is an effective method of changing behaviors. If a child sucks the thumb until it is chapped, adults can try to keep the child's hands busy with interesting toys and objects to manipulate. In this way, they reinforce incompatible behaviors; but they need not seem punitive as they do so. Sometimes several things are reinforcing the undesirable behavior, and adults need to really analyze why something like thumb sucking seems so rewarding to a child.

Adults may also *remove* the child or object from a situation that rewards inappropriate behaviors. This is what they are doing when they send a child to the other room or have the child go to the corner to calm down. Such periods of isolation should be very brief as more problems generally result from long periods of isolation. Little children can be "isolated" just by having them sit still on a chair for thirty seconds. If the adult seems firm and even awesome and ignores the child, the little isolation period may be taken very seriously by a child.

It is possible to act out that firm and awesome countenance without really feeling anger. Anger is not appropriate in a goal-oriented training program. Nor do feelings of guilt follow in consequence of a training program, because no feelings of hostility are involved. When a person angrily tries to change other people, many problems arise. They feel anger too. Resentment, passive resistance, revenge, lying, avoidance, and acts of aggression may result when children begin to perceive someone as a "punisher."

Punishment can be used in a training program, but it must be carefully done. Spanking is often discussed in this regard. If parents choose to include spanking in a training program, the spanking should be done with three fingers applied quickly to the child's buttocks. This stings, but no damage may be done. Such symbolic punishment is so mild, it is ridiculous to feel anger while using it.

One further comment may be made about using punishment. If a child is punished for a behavior and that behavior persists, the child is finding something rewarding in the punishment. It may be the attention. Remember, it is not really a punishment unless it causes the behavior to stop.

Once adults have decided what the child likes and dislikes, they are ready to decide what behaviors they want to increase or decrease. They must observe the child for several days to establish how often the behavior occurs and whether or not the behavior is changing. They should keep data during the periods they observe. The worksheets in Chapter 2 can be used for this record keeping. The child's behavior should be observed for several days before starting the training program, again during the program, and after the training program is completed. This record keeping will demonstrate whether or not a change has really taken place.

As practitioners find the things the child enjoys or considers rewarding and the things the child dislikes and tries to avoid, they may begin to consider how they will use these likes and dislikes in a training program. Whatever devices they choose to use, they must (1) know what effect they will have on the child, (2) be able to make them as automatic as possible, (3) make them be closely related to the behavior they are working on, (4) be *very* consistent, (5) immediately apply them, (6) use them appropriately (neither too much nor too little), and (7) be ready to reward the improvement as the behavior gradually evolves.

When trying to change behaviors or teach new skills, adults must also remember to reinforce the child every time there are approximations of the desired behavior. The child must be rewarded every time the total behavior is accomplished. After a while the behavior should be reinforced every second or third or fourth time it occurs. Finally, the behavior is rewarded occasionally. This intermittent reinforcement is the most effective method of changing behaviors. Unfortunately, people use intermittent reinforcement whenever they are inconsistent. No wonder so many training programs fail! Practitioners must totally prepare themselves for the time and effort involved in order to be consistent.

Remember that certain behaviors are those likely to occur in particular types of situations. Children are more likely to cry for what they want when doting grandparents are present. Remember that once a training program is begun, the behaviors practitioners are trying to eliminate are likely to increase for a while as the child tests their resolve. There is no need to panic. If the consequences were carefully chosen, the behavior will gradually change once the child knows they will remain firm and consistent.

Teaching a New Behavior

The previous paragraphs discussed the principles that come into play when people want to influence others' behaviors. Those principles of reinforcement also apply when teaching new skills or behaviors to children. The steps involved in such a process are outlined in the following LIVING SKILLS PROCEDURE:

1. Think through and list *every movement* of a body part. This includes the child's ability to attend (focus or pay attention) to what is expected at any point in the activity.
   a. *every step* involved in a skill
2. Test each step to see what parts the child is already able to perform.

3. Teach those steps in the skill that are new or difficult for the child by:
   a. demonstrating how to do it and permitting the child to imitate
   b. shape the behavior by helping the child do it
   c. gradually fade out adult help step by step; shaping is called the PROGRAMMING PROCEDURE in this text, which simply means to
      • give the child a short, simple command or language cue
      • when the child does not respond, cue again, then *shape* or help the child do it
      • reward immediately
      • continue this process; reward approximations until child responds to the command and performs the skill
      • reward immediately and consistently. (This method of teaching can be charted as shown in Chapter 2 on the worksheet under the heading, "Programmed Activities.")
4. Help the child combine or chain these steps together until the entire skill is mastered.

Additional Suggestions

Practitioners can help children perform a skill and fade out their help step by step.

1. Let the child do the first or the last step. Then the next ones as the child is able. The reward is in the success.
2. Use STP (Smiling, Touching, Praising) to reward the child's efforts each step of the way. Other reinforcers are also appropriate.
3. Be quiet while demonstrating skills. Find a quiet place to teach, and remove all distractions.
4. Carefully choose a few basic cues or a key word to use each time they command or show a step.

Principles

Everything people do is a skill they wanted to learn and, therefore, practiced at some time in their lives. That skill may be broken into steps for learning and becomes automatic after much repetition. People develop only those skills and behaviors that have satisfying consequences or rewards. They eliminate behaviors when they don't like their results. Behaviors can be maintained when they are sufficiently rewarding.

When helping children learn, adults must care enough to really observe and accept the child's abilities, likes, and dislikes. Then they can plan

Exhibit 4-5 Exercise II

1.	Hazel enjoys listening to the sound of the bell ringing. She and her mother are on the floor playing. Her mother wants Hazel to roll and uses the bell as a (positive/negative) reinforcer.
	Hazel will roll toward the positive reinforcer because she likes the bell.
2.	Hazel and her mother were sitting on the floor together watching TV. Hazel was propped between her mother's open legs, and she was stabilizing her body with her hands on her shoulders gently curving them forward. As Hazel lifted her head to look at TV and held her head up for 30 seconds, her mother said, "Good head up, Hazel," and gave her a bite of banana. She is coupling (_____) reinforcers with the secondary reinforcer of praise.
	Combining primary and secondary reinforcers is an effective way to teach a new behavior.
3.	Every time Hazel lifts her head up for 30 seconds, her mother says, "Good head up, Hazel," Hazel's mother is using language (____) to reinforce Hazel.
	The consistent use of cues is necessary for the child to know what is expected her.
4.	Both the banana and the praise used by Hazel's mother are (___) for Hazel.
	Reinforcers must be used to teach a new behavior.
5.	Susan and her sister were building block towers. Susan stacked four blocks and they fell down. She laughed, built the tower again, and purposefully kncked it down. When she again laughed, her sister simply turned her head away and wouldn't look at Susan. Susan's sister (was/was not) ignoring the inappropriate behaviors.
	Susan's sister was ignoring Susan's laughter because it was an inappropriate behavior.

Exhibit 4-5 continued

6.	Tommy was playing in his playpen while his mother ironed. She was talking to him as he played with his toys. During long conversational lulls, Tommy began to throw his toys out of the playpen to get his mother's attention. Instead of picking up the thrown toys and giving them back to Tommy, his mother was (_____) his throwing because it was inappropriate. She only spoke to Tommy again when the throwing stopped.
	Ignoring inappropriate behaviors will decrease the frequency of the behavior.
7.	Both Susan and Tommy were using (_____) behaviors to get attention; and their sister and mother (_____) their misbehaviors.
	If an inappropriate behavior is not harmful to the child, one of the most effective ways it can be handled is to ignore it.
8.	When Sam was bored or his toys were out of reach, he would wave his hands in front of his face for stimulation. His parents found this annoying. To decrease the hand waving, they kept the radio on and the toys within reach. The parents (were/were not) reinforcing the incompatible behavior of playing with the toys instead of waving his hands in front of his face.
	The parents were reinforcing the incompatible behavior of toy playing instead of hand waving.
9.	Tommy enjoyed making screeching noises because it gave him vibrational stimulation. The noises irritated his mother. She bought a set of headphones for him to wear, and she plugged the headphones into the stereo. His screeching stopped when he wore the headphones. His mother was reinforcing the (_____ _____) of wearing the headphones.
	Reinforcing the incompatible behavior of wearing the headphones reduced the irritating screeching noises.
10.	If a child is engaged in a desirable behavior, the child will be unable to continue an undesirable behavior at the same time. This is known as (_____) an (_____ _____).

Exhibit 4-5 continued

<u>Reinforcing</u> an <u>incompatible</u> <u>behavior</u> is an effective way of eliminating undesirable behaviors.	

11. Paul had been watching TV for an hour. It was time to turn the set off, but Paul still wanted to watch more TV. He began to cry and soon was having a full-blown temper tantrum. Paul's mother carried him to his room, placed him on his bed, and shut the door. His mother (did/did not) remove Paul until he could control his own behavior.

Removing the child from the activity, or the activity from the child <u>did</u> decrease an undesirable behavior.	

12. Susan and her mother were pointing to and naming parts of the face. Susan was being unusually stubborn and refused to pay attention to her mother. Her mother said, "Susan, look at me." When Susan did not, her mother turned her head around, pointed to her mouth, and repeated "Look at me." Susan's mother (did/did not) shape Susan's behavior.

When Susan's mother turned Susan's head around, she <u>did</u> shape the behavior by helping Susan do it.	

13. In using the phrase, "Look at me," Susan's mother (was/was not) cueing Susan.

Susan's mother <u>was</u> cueing Susan by giving her a simple language cue.	

14. When Susan refused to pay attention to what her mother wanted her to do, she (was/was not) attending.

Susan <u>was not</u> attending to the task when she refused to pay attention to her mother.	

15. Until a child is (_____) to the task being taught, the child will be unable to learn the task.

Exhibit 4-5 continued

	Attending to the task is a requirement for learning.	
16.	Hazel's parents are watching her for several periods of five minutes a day. They are observing her to see how often she lifts her head while she lays on her tummy. They (do/do not) mark each head lift on the worksheets in order to chart this behavior.	
	They do mark the worksheets or other chart so they can prove progress after a training program.	
17.	Although her parents want her to raise her head 45 degrees, they (do/do not) reinforce her approximations of the skill.	
	They do reward the approximations requiring a little more effort as Hazel grows stronger.	
18.	Tommy does not yet have a true creeping skill. His parents still reward his (_____) in order to encourage him.	
	They reward his approximations.	
19.	Paul knows he must not whine when he wants his mother's attention. She usually ignores him, but sometimes gives him what he wants to quiet his whining. The behavior continues. This (is/is not) an example of intermittent reinforcement.	
	This is an example of very powerful intermittent reinforcement.	
20.	Hazel has become quite good at lifting her head to make the bells ring. Now her parents reinforce her irregularly for her efforts. They are using (_____ _____).	
	Hazel's parents are using intermittent reinforcement to strengthen her head lifting abilities.	

Exhibit 4-5 continued

21.	Sam's parents have begun a training program to stop his "flapping" behaviors. They have noticed that the flapping has (_____) since the program began. They are concerned that they may be reinforcing the wrong behavior.
	They need not be concerned yet. Behaviors often <u>increase</u> for awhile when training programs first begin.
22.	Paul's mother is determined not to respond to his whining. She has been consistent for three hours. Now the whining is worse then ever. This is an example of the (_____) of behaviors that often occurs during training programs.
	This is an example of the <u>increase</u> or <u>escalation</u> of a behavior before it is discarded as nonrewarding.
23.	Susan likes Cheerios and does not like to sit still. Her parents (do/do not) reward her with Cheerios when she tries hard to take a few steps. They (do/do not) make her sit for thirty seconds when she knocks over her brother's block walls.
	Parents <u>do</u> reward children for appropriate behaviors with foods the children like. They <u>do</u> use quiet sitting when the child has behaved inappropriately.
24.	Tommy does not like to be hungry. He does enjoy eating. His mother works on his sitting program at meal times. When he (does/does not) sit up, she feeds him. When he slumps, she (does/does not) feed him. Sometimes she "shapes" and rewards the behavior she wants. She always cues, "Sit up, Tommy," while she trains him.
	Tommy's mother <u>does</u> feed him while he sits up and when he responds correctly to the cue. She <u>does not</u> feed him when he slumps.

rewarding training programs. A training program allows for the good planning, time, and the effort required to effect change. For this reason, adults can be more patient, accepting, happy, and enthusiastic. Their enthusiasm and pleasure will also prove rewarding to the child. More progress will result because of these particular attitudes of love—for love effects change.

FIVE NATURAL TEACHING TOOLS

Manipulation

People learn well when they learn using their hands. They gain information, understanding, and concepts of relationships as they handle objects because objects can be recognized by their senses—they are concrete. They are not abstract like ideas. Adults help children learn by giving them objects to handle or manipulate. *Manipulation* of concrete objects is a powerful teaching tool. Abstract concepts can be learned by many young children if the teaching materials used can be manipulated.

Discovery

Most children are curious and love to learn about the things they *discover* in the world around them. Adults can "plant" objects they want the child to discover in the play pen, in socks, on the floor nearby, under a pillow in the bed, or any place where the child will encounter it. When the child discovers the new toy or learning material, the practitioners name the object several times. If the child has language problems, they place their faces on the child's level and say the word so the child can watch them. They can help the child really "discover" the qualities of the object by smelling, touching, tasting, listening to, and looking at the material whenever this is possible and safe. They show the child what can be done with the object, and name it again. They are enthusiastic and interested. Pleasure is catching. So is boredom.

Imitation and Demonstration

Children learn by observing and imitating others. Adults use this learning tool when they demonstrate skills. Their demonstrations are most effective when they plan how to teach the skill one step at a time and practice before showing the child. When demonstrating a skill, adults should be quiet, precise, and move slowly. They can let the child try the first or last step in the process. Often a child will try to do or imitate adults' activities without any demonstrations, which is why it is important for little children to stay around family activities and be included in any possible way.

Games

Children love playing *games*. Parents enjoy them too. Pleasure increases learning efficiency. It is valuable to make up little games, songs, poems, fingerplays, and activities to help a child reach appropriate developmental goals.

Repetition

Little children enjoy repetitious games and activities, which is good because everything an adult does is a skill that was learned through repetition or practice. Adults practice rolling, smiling, reaching, walking, singing, combing their hair, driving the car, and algebra. First, they must want to do or learn something. Then they must be willing to try and fail again and again. Occasionally, they will succeed and then fail again. Finally, through repetition or practice, they will succeed most of the time and only fail occasionally.

The Principle

Children learn through manipulation, discovery, imitation, and games because they are pleasurable and immediately satisfying. The fun of the learning makes it worth the repetition and effort. These learning techniques involve the mind, the hands, the environment, and social contact with the important people the child loves. Love and happiness work as one. People are happiest in a loving environment and so, they enjoy repeating the things that give them pleasure. Learning through manipulation, discovery, imitation, and games gives pleasure in a naturally rewarding fashion, and these are important teaching tools.

LEARNING THROUGH THE SENSES

People learn through tools called *senses*. They depend upon their five major senses for their knowledge of the world and how to live in it. Those major senses are sight, hearing, touch, taste, and smell. If a child is born with deficiencies in any of these sensory areas, the learning process may be delayed. That learning process will certainly be made more difficult.

Exhibit 4-6 Exercise III

1.	Sam's mother gave him two wooden blocks to hold. He turned them around and touched them all over with his fingers. Sam (is/is not) learning through manipulation.
	Sam is learning through manipulation by touching the object.
2.	Paul enjoys playing with formboards. His mother places several on his bed for him to play with. He enjoys going around the shapes with his (_____) as well as using his fingers to feel the spaces in the board.
	Paul is learning by manipulation since he is touching the objects with his fingers or hands.
3.	Susan found a bell on the floor. She picked it up and heard it ring. She became excited and quickly was (_____) the clapper in an attempt to find out what made the bell ring.
	Susan was trying to find out what makes a bell ring by touching or manipulating the clapper.
4.	Hazel is unable to hold most objects in her hands although she does get pleasure from sound toys or bells. Hazel (will/will not) be able to use manipulation to learn about objects.
	Because of her physical limitations, Hazel will not be able to manipulate objects.
5.	Sam cannot see the objects his mother gives him to play with. However, she has selected toys that have texture or some other distinctive feature so he can learn about them through (_____).
	Sam can gain a great deal of information about his toys by manipulating or touching them.
6.	Hazel does not move much. Her mother puts toys around her and helps her reach to (_____) the toys by her side.

Exhibit 4-6 continued

Children can be guided to <u>discover</u> things in their environment.	

7.	Hazel's mother moves the baby's hands over the toy so she can learn by the (_____) of (_____).

Children can be guided to dis-cover the nature of things through the <u>sense</u> of <u>touch</u>.	

8.	Tommy is barely able to crawl. He generally rolls or drags himself around the room. Sometimes he gets under the table. His parents leave rattles, stuffed toys, or textured fabrics with bells on them for him to (_____) under the table.

Parents can "plant" things around a room for a child to <u>discover</u>.	

9.	Susan is trying to learn to walk on the grass. It is hard for her. Her parents make it fun for her by putting (_____) in the yard for her to discover.

A child can be motivated to move by putting new or old <u>toys</u>, bells, textured animals in the yard to discover.	

10.	Susan pokes into everything. Her parents leave plastic alphabet letters for her to (_____) just under the edge of the couch. When she finds the letters, her parents get down on her level, look directly into her face and (_____) the letters.

Letters and numbers can be left around furniture for children to <u>discover</u>. Parents should <u>name</u> the letters again and again.	

11.	Paul spends a lot of time in bed. When he comes back from the doctor's, he often discovers a new (_____) under his pillow or sheet.

Exhibit 4-6 continued

Many <u>objects</u> can be left for a child to discover under his pillow or sheet.	

12.	Paul's parents help him (_____) more about the item by having him touch it, listen to it, look at it, smell it, and taste it whenever possible.

Children <u>learn</u> or <u>discover</u> more about things by using as many of their senses as possible.	

13.	A father brought a kitten home for his daughter. "Why does my kitten run around sniffing and touching everything?" she asked. Her father replied that the kitten was just like Marco Polo. "What's a Marco Polo?" she asked. "Marco Polo was a great explorer who wanted to (_____) China. Your kitten is curious and wants to (_____) her world too." "Oh," said the little girl. Later, she named the kitten Marco Polo.

The father taught his daughter about adventure and exploration when he compared Marco Polo's desire to <u>discover</u> China with the kitten's need to <u>discover</u> its new home.	

14.	When Sam discovered a small vibrator on the couch, his father would (_____) it, turn it on, and (_____) the boy how to use it on his leg.

Parents <u>name</u> new objects and <u>show</u> children how to use them.	

15.	When Sam discovered a set of bells, his mother (_____) them, showed him how to ring them, and laughed with him as they played.

Children learn better when their discoveries are <u>named</u> when they are shown how to use them and when parents laugh and enjoy the discovery too.	

Exhibit 4-6 continued

16.	Susan's father gave her a pegboard to play with. First, he took all the pegs out and put them back in again. Then he took the pegs out and handed them to Susan. This (is/is not) an example of demonstration.	
	Susan's father <u>is</u> demonstrating how to put pegs in a pegboard.	
17.	Susan's mother was dusting the furniture. Susan picked up a tissue and rubbed it over her toy drum, (_____) her mother's actions.	
	Susan is <u>imitating</u> her mother's dusting.	
18.	Sam's father gave him a party noisemaker to hold. He told him what it was, how it made noise, and then put his hand over Sam's causing the object to make a loud sound. This (_____) helped Sam to learn to play with his new toy.	
	Through a <u>demonstration</u> of how the toy worked, Sam's father was helping him to learn.	
19.	Tommy's older brother wants to help Tommy learn to roll a ball. He takes the ball in his hand, shows it to Tommy making sure Tommy is looking at it, and then (_____) rolls the ball toward their father.	
	When demonstrating something to a child, do it precisely and <u>slowly</u> so the child can see what you are doing.	
20.	Paul's grandmother sang a cheery tune while she cleaned Paul's room. Paul laughed and tried to sing the same song. He really enjoyed (_____) his grandmother's song.	
	Children get a great deal of pleasure <u>imitating</u> adults.	
21.	Hazel's mother is getting ready to give Hazel a bath. As she gets the bath-time basket together, she gets Hazel's attention by making a "motor boat" sound with her mouth. Hazel imitates this and her mother makes a fuss over the (_____) that they are playing.	

Exhibit 4-6 continued

A <u>game</u> is fun for both parents and children.	

22.	When Paul's father gives him a bath, he sings a song about Paul's body parts. Paul's father (is/is not) using a game activity to help Paul learn all his body parts.

Using a song or other activity <u>is</u> a game to help children enjoy learning.	

23.	Hazel's aunt made a sound mobile to hang in Hazel's crib. When Hazel waves her arms, she often brushes the mobile and causes the tiny bells to ring. Whenever her aunt is around and this happens, her aunt tickles her with a feather. This (_____) brings both Hazel and her aunt much pleasure.

A <u>game</u> helps increase the efficiency with which children learn.	

24.	Susan's sister was using finger puppets to point to Susan's nose, hands, ears, and so on. This game (will/will not) help Susan learn to name her body parts.

Children enjoy learning when it is fun. Games <u>will</u> help children reach appropriate developmental goals.	

25.	When the important people in children's lives take the time to make up games, songs, or poems to teach children, they are actually helping to (_____) learning efficiency.

Pleasure can definately <u>increase</u> the learning efficiency of children.	

26.	Susan's mother is trying to teach her to build a tower of blocks. They do this every day over and over again to the delight of both of them. This (is/is not) an example of repetition.

Exhibit 4-6 continued

Doing an activity over and over again and making it fun <u>is</u> an example of repetition.	
27. Paul's grandmother is trying to teach Paul to recognize colors. She is doing this in many ways, although the goal remains to have Paul learn colors. This is strong evidence that (_____) need not be boring and can, in fact, be fun.	
<u>Practice</u> or <u>repetition</u> can be made fun if the method of practicing the skill is varied.	
28. Tommy is trying to learn to creep. His family is helping him by holding his stomach off the floor while Tommy is trying to master this skill. They have a schedule when they practice with him. Repetition (will/will not) speed the learning process.	
It is a principle of learning that practice <u>will</u> hasten learning.	
29. When Paul's grandmother was teaching him his colors, Paul would often make mistakes. He would get frustrated and not want to continue, but his grandmother would try another activity. Even though Paul failed on one activity, it is important to continue to give opportunities to (_____) the skill until it is completely mastered.	
Continual <u>practice</u> or <u>repetition</u> is important to skill mastery, even if failure occurs occasionally.	
30. The important people in the lives of Hazel, Tommy, Susan, Sam, and Paul help learning by using manipulation, discovery, imitation and demonstration, games, and repetition. They are making use of five very important teaching (_____).	
Five <u>tools</u> of teaching are manipulation, discovery, imitation and demonstration, games, and repetition.	

Practitioners try to help the child develop any remaining ability in the area of loss. They train the child to maximize the potential of the remaining senses. Many activities are suggested in this text to stimulate the use of those senses and encourage the child to "attend" to language and other sensory stimuli.

Suggestions follow for the stimulation of each of the major five senses. It is advisable to cease the activities just before the child loses interest. They should be done daily with a sense of pleasure and mutual communication. Language cues should be given throughout. The RHYTHM PROCEDURE described hereafter is useful to encourage memory and other cognitive skills. Many more ideas are included in the section of this text entitled "Activities That Enrich Our Lives."

Rhythm Procedure

Sensorial activities can be done in many possible patterns. For example: long-short-long-short, then short-long-short-short. Eventually expose the child to a number of these patterns. Use them while brushing the skin, flashing lights, and so on.

Physical Stimulation Procedures

1. Visual Sensory Activities
   - Put posters on the bedroom walls or where child sleeps. Move them around. Paint walls in bright colored stripes or patterns. Put pictures on the ceiling. Hang mobiles from the ceiling.
   - Move the bed or crib about once a week around the room. Buy sheets with different colors and patterns.
   - Construct crib mobiles. Loosely tie string or cord from mobile and attach to elastic placed around infant's wrist or ankles. Baby will be able to move the parts of the mobile.
   - Place colored cellophane in windows. As light comes in, the room colors will change.
   - Play flashing games at night with the light switch when the room is dark.
   - Use RHYTHM PROCEDURE. Test to see if child becomes upset when the pattern is occasionally changed.
   - Permit child to follow the pattern of a small flashlight. Use the light to help the infant reach the goals of the phase he is in at the time.
   - Construct three by three inch black and white pictures of faces using black and white construction paper and cover with clear contact paper.
   - Also make pictures of shapes, numbers, and alphabet letters, too. Put them on the bumper of the crib at infant's eye level.

2. Listening Sensorial Activities
   - Place a wind chime near an air source in the infant's room. It will catch a breeze and ring gently.
   - Talk, coo, laugh, play and sing soft music.
   - Make varieties of sounds that are soft and loud, low and high, crying and laughing. Talk about them!
   - Sing at feeding or bottle time. Use old favorites, songs of faith, happy songs, or sad songs. Leave a little clock to tick in the child's room.
   - Make "feeling" sounds to go with these words: delicious, happy, sad. Make these activities into imitative games when possible.
   - Teach poems, nursery rhymes, and scriptures. Repeat them frequently or put them on tapes. Repeat during feeding and the short little period of time between feeding the child and sleep.
   - Use the RHYTHM PROCEDURE whenever it is possible.
3. Touch and Spatial Sensorial Activities
   - Give the little child many things for touching or feeling. Help move the child's hands over them. This is called the Touch Procedure I. Use warm and cold objects.
   - Consider the massage process described in Leboyer's book, *Loving Hands* (1979).
   - Hold and cuddle child's bare skin. Lightly tickle the infant, soothe, give little pinches or backrubs. Lightly brush child's skin, head, back and spine, arms and legs, tummy and chest, toes and fingers. Use soft materials and then rougher ones. Try soft brushes, sponges, scrapers and scrubbers, and varieties of fabrics.
   - When the child indicates interest in the hand, put little bells on elastic or ribbons for the wrist. Make mittens using little stockings. Sew shapes, colors, and numbers onto the mittens. Talk, talk, talk with the child during hand play.
   - TOUCH PROCEDURE II. Should the child have problems with language development, touch hands of child and adult on mouth, throat, and jaw areas of both while making sounds.
   - Texture blanket. Sew scraps of fabric as a quilt or blanket. Sew elastic, bells, and buttons on very carefully and firmly. Put knitting, lace, and cording on the pad, too. Lay this blanket on the floor and lay the child on it. Use scents and/or perfume near the edges to add more stimulation for the senses—garlic oil, vanilla, or extracts! Always keep safety in mind.
   - BATHTIME PROCEDURE. Put food colors in the child's bath water. Use vanilla, perfumes, and extracts in the water. When the child is dry, wrap up in fabrics that differ from toweling. Brush all

the child's skin. Brush the feet and hands, the spine. Try soft brushes, wigs, fabrics, and sponges. Brush between and around fingers and toes using a soft brush. Stroke with RHYTHM PROCEDURE when possible.

4. Smell Sensorial Activities
   - Take the child outside and permit the child to smell flowers, and newly cut lawn.
   - Take the child to the kitchen to smell cooking materials. Give a whiff of the vinegar (from a distance), the onions and the garlic (from a distance of several inches), salad oil and any other ingredients that may go into a salad.
   - Devise "smell bottles" or just let the child smell perfume bottles, spice bottles, dusting powders, or shaving lotions.
   - Rub the child with various oils and powders after bath time. Talk about the odors.

5. Taste Sensorial Activities
   - Provide opportunities for the child to "mouth" objects that are too large to swallow. Be careful. Different rubber tubes or nipples are safe examples. Put various flavors on the tip of the nipple or finger. Honey, vinegar, salt, yogurt, mashed cottage cheese, and juices may be used.

Principle

Learning is accomplished through the senses. Many simple and inexpensive devices may be used for physical stimulation activities. Those materials are already in most homes and become very effective teaching materials when used appropriately in a child's program of intervention. They are most effective when applied with patient acceptance and pleasure.

BASING TEACHING GOALS ON DEVELOPMENTAL PRINCIPLES

A butterfly develops in stages. An egg becomes a caterpillar; the caterpillar spins a cocoon; the butterfly emerges from that cocoon. The needs of the butterfly differed according to the stage. Indeed each growth period had requirements that were only appropriate at that time.

People also develop in stages or phases. Those phases are especially noticeable in the first years of life. In this text "Phases I and II" denote the skills developed during the first eight months of life. Those who function on these phase levels develop their abilities to interpret the world through their

Exhibit 4-7 Exercise IV

1.	Tommy is deaf. Because of his handicap, it is likely that his ability to learn language will be (_____).
	If a child is born with problems in any of the sensory areas, the learning process may be <u>delayed</u>.
2.	Susan's mother has put posters on the wall of her bedroom. She also has hung several mobiles where Susan can see them. This is an example of (____) sensory activities.
	<u>Visual</u> sensory activities can **assist** the child to learn about the environment.
3.	Paul's uncle made a complex mobile that he hung near Paul's bed. With the string tied near the mobile, Paul can pull on it and watch it move. This (is/is not) an example of a visual sensory activity.
	It <u>is</u> important for the child to learn about the world through the visual sense.
4.	Hazel's mother placed a wind chime near the air conditioning vent in the bedroom. Each time air circulates through the vent, the chimes ring gently. This (is/is not) an example of a listening sensorial activity.
	It <u>is</u> important for children to learn to attend to auditory stimuli.
5.	Sam's parents read him stories every night. They realize that since Sam is blind, he will need extra help in learning. Reading is an example of a (____ _____ ____).
	Various <u>listening sensory activities</u> are crucial to the development of listening skills.
6.	Sam's mother made him a texture blanket. When they play with it, his mother tells Sam what the different textures are and is even teaching him to name his favorite smells. This is an example of a (____ ____ ___).

Exhibit 4-7 continued

<u>Touch sensorial activities</u> are extremely beneficial to visually impaired babies.	
7. The Touch Procedure I (is/is not) a valuable teaching strategy to assist small children in gaining information by manipulating objects.	
Allowing a child to feel the different characteristics of objects and shapes <u>is</u> called the Touch Procedure I.	
8. One way of helping little children to learn quickly and effectively is to make use of daily or natural activities such as feeding, diapering, or bathing. Susan's mother often puts perfume or food coloring in the bathtub. This is an example of the (___) procedure.	
The <u>bath-time</u> procedure can be used to make bathing fun and also a real learning experience.	
9. Paul's mother made a small set of bottles in which she has placed various common scents. Then she lets Paul smell them and try to guess the scent. This is an example of a (___ ____ ___).	
<u>Smell Sensory Activities</u> include rubbing different smelling powders or oils on the baby after the bath.	
10. The use of all the (_____) in the child's total developmental or educational program can greatly assist learning. Parents who use the child's total environment and intact sensory systems will be maximizing educational opportunities.	
People all learn through tools called the five <u>senses</u> of sight, hearing, touch, taste, and smell.	

senses. They are also just beginning to understand and attempt to imitate language. They lay the foundation for all later learning based upon their sensorimotor abilities.

Once this foundation is well laid, the child builds upon it with the highly complex skills that emerge between the critical period generally observed between. the ages of eight to eighteen months (Phase III). The sensorimotor skills become important at this time, and movement becomes a major developmental goal. A burst of language often emerges as a child nears the age of two. A seeking for independence and self-esteem then becomes typically important even as a child begins to learn social skills. Indeed, the developmental goals of a child in Phase IV and Phase V lead to the emergence of a total, if young, personality.

Those five periods or phases of growth may be observed in five areas of human development. People's reflexes develop into their large body movements (gross motor skills). These developmental goals or skills are grouped together in this curriculum as reflex/gross motor skills (RM). Their eyes and hands become able to work together, and are called perceptual/fine motor skills (PFM). People begin to think and have an effect upon their environment. That process of cognition is outlined in the sensory/cognitive (SC) portion of this text. Language (L) also develops as do personal, social and the self-help skills (P/S/SH) that lead to independence.

Principle

Practitioners can enjoy and accept the children they work with when they really understand the children's exact point of development and the skills that are appropriate to them. The developmental checklists included at the end of Chapter 2 help practitioners gain a valid idea of the child's abilities. They can then plan appropriate intervention using many of the activity suggestions in the curriculum section of this text.

PERCEPTUAL AND MOTOR SKILLS ACTIVITIES

Two of the most important things a child must try to do are master the movements of body parts and coordinate those movements purposefully. The basic movements themselves originate in the reflexes present at birth. Young children must master movements of the whole body as well as the arms and legs. These movements are referred to as gross motor skills (RM). Young children must also bring under control the purposeful movements of the hands. These activities are referred to as perceptual or fine motor skills (PFM).

A child must also develop a sense of spatial relationships. They need to know how much space they occupy as they move. They must develop a feel for their own bodies and a sense of relationship to other people and things.

When adults encourage children to develop their gross and fine motor skills as well as their sense of space, they are also encouraging cognitive or

Exhibit 4-8 Exercise V

1.	Tommy is beginning to learn to crawl. His parents work diligently practicing this skill with Tommy. They realize that his development is occuring in (____).
	Human beings develop in <u>phases</u> or <u>stages</u>.
2.	During Phase I and II, or the first (____) months of life, children learn largely through sensorimotor activities and also begin to imitate certain language activities.
	The first <u>eight</u> months of life are important as a foundation for all later learning.
3.	Between the ages of eight and 18 months, or Phase (____), movement or motor activities become a major developmental goal.
	Phase <u>III</u> is important because of the increase in the child's mobility.
4.	The five phases of growth can be observed in (____) areas of human development. The goals or skills in each phase are grouped according to a specific developmental area.
	The <u>five</u> areas of growth are reflex/gross motor, perceptual/ fine motor, sensory/cognitive, language, and personal/social/ self-help.
5.	When taken together, the goals and activities in the five phases and the five areas of growth lead to the emergence of the child's total (_____). Individual's working with children must accept and understand the child's exact point of development.
	<u>Personality</u> development occurs as the result of progression through the five phases and areas of growth.

Exhibit 4-8 continued

6.	Hazel's parents note on the developmental checklists that she lifts her head and is beginning to roll. Her motor (RM) development is within the range of goals found in (_____) I.
	Hazel's motor development is typically <u>Phase</u> I.
7.	Tommy is trying to crawl and sit. He is also following objects with his eyes and banging, splashing,and grasping objects. His development in these two areas (is/is not) typical of Phase II.
	Tommy's development in these areas <u>is</u> within the Phase II range of goals.
8.	Susan is beginning to work. This is typical of Phase III. She is interested in turning book pages and she scribbles. These activities are within the (_____) range of Phase IV.
	Children may perform at different <u>developmental</u> levels when they have problems and special needs.
9.	Sam's vocabulary includes 200-300 words, and he combines them in 2-3 word sentences. He is still learning to walk. Sam (is/is not) able to use language on a Phase V level while his motor development remains at Phase III.
	Sam's language <u>is</u> at the developmental level shown in Phase V.
10.	Paul is unable to develop his gross motor skills. They remain on a (_____) level. His fine motor skills include building towers of 6-7 cubes, scribbling in circular motion, working simple puzzles. He shows a definite preference for handedness. These skills are at the Phase V developmental level.
	Paul is at <u>Phase I</u> level in motor skills,and his perceptual fine motor work is typically Phase V.

Exhibit 4-8 continued

11.	Hazel's parents continue to do sensorimotor activities for her individualized (____) as these are appropriate for her level of development.
	Hazel's individualized <u>program</u> is appropriate for her level of development.
12.	Susan's parents spend a great deal of time with walking activities. This (is/is not) appropriate for her individualized program.
	This <u>is</u> appropriate as Susan's motor skills are developmentally delayed.
13.	Sam's parents recognize that his language development is quite advanced. They continue encouraging these skills as they see them as a great strength and advantage for him. They (do/do not) spend a great deal of time encouraging him to become confident enough to walk as this is an area where his development is (_____).
	Sam's parents <u>do</u> spend time encouraging his motor development which is <u>delayed</u>.
14.	Paul's parents note that his temper tantrums are frequent, that he is beginning to enjoy routine in his life, and that he is doing well at self-feeding. They are pleased that his personal/social/self-help (is/is not) well within the developmental goals of Phase V.
	Paul's social and self-help development <u>is</u> within the range of Phase V.
15.	Paul's parents continue to (encourage/discourage) the development of his social and self-help skills as they feel he needs the independence and confidence these skills develop.
	Paul's parents <u>encourage</u> his independence skills as they lead to sound self-esteem.

mental growth and a concept of self. These are marvelously rewarding concepts. They do require practice for children with special needs. These following suggestions may provide useful ideas for parents and professionals who would help children develop motoric skills.

Activities for Spatial Concepts

- When the child is bathing, talk about the things you are doing. Talk and move the wash cloth or sponge *between* the *legs, around* the *arms, down* the *back, around* the *neck, over* and *under, on, through,* and *off* the *hands, head, toes, fingers,* etc.
- Brush the child's body after the bath. Talk about the rough and smooth, hard or soft feelings. Identify body parts. Use the RHYTHM PROCEDURE.
- Wrap child in variety of fabrics.
- Move the child between your legs, under your arms, on your shoulders. Talk as described above.
- Set up obstacles for the child to crawl through. Cut big and little holes or shapes into boxes. Cover boxes with contact paper. Place toys inside for the baby to discover.
- Teach spatial concepts with a small box or basket. Place a toy on it, off it, in, out, under and beside.

Activities for Gross Motor Development

These activities are taught like games—not as lessons that must be done. Control of error becomes the fun in the game. Often trainers can begin doing the activities and the child will try to imitate. They are appropriate for children able to function in Phases IV and V.

- Carry or dance with the child to music.
- Dance out stories. Act like animals. Act out feelings. Walk on tip toe, up and down, and over and under.
- Let able child move small pieces of furniture quietly.
- Practice walking, crawling, rolling between objects without touching. When possible, walk or crawl or roll on mounds outdoors.
- Sports, gymnastics, or yoga activities may be *attempted* as parents practice.
- Acting out may be done in front of a low mirror.
- Begin basketball and other sports in Phases III or IV. Let the child drop the ball in laundry baskets or waste baskets. They must get the ball past someone who tries to block it. Roll ball to baby. Let the baby "win."

- Hand clapping, acting out verbal commands, foot tapping, imitation of animal actions, scooting and relay games, body awareness games, and follow-me games—play games so the little children win frequently and see themselves as "winners."
- Walk on a line. Lay a strip of tape on a floor. Let child walk on the tape carrying a bell. Don't let the bell ring. Carry objects on trays while walking on the line. Walk with a flag.

Activities for Perceptual/Fine Motor Development

- Encourage reaching and hand use by placing toys near a child. Keep the environment as stimulating as possible.
- Little bells or patterns may be securely sewn on little mittens, then worn on the infant's hands. This may draw the child's attention to the hand.
- See the PHYSICAL STIMULATION PROCEDURE and other suggestions in the section of this chapter entitled "Learning through the Senses."
- Many toys are fine instruments for developing fine motor skills. Puzzles, formboards, rings and hoops, nesting cups, and blocks utilize perceptual skills.
- Review the Perceptual/Fine Motor Activities and the activities listed under Sensory/Cognitive Skills in this curriculum.

Practical Life Skills

Skills of practical living combine gross, fine, and spatial abilities. Review the TRAINING PROCEDURE materials under MOTIVATION in this chapter. More suggested activities are given in the Personal/Social/Self-Help (P/S/SH) section of the curriculum.

Remember to get down on the child's physical level to demonstrate. Remember to make the experiences as happy and successful as possible.

- OPENING AND SHUTTING—cupboards, doors, locks, hooks.
- CARRYING—trays, chairs, tables, bells, fine objects.
- POURING—beans, rice, water, salt, vanilla (fine).
- SOCIAL SKILLS—shaking hands, setting the table, folding napkins, getting a chair, excuse me, thank you, table manners, serving.
- HOUSEKEEPING SKILLS—vacuuming, dusting, polishing floors, sweeping, polishing shoes, silver, furniture, flower arranging, washing clothes and woodwork, ironing-peg 180 degrees, sponging up and wringing out, washing dishes, raking, digging, scissors, hammer, sawing using styrofoam.

- SELF-CARE SKILLS—toileting, washing themselves, feeding, combing hair, cleaning nails, polishing nails, buttons, shoes, ironing clothes, washing hands, and dressing skills.
- COOKING—scraping, cutting, peeling, stirring, pouring, shelling peas.

Principle

Perceptual and motor skill activities are vitally important as practitioners seek to help children gain a concept of themselves and their spatial place in the world. Gaining this understanding is one of the major developmental goals for all children during the early years of life. A child's problems may present some difficulties in this area of development, but many simple and inexpensive activities may be devised to overcome and circumvent those limitations.

GIVING LANGUAGE

Children with speech and language problems often need a great deal of help and motivation in order to learn language. People tend not to realize how much effort is required to master languages because most children are naturally motivated to express themselves and want to understand what others are saying to them, which is the purpose of communication.

People often think of communication as knowing words. Actually, people must also learn to move their bodies and make gestures that are socially appropriate as well. These gestures or *receptive* language help people understand the real meaning of what is being said, which is called *expressive* language.

Adults can do a number of things to help their children develop better speech and language. They can talk a great deal to the child. They can often place their faces where the child can see them speaking, which is especially important in the case of a child with a hearing loss. The child's smallest efforts can be rewarded consistently, appropriately, and immediately. Adults can give the child interesting enrichment activities. They can repeat single words until they are recognized. Then parents can use the NAMING PROCEDURE to give more information. "Ball." "This is a ball." "Ball." "This is a red ball." "This red ball has a white stripe." Adults can help the child handle the object as they describe it. They can wait a moment or two to give the child time to attempt a sound or repetition of the word.

Games can be used to teach language. Imitation games are enjoyed by babies and young children. Adults can imitate the child's sounds or make sounds of their own for the child to try to imitate. They can face the child so

Exhibit 4-9 Exercise VI

1. People learn a great deal about their world by moving their bodies around their environment. When they move the large muscles, including the arms and legs, we are practicing (_____) motor skills.

   Gross motor activities are important to overall body development.

2. Hazel's mother is trying to teach her to grasp small objects. She places various objects in Hazel's hands and encourages her to grasp them. This is an example of (_____) motor skill development.

   Activities using the fingers and hands are called fine motor skills.

3. Sam is trying to develop his walking skills. One of his major difficulties involves his ability to orient himself to his environment. It will be necessary for him to develop (_____) relationships or a feel for his own body.

   Spatial relationships or knowing how much space a person's body occupies as it moves, is crucial to motor skill development.

4. When Sam's father is bathing him, he always tries to remember to talk about the things he is doing. For example, he will say, "Sam, the wash cloth is on your toes," or "I am washing around your neck." This is an example of an activity that can be used to teach (_____) relationships.

   Identifying body parts helps the child to acquire a knowledge of Spatial relationships.

5. Tommy's parents have set up cardboard boxes for Tommy to crawl around and through. This (is/is not) an activity designed to develop a concept of spatial relationships.

   Being able to navigate around obstacles is indicative of good spatial relationships.

Exhibit 4-9 continued

6.	Susan's sister is trying to help her learn to walk. She will place favorite objects out of reach and encourage Susan to get them. They do this as a game. This (is/is not) a gross motor activity.
	Practicing walking skills <u>is</u> a good gross motor activity.	
7.	Paul's father has set up a small basket and backboard on a stand. He put it near Paul's bed and allowed him to throw a small ball into the basket. This (_____) motor activity is really enjoyed by both Paul and his father.
	<u>Gross</u> motor activities are important for all children.	
8.	Paul's grandmother enjoys doing small puzzles with him. They often do this for hours as Paul is really learning to do (_____) motor activities well.
	Puzzles, formboards, and blocks are all excellent materials for developing <u>fine</u> motor skills.	
9.	Teaching children to carry objects or do housekeeping skills are good examples of (_____) life skills. These skills will help the child become less dependent on adults.
	<u>Practical</u> life skills are essential to normalizing a child's life.	
10.	Parents of children with special needs must be aware of the necessity of teaching skills such as toileting, washing hands, feeding, dressing, and so on. These (___-___) skills are crucial to the development of the total child.
	Many <u>self-help</u> skills can be learned as a part of a child's daily routine.	

their lips are within the child's reach. The child can be guided to touch adult's neck and face and feel where the sounds are coming from. Adults' pleasure and enthusiasm will reward the child's imitative efforts.

Adults also need to encourage the child who is speaking by listening with consideration and accepting those first efforts without criticism. Rather than correcting the child, they can merely repeat the sentence or word properly in their conversation.

The WORD COMMAND PROCEDURE is important because it is simple and useful in conditioning children to respond in a definite way to certain words. Teach command words like come, stop, and wait as a game and keep it fun. Always give the command in the same tone of voice. Reward the baby again and again until the response to the command is automatic. Begin the games next to the child and then move further away as the child masters the correct response. Repeat the games frequently for fun even though the child may perform well 80 to 85 percent of the time.

Given this training, the child will associate certain words with behaviors and ideas, as well as gestures or movements. A wave is a greeting. A hand held up and out is a signal to stop. These and other forms of body language begin as small gestures in infancy. A baby may only be able to give a small movement of an arm as a reaching gesture. When adults recognize or interpret that movement as a communicative effort, they begin to reinforce the reaching.

Those gestures may be strengthened and developed into entire sign languages that are helpful to those who are severely/profoundly deaf or mentally retarded. Moreover, sign languages are used to help the deaf-blind communicate.

Adults also communicate with written symbols. Some children may not be able to speak, but still may acquire concepts by learning to read written symbols. All children with the potential to read may well be exposed to the PHONETIC SYMBOL PROCEDURE because it uses the manipulation of concrete objects that represent sound symbols. Although adaptable to the individual child's needs, the basic elements of the PHONETIC SYMBOL PROCEDURE encourage language development through the involvement of a variety of senses.

1. Imitate the child's sounds.
2. Imitate the child's sounds while placing the child's hand on the source of sound while vocalizing.
3. Place child's hand on source of sound during child's vocalization.
4. Give child phonetic symbols for the sounds being made. Allow child to play with the symbols and include them in daily living activities.

Materials: Phonetic symbols m, b, p (probable) and others. May be constructed of construction paper covered with clear contact paper on both sides.

Cue: "Here is your *b*."
   "Chew your *b*."
   "Where is your *b*?"

It is preferable to use the sounds of letters rather than the alphabet names of letters.

Comment: Environmental use of symbols.

1. Introduce with the grasping reflex.
2. Leave symbols around infant's crib and play area as well as general environment.
3. Put symbols on the walls at eye level for infant.
4. Hang symbols on mobiles in view of child's eyes.
5. Direct child's limbs to outline shapes of symbols.
6. Direct child's hand over symbols.
7. Emphasize symbol and sound throughout the day.

Language abilities are also strengthened through sharing stories, poems, songs, and fingerplays. They may be tape recorded along with words being stressed in the language program. The tapes may be played repeatedly. This is called the TAPE PROCEDURE in the curriculum section of this manual. Many children love the tapes. They enjoy hearing their names called and they also enjoy hearing their own voices. Children in Phases I and II may benefit by listening to the sounds of other little children babbling or trying to speak. The general language stimulation and repetition on the tapes may be most effective when combined with the PROGRAMMING PROCEDURE and used to help teach precise sound and word approximations.

Principle

The greatest motivating factor in language acquisition is the desire to communicate with others. Patience, acceptance, the setting of long-term goals and prolonged enthusiasm must be combined with good reinforcement procedures when adults help a child learn to communicate.

Exhibit 4-10 Exercise VII

1.	Tommy is trying to "talk" and tell his mother something. This attempt at communication is (receptive/expressive) language.
	Saying what we mean is called <u>expressive</u> language.
2.	Sam is learning to walk. He often discovers objects his parents have "planted" for him. When he finds a ball or a toy, his parents say, "Sam, that is a ball." We call this teaching method the (____ ____).
	The <u>NAMING PROCEDURE</u> is used to teach children the names of objects.
3.	Paul is playing with plastic geometric shapes. His grandmother hands him another and says to him, "Paul, this is a small, red square." This (is/is not) an example of the NAMING PROCEDURE.
	The NAMING PROCEDURE <u>is</u> used to give a child more information about an object.
4.	Susan has been slow to develop language skills. Yet, she is enthusiastic about speaking and often puts together two sounds which sound a little like words. Her family is happy she is trying to speak and they (_____) her efforts without criticism.
	When we <u>accept</u> the child's early language efforts, we can shape better expressive language.
5.	When Tommy's father speaks to him, he always faces Tommy so he can see his lips and mouth. Often his father will take Tommy's hands and place them on his (____ and _____) to feel where the sounds are coming from.
	Placing a child's hands on your <u>face</u> and <u>neck</u> will help him "feel" the sounds of language.
6.	Sam was on the second floor of his home walking along the rail. When he got near the steps, his mother said "Sam, stop!" and firmly grasped his arm. After several situations like this, Sam will stop when told to do so. This is an example of the (_____ _____ ___).

Exhibit 4-10 continued

The <u>WORD COMMAND PROCEDURE</u> conditions children to respond in a definite way to certain words.	

7.	Susan is practicing her walking skills. Her sister is across the room from her. Her sister says "Susan, come." and holds out her arms as a cue. This (is/is not) an example of the <u>WORD COMMAND PROCEDURE</u>.

The WORD COMMAND PROCEDURE is practiced until the child's response becomes automatic.	

8.	Even though Tommy is still very young, his parents want to use a variation of the WORD COMMAND PROCEDURE to help him learn language. When Tommy rolls or crawls near a dangerous object, his parents position themselves where Tommy can see, and they hold their hand up and out while telling him to stop. It is important to use (_____) to teach children with hearing losses.

<u>Gestures</u>, <u>movements</u>, or <u>signs</u> may be combined with language to eventually form a sign language and give an understanding of language.	

9.	Hazel attempts to reach out for objects or her mother when she hears her coming. Hazel's mother tries to remember to reinforce this effort at (_____) so that Hazel's gestures or movements can begin to have meaning to her and her family.

<u>Communication</u> includes not only words, but also movements, gestures, and signals.	

10.	Paul's grandmother made some cardboard letters out of construction paper. She gives them to Paul and tells him the sounds they make. This use of the (____ _____ _____) will help Paul learn communication skills.

The <u>PHONETIC SYMBOL PROCEDURE</u> may be used to teach children with the potential to learn to read.	

Exhibit 4-10 continued

11.	Parents can leave symbols around the child's environment. Solid letters or cut-outs can be planted in the child's favorite places. When the child finds these symbols, they should be immediately identified. This (is/is not) an example of the PHONETIC SYMBOL PROCEDURE.
	The PHONETIC SYMBOL PROCEDURE <u>is</u> an excellent technique for teaching letter sounds and names.
12.	Children should be allowed to see and feel symbols. The phonetic symbols should also be identified by the sounds they make. The PHONETIC SYMBOL PROCEDURE is an excellent teaching process because it allows the child to use most of his (____) in the learning activity.
	The PHONETIC SYMBOL PROCEDURE encourages language development through a variety of <u>senses</u>.
13.	Hazel's mother bought a cassette recorder and made a tape of another infant babbling and cooing. She plays this tape in Hazel's room to encourage the development of Hazel's language. This (is/is not) an example of the TAPE PROCEDURE.
	The TAPE PROCEDURE <u>is</u> one of many language enrichment activities.
14.	General language stimulation and repetition using the (____ _____) in combination with the PROGRAMMING PROCEDURE enhances the effectiveness of this teaching approach.
	The TAPE PROCEDURE encourages the development of language.
15.	Language acquisition is greatly enhanced by the motivation of the child to (_____) with others.
	To communicate is one of the great needs of human beings.

Exhibit 4-10 continued

16.	Paul's mother has made a tape recording of Paul's favorite nursery rhymes set to music for Paul to sing and memorize with the tape. This is an example of using the (_____) PROCEDURE to enrich learning.
	The <u>TAPE</u> PROCEDURE is a good learning tool to enrich language development.
17.	When Hazel is fed her meals, her mother continually talks with her about the foods Hazel is eating, naming the foods, describing them as to color, texture, and taste. Hazel's mother (is/is not) building a receptive language vocabulary of understanding in her child.
	A receptive language vocabulary <u>is</u> necessary for Hazel to learn to understand and to talk.
18.	Sam and his mother went to visit a farm so that Sam could see what the animals really sounded like and so he could touch and pet them and feel their fur and their size. On the way home, Sam and his mother talked about the animals they had visited. Sam added four new words to his expressive vocabulary as a result of the visit to the farm. In creating new experiences for Sam, his mother (did/did not) add new words and concepts to Sam's vocabulary.
	Sam increased his expressive vocabulary because his mother <u>did</u> enlarge his world in creating new experiences for him to share and in discussing it with him.
19.	Susan is learning the names of fruits. Her mother has chosen 3 of Susan's favorites: apple, banana, and grapes. Mother set out the apple in front of Susan and said, "Apple." Susan's response was an approximation of apple when she said, "A-ow." "Good talking, Susan. Give me the apple." Susan did. Mother put the apple and the banana in front of Susan. "Give me the apple, Susan." Susan gave her mother the apple. Mother again asked "What is this, Susan?" "A-ow," replied Susan. This is an example of the (_____ _____ _____).
	Susan's mother used the <u>WORD LEARNING</u> PROCEDURE to increase Susan's receptive and expressive vocabulary.

Exhibit 4-10 continued

20.	Tommy is beginning to make some nice cooing sounds and squeals. His father has begun to imitate Tommy's sounds in response. When father does this, he takes Tommy's hand and places it on his own (father's) throat and jaw so that Tommy will feel the vibrations necessary to produce the sound. Tommy is beginning to enjoy the game. He can feel the vibrations in his father's face and neck and is beginning to receive tactile feedback for sounds he cannot hear. Tommy's father (is/is not) stimulating other senses to compensate for Tommy's hearing impairment.

Tommy's father _is_ improving Tommy's language potential by utilizing as many of the senses as possible.	

ACTIVITIES THAT ENRICH LIVES

People can learn only what they experience directly or vicariously. They absorb much of what they learn just by being exposed to the environment of their family homes. Here are some suggestions that may help in enriching the learning environment for children who function within developmental phases I, II, and III.

- Keep the child near the family, not in a back room. Buy a "body carrier" and keep the baby with the family. This helps combat boredom and loneliness. It also increases a sense of up/down and body motion for children with severe visual problems.
- Add interest to the baby's sleeping and play areas. Move the crib from time to time. Put up posters. Change the pictures on walls. Have a little clock ticking nearby. Hang mobiles. Record family voices singing, talking, saying scriptures or poems. Play the tapes frequently for the baby. Paint the room in bright colors.
- Talk, talk, talk for the child. Talk about what you are doing with the child, the toys, everything. Remember the NAMING PROCEDURE.
- Give the child many sensory experiences. Make them safe.
- Put all kinds of fabrics under the child when placed on the floor. Do not use just the pastel blanket.
- Put the child on the floor, but in a place that makes observation possible.

- Encourage the child to move as much as is possible, but be sure the house and yard have been made safe.
- Remember the DISCOVERY PROCEDURE. "Plant" things that you want the child to learn (numbers, shapes, phonetic symbols, colors).
- Devise happy games that teach shapes, words, colors, or numbers.
- Teach with the child's body—outlined numbers or shapes, with the baby's arms, hands, and legs.
- Use the child's senses as much as is possible when teaching and playing.
- Train the child to mind before walking begins. Note the WORD COMMAND PROCEDURE.
- When the child can move around the house, teach the names of objects. Ask "where" this or that is. Let the child go to it, then show it to you. Be excited.
- Reward the child's successes. Ignore the child's failures.
- Read to the child briefly. At first buy strong cardboard books that have good pictures and few words.
- Sing with the child and play music frequently. Waiting times are happy times for singing little songs.
- When the child begins scribbling, make an "Art Gallery." Put up postcards and pictures by artists. Add the child's scribbles, too. Talk about the pictures. Name the artists.
- Praying with the child is appropriate if religion is important in the home. Memorize poetry and scriptures and practice when the child can listen to them repeatedly.
- Encourage a sense of order. Provide low, open shelves for the child's belongings and low rods for hanging clothes. Tables and chairs need to be 17 to 21 inches high.
- Make the outdoor play area truly a child's garden. The yard can be attractive and still include play areas for the child. Examples include trees, a little hill with grass, shade, rocks to climb, a shallow water pool for wading and water play, a sand pile in the shade, balance boards or fencing to walk on, little bells to tinkle in the breeze, a pet, a bird house or feeder, things to push, objects to roll and crawl after, things to pull and carry, things to hunt for, and objects left in the garden to discover.

Stories, songs, fingerplays, and poems may be used appropriately in many situations. They may be begun even in the first months of life. Parents can repeat them as they feed the child. The more they are repeated, the more the little children seem to enjoy them.

Children functioning in Phases IV and V enjoy them even more. They are such an enjoyable part of any learning situation that it is wise to incorporate them when teaching readiness for academic subjects. For example, it is possible to make little books for children by taking Polaroid pictures of special events they experience and then writing simple sentences next to the pictures. The pages may be stapled together into book form for the child.

The child may be prepared for more academic learning by using the natural methods of discovery, manipulation, imitation, and games. Symbols for numbers, shapes, letters, and colors may be planted in the yard and around the house. Just name the symbol as you would any other object. Let them be played with just like any other toys. People do not fear the familiar. They grow familiar with the objects that are around them daily.

As it is often difficult to know what little children have really learned, it helps adults to structure themselves to teach in terms of units. The UNIT ACTIVITIES PROCEDURE merely helps trainers organize many small concepts with a large one. For example, TRANSPORTATION is a major concept with many parts comprised of cars, boats, buses, trains, and airplanes. A child in Phases IV or V may be able to learn these concepts. A very talented child can learn how we go places, how food and clothing are brought to us, and the names of people who control the modes of transportation. All these concepts are appropriate in a unit on transportation. Units can be tried at the rate of one unit a month. They don't take much work, but trainers will know what the child has been exposed to.

Principle

It is most gratifying to share enrichment activities with children. They are fun. They are not drudgery. The child perceives the adult as an interesting person rather than just a disciplinarian and caretaker. Children tend to listen more closely and watch carefully those they love to be with. But this is just another facet of accepting and loving. Love brings about change. Love is worth the effort. People have no way of knowing the true potential of a human being until they have given that potential time and opportunity to flourish. The first years of any child's life are vital to all future growth and development. This is true for all children, as all children are special in one way or another.

LOOKING TOWARD THE TOTAL CHILD

Acceptance

Acceptance does not mean resignation. Acceptance does not negate hope. Acceptance says, "Here is where we start. This is what we have to work with. This is the speed at which we may be expected to move. But move we shall."

Exhibit 4-11 Exercise VIII

1.	Hazel's parents have made a language tape for her. They have recorded songs, poems, babbling sounds and have put cues for commands they will train her to obey for skills. They find the tapes helpful as children on Hazel's level of development (do/do not) enjoy repetition of sounds.

	Hazel's parents are using tapes because children at Hazel's developmental level <u>do</u> enjoy repetition of sounds and often eagerly anticipate their names and words they recognize on such tapes.

2.	Sam's mother enjoys singing. She teaches him many little songs, and he enjoys singing with her. She also is teaching him rhythm and letting him learn the conducting patterns for music. She is (___) his environment and does not limit his learning because of his problems or age.

	Sam's mother is <u>enriching</u> his environment with the music she and he both enjoy.

3.	Sometimes Sam's mother sings when he is along on the patio outside the kitchen. He hears her voice and (is/is not) able to find his way to the door. Often enrichment activities serve to loneliness and a sense of isolation.

	Sam <u>is</u> able to hear her voice, and <u>it</u> guides him to the open kitchen door.

4.	Tommy's parents move his crib around his room regularly. They change the posters on the walls and vary the mobiles hanging from the ceiling. They have cut cellophane in shapes and taped them on the bedroom window. They have prepared a very (_____) environment for Tommy when he is in his room.

	Tommy's parents have prepared a stimulating, fun, <u>enriched</u> environment for Tommy when he is in his room.

Exhibit 4-11 continued

5.	Paul's parents have encouraged his interest in the stories he has enjoyed since he was eight months old. Now they take polaroid (_____) when he goes to the doctors or for outings. They mount the pictures, write simple sentences next to the pictures, and staple them together in book form. Paul calls these his own "Life" books.

The polaroid <u>pictures</u> are used to remind Paul of his experiences, and he becomes familiar with the words and sentences that are next to the pictures as they are repeated often.	

6.	Hazel is much too big for the back carrier her mother used to use. Still her mother keeps her nearby wherever she works. When she cooks she puts Hazel in her high chair and places her nearby. As she cooks, Hazel's mother lets Hazel smell the ingredients of the recipes. She lets her finger-play on the tray with some of the ingredients. Hazel's mother is helping Hazel use her senses to (_____) her environment.

Hazel's mother is helping Hazel use her senses to <u>enrich</u> Hazel's environments.	

7.	Tommy's parents have purchased several small cardboard books for him. When he is quiet and relaxed before sleeping, they seat him where he can see their lips and the picture books. They read to him for brief periods and make this (_____) activity brief,but pleasant.

This <u>enrichment</u> activity is kept brief, but Tommy and his parents do enjoy the pictures and the shared times.	

8.	Sam's parents leave wooden shapes in various places for him to (____). Sometimes he finds his cube on the coffee table. Once he found his ovoid on the high chair tray as he waited to eat. The hemisphere was on the couch as he crawled up one day.

Sam's parents let him <u>discover</u> the shapes he enjoys feeling. Later they will help him organize concepts of objects pointing out that they are similar to the cube, sphere, cylinder, and other basic shapes.	

Exhibit 4-11 continued

9.	Susan's mother enjoys art. Susan's sister often finger paints and draws, and Susan loves to scribble alongside. The children's mother has put corkboard along the bottom three feet of wall in the hallway. She keeps an "art gallery" of prints of masterpieces taped on the corkboard in order to (_____) the children's lives. She includes Susan's scribbles and her sister's efforts on the corkboard. She wants the girls to feel good about their "art work" too.
	Susan's mother uses the prints and the corkboard to <u>enrich</u> the girls' lives and build their self-esteem.
10.	Paul so enjoys little stories and poems that he wants to make them up. His mother writes his "poems " on cards for him and puts them in a file near his bed. He pretends to read them. She does read them to Daddy when he comes home at night. They enjoy sharing this (____ _____) together as a family.
	The family enjoys sharing this <u>enrichment activity</u>.
11.	Susan's parents are deeply religious. They have placed scriptures and uplifting proverbs on tapes to help their memorization. They play the tapes while Susan plays with her toys. They hope she will (____) some of these sayings and that they may become meaningful to her at some time in the future.
	Susan's parents hope she will <u>absorb</u> some of these word patterns and that they will be able to teach them to her in association with her later life experiences.
12.	Paul loves to go for rides. He has started showing interest in the cars and trucks he sees along the way. His parents have decided to plan a transportation unit to enrich his life. Such a unit (may/may not) include activities with boats, planes, trains, and buses.
	A transportation unit <u>may</u> include activities with a variety of objects that are used to transport people and materials in our society.

Exhibit 4-11 continued

13.	Paul's parents are planning several outings this month, and they are basing them upon the transportation (_____). They will take him to see the trains at the railroad station, the buses at the depot, the airplanes landing, the trucks at the movers, and the boats at the lake.
	Outings are a means of making a <u>unit</u> such as transportation real through experience. The more real or concrete an experience the better the learning that will result.
14.	Paul's parents took pictures of Paul on each of the outings. They were polaroid pictures and were mounted in little books with a short appropriate (_____) next to each picture. If Paul wanted something included in his experience book that did not have a picture, his parent's made a simple sketch to go with the sentence.
	The short, appropriate <u>sentence</u> is combined with the experience and the pictures to make written words meaningful to Paul.
15.	Paul's parents have bought several sets of small, inexpensive trucks, cars, planes, boats, and other (_____) that he can play with as a part of the transportation unit.
	Appropriate <u>toys</u> are a vital part of the unit method of teaching as they are concrete and may be manipulated, and this learning takes place through experience.
16.	Paul's parents name the different types of toy boats, cars, trains, and trucks in order to enlarge his (_____), which is an important part of language enrichment.
	Increasing the <u>vocabulary</u> is an important part of language building.
17.	Paul's parents have purchased some simple, inexpensive books on cars, boats, trucks, trains, and airplanes to enrich his learning through the (___ _____) of teaching.

Exhibit 4-11 continued

The <u>unit method</u> of teaching is an outstanding way to enrich a child's vocabulary and knowledge of the world.	
18. Paul's parents talk to him about the concepts they are teaching him in the transportation units. They (do/do not) point out these modes of transportation when they are shown on TV.	
Paul's parents <u>do</u> point out anything on TV that can <u>add</u> to Paul's vocabulary or understanding of simple concepts involved in transportation.	

Accept and move on is the goal of the great movement now revolutionizing options for the handicapped throughout the Western world. That revolution enjoins a philosophy of acceptance and insists that everyone is entitled to the option to learn and find a place in society. That philosophy is commonly called "normalization." Its disciples are those who seek as normal a life as possible for others whose limitations seem so frightening to much of society.

If adults are to enable children with problems to enter into the mainstream of society, they must do the work necessary to alleviate that social fear. At the same time they must strengthen the children so that they can eventually prove themselves and their worth to society. The change in attitude must begin with those who care for the children. The work begins in the earliest years of their lives.

That work must look to the development of the total child. It must focus on the present possibilities, yet direct itself to the development of personality as well as a body—in other words, the total person who must someday play some role in relation to others and society.

Those children deserve to have opportunities to develop their potentials in the emotional, aesthetic, social, and spiritual aspects of life to whatever degree is possible. Often their progress is limited by others' attitudes.

Trainers are prone to see only the problems in a situation. But when they focus their minds on their load of care, they are held back from recognizing all the potential for love and growth that may exist in a situation. The child is not the problem. The problem is fear of the unknown, of the difficulty, and of failure. Once trainers overcome those fears and accept the fact that possibilities still remain, they can help the child develop, not only physically and mentally, but also socially, aesthetically, and spiritually.

These last areas of growth have been little explored in special education. Very little guidance is available. However, the majority of parents who have raised children with special needs can testify that those children do respond to love and beauty and companionship.

How then might trainers best go about helping the child develop a love of beauty or aesthetics? Simply, expose the child to their caring for what is beautiful. They can demonstrate their caring in the way they lovingly, slowly, and carefully handle beautiful objects. The expression on their faces, in the tone of their voices, can denote all that they find special in a flower. They can use training programs to teach that reverence to the children. Imitation, repetition, manipulation, games, and even the discovery method of teaching may be employed to this end.

Manipulation, imitation, and repetition are also useful in teaching spiritual concepts. The same full use of the senses is important. Trainers can make dolls or pictures of those they honor spiritually. They can devise teaching materials to teach many aspects of kindness, gentleness, and consideration. They can demonstrate those qualities as they teach these concepts. They can demonstrate those qualities as they live before these children. Many of their souls will understand example.

Trainers can study the developmental abilities of a child functioning at any particular level and utilize this understanding no matter what the subject matter. They can teach in a meaningful way given knowledge of the thinking processes involved from birth on. Piaget notes that different types of thinking occur at different stages of development. His insights are briefly explained in Chapter 1. Trainers can teach to that quality of thinking and do it appropriately if the developmental levels of the child are clearly understood, if they make the subject concrete, and if they demonstrate the appropriate attitude physically and emotionally.

Again, it is through example and careful training that adults can help the children grow socially. That training must be appropriate for the child's present stage of development. But the child will change and so will the demands of society. Children will eventually be expected to care for themselves as much as possible. Adults do not help them if they overprotect and overserve them when they are young but able to begin to learn self-helping skills.

The Importance of Self-Help

Teaching a child to do all that is possible in the way of self-care is vitally important if adults are truly concerned about the total personality and development of a child. Again, adults' own attitudes are often a problem.

One such attitude is that of comparing a handicapped child with children of the same physical or chronological age. Rather, parents accept the *developmental* age of their child's functioning. They can read about children at *that* stage and begin to encourage their children to do all that that stage of development makes possible. When parents observe children, they can observe children who are developmentally similar to their child. They can compare only to be certain they are encouraging their child to live within the full range of possibilities available at that point.

Parents must also expect the same of their child as they would of any other child functioning at that developmental level. This may seem harsh because the child must often overcome a great deal in order to accomplish any skills. Nevertheless, consider if any other child living at an 18-month old level is expected to begin picking up toys. Yes, of course. So then must special children be taught to care for their own things at a similar point in development. Even a bedridden child can frequently put books and toys into a nearby box. Admittedly, a handicapping condition will make it more difficult to make such self-care possible. The skill will take longer to master. It will require time, practice, and patience. But this effort is well worth it as one of the most important factors in personality growth is self-esteem.

Independence Leads to Self-Esteem

People like themselves better every time they learn to do something for themselves. There is great satisfaction in having some control over themselves and their environment. This principle relating independence to sound self-esteem applies even to children in their cribs.

A very helpless child can have a little mobile of toys and bells hung across the bars of the crib. This simple device can be easily made by parents. Bells

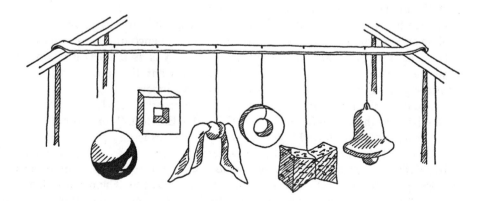

can ring and objects move when the child makes the least motion as it hangs low enough in the crib so that the moving hands generally touch something. No one else needs to come and wind it. No one else must be depended upon. The articles may be changed frequently. Many toys can be used as well as bells, fabrics, sponges, and balls. Safety must be considered in all cases. The crib device is simply made of one-inch wide elastic with yarn or elastic thread used to hang the sensory objects.

A length of yarn or string may be attached to a mobile above the bed and to the child's wrist or ankles. Again, the child's movements will effect a movement of the mobile, which in turn will ring light bells and turn objects for the child.

These simple devices are included here to stress the principle that no one need to be totally helpless. Others can try to help a child satisfy the need to have some control and some effect upon the immediate environment. This is an important point for children with special needs. Two factors must be considered.

First, it takes time and effort to train a child in necessary self-help skills. It is much easier to just do something for the child. It is particularly difficult to stand by and watch the heart-breaking, but courageous efforts of a child with problems. This difficulty may be overcome in most cases by knowing adults can help with good training programs. They truly help when they teach. Adults only prolong or increase the problems when they refuse to encourage independence.

Second, the problems may become worse when the child goes through periods of frustration and discouragement. At such times the child may even refuse to try. Plateaus may also slow the apparent progress of the program. They seem to last forever. Review the section on motivation. Be patient. Things will move again. The smallest gain is progress. Be enthusiastic. It must be interpreted as a victory to the child.

Remember that self-esteem will develop as adults encourage self-help despite such setbacks. Good programs are devised to encourage as normal a development as possible. The growth of personality is as important as any other facet of the child's program. No matter what the limitations, all children can be encouraged to see themselves as winners.

The children will win more often as adults master the TRAINING PROCEDURE and the LIVING SKILLS PROCEDURE. All skills are taught the same basic way. Review and practice these procedures from time to time. It will make a difference in the child's progress.

The following outline is suggested as an example of overall planning for the development of a skill. In this case the skill is toileting. The overall plan is divided into five stages. Those stages include (1) readiness assessment, (2) preparation for training, (3) the actual training period, (4) training for dryness following naps, and (5) nighttime dryness.

The suggestions for this program have been collected from a number of families and sources (Hart, 1974; Dodson, 1970; Portage Project, 1976; Bender & Valletutti, 1976; *Wabash Manual*, 1969). There is no need to try all these ideas. Simply realize that there is no end to the various approaches available to help children learn any skill. Be open and focus on the child's assets. Use them to help the child progress to as full a potential for life as is possible.

Principle

Acceptance, faith, and hope are vital components in any program of intervention on behalf of young children with special needs. The total personality growth of the child includes training in sensitivity to aesthetic and spiritual values as well as those self-help skills that will enhance the child's self-esteem and eventual place in society.

Stage I. Readiness Assessment

Answer the questions on this list. *Potty training may be considered when the child qualifies on these points:*

	Yes	No
Can the child wait for gratification of wants?	___	___
Can the child wait approximately two minutes?	___	___
Does the child like to imitate adults?	___	___
Does the child like to try to be independent?	___	___
Does the child understand simple directions?	___	___
Does the child enjoy trying to please you?	___	___
Is the child aware of and proud of his/her own accomplishments?	___	___
Is the child functioning at late Phase III or Phase IV stages?	___	___
Does the child stay dry two hours at a time?	___	___
Is the child aware of wetness?	___	___
Is the child aware of wetting or bowel movements?	___	___
Can the child sit still for five minutes at a time?	___	___
Can the child lower pants and/or raise own skirts?	___	___
Can the child get to the toilet alone?	___	___
Can the child express needs verbally or by gesture?	___	___

List the items that need work and date them when accomplished.

Skill	Date
Skill	Date
Skill	Date
Skill	Date
Skill	Date

Stage II. Preparation Period

These activities are done for a week or two prior to the actual period of toilet training. Begin by charting or keeping data on the child's normal voiding pattern.

Check the child's diapers every 15 to 30 minutes for several days. Mark the times wetness occurs on the chart. (Sample charts follow.) A pattern sometimes becomes obvious and can help adults recognize when the child normally urinates or has bowel movements. Mark "U' and "BM" on the chart at those times.

Choose certain cues or "key" words and phrases to be used consistently by all the family and with the child during this preparation period and during toilet training.

Examples: Now you are wetting in your diapers.
You are wet.
You are having a BM.
You had a BM.
I need to wet.
I wet. Etc.

Give the child the appropriate language while he wets or has a bowel movement during this period. Choose certain gestures to indicate toileting needs. Have all members of the family use them around the child at this time.

Have family members "model" or show the child the toileting process. Use the same words and gestures. Show the child what to do. Include the wiping process and the washing of hands.

Get little steps so the child will be able to go to the sink and wash hands as part of the toileting process.

Try to keep the child as dry as possible during this period. Let child wear training pants briefly right after child has urinated. Help the child pull the training pants up and down. Use this occasionally as a treat.

Let the child become familiar with the potty seat. Keep it near the toilet. Some children are afraid to sit on the large toilet so don't try that yet. If you use a child's seat on the large toilet, provide steps so that the child's feet are supported.

Stage III. Training Period

Choose two weeks for a concentrated effort to toilet train the child. Do this when you are not terribly busy with other projects or under stress from other problems. Keep your home and yourself as happy as possible during this period. Enjoy spending the extra time and effort with the child.

Always use the key words and phrases that you chose during the preparation period. If the child begins verbalizing for his toilet needs, use those sounds, too.

Always use the gestures you chose during the preparation period. If the child comes up with gestures of his own, use them too. Just remember the child will also use these gestures in public. Don't encourage them if you don't like them.

The child does not wear diapers during the days while in this stage. Training pants are appropriate.

List rewards the child really enjoys. Use them *immediately* after child makes efforts to potty or actually does succeed. If food is a good reward, spread the meals out over a period of hours and use for reinforcement.

Study the charts to see the child's normal schedule. Seat the child on the potty for five minutes at a time during the times indicated by the charts.

Use the child's natural body rhythms for your scheduling, *not* times that are convenient for adult schedules. If the child does not have consistent patterns, place the child on the potty every 45 minutes.

Sometimes it helps to place the child's hand in a little warm water during the wait on the potty.

Sometimes it helps to let water run in the sink while the child sits on the potty.

Pay attention to the child while the child sits on the potty. Really talk and listen.

Sometimes it helps to give the child liquid 10–20 minutes before pottying time.

It is easier to learn to control bowel movement than urination. This is because the child can really feel the pressure on the bowels and is quickly rewarded for "pushing" efforts.

Family members should continue to "model" the toileting procedure for the child.

Little boys can be taught to urinate standing up to the toilet. Provide steps.

Ping-pong balls and/or little paper ships can be placed in the water for little boys to aim at.

Guide child's hands to teach wiping skills. Teach little girls to blot for urination. Teach them to wipe from front to back for bowel movements.

Guide child's hands through washing procedure after toileting. Be sure to provide steps for the child.

Chart the child's successes and failures. The chart can be used as one of the rewards for the child.

Continue putting child in training pants after urination. When the child has succeeded in using the potty several times, leave him in training pants. The training pants can also be used as a reward.

Check the chart at about ten days into the training program. If the chart shows that the child is not mastering toileting skills, stop the program. Wait for several months and then try again as some children are not able to potty train due to physical limitations.

Stage IV. Training for Dryness after Naps—Phase IV and V

When the child has good toileting patterns, encourage the child to stay dry during naps.

Do not give liquids 15–30 minutes before nap time.

Potty the child just before naptime.

As many children wet just while they are waking up, go in and have the child toilet immediately when you hear the child awaken.

Reward the child with praise for staying dry. Stronger rewards may also be used. Charting successes will encourage parents and the child.

Don't punish the child for wetting the bed. Use a plastic mattress cover. Let the child help parents change the sheet.

Stage V. Training for Nighttime Dryness—Phase V and Beyond

Many people are comfortable with the idea that a child may sleep through the night in diapers until generally found dry in the mornings. Those who wish to have a training program for this skill may consider the following suggestions.

Cut down on liquids given child after evening meal.

Potty the child again just before parents go to bed.

Exhibit 4-12 Chart for Toilet Training

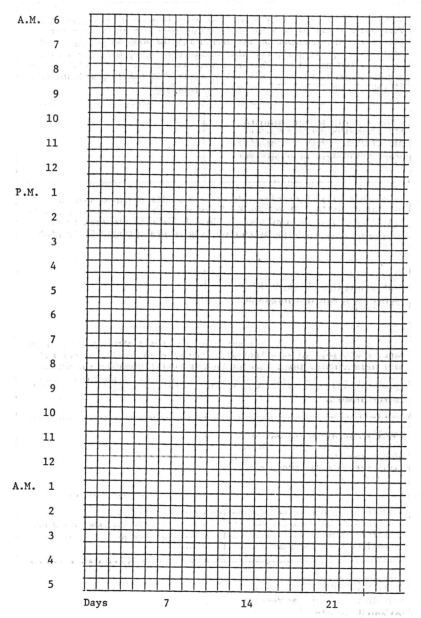

Exhibit 4-13 Exercise IX

1.	Tommy's parents were very upset when they learned of his hearing loss. They watched him as he grew and realized he had a great zest for learning. They decided to enrich his life as much as possible and began language programs for him immediately. They make his life as (_____) as possible. They also work hard to see to it that he can see their faces as they talk. They reward his babbling and see to it that he wears his aids as much as possible.

Tommy's parents have accepted his strengths and are making his life as <u>normal</u> as possible while enriching his environment as he loves to learn.	

2.	Although Paul is bedridden, his parents invite children over to play continually. They take Paul out of the house whenever possible and discuss what he experiences. They believe in the principles of normalization and (are/are not) helping Paul prepare for a place in society.

Paul's parents <u>are</u> helping Paul prepare for a place in society and are in accord with the princples of normalization.	

3.	Hazel's parents realize that she loves to listen although many of her other abilities are very limited. They play the radio for her and have made special tapes that include beautiful thoughts and songs. They help her touch objects and use a great deal of physical stimu-lation in her program as they (are/are not) stressing her strengths in her program.

Hazel's parents recognize that Hazel learns on a sensorimotor level, and they <u>are</u> stressing her abilities in their program of intervention.	

4.	Susan's parents take her for nature walks regularly. They repeat the names of flowers for her and (do/do not) show her how to handle beautiful objects with care. They smile and show great enthusiasm themselves over the many facets of nature.

Susan's parents <u>do</u> show her their love of beauty. Their example will help her develop aesthetic values.	

Exhibit 4-13 continued

5.	When Susan's parents get home they let her help them put some flowers in a vase on the table. They point the flowers out to her and repeat the names. They (have/have not) limited her by deciding she will not be able to learn about or appreciate the beauties of nature.
	They <u>have not</u> limited Susan, and she may become quite capable of doing certain kinds of work as a florist if her parents continue to believe that normalization is possible for Susan.
6.	Susan's mother has cut out felt flowers for Susan to play with. She has also made toss pillows for the room that have the shape of flowers. These objects are concrete, and Susan is able to handle and (_____) them.
	Because these objects are concrete, Susan can <u>manipulate</u> them. This gives them more meaning for her. It also makes it possible for her parents to name the flowers as they are there in pillow and toy form.
7.	Sam's parents know that despite his slowness in motor development and his poor vision, he is a very capable child. They recognize that other children on his developmental level pick up toys so they keep a toy box near his play areas. When he is done playing, they (do/ do not) help him pick up his toys.
	Sam's parents <u>do</u> help him learn to pick up his toys. They recognize this as a normal practice and are preparing him to live like others in society as much as is possible.
8.	Sam does not like to feed himself. His parents have determined that they will stop catering to him in this matter. They realize that other children at his (____) level try to self-feed, and they are now initiating a training program to help Sam accept this responsibility for his own care.
	Other children at Sam's <u>developmental</u> level feed themselves. Sam's parents wisely expect him to do all he can for himself that is common to children at his level of development.

Exhibit 4-13 continued

9. Hazel's parents have taught her how to hit the objects hanging from a crib mobile they made for her bed. She (is/is not) able to have some control and effect upon her environment.	
Hazel <u>is</u> now able to affect her environment and entertain herself when she chooses.	
10. Paul's father loves sports. Despite Paul's physical problems, he knows his son is bright and can share the intellectual aspects of this important facet of society. He has put boxes at either end of Paul's bed. They toss balls into the boxes. They also try to stop each other from making it. Both enjoy the game. Paul's father sees to it that Paul succeeds most of the time. He (does/does not) want Paul to be competitive and see himself as a winner in life and society.	
Paul's father <u>does</u> want Paul to understand the sports world and see himself as a winner in life.	
11. Susan's parents checked to see if she was ready for potty training. She can wait and is generally dry for one or two hours at a time. However, she cannot yet walk well enough to get to her potty, nor can she maintain balance while pushing down her training pants. Her parents have decided she (is/is not) ready for a toileting program.	
Susan <u>is not</u> ready for a successful toileting program. Her parents have wisely decided to wait.	
12. Sam's mother charted his urination and bowel patterns for several days. When she saw his pattern and knew that he was capable of most of the items on the (_____ _____) chart, she decided to prepare him for potty training.	
Sam was able to complete all those items on the <u>readiness assessment</u> chart although his vision made imitation and the location of the potty difficult. Despite these difficulties, he was ready for toilet training.	

Exhibit 4-13 continued

13.	Sam's parents and older brother decided to use the same words for Sam's toileting program. They are modeling the skill for him using his senses of touch and hearing as their major teaching devices. They are not yet requiring him to use the toilet as they are in the (_____) period.
	Sam is not expected to use the potty yet as he is in the <u>prepar-ation</u> period.
14.	When Sam's mother felt he was interested in and ready for toilet training, she cancelled her many appointments for 10 days, organized her household, and prepared herself for the time involved to make Sam's toilet (_____) program as successful and easy as possible.
	Sam's mother prepared Sam and then herself for a successful toilet <u>training</u> program.
15.	After ten days, Sam's mother found he was successful in using his potty 85 percent of the time. She felt the program was successful. She then helped him get up dry from naps by (giving/not giving) him liquids for 30 minutes before he slept and by getting him to the potty immediately when he awakens.
	Sam's mother is <u>not giving</u> him liquids as she wants him to be able to stay dry during his naps.

Potty the child once again during the night if this is necessary.

Stop using diapers when the child begins arising dry in the morning.

Protect the mattress with a plastic cover.

Check the child every two hours of the night. Chart when child is wet. Begin taking child to the potty at that time every night.

Reward the child for successful nights. Have the child help change the bed when he has accidents. Remember some children are limited physically in their ability to perform this skill.

Toileting Tips

1. Regular bowel movements need not be daily in early childhood.
2. Most children are three years old before they remain dry all day.
3. Night wetting may occur until a child is four years old.

4. No matter how well the toilet training may seem to go, there will be lapses. Remain calm, casual, and patient.
5. Let child know where the toilet is when taken to strange places.
6. Some suggest that, for the first few weeks, you wait to flush the child's BM down the toilet until the child is not there to see.

SUMMARY

This chapter presented a coherent series of teaching principles that can be used by a nonprofessional or parent practitioner. Interwoven among these principles, and certainly the underlying theme, is the need for the practitioner to have a positive attitude, to be accepting of the child wherever he or she is functioning, to have patience, for eventually the child will accomplish some goals adults have established, and finally, that we must not set limits on the child's potentials. Remaining optimistic and open to the child's potential will allow adults to keep working even if progress is delayed or slowed by various difficulties and growth plateaus.

Part II

Using the Curriculum Lesson Plans

The curriculum is intended to be a flexible teaching aid for use by parents, paraprofessionals, and professionals. Within each of the five curriculum areas, there are five developmental phases. The phases and corresponding age levels are as follows:

Phase I.   Birth to between 16 and 20 weeks.
Phase II.   16 to 20 weeks to between 32 and 36 weeks.
Phase III. 32 to 36 weeks to between 15 and 18 months.
Phase IV.   15 to 18 months to between 21 and 24 months.
Phase V.   21 to 24 months to 36 months.

Each of the five developmental skills areas, reflex/gross motor, perceptual/fine motor, sensory/cognitive, language, and personal/social/self-help, contains developmental tasks related to important functional milestones of human growth and development. The tasks are arranged in a generally sequential order from birth to three years of age developmentally.

Prior to employing the curriculum, the trainer must determine the child's present functional level. The Developmental Checklist described may be used for this purpose.

After the child has been evaluated developmentally, the trainer notes the skills the child does not possess that are crucial for later development. Since the skills listed on the checklist correspond exactly to those in the curriculum, the trainer can immediately determine a starting point for instruction. These designated target skills in the five areas of development then become the child's educational program. This process allows instruction to begin at a level commensurate with the child's present functional level.

Once these activities are completed, the trainer is ready to proceed with program implementation. This process begins by selecting the skill areas to

163

be taught, projecting an instructional time frame, and initiating the suggested activities listed under each skill area. These activities should be viewed as suggestions to be employed in obtaining mastery of the developmental tasks. However, it must be clearly understood that individualized and detailed task analyses for each objective must be completed before the actual teaching is undertaken. Task analysis may be reviewed as explained in Chapter 4.

The individual lesson plans are divided into five sections corresponding to the developmental areas and phases. The design of each lesson plan is arranged so that it may assist in the planning of an individual program. Each lesson plan has a title, two numbers, and a skill area code. The areas are coded as follows: RM—reflex/gross motor; PFM—perceptual/fine motor; SC—sensory/cognitive; L—language; and P/S/SH—personal/social/self-help. The Roman numerals I through V designate the phase (and thus the developmental level at which the skill is usually acquired), while the arabic numerals suggest the sequence that the skill development usually follows. The lesson plan title is the same as the wording of the skill (on the Developmental Checklist) with which it corresponds. Additionally, both a general and specific behavioral objective are presented.

Other parts of the lesson plans include suggested activities designed to aid in the achievement of the skill, the materials or tools needed to conduct the instruction, language cues or commands related to the activity in order to facilitate development of language and language association, and notes to describe, clarify, or suggest additional activities or reinforcement to be used. Many of the lesson plans recommend the use of different PROCEDURES that are teaching processes that apply repeatedly to many of the developmental skills. Those PROCEDURES are explained in detail throughout Chapter 4 and identified by page number in the Index.

Some of the lesson plans include cross-references. These refer to skills that are found in two different areas of development. For example, the skill of building a tower of four cubes is found in the perceptual/fine motor area as PFM IV 3. It is placed there because it teaches the skills of fine motor manipulation and eye-hand coordination involved in stacking cubes. The same skill is found in the sensory/cognitive area as SC IV 2 because it provides skill training in seeing a design and perceiving what is seen to reproduce a tower. Even though the skill is included in each of the two areas for different reasons, the methodology of teaching the skill is exactly the same.

One other aspect of the lesson plan format warrants some explanation. Each lesson plan includes a section for additional suggestions and evaluation of each activity attempted with the child. This section has purposefully been left open for the professional to incorporate the evaluation plan of his or her particular educational agency or school. The user of the curriculum may choose to record the performance in terms of the percentage of correct responses in a given set of five or ten trials or employ some other system to account for a child's performance over a given period of time. Whatever system is chosen, it is essential to have an accurate record of performance in order to determine which aspects were unsuccessful so that modifications in the program can be initiated. The authors of this curriculum are well aware of the worthy efforts of other educational program planners and teachers who have developed their own programs and procedures for the evaluation of early childhood educational programs. However, the commonality of developmental sequential growth allows other professionals to employ the lesson plans of this curriculum in conjunction with any other chosen form of program planning and evaluation.

These, then, are the steps that should be taken to use the curriculum quickly and simply:

1. Complete the Developmental Checklist (as described in Chapter 2).
2. Select the developmental goals for training program and list by number.
3. Read the corresponding lesson plan activities for general ideas.
4. Apply LIVING SKILLS PROCEDURE for a detailed task analysis of the individual child's existing skills as involved in the goal (as described in Chapter 4). When the child has the necessary prerequisite skills, proceed to work on the new goal.
5. Be aware of the suggested language usage in each skill. Always stress language as a part of the training program.
6. Evaluate the child's performance and training progress using the worksheets described in Chapter 2.

REFLEX DEVELOPMENT IN INFANCY

Nonhandicapped infants are born with a variety of primitive reflexes. These reflexes are involuntary motor responses that may be elicited by appropriate stimuli. Indeed, Piaget (1952) suggests that the first few weeks of life of the infant are a period in which only simple reflexive movements are possible. Many of these primitive reflexes are present in newborn or appear soon after and then follow a rather orderly sequence of appearance and disappearance. Reflexes eventually become thoroughly integrated into voluntary motor control, thus disappearing after infancy.

While most primitive reflexes disappear around six months of life, both mental retardation and cerebral palsy can delay the time sequence for primitive and postural reflexes. Reflexes are considered in this particular textbook because a careful evaluation of them is an essential prerequisite for development/reduction leading to improved motor function (Gillete, 1969).

This section adapts and adopts the seven reflexes in the experimental profile developed by Capute, Accardo, Vining, Rubenstein, and Harryman (1978) because these reflexes focus upon the period of approximately six months of age, when the reflexes are at their maximal developmental velocities. Thus these reflexes are evaluated with significant findings occurring outside the immediate newborn period when neurological signs are at best transitory. Yet with careful evaluation, diagnosis may be made prior to age one, thus facilitating the application of early intervention programs. Further, various authorities suggest that the seven reflexes in the profile have the greatest predictive value for later motor function (Capute et al., 1978). To this group of seven reflexes, four others are added to bring the total to 11 reflexes. As discussed in the section on evaluation of child progress or status, careful evaluation of motor functioning including reflexes should be conducted by a registered physical therapist (RPT). Paraprofessionals and parents are advised to be cautious with infants during the early periods of motoric development. Activities must be appropriate for the ability level and special needs of the infant. Ongoing program planning with physicians and physical therapists is most strongly advised.

For the purposes of this section, the reflexes will be described along with the eliciting stimulus that causes the reflex to appear. In those cases where suggestions can be made to enhance the demonstration of the reflex or enhance its inhibition, these will be presented as activities. The reflexes are as follows:

- sucking reflex
- palmar grasp reflex
- asymmetrical tonic neck reflex
- symmetrical tonic neck reflex
- tonic labyrinthine reflex
- positive support reflex
- segmental rolling
- Moro reflex
- Galant reflex
- reaching reflex
- walking reflex

	Behavioral Objectives	RM I 1

RM I 1	SUCKING REFLEX	Comment
Description	The infant will use a sucking motion on a nipple placed near his lips.	May be weak during the first two or three days after birth. Medical or RPT consultation may be advised, particularly if infant has medical problems.

Activities

RM I 1.1	Adult puts finger or nipple in infant's mouth. Massages infant's cheeks with "back and forth" motion.	Evaluation
Cue	Suck.	
Material	Nipple.	
RM I 1.2	Gently spread infant's lips apart with index finger above top lip and thumb just under lower lip.	Evaluation
Cue	Suck.	
RM I 1.3	Touch infant's lips with cold objects.	Evaluation
Materials	Ice cubes, very cold cloth.	
RM I 1.4	Use small amount of corn syrup on tip of pacifier and put in infant's mouth. Move pacifier in and out. Add corn syrup and repeat.	Evaluation
Materials	Corn syrup, pacifier.	
Cue	Suck.	
RM I 1.5	Gently rub infant's throat from chin down to base of throat to aid swallowing.	Evaluation

Cue	Swallow.
Comment	If infant is being breat-fed, press infant's mouth closer to breast to make an air seal.
Comment	Change infant's feeding position.

Behavioral Objectives   RM I   2

RM I 2	PALMAR GRASP	Comment
Description	When an object is placed jn the infant's palm, he will involuntarily grasp it.	Medical or RPT consultation may be advised, particularly if infant has medical problems. Birth to 2–3 months.

Activities

RM I 2.1	Adult puts a finger in each of the infant's hands from the outside. Infant curls fingers around adult finger.	Evaluation
RM I 2.2	Adult gently pulls on infant's hand while in Palmar Grasp. Relax and pull again. Repeat.	Evaluation
Cue	Pull.	
Comment	Use with rhythm and duration patterns.	
Comment	Infant may release hand from finger for a second or two.	

Behavioral Objectives   RM I   3

RM I 3	ASYMMETRICAL TONIC NECK REFLEX	Comment
Description	When the infant is lying on his back, the head is turned to one side with the arm and	To be observed and

leg extended on that side. It is sometimes called the fencer position.

exercised.

Reflex inhibits rolling.

Birth to 2–3 months.

Medical or RPT consultation may be advised, particularly if infant has medical problems.

Activities

RM I 3.1

Adult places infant on back.
Adult turns infant's head to left.
Infant's head turns left.
Right arm goes out straight.
Right knee may bend up.
Reverse.
Repeat.

Evaluation

Behavioral Objectives   RM I 4

RM I 4

SYMMETRICAL TONIC NECK REFLEX

Comment

Description

With the infant sitting, the head is extended in the midline, the arms will extend and the legs are flexed or drawn up. If the head is flexed (pushed down) the arms will flex and the legs will extend straight outward.

To be observed and exercised.

Birth until infant crawls. Medical or RPT consultation may be advised, particularly if infant has medical problems.

Activities

| RM I 4.1 | Adult places infant in kneeling position.
Adult raises infant's head.
Infant may stretch out arms and bend up legs. | Evaluation |

Behavioral Objectives　　　　RM I 5

| RM I 5 | TONIC LABYRINTHINE REFLEX | Comment |
| Description | The infant is supine or prone and the extremities are changed in position relevant to the head. If the neck is extended 45°, the limbs will extend out; with the neck flexed 45°, the limbs will flex. | To be observed and exercised.
Medical or RPT consultation may be advised, particularly if infant has medical problems. |

Activities

| RM I 5.1 | Lay infant on stomach.
Raise infant's head gently.
Infant will resist the movement. | Evaluation |
| Cue | Up. | |

| RM I 5.2 | Lay infant on back.
Raise infant's head gently.
Infant will resist the movement. | Evaluation |
| Cue | Up. | |

Behavioral Objectives　　　　RM I 6

| RM I 6 | POSITIVE SUPPORT REFLEX | Comment |
| Description | When the infant's feet are stimulated, there is a contraction of muscle groups causing the joints in the lower leg to become set in a position capable of supporting weight. | To be observed and exercised.
Birth to 4 months. |

Medical or RPT consultation may be advised, particularly if infant has medical problems.

Activities

RM I 6.1   Hold the infant firmly around the chest with the head in a midline flexed position.   Evaluation

Gently bounce the infant on the balls of the feet.

RM I 6.2   Next bring the balls of the infant's feet in contact with the table.   Evaluation

The infant should maintain the weight for 30 seconds or longer.

Behavioral Objectives   RM I 7

RM I 7   SEGMENTAL ROLLING   Comment

Description   When rotation is applied along the infant's body axis (at the head or on the legs), the body turns to untwist itself at the waist so that only one segment needs to turn at a time.   To be observed and exercised.

Medical or RPT consultation may be advised, particularly if infant has medical problems.

Activities

RM I 7.1   With the infant in a supine position the head is gently moved to a 45° position and slowly rotated in order to turn the shoulders.   Evaluation

Comment   The head is manipulated with one hand on the side of the face near the chin.

Confirm activity with RPT and/or physician.

RM I 7.2	The infant's one leg is flexed at the hip and knee. The leg is held below the knee and with that leg, the infant is rotated.	Evaluation
Comment	The infant will turn the pelvis toward the midline.	

Behavioral Objectives   RM I 8

RM I 8 Description	MORO REFLEX—STARTLE RESPONSE When the head is suddenly extended, there is a rapid and symmetrical upward and outward movement of the arms. The hands open and there is a gradual inward and bending movement of the arms into a clasping position.	Comment To be observed and exercised. Birth to 2-3 months. Medical or RPT consultation may be advised, particularly if infant has medical problems.

Activities

RM I 8.1	Place infant on back. Lift infant's head with adult hand about one inch off the surface. Quickly drop hand under head just a tiny bit. Infant's arm moves out, hands open but fingers usually still curl. Then infant's arms often move in and cross over chest. Infant may cry, move legs, and stretch body.	Evaluation

Behavioral Objectives   RM I 9

RM I 9 Description	GALANT REFLEX When the infant is stroked along the area slightly to the left or right of the midline along the back, the infant's trunk is arched toward the stimulated side.	Comment To be observed and exercised. Birth to 2-3 months.

Medical or
RPT consulta-
tion may be
advised, partic-
ularly if infant
has medical
problems.

Activities

RM I 9.1   Adult places infant in prone position or on   Evaluation
stomach.

Adult strokes infant's back from the side to
the spine.
Infant's body draws up toward direction of
strokes.

Materials   Hand, fingers, feathers, sponge, net, brushes.

Comment   RHYTHM PROCEDURE may be tried.

Behavioral Objectives   RM I   10

RM I   10   REACHING REFLEX   Comment

Description   When a dangling object is placed within the   Will appear
infant's field of vision, the infant will reach   during the first
out to touch (and may even grasp) it.   few weeks of
life, disappears
at four weeks,
only to reap-
pear at 20
weeks.

Medical or
RPT consulta-
tion may be
advised, par-
ticularly if in-
fant has med-
ical problems.

Activities

RM I   10.1   With the infant in a supine (on the back) posi-   Evaluation
tion, dangle an attractive object in his visual
field until he reaches out for it. Repeat.

Material   A dangling object.

Comment   Infants who practice reaching during this time
                  will be better at reaching when the ability
                  reappears at 20–24 weeks.

                  In addition, if given this early practice, the
                  reaching will reappear some five to six weeks
                  sooner than for the infant who had no prac-
                  tice.

Behavioral Objectives   RM I   11

RM I   11   WALKING REFLEX   Comment

Description   If the infant is held supported under the arms   Will appear
                  with her feet on a flat surface, she will walk   during the first
                  across the surface.   few weeks of
                                                                     life, usually
                                                                     disappears at
                                                                     eight weeks,
                                                                     will reappear
                                                                     towards the
                                                                     end of the first
                                                                     year.

                                                                     Medical or
                                                                     RPT consulta-
                                                                     tion may be
                                                                     advised, par-
                                                                     ticularly if in-
                                                                     fant has med-
                                                                     ical problems.

Activities

RM I   11.1   Hold the infant under the arms (facing away   Evaluation
                  from you) and allow her to walk across the
                  surface of a table. Repeat and practice.

Comment   It has been shown that if the infant practices
                  walking at this early age, the experience will
                  accelerate the appearance of walking later on.

Behavioral Objectives	RM I 12

RM I 12	RELAXES FOR TOUCH AND MASSAGE	Comment
General Objective	To develop infant's ability to relax and be soothed by touch.	Medical or RPT consultation may be advised, particularly if infant has medical problems.
Specific Objective	The infant will relax and enjoy touch, massage, and physical stimulation.	

Activities

RM I 12.1	Relax infant by gently patting him all over, lightly bouncing arms and legs. Determine which movement most relaxes the particular infant—fast or slow and smooth.	Evaluation
Cue	Identify body parts as touched.	
Comment	Speak in a soothing tone of voice or speak softly.	
RM I 12.2	Massage infant. There are various ways to massage infants. Most involve the use of some gentle oil which is wiped off following the massage.	Evaluation
	Movements are generally smooth, slow, and gently stretching.	
	At first, gently touch or slightly rub the infant for several days before beginning massage. When infant shows pleasure in touch, begin massage.	
	Massage the trunk and infant's body and move to arms and legs. Include massage of fingers and toes and back. Keep a terry cloth towel or diaper available should infant urinate during massage.	
Materials	**Oil.** Diaper or terry cloth towel.	

Cue	Name body parts being massaged. Speak in a soothing tone of voice.
	Hum or sing softly.
Comment	Massage is not usually attempted until the infant's naval area has healed.
Comment	If the infant has special physical problems, discuss massage with physician or physical therapist.
RM I 12.3	Lightly brush infant's body following massage and on several occasions daily. Include all body parts. Gently brush infant's head, spine, fingers, and toes as well as trunk and limbs of body.	Evaluation
	Use a variety of brushes and fabrics.
Cue	Name body parts being brushed.
	Speak in a soothing tone of voice.
	Hum or sing softly.
RM I 12.4	Place infant's head on adult's forearm, adult's hand supporting infant's arm and back. Other adult arm may hold infant's buttocks. Support infant in tub of water, warmed to a comfortable temperature. Permit infant to relax and play in the warm water while held by adult arm under infant's head and arm.	Evaluation
Material	Comfortably warm tub of water.
Comment	Should there be any question about infant's health, consult with physician.

	Behavioral Objectives	RM I 13
RM I 13	GENERAL EXERCISE PROCEDURE	Comment
General Objective	Development of infant's movement and general physical strengthening.	
Specific Ojective	The infant will develop movement and become physically stronger.	

Activities

RM I 13.1	Lay infant on back.	Evaluation

Move infant's limbs according to patterns shown below. Speed of movement will depend upon physical condition of infant. *If the infant is known to have medical problems, consult with physician and/or physical therapist.* Generally movements are slow, smooth, and slightly stretching.

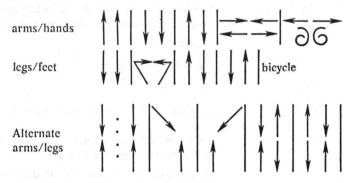

arms/hands

legs/feet   bicycle

Alternate
arms/legs

RM I 13.2	Include RHYTHM PROCEDURE in exercises whenever possible. Slow to fast, etc; counts; in ordered pattern.	Evaluation

Behavioral Objectives   RM I   14

RM I 14	LIFTS HEAD PRONE	Comment
General Objective	Develop ability to lift head prone.	Medical or RPT consultation may be advised, particularly if infant has medical problems.
Specific Objective	When in the prone position, the child will demonstrate the ability to lift his head.	

Activities

RM I 14.1	Infant is placed face down with legs out straight.	Evaluation
	Head is lifted gently with side to side movement.	
	Repeat several times.	
Cue	Up.	
Comment	Give only as much assistance as needed.	
RM I 14.2	Use sound toy in front of head while helping child to lift head and find toy with eyes.	Evaluation
	Repeat.	
Materials	Shaker, bell, rattle, etc.	
Cue	Up.	
Comment	Give only as much assistance as needed.	
RM I 14.3	Infant placed face down in crib, with head and shoulders over rolled towel.	Evaluation
	Help infant lift head and look in direction of bright objects, sound toys, or adult voice. Increase the size of the roll as infant becomes stronger.	
	Increase the time on the roll as infant becomes stronger.	
Materials	Black and white symbol cards, rattles, bright objects, mirror, etc. Towel.	
Cue	Up. Name object.	
	Look at the _____ .	
Comment	Give only as much assistance as needed.	
RM I 14.4	Infant on couch, head extended over edge.	Evaluation
	Lower head enough to put a little stretch on neck muscles.	
	Help infant lift head.	
Cue	Up.	
Comment	Give only as much assistance as needed.	

RM I 14.5	Attach jingle bells or light sound maker to girls' "stretch" headband.	Evaluation
	Place on infant's head with bells turned to the back. Place infant on stomach.	
	Bells ring when infant moves head.	
Materials	Girls' stretch headband.	
	Jingle bells.	
	Pin.	
Cue	Up.	
	Turn.	
	Turn your head.	
RM I 14.6	Attach jingle bells to small animal collar or to a girls' stretch headband.	Evaluation
	Buckle or pin collar or headband around infant's neck in a comfortable way using cotton under collar to prevent rubbing.	
	Position bells at back of neck.	
	Place infant on stomach.	
	Bells ring when infant lifts and moves head or shoulders.	
Materials	Girls' stretch headband.	
	Plain animal collar.	
	Jingle bells.	
	Pin.	
	Cotton.	
Cue	Up.	
	Move.	
	Lift your head.	
Comment	Do not use collars with insect poisons.	

Behavioral Objectives   RM I   15

RM I 15	PUSHES ADULT HAND WITH FEET	Comment
General Objective	Develop ability to push adult's hand with infant's feet.	

Specific Objective	The infant will demonstrate the ability to push feet against adult's hand.	
Activities		
RM I 15.1	Place infant on stomach. Grasp ankles. Gently bend and straighten hips and knees. Move both legs together several times. Alternate.	Evaluation
Comment	Use RHYTHM PROCEDURE	
RM I 15.2	Place infant on back. Place hand against infant's foot. Direct leg and foot against adult's hand.	Evaluation
Cue	Push.	
Comment	Adult should encourage strength in the push.	

	Behavioral Objectives	RM I 16
RM I 16	MARKED HEAD LAG WHEN PULLED TO SITTING POSITION	Comment To be observed.
General Objective		
Specific Objective		
Activities		
RM I 16.1	Place infant on back. Hold infant by shoulders. Slowly raise infant; infant's head will fall back.	Evaluation
Cue	Up.	
Comment	Do not allow to fall back to table surface.	
Comment	Only lift baby slightly.	
RM I 16.2	Repeat.	Evaluation

RM I 17	PRONE, HEAD UP 45°	Comment
General Objective	Initiate the development of head control.	Medical or RPT consultation may be advised, particularly if infant has medical problems.
Specific Objective	When placed in the prone position the infant will raise her head 45° (half way up).	

Activities		
RM I 17.1	Infant placed face down, adult's hand on backside.	Evaluation
	Adult makes sound in front of infant's eyes, starting from eye level up.	
Materials	Bells, clackers, shakers, etc.	
Cue	Up, look, etc.	
Comment	Give only as much assistance as needed.	
RM I 17.2	Infant placed face down with knees under tummy.	Evaluation
	Repeat as above.	
Materials	As above.	
Comment	Give only as much assistance as needed.	
Comment	Finger snapping may also be used.	
RM I 17.3	Infant placed face down.	Evaluation
	Adult behind child places adult's finger in each of infant's hands.	
	Gently outstretch and raise infant arms.	
Cue	Up.	
Comment	This activity will encourage infant to lift her head and back.	

RM I 17.4	Infant placed face down.	Evaluation
	Use sound toys to encourage infant to lift and move head to the right, to the left, and straight ahead.	
Materials	Shakers, bells, etc.	
Cue	Up, look.	
Comment	Encourage infant to attend to source of sound in each direction. If child has difficulty, use PROGRAMMING PROCEDURE.	

Behavioral Objectives   RM I   18

RM I 18	HOLDS HEAD ERECT FOR A FEW SECONDS	Comment
General Objective	Initiate development of head control.	Medical or RPT consultation may be advised, particularly if infant has medical problems.
Specific Objective	When placed in the prone position the infant will demonstrate the ability to hold his head erect for a few seconds.	

Activities

RM I 18.1	Infant placed face down. Adult makes sound in front of infant's eyes, then raises to 90°.	Evaluation
	Repeat.	
Materials	Shakers, bells, etc.	
Cue	Up.	
Comment	Attempt to get infant to hold head erect for a few seconds.	
	Repeat activity and reward infant for holding head erect.	

RM I 18.2	Infant held upright with back support.	Evaluation
	Gradually reduce support, keeping adult's hand near head.	
	Occasionally let baby support his own head for a few seconds.	
RM I 18.3	Hold infant upright.	Evaluation
	Have another person make sounds at eye level to encourage infant to hold position.	
Materials	Shakers, sound toys.	
Cue	Up, look.	

Behavioral Objectives   RM I   19

RM I 19	LANDAU REFLEX—HEAD COMES UP FROM VENTRAL SUSPENSION	Comment
General Objective	Initiate the development of head control.	Medical or RPT consultation may be advised, particularly if infant has medical problems.
Specific Objective	The infant will demonstrate the ability to control head when placed in ventral suspension.	Three to twelve months.

Activities

RM I 19.1	Hold infant in air, support knees and chest. Infant's head, spine, and legs stretch out.	Evaluation
	Gently push down infant's head while held out.	
	Hips, knees, and elbows flex when head is lightly pushed down.	
RM I 19.2	Place infant's stomach on small tapering cushion.	Evaluation
	Place infant's hands or forearms in position to be leaned on.	
	Run adult's hand along infant's back to help infant raise her back and head.	

Materials	Small tapering pillow.
	Brush.
	Fabrics.
Cue	Up.
Comment	Back rubs to include rhythm and duration patterns.
Comment	Fabrics and brushes may be used for back rub/strokes.

RM I 19.3	Place one adult hand on infant's knees. Place one adult hand on infant's stomach and chest.	Evaluation
	Lift infant.	
	Encourage infant to control head.	
	Lower infant.	
	Repeat.	
Cue	Up.	
Comment	Apply RHYTHM PROCEDURE.	
Comment	As infant grows stronger, "bounce" in air, move slowly in circle, hold to mirror, etc.	

	Behavioral Objectives	RM I 20
RM I 20	PRONE, HEAD UP 90°	Comment
General Objective	Development of head control.	Medical or RPT consultation may be advised, particularly if infant has medical problems.
Specific Objective	When placed in the prone position, the infant will demonstrate the ability to lift his head 90°.	

Activities

		Evaluation
RM I 20.1	Place infant on stomach.	
	Hold sound toy at eye level, move slowly upward until infant's head is erect.	
Material	Sound toy.	
Cue	Up.	

		Evaluation
RM I 20.2	Infant on stomach. Adult places face in front of infant's face.	
	Move up slowly so child will follow to hold eye contact.	
Cue	Up.	

		Evaluation
RM I 20.3	Infant on stomach, place rolled up towel or small pillow under arms.	
	Dangle sound toy in front of child.	
	Slowly move toy up until child's head is erect.	
Materials	Towel, pillow, sound toy.	
Cue	Up.	
Comment	Stroke infant under chin to encourage him to lift head.	
Comment	Place infant on stomach at least 45 minutes per day to allow for practice in head lifting and head control.	

Behavioral Objectives   RM I 21

RM I 21	PRONE, CHEST UP WITH ARM SUPPORT	Comment
General Objective	Development of control of upper body.	Medical or RPT consultation may be advised, particularly if infant has medical problems.

Specific Objective	When placed in the prone position the infant will demonstrate the ability to raise her chest with arm support.	

Activities

RM I 21.1	Infant on stomach, place pillow or rolled towel under arms to hold head and chest up.	Evaluation
	Dangle sound toy in front of her.	
Materials	Pillow, towel, sound toy, rattle, shaker, etc.	
Cue	Up, look.	
RM I 21.2	Infant on stomach, place colorful object or sound toy in front of child.	Evaluation
	Encourage child to hold her head up to see it.	
Material	Sound toy.	
Cue	Up, look.	
RM I 21.3	Place infant on stomach, prop her on her forearms.	Evaluation
	Help support head with adult's hands.	
Materials	Pillow, towel.	
Cue	Up.	
Comment	Reduce adult support as infant increases her ability to do task.	
	Use smiles, touches, and pleasure only when child is supporting her own head and shoulders.	
RM I 21.4	Infant on stomach, head and shoulders reaching out over table edge.	Evaluation
	Adult hand on buttocks, other hand supporting infant's forearms.	
	Dangle sound toy in front of child to encourage raising up.	
Material	Sound toy.	
Cue	Up, look.	
Comment	Gradually reduce adult support.	

Comment   As infant increases her ability to do task, gradually move child out over table edge until entire upper part of body is unsupported.

Behavioral Objectives   RM I 22

RM I 22   SOME HEAD LIFT ON BACK   Comment

General Objective   Development of neck muscles for head control.

Specific Objective   When placed in the supine position, infant will lift head slightly.

Activities

RM I 22.1   Place infant on back, dangle sound toy beyond reach of his outstretched hands.   Evaluation
Encourage child to reach for toy.

Materials   Sound toy, doll, or other bright objects.

Cue   Touch the toy.

RM I 22.2   Infant on back in crib.   Evaluation
Hang toy or cradle gym over crib so baby can reach for it.

Materials   Sound toys, cradle gym, bright objects.

Cue   Touch the toy.

Comment   Give infant plenty of opportunities to reach for toys on his back.

Comment   Infant will only be able to lift his head slightly. The object of this activity is to develop the neck muscles for later RM activities.

Behavioral Objectives   RM I 23

RM I 23   ROLLS SIDE TO BACK   Comment

General Objective   Development of the ability to roll over.

Specific Objective   When placed on her side, the infant will roll to her back.

Activities		Evaluation
RM I 23.1	Place infant on side.	
	Show her bright toy.	
	Place toy out of reach level with top of head.	
	Encourage child to reach for toy with upper arm.	
Materials	Bright objects or sound toys.	
Cue	Touch the toy.	
Comment	After child rolls over, let her play with toy. Reposition infant and repeat.	

RM I 23.2	Repeat as above, alternate sides.	Evaluation
Materials	As above.	
Cue	Touch the toy.	
Comment	Use smiles, touches, and pleasure for successful attempts.	
Comment	Always allow child to play with toy after successful attempts.	

	Behavioral Objectives	RM I 24

RM I 24	SITS WITH SUPPORT, HEAD STEADY	Comment
General Objective	Development of head control in a sitting position.	
Specific Objective	When placed in a supported sitting position, the infant will hold his head steady.	

Activities		
RM I 24.1	Place infant in corner of sofa or stuffed chair.	Evaluation
	Prop him with pillows.	
	Place head and shoulders upright.	
	Hold bright toys in front of child to help maintain head support.	
Materials	Sound toys, pillows.	
Cue	Look.	

RM I 24.2	Place infant in adult's lap.	Evaluation
	Support head with hand.	
	Show him bright toy.	
Material	Sound toy.	
Cue	Look.	
Comment	Gradually reduce adult support.	
Comment	Stop when infant loses balance and begin again.	
RM I 24.3	Place infant in adult's lap, support head.	Evaluation
	Tilt him diagonially back to one side until he loses head balance.	
	Slowly bring him back to upright, encouraging him to regain head control.	
Cue	Hold your head up.	
Comment	Make it a game, with plenty of smiles, touches, and pleasure for successes.	
RM I 24.4	Repeat 24.3 to the other side.	Evaluation

<table>
<tr><td></td><td align="center">Behavioral Objectives</td><td align="right">RM I   25</td></tr>
</table>

RM I 25	ROLLS OVER STOMACH TO BACK	Comment
General Objective	Development of the ability to roll over.	Medical or RPT consultation may be advised, particularly if infant has medical problems.
Specific Objective	When placed on stomach, the infant will roll to her back.	

Activities

RM I 25.1	Place infant on stomach.	Evaluation
	Gently fold right arm under chest.	
	Infant will roll to back.	

Cue	Roll over.	
Comment	For the first few times, support infant's head.	
RM I 25.2	Repeat on other side.	Evaluation
RM I 25.3	Place infant on stomach.	
	Gently roll her back and forth until gravity rolls her on her back.	
Cue	Roll over.	
Comment	Repeat from side to side.	
RM I 25.4	Place infant on stomach.	Evaluation
	Place a toy out of reach. Encourage her to reach for and grasp object.	
	Move toy until infant rolls over.	
Material	Sound toy.	
Cue	Roll over.	
Comment	Allow infant to play with toy after successful attempt.	
RM I 25.5	Place infant on stomach.	Evaluation
	Slowly pass toy over head to encourage her to roll over.	
Material	Sound toy.	
Cue	Roll over.	
Comment	As above.	
RM I 25.6	Place infant on stomach.	Evaluation
	Adult sits to one side and stretches arms out to infant.	
	Adult talks to infant and encourages her to roll over.	
Cue	Roll over.	
Comment	Use smiles, touches, and pleasure for success.	

Behavioral Objectives RM I 26

RM I 26	HANDS ENGAGE AT MIDLINE	Comment
General Objective	Development of ability to utilize both hands.	Medical or RPT consultation may be advised, particularly if infant has medical problems.
Specific Objective	When placed in a sitting position, the infant will bring his hands together at the midline.	

Activities

RM I 26.1	Place infant in a sitting position with support if necessary.	Evaluation
	Rub each palm briskly with fingertips; open his hands if necessary.	
	Place his hands together.	
	Put infant's hands with your hands.	
	Rub his hands together.	
Comment	Talk or sing to infant during the activity. Always make it a game.	
RM I 26.2	Place infant as above.	Evaluation
	Hold toy or bright object directly in front of him at midline.	
	Encourage him to reach for toy at midline with both hands.	
Materials	Sound toys.	
Cue	Reach for the toy, ball, etc.	
Comment	Encourage infant to use both hands.	
Comment	Adult may use hands over infant's hands to grasp for an object.	
Comment	Gradually reduce adult support on hands.	
Comment	Use smiles, touches, pleasure for success and always allow him to play with toy after a successful attempt.	

Behavioral Objectives   RM II   1

RM II 1	PULLS TO SIT, NO HEAD LAG	Comment
General Objective	Development of head control.	To be observed.
Specific Objective	When pulled to a sitting position, the infant will have no head lag.	

Activities		
RM II 1.1	Practice RM I 17, 18, 24 activities.	Evaluation
RM II 1.2	When infant has developed sufficient head control and muscle strength, the adult should be able to grasp the infant's hand and slowly pull infant to sitting position.	Evaluation
Cue	Up.	
Comment	Note the head lag. If the infant appears to still have head lag, continue to repeat the activities in RM II 1.1.	

Behavioral Objectives   RM II   2

RM II 2	LIFTS HEAD AND CHEST, WEIGHT ON HANDS, LEGS EXTENDED (PRONE)	Comment
General Objective	Development of head and upper body control.	
Specific Objective	When placed in a prone position, with legs extended, the infant will lift his head and chest supporting his weight on his hand.	

Activities		
RM II 2.1	Practice RM I 20 activities.	Evaluation
RM II 2.2	Adult places infant on stomach.	Evaluation
	Lift hips slightly so that he can pick his chest off the floor, putting his weight on his hands and arms.	
	Encourage him to move forward on his hands by placing a colorful toy in front of him.	

Materials	Toys, stuffed animals.
Cue	Get the toy, etc.

RM II 3	ROLLS FROM BACK TO SIDE	Comment
General Objective	Development of ability to roll from back to stomach.	Medical or RPT consultation may be advised, particularly if infant has medical problems.
Specific Objective	When placed on her back, the infant will roll to her side.	

Activities

RM II 3.1	Adult places infant on her back.	Evaluation
	Lift her right (or left) leg with the knee bent and cross it over to her left.	
	Press her knee toward the mat until her hip is raised.	
	Hold in the position until infant rolls to her side.	
Cue	Roll.	
Comment	At first the infant's head may have to be turned in the direction of the roll.	
Comment	Give only as much assistance as is necessary. Gradually fade assistance.	
Comment	Reverse the procedure to give infant equal practice in each direction.	
RM II 3.2	With infant on her back, present a sound toy just out of reach.	Evaluation
	Move the toy to the side but still in the line of vision.	
	Tell her to get the toy.	
Material	Sound toy.	

Cue	Get the toy.	
Comment	Reverse sides for equal practice.	

Behavioral Objectives	RM II 4

RM II 4	TURNS HEAD FULLY, SITTING IN CHAIR	Comment
General Objective	Development of head control.	Medical or RPT consultation may be advised, particularly if infant has medical problems.
Specific Objective	When placed in a sitting position in a chair, the infant will be able to turn his head.	

Activities		
RM II 4.1	Place infant in infant seat or high chair. Walk back and forth shaking a rattle or ringing a bell.	Evaluation
Materials	Rattle, bell.	
Cue	Look at the bell, etc.	
Comment	Observe if child follows the movement. Use smiles, touches, and pleasure for success.	
RM II 4.2	Place infant in area where there is much activity, for example, the kitchen.	Evaluation
	Make noises, talk to child, move around the area.	
	Encourage him to look at movement, or look around.	
Comment	As above.	

Behavioral Objectives	RM II 5

RM II 5	SITS IN HIGH CHAIR WITH SUPPORT	Comment
General Objective	Development of ability to sit unsupported.	

Specific Objective	When placed in a high chair, the infant will be able to sit.	

Activities

RM II 5.1	Repeat exercise in RM I 24.1.	Evaluation
RM II 5.2	Place infant in high chair with toy and/or restraining strap.	Evaluation
Comment	Observe the degree to which the infant can: 1. control her head 2. maintain balance.	
Comment	If the infant has difficulty, continue activities described in RM I 24.1.	

Behavioral Objectives   RM II 6

RM II 6	BODY BALANCE WHILE HELD EXTENDED	Comment
General Objective	Development of overall body balance and control.	Medical or RPT consultation may be advised, particularly if infant has medical problems.
Specific Objective	When held in an extended position, the infant will maintain body balance.	

Activities

RM II 6.1	Adult places infant on stomach across the lap, supporting the infant. Gently bounce him up and down and from side to side.	Evaluation
Comment	Make it a game by using nursery rhymes.	
Comment	Use RHYTHM PROCEDURE.	
RM II 6.2	With arms extended, adult holds infant outward. Hold infant in this position for a few seconds. Carefully and gently lower either upper or lower part of infant's body.	Evaluation

Comment   Infant should attempt to regain balance by body movement.

Behavioral Objectives   RM II   7

RM II 7	BEARS SOME WEIGHT ON LEGS	Comment
General Objective	To develop support reflex activity of legs and feet.	Medical or RPT consultation may be advised, particularly if infant has medical problems.
Specific Objective	When infant is held erect with feet touching floor, she will attempt to bear some of her weight on her legs.	

Activities

RM II 7.1	Adult holds child erect with hands under infant's armpits and the infant's feet touching the floor. Lower and raise her, keeping feet in contact with floor.	Evaluation
Cue	Stand up.	
Comment	Make this activity a game. Sing or talk to child.	

Behavioral Objectives   RM II   8

RM II 8	ROLLS BACK TO STOMACH	Comment
General Objective	Develop ability to roll from back to stomach in either direction.	Medical or RPT consultation may be advised, particularly if infant has medical problems.
Specific Objective	When placed on his back, the infant will roll to his stomach.	

Activities

RM II 8.1	Place infant on back.	Evaluation
	Lift his right (or left) leg with knee bent and cross over to other side.	
	Press knee toward mat on floor until hip is raised.	
	Hold until infant rolls over.	
Cue	Roll over.	
Comment	At first, infant's head may have to be turned in the direction of the roll.	
Comment	Gradually fade your help as quickly as possible.	
Comment	Repeat to other side.	
RM II 8.2	With infant on his back, pass a toy or colorful object over his head.	Evaluation
	Encourage him to roll after the toy.	
Materials	Sound toy, etc.	
Cue	Roll over and get the toy.	
Comment	Repeat to other side.	

	Behavioral Objectives	RM II 9

RM II 9	TOE PLAY	Comment
General Objective	Development of body image.	Medical or RPT consultation may be advised, particularly if infant has medical problems.
Specific Objective	When placed on her back, the infant will play with her toes.	

Activities

RM II 9.1	Adult plays with infant's toes.	Evaluation
	Gently lift feet so that infant can see her toes.	
	Gently move her toes toward her hands until infant can touch her toes.	
Cue	Touch your toes.	
Comment	Use smiles, touches, and pleasure when infant touches her toes.	
RM II 9.2	Adult ties little bells or colored yarn to the infant's toes.	Evaluation
	Encourage the infant to touch the bell or the yarn.	
Materials	Yarn, little bells.	
Cue	Touch the yarn.	
Comment	Let the infant play with the yarn or bell.	
Comment	Gradually fade the use of the yarn until infant will play with her toes.	

	Behavioral Objectives	RM II 10

RM II 10	FIRST CRAWLING REACTION, DRAWS UP KNEES, PUSHES ON HANDS	Comment
General Objective	To develop ability for crawling.	Medical or RPT consulta- tion may be advised, par- ticularly if in- fant has med- ical problems.
Specific Objective	When placed in the prone position, the infant will demonstrate the crawling reaction by drawing up his knees and pushing on his hands.	

Activities

RM II 10.1	Place infant on stomach.	Evaluation
	Grasp his legs around the calves and push them up to either side into a bent-knee position.	
	Return legs to extended position.	
	Repeat.	
RM II 10.2	Place infant on stomach.	Evaluation
	Put a squeeze toy or colorful object out in front of infant.	
	Help him to draw one leg up while providing pressure to the sole of the opposite foot.	
	Alternate legs until child reaches the toy.	
Materials	Squeeze toy, rattle.	
Cue	Crawl to the toy.	
Comment	Don't be too concerned about arm movements as they tend to parallel leg movements.	
Comment	Use smiles, touches, and pleasure for success.	
	Allow child to play with toy when he reaches it.	

Behavioral Objectives   RM II 11

RM II 11	PARACHUTE REACTION	Comment
General Objective	Encourage and exercise infant's Parachute Reaction.	Medical or RPT consultation may be advised, particularly if infant has medical problems.
Specific Objective	Infant will demonstrate Parachute Reaction.	6-9 months.

Activities

RM II 11.1	Adult holds infant in air supporting stomach/chest area.	Evaluation
	Suddenly lower infant.	
	Infant's arms and legs stretch out.	

	Behavioral Objectives	RM II 12

RM II 12	HELD STANDING, BEARS WEIGHT AND BOUNCES	Comment
General Objective	Develop infant's ability to be held standing, bearing weight and bouncing.	Medical or RPT consultation may be advised, particularly if infant has medical problems.
Specific Objective	Infant will be able to bear weight and bounce when standing.	

Activities

RM II 12.1	Bounce infant on knee in sitting position until infant has feel for "bouncing."	Evaluation
Cue	Bounce, bounce, or bouncy, bouncy.	
RM II 12.2	Sit infant on floor.	Evaluation
	Have infant grasp adult thumbs.	
	Adult fingers wrap around arms of infant.	
	Pull infant to standing position.	
	Bounce on knee.	
	Hold for a few seconds.	
	Lower infant to floor.	
	Repeat.	
Cue	Up, Up you go, Come, Come up.	
	Counts 1,2,3, etc.	
RM II 12.3	Stand infant on floor or on adult lap and bounce with adult supporting infant around waist.	Evaluation

Cue	Up, bouncy-bounce; Songs—"Ride a Cock Horse", etc.	
Comment	If infant has trouble feeling "bounce," second adult shapes bend in knees while game is played.	
RM II 12.4	Stand infant on edge of crib and shape bounce.	Evaluation
Cue	Bounce.	
Rm II 12.5	Place infant in standing toys. Help infant bounce until he feels rhythm.	Evaluation
Materials	Teeter-babe. Jolly jumper. Baby Tenda.	
Cue	Bouncy-bounce, etc.	
RM II 12.6	Place toys on low table top. Place infant by edge of table. Support infant during play with toys.	Evaluation
Materials	Toys, low table.	

Behavioral Objectives		RM II 13
RM II 13	ROLLS BACK TO STOMACH, STOMACH TO BACK	Comment
General Objective	Develop infant's ability to roll from stomach to back and back to stomach.	Medical or RPT consultation may be advised, particularly if infant has medical problems.
Specific Objective	The infant will be able to roll from back to stomach and from stomach to back.	

Activities

Rm II 13.1	Place infant on back.	Evaluation

Place adult's right hand under bending left knee of infant while wrist holds back right leg.

Roll left hip to right while raising infant's right hip up and out.

Roll infant over to stomach.

With infant on stomach, move infant's right shoulder under her chest, push infant's hip to right with adult's opposite hand.

Roll will follow.

Repeat full activity on other side.

Cue   Roll, Roll over.

Behavioral Objectives   RM II   14

RM II 14	SITS ALONE MOMENTARILY LEANING FORWARD ON HANDS	Comment
General Objective	Development of the ability to sit unsupported.	Medical or RPT consultation may be advised, particularly if infant has medical problems.
Specific Objective	When placed in a sitting position infant will sit unsupported momentarily while leaning unsupported on his hands.	

Activities

RM II 14.1	Sit on floor.	Evaluation

Sit infant on floor between adult's legs.

Help infant gain support by leaning on adult's legs.

Place interesting toy between legs to encourage infant to stay and sit.

Materials   Toys.

Cue   Sit, Sit up.

RM II 14.2	While sitting on floor, place infant's hands on surface, palms down.	Evaluation
	Push lightly on infant's shoulders to give feeling of catching on his hands.	
Cue	Stay up.	
RM II 14.3	Sit infant on exercise ball with hands supporting palms down, adult hands supporting infant on waist, then over hands.	Evaluation
	Tilt ball to either side.	
Material	Exercise ball.	
Cue	Sit up. Stay up.	
RM II 14.4	Sit infant on edge of table.	Evaluation
	Support infant with adult's body against infant's legs.	
	Take infant's hands in adult's hands.	
	Play "airplane." Move infant to either side but use infant's strength to get up again when possible.	
Materials	Table.	
	Toy airplane to show infant.	
Cue	Airplane "noises."	

Behavioral Objectives	RM II 15

RM II 15	LIFTS HEAD ON BACK	Comment
General Objective	Development of infant's ability to lift head when placed on back.	Medical or RPT consultation may be advised, particularly if infant has medical problems.
Specific Objective	Infant will increase in ability to lift head while on back.	

Activities

RM II 15.1	Lay infant on back on tapering cushion or on floor or bed.	Evaluation
	Raise infant's head and/or shoulders, then lower.	
	Begin with small movement. Increase as infant strengthens.	
Material	Tapering cushion.	
Cue	Up. Come up.	
RM II 15.2	Lay infant on back.	Evaluation
	Raise infant by pulling gently on infant's arms.	
	Lower gently.	
	Begin with small movement, increase as infant strengthens.	
Cue	Up. Come up.	
RM II 15.3	Place infant on back on exercise ball.	Evaluation
	Grasp infant by knees.	
	Bend knees up and roll ball toward adult at same time.	
Material	Exercise ball.	
Cue	Up. Hold on.	
Comment	Keep infant's back flat on ball.	
Comment	Watch that infant doesn't get too tired.	

	Behavioral Objectives	RM II 16
RM II 16	SITS ALONE MOMENTARILY	Comment
General Objective	Develop ability to sit without hand support.	
Specific Objective	When placed in a sitting position, the infant will sit without support for a short while.	

Activities

RM II 16.1	Adult sits with infant on floor with arm behind infant's back.	Evaluation
	Encourage him to manipulate a sound toy.	
Material	Sound toy.	
Comment	Gradually reduce amount of support.	
RM II 16.2	Adult places infant in sitting position between legs.	Evaluation
	Allow infant to place hands on adult's legs for support.	
Cue	Sit up.	
Comment	As child becomes steadier, encourage him to play with a toy so he does not use hands for support.	
RM II 16.3	Sit infant on floor with pillows all around him.	Evaluation
Comment	Make sure legs are stretched out for balance. Use STP for success.	

Behavioral Objectives   RM II   17

RM II 17	BRIEFLY SUPPORTS ENTIRE WEIGHT ON LEGS WHEN HELD	Comment
General Objective	Develop infant's ability to support weight while standing.	Medical or RPT consultation may be advised, particularly if infant has medical problems.
Specific Objective	When placed in a standing position with support, the infant will hold her entire weight on her legs.	

Activities

RM II 17.1	Repeat RM II 7 activities.	Evaluation
RM II 17.2	Adult holds infant in standing position with feet on floor.	Evaluation
	Allow knees to bend, then lift to erect.	
	Encourage her to straighten knees as she is lifted to standing.	
Cue	Stand up.	
Comment	Attempt to get her to bear increasing amount of her weight.	
RM II 17.3	Adult places infant on back.	Evaluation
	Sit at her feet, with thighs at right angles to her feet.	
	Grasp knees and pull her toward you until hips and knees are bent but feet are flat on floor.	
	Pull her forward to standing position.	
	When her knees buckle, lower her to sitting, then to lying.	
	Repeat.	
Cue	Stand up.	
Comment	Provide support and assistance as necessary.	

Behavioral Objectives	RM II 18

RM II 18	ATTEMPTS BELLY CRAWL USING HANDS AND FEET	Comment
General Objective	Develop ability to crawl.	Medical or RPT consultation may be advised, particularly if infant has medical problems.

Specific Objective	The infant will attempt the belly crawl using hands and feet.	

Activities		
RM II 18.1	Place infant on belly.	Evaluation
	Place a toy or bright object out of reach.	
	Encourage him to get the toy.	
Material	Toy.	
Cue	Crawl for the toy.	
Comment	Allow him to play with toy when he reaches it.	
Comment	Provide assistance if necessary by:	
	1. Pulling him forward by pulling lightly under upper arms.	
	2. Rocking him back and forth to initiate movement.	
Comment	The infant should spend at least two hours per day on his belly to stimulate crawling.	

	Behavioral Objectives	RM II 19

RM II 19	PROTECTIVE REACTION, SITTING BALANCE SUDDENLY DISTURBED LATERALLY	Comment
General Objective	Development of independent sitting balance.	
Specific Objective	When infant's sitting balance is disturbed, the infant will respond with a protective reaction of extended arm.	

Activities		
RM II 19.1	Sit infant on floor surrounded by pillows for support.	Evaluation
	Gently push her shoulder forward to disturb balance.	
	Encourage her to use her arms for props.	
	Repeat with other shoulder.	

RM II   19.2   Sit infant on same position as 19.1. Place a   Evaluation
                      bright toy just out of reach.

                      Encourage her to get the toy.

                      As she leans forward, and her balance is
                      disturbed, encourage her to use her arms for
                      support.

                      Repeat.

Behavioral Objectives	RM II 20

RM II 20	BODY RIGHTING REFLEX	Comment
General Objective	Encourage infant's ability to right himself.	Medical or RPT consultation may be advised, particularly if infant has medical problems.
Specific Objective	Infant will increase ability to right himself.	7–12 months

Activities

RM II 20.1	Hold infant up.	Evaluation
	Tilt infant to one side.	
	Infant's head and trunk will move toward upright position.	
	Reverse sides.	
	Repeat.	
Materials	Developmental Exercise Ball. Rocking chairs.	
Comment	Important in learning to sit and stand.	

Behavioral Objectives	RM III 1

RM III 1	SITS INDEFINITELY, GOOD COORDINATION	Comment
General Objective	Develop infant's ability to sit unsupported.	To be observed.

| Specific Objective | When in the sitting position, the infant will maintain the position indefinitely with good coordination. | Medical or RPT consultation may be advised, particularly if infant has medical problems. |

Activities

RM III 1.1	Place infant on floor with pillows around her in case she falls over.	Evaluation
	Place a toy in front of her to gain her attention.	
	Adult sits facing infant and rolls a ball towards her.	
Materials	Pillows, toy, ball.	
Comment	Note if infant can sit well a long time without losing her balance or tipping over.	
RM III 1.2	Place infant in sitting position on a rocker board or exercise ball. Place infant's hands on board or ball. Support infant around waist.	
	Rock board or ball.	
Materials	Rocker board, exercise ball.	
Cue	Back and forth. Rock, rock.	
Comment	STP for successful efforts.	

| | Behavioral Objectives | RM III 2 |

RM III 2	UP ON KNEES, BELLY CRAWL	Comment
General Objective	Develop ability to crawl.	
Specific Objective	When placed on his stomach, the infant will get up on his knees and belly crawl.	

Activities

RM III 2.1	See also RM II 18 activities.	Evaluation
RM III 2.2	Place infant on scooter board so his stomach is flat on board.	Evaluation
	Aid infant to move by moving his arms.	
	This will propel the board.	
	Place some food or a favorite toy in front of the infant and encourage him to move the board to get the object.	
Materials	Toy, scooter board.	
Cue	Crawl after your toy.	
RM III 2.3	Place a rolled-up towel under the infant's belly.	Evaluation
	Gently roll the infant back and forth.	
	Encourage the infant to support himself with hands and knees.	
Material	Towel.	
Comment	As the infant becomes able to support himself, reduce assistance.	

Behavioral Objectives	RM III 3

RM III 3	GETS TO AND FROM SITTING INDEPENDENTLY	Comment
General Objective	To help infant to achieve the sitting position independently.	
Specific Objective	The infant will be able to get to and from the sitting position independently.	

Activities

RM III 3.1	Place infant on her side. Get behind her hips and bend her knee toward her chest.	Evaluation
	Grasp her upper hand and gently pull her up sideward toward sitting.	

Cue	Sit up.
Comment	Give only as much help as is necessary.
Comment	Work from both sides equally.

RM III 3.2	Place infant on stomach. Pull one arm across under her head and chest.	Evaluation
	The infant will roll to her side and complete the movement as in RM III 3.1.	
Cue	Sit up.	

RM III 3.3	Place infant on her back.	Evaluation
	Encourage her to roll to her side and complete through to sitting as in 3.1.	
Cue	Sit up.	

RM III 3.4	Place infant in sitting position.	Evaluation
	Put her arm out to the right (left), having her lean in that direction and bending or collapsing her elbow.	
	This will put the infant on her side, where she can roll on her back or stomach.	
Comment	Help the infant only as much as necessary.	

Behavioral Objectives   RM III 4

RM III 4	PULLS TO STAND	Comment
General Objective	Develop the ability to pull to a standing position.	Medical or RPT consultation may be advised, particularly if infant has medical problems.
Specific Objective	When provided with a support object, the infant will pull himself to a standing position.	

Cue	Creep to the _____ .	
Comment	Assist infant only as much as necessary.	
RM III 6.3	Stimulate infant's creeping by assisting balance by holding on to waistband of his pants.	Evaluation
Comment	Gradually use lighter hold on waistband until infant creeps unassisted.	
RM III 6.4	Use cardboard box to build a long tunnel.	Evaluation
	Place the infant at one end of the tunnel.	
	Position yourself at the other end of the tunnel with some food or a toy.	
	Encourage the infant to creep through the tunnel.	
Materials	Cardboard boxes shaped into a tunnel; rolled up playpen mattress; blanket thrown over a row of chairs.	

Behavioral Objectives	RM III 7

RM III 7	PROTECTIVE REACTION, SITTING BALANCE DISTURBED BACKWARDS	Comment
General Objective	Stimulate infant's protective action to having sitting balance disturbed.	Medical or RPT consultation may be advised, particularly if infant has medical problems.
Specific Objective	When the infant's sitting balance is disturbed backwards, child will initiate a protective hands-out reaction.	

Activities		
RM III 7.1	Place or tell infant to sit on floor.	Evaluation
	Put some large soft pillows behind her on the floor.	

Tell her you are going to play a game where you try to push her over, but she must keep from falling.

Gently push her shoulders and encourage her to stop herself from falling.

If necessary show her how to put her hands out to stop herself.

Materials	Soft pillows.
Cue	Don't let me push you over.
Comment	Make it like a game, but be sure the infant is able to put hands out to keep from tipping over. Repeat this activity until infant can keep from falling.

Behavioral Objectives   RM III   8

RM III 8	CAN STAND HOLDING ON TO FURNITURE	Comment
General Objective	Develop infant's ability to stand well supported.	
Specific Objective	When holding on to furniture, the infant will be able to stand well.	

Activities

RM III 8.1	Place infant standing in front of couch or chair. Present some of his favorite toys on seat of chair. Encourage him to stand and play with toys using couch for support.	Evaluation
Materials	Toys.	
Cue	Stand up and hold on.	
RM III 8.2	Provide opportunities for the child to stand in his crib or playpen by hanging attractive toys in a position where he must stand to play with them.	Evaluation

Comment	Use much STP when the infant stands to play.
Comment	Remember the infant will not be able to let himself down from standing without help for some time.
	It will be necessary to assist the infant into a sitting position.

Behavioral Objectives   RM III   9

RM III 9	BEGINNING OF HIP ROTATION, LEADS WITH HIPS WHEN TURNING	Comment
General Objective	Develop covert movement for supported walking.	
Specific Objective	When turning in a supported standing position, the infant will begin to demonstrate hip rotation.	

Activities

RM III 9.1	Place the infant in a standing position.	Evaluation
	Stand behind the infant with your hands on her pelvis.	
	Make her turn the upper part of her body to one side while you help to rotate her hips in that direction.	
	Repeat to the other side.	
Comment	Give the infant only as much help as necessary.	
Comment	Gradually fade assistance as infant is able to begin hip rotation by herself.	
RM III 9.2	Place the infant in a standing position in front of the sofa.	Evaluation
	Stand behind her and speak soothingly.	
	Present a favorite toy to her left or right side.	
	Place your hands on her hips and rotate them in the direction of the toy.	
	Repeat to the other side.	
Material	Toy.	

Comment	Gradually fade assistance as infant is able to begin hip rotation by herself.	

	Behavioral Objectives	RM III 10

RM III 10	CRUISES SIDEWAYS HOLDING ON	Comment
General Objective	Develop ability for supported walking.	
Specific Objective	When standing holding on to furniture, the infant will demonstrate the ability to cruise sideways holding on.	

Activities

RM III 10.1	Place infant standing in front of sofa. Place his favorite toy on the sofa just out of reach. Encourage him to move a sideward step to reach the toy.	Evaluation
Material	Toy.	
Cue	Step over to the toy.	
Comment	As the infant gains skill in cruising, encourage him to cruise along the front of the sofa or around a table, etc.	
RM III 10.2	Provide opportunities for him to cruise around objects in your home (or in the classroom). Examples: Kitchen table, chairs, tables, along kitchen cabinets, etc.	Evaluation
RM III 10.3	When the infant starts to cruise well and indicates he wants to transfer support to another nearby object, encourage him to cruise to the object by offering minimal support.	Evaluation
Cue	I'll help you step to the _____.	
Comment	Offer only as much help as is necessary.	

Behavioral Objectives   RM III   11

RM III 11	WALKS TWO HANDS HELD	Comment
General Objective	Develop ability to walk well with support.	
Specific Objective	When an adult holds the infant's hands, the infant will be able to walk forward.	

Activities

RM III 11.1	Place infant in standing position.	Evaluation
	Position yourself in front of infant grasping both hands forward at her shoulder level.	
	Gently pull her forward as you walk backwards.	
	Second adult may help move infant's legs.	
Cue	Use RHYTHM PROCEDURE to keep time as infant walks.	
RM III 11.2	Place infant's hands on firm ring or hula hoop. Lead infant by the hoop.	
Material	Hula hoop.	
Cue	Come.	
	Walk.	
	Here we go.	
	Let's go. Let's walk.	
RM III 11.3	Place a firm rod in each of infant's hands. Adult moves rod with infant.	Evaluation
Materials	Two dowels four inches by one inch, painted, bells, as desired.	
Cue	Come.	
	Let's walk, etc.	
RM III 11.4	Adult places rhythm band castinets on floor in front of infant. Infant holds on to adult's hands. Lifts one foot at a time to castinets, presses, and makes sound.	Evaluation
	Second adult may help infant move leg.	

Materials	Rhythm band castinets.
Cue	Step.
	Step here.
	Make it clap.

	Behavioral Objectives	RM III 12

RM III 12	WALKS FORWARD—ONE HAND HELD	Comment
General Objective	Develop ability to walk well with support.	
Specific Objective	When an adult holds one hand, the child will be able to walk forward.	

Activities

RM III 12.1	Practice activities from RM III 11.	Evaluation
	Progress to giving infant support with only one hand from the side.	
Cue	Walk with me.	
Comment	The infant may walk better with support from one side than the other.	
	Always start with his preferred side.	
RM III 12.2	Repeat activities but gradually reduce grasp of infant's hand to having him hold on to your finger(s).	Evaluation

	Behavioral Objectives	RM III 13

RM III 13	STANDS ALONE	Comment
General Objective	Develop ability to stand without support.	
Specific Objective	The child will stand without support.	

Activities

RM III 13.1	Pull child to standing position with support.	Evaluation
	Gradually withdraw support by offering her a favorite toy so she will let go of your hands.	
Comment	Use STP for success.	
RM III 13.2	Give the child two toys to hold in each hand. Encourage and praise her for standing alone.	Evaluation
Cue	See how well (child's name) stands all by herself.	
Comment	Gradually increase the amount of time the child stands alone.	

Behavioral Objectives	RM III 14

RM III 14	WALKS ALONE	Comment
General Objective	Develop ability to walk without support.	
Specific Objective	The child will be able to walk without support.	

Activities

RM III 14.1	Stand child with his back to the wall or against the refrigerator.	Evaluation
	Stand a few feet away from the child ready to catch him if necessary and offer him a bit of food or a toy.	
	Tell him to come to you and hold the object or food out where he can see it.	
Materials	Food, toy.	
Cue	Walk over to Mamma, etc.	
RM III 14.2	Allow the child to push a small child's chair (a sturdy cardboard box will do) across the floor.	Evaluation
	Encourage him with praise.	
Materials	Child's chair, cardboard box.	

Cue	See how well (child's name) walks by himself.	
Comment	This activity will help the child learn to walk without adult support but will still allow for some support.	
RM III 14.3	Stand child just far enough from a floorlength mirror that the child must make an effort to walk to get to see his own reflection in the mirror.	Evaluation
	As child begins stepping alone, gradually place child further and further from the mirror.	
Material	Mirror, floor length.	
Cue	Get the baby.	
	Go see baby _____ .	
	Walk.	
	Walk to the baby, etc.	

Behavioral Objectives   RM III 15

RM III 15	CREEPS UPSTAIRS	Comment
General Objective	Develop ability to creep upstairs.	
Specific Objective	The child will be able to creep upstairs unaided.	

Activities

RM III 15.1	Place the child at the bottom of stairs.	Evaluation
	Encourage the child to creep up the steps by placing one knee on the first step and showing her how to pull herself up.	
Cue	Up the stairs you go.	
RM III 15.2	Place the child before the stairs.	Evaluation
	Put a favorite toy on the second step and tell her to get the toy.	
Material	Child's favorite toy.	

Cue	Creep up to get your toy.	
Comment	If necessary assist the child as you did in 15.1.	
Comment	Give only as much help as necessary.	
Comment	Gradually fade your help.	
RM III 15.3	Repeat 15.2 but put the toy on a higher step to increase the number of steps she must creep.	Evaluation
Material	Child's favorite toy.	
Cue	Creep up to get your toy.	
Comment	If necessary assist the child as you did in 15.1.	
RM III 15.4	Mom (Dad) sits at the top of stairs and calls to the child. Encourage her to come to you.	Evaluation
Cue	Come to Mama, Dad, etc.	
Comment	It is a good idea to have someone (Mom, Dad, brother, sister) stand behind the child in case she falls.	

	Behavioral Objectives	RM III 16

RM III 16	LOWERS SELF FROM STANDING TO SITTING WITH SUPPORT	Comment
General Objective	Develop child's ability to get from a standing to a sitting position.	
Specific Objective	The child will demonstrate the ability to lower himself from a standing to a sitting position.	

Activities

RM III 16.1	Place the child in a standing position; position yourself directly in front of him in a squatting position. Place your hands on the child's hips and gently pull him to a squatting position. Then lower him to a sitting position.	Evaluation
Cue	Let's sit down.	

Comment	Make it like a game.
Comment	You may assist child by tapping behind his knee so he will bend his knees, but only give as much help as is necessary.

RM III 16.2	With the child in a standing position, show him a favorite toy.	Evaluation
	Place the toy on the floor and encourage him to sit down and play with it.	
	Repeat the procedure described in 16.1 to help the child to sit.	

Material	Child's favorite toy.
Cue	Sit down and play with your _____ .
Comment	Make it like a game.
Comment	You may assist child by tapping behind his knee so he will bend his knees, but only give as much help as is necessary.
Comment	Give much STP for successful attempt.
Comment	Gradually fade your help as child becomes confident to sit by himself.

Behavioral Objectives	RM III 17

RM III 17	SUPPORTS WEIGHT ON ENTIRE SOLE SURFACE AND WALKS	Comment
General Objective	Improvement of independent walking once child has achieved it.	
Specific Objective	The child will demonstrate the ability to walk well by supporting her weight on entire sole surface of her feet.	

Activities

RM III 17.1	Encourage the child to practice her walking skills.	Evaluation
	You may lead her by the hand but encourage her to take the last few steps herself.	
Cue	See how (child's name) walks by herself.	

RM III 17.2	Provide the child with musical or sound-making toys to pull around.	Evaluation
Materials	Pull toys (musical).	
Comment	Use much STP for success.	
RM III 17.3	With another adult, play a game where the child takes an object from one adult to the other.	Evaluation
	Use exaggerated talk as well as the RHYTHM PROCEDURE to carry out this activity.	
Cue	Take the ball to _____ .	
RM III 17.4	Take the child into the yard or outside area so she may practice walking on grass, sidewalks, and other surfaces.	Evaluation
Comment	For all these activities, you can expect the child to fall. Do not become overly concerned, rather indicate to the child that falling is just part of learning how to walk.	

Behavioral Objectives   RM III   18

RM III 18	KNEELS ALONE WITH BALANCE	Comment
General Objective	Develop child's ability to kneel independently.	
Specific Objective	The child will demonstrate the ability to kneel with balance.	

Activities

RM III 18.1	Place child in kneeling position in front of a low table.	Evaluation
	Put some toys on the table and encourage the child to play with the toys.	
	Place a pillow behind the child in case he falls.	
Materials	Toys, low table, pillow.	
Comment	Encourage child to use table for support at first.	

RM III 18.2	Place child in kneeling position; provide support if needed. Evaluation
	Hand him a toy to play with (and keep his attention).
	Gradually reduce your support until child can kneel alone.
Material	Toy.
RM III 18.3	Place child in kneeling position. Evaluation Kneel, directly facing child.
	Play a game like "patty-cake" where the child will not only play the game but maintain balance as well.

Behavioral Objectives   RM III   19

RM III 19	STOOPS AND RECOVERS	Comment
General Objective	Develop large muscle strength and balance.	
Specific Objective	The child will be able to stoop and recover to a standing position.	

Activities

RM III 19.1	Have the child stand with hands on hips and Evaluation feet together.
	You position yourself in front of her the same way.
	Demonstrate a knee bend and stand straight again.
	Encourage the child to do the same.
Cue	Watch me do this. Now you do it.
Comment	Assist the child to bend her knees and return to standing if necessary.
Comment	Give only as much help as necessary and gradually fade your assistance.
Comment	The child may lose her balance at first; be prepared to catch her *if necessary*.

Comment	Make it like a game and put the movement to music (RHYTHM PROCEDURE).	

	Behavioral Objectives	RM III 20

RM III 20	WALKS PUSHING LARGE WHEEL TOY	Comment
General Objective	Improve independent walking skills.	
Specific Objective	The child will demonstrate the ability to walk while pushing a large wheel toy.	

Activities		
RM III 20.1	See also RM III 14.2 for practice activity.	Evaluation
RM III 20.2	Provide the child with a large wheel push toy. Put his hand on the toy with your hand over his (standing behind him). Push the toy forward until child gets the idea.	Evaluation
Material	Large wheel toy.	
Cue	Push the _____ .	
Comment	Give only as much help as is needed; gradually reduce your assistance.	
RM III 20.3	Give the child the toy and stand a few feet away from him. Tell him to push the toy over to you.	Evaluation
Material	Large wheel toy.	
Cue	Push the _____ to me.	
Comment	STP for successful efforts.	

	Behavioral Objectives	RM III 21

RM III 21	STANDS SELF UP USING SUPPORT	Comment
General Objective	Develop child's ability to get to a standing position with minimal support.	

Specific Objective	The child will be able to get to a standing position using minimal support.	

Activities

RM III 21.1	Place the child in a sitting position near a wall or refrigerator, etc.	Evaluation
	Place her hand on the wall and tell her to stand up by encouraging her to push against the wall.	
Cue	Stand up.	
Comment	You may help child but only give as much help as necessary.	

Activities

RM III 21.2	Place child in a sitting position near a table leg or crib bar. Show child how to grasp and pull straight up or alternate her hands, pulling up the leg or bar.
	Command: Stand up and pull up. Note: Give as much help as is necessary.

	Behavioral Objectives	RM IV 1

RM IV 1	STOOPS TO PICK UP OBJECT WITHOUT LOSING BALANCE	Comment
General Objective	Develop coordination and balance.	
Specific Objective	When the child stoops to pick up the object, she will pick up the object without losing balance.	

Activities

RM IV 1.1	Begin by playing games that require the child to squat and return to a standing position. In the beginning hold both the child's hands, but gradually reduce the amount of your help as the child becomes more proficient at this skill.	Evaluation
	Repeat.	

Cue	Bend down.	
Comment	Make this like a game; use RHYTHM PROCEDURE.	
RM IV 1.2	Place some of the child's favorite toys on floor. Stoop down and pick one up. Encourage the child to imitate you. Assist her if necessary, but only give as much help as needed.	Evaluation
Materials	Toys.	
Cue	Bend down and pick up your _____ .	
Comment	As above.	

Behavioral Objectives

RM IV   2

RM IV 2	SITS IN LOW CHAIR	Comment
General Objective	Develop child's ability to sit in low chair unaided.	
Specific Objective	The child will demonstrate the ability to climb into a low chair unaided.	

Activities

RM IV 2.1	Begin by placing child next to a low child's chair. Encourage him to sit in the chair. Children often will hold to the back of a chair with one hand, hold the seat with the other, and get onto one knee on the seat.	Evaluation
	Then he will pull himself up to meet the seat, turning himself around to sit down.	
Material	Child's chair.	
Cue	Sit down by yourself.	
Comment	Guide the child through the movement if necessary; help him only as much as needed.	
RM IV 2.2	Place a large chair next to the child's small chair. Sit slowly in the chair so the child can see how it's done.	Evaluation
	Tell the child to sit in his chair.	

Provide help if necessary; for example, guide the child into the chair by placing his hands behind him, grasping the seat and slowly sitting down.

Behavioral Objectives	RM IV 3

RM IV 3	WALKS ABOUT WELL WITH IMMATURE GAIT	Comment
General Objective	Develop child's independent walking skills.	
Specific Objective	When the child walks, she will walk about well with an immature gait.	

Activities		
RM IV 3.1	Provide opportunities for child to walk from place to place in the classroom, home, and play area.	Evaluation
	Provide musical toys to be pulled from place to place.	
	Give her an opportunity to play games that require her to walk from object to object or person to person.	
Materials	Musical toys.	
Cue	Walk to the _____ . Walk like me.	

Behavioral Objectives	RM IV 4

RM IV 4	WALKS FAST OR RUNS STIFFLY	Comment
General Objective	Develop child's independent walking skills.	
Specific Objective	The child will demonstrate the ability to walk fast or run stiffly.	

Activities		
RM IV 4.1	Take the child outside and tell him you are going to play a game.	Evaluation

	Encourage him to walk fast beside you as you walk along.	
Cue	Hurry, hurry! Walk fast!	
RM IV 4.2	Take him to a grassy slope.	Evaluation
	Put him on the top of the slope and have him walk down to you.	
	The slope will make him run, and with you there to catch him he will be more secure.	
RM IV 4.3	Play games where you "run" with the child to an object.	Evaluation
Cue	Beat me there!	

Behavioral Objectives   RM IV 5

RM IV 5	WALKS UP STAIRS, ONE HAND HELD	Comment
General Objective	Encourage child to walk up stairs with support.	
Specific Objective	When placed before stairs, the child will be able to walk up the stairs with one hand held.	

Activities

RM IV 5.1	Stand with the child at the bottom of a stairwell.	Evaluation
	Place the child's hand on the rail; you grasp her other hand.	
	As you walk up, gently tug the child's hand and tell her to step up. Assist the child to lift her legs if necessary.	
Cue	Step up.	
Comment	Use STP for success.	
RM IV 5.2	Repeat until child becomes skilled at walking up stairs.	

RM IV 6	WALKS CARRYING TOY	Comment
General Objective	Increase child's independent walking skills.	
Specific Objective	The child will demonstrate the ability to walk while carrying a toy.	

Activities

RM IV 6.1	Present the child with a toy. Go to one end of the room and ask the child to walk to you carrying the toy.	Evaluation
Material	Small toy.	
Cue	Carry the toy to me.	
RM IV 6.2	Repeat 6.1 but put the toy in the child's other hand so he experiences carrying something in each hand.	Evaluation
Material	As above.	
Cue	As above.	
RM IV 6.3	Repeat 6.1 and 6.2 outdoors on even and uneven surfaces so the child may practice this skill.	Evaluation
Material	As above.	
Cue	As above.	

RM IV 7	PULLS/PUSHES TOY WHEN WALKING	Comment
General Objective	Increase child's existing skill in walking.	
Specific Objective	The child will demonstrate the ability to push or pull a toy while walking.	

Activities

RM IV 7.1	Provide the child with a doll buggy.	Evaluation
	Place both hands on the handle, go across the room and tell the child to push the buggy over to you.	
Material	Doll buggy.	
Cue	Push the dolly buggy to me.	
RM IV 7.2	Repeat 7.1 with other push or pull toys.	Evaluation
	It is helpful if the toys make noise or music as this will be reinforcing.	
Material	Musical push/pull toy.	
Cue	Push/pull the _____ over here.	
Comment	Make this activity like a game—use RHYTHM PROCEDURE.	

Behavioral Objectives   RM IV   8

RM IV 8	CLIMBS STAIRS WITH RAIL	Comment
General Objective	To help the child become independent in climbing stairs.	
Specific Objective	When climbing stairs, the child will be able to go up stairs holding the rail.	

Activities

RM IV 8.1	Repeat activities listed in RM IV 5.	Evaluation
RM IV 8.2	With child at bottom of steps, tell him to place his hand on the rail.	Evaluation
	Stand behind him and encourage him to climb the stairs.	
	Follow the child up the stairs so he feels secure.	
Cue	Climb up the stairs.	
RM IV 8.3	Stand up at the top of the stairs.	Evaluation
	Tell the child to climb up to you.	

Have another adult accompany child to provide security.

Cue   As above.

Behavioral Objectives   RM IV   9

RM IV 9   **CREEPS BACKWARDS DOWN STAIRS**   Comment

General
Objective   Encourage child to go down stairs independently and safely.

Specific
Objective   When attempting to descend stairs, the child
will creep down the stairs feet first.

Activities

RM IV 9.1   Kneel on the third step, with the child on the   Evaluation
bottom.

Have her watch you creep down a few steps.

Cue   Oh is that fun!

RM IV 9.2   Place the child on the third step from the   Evaluation
bottom.

Place your hands on her hips and physically
guide her through the movements to crawl
down the steps.

Cue   Crawl down like this.

RM IV 9.3   Repeat 9.2, but give less and less assistance as   Evaluation
the child becomes more able to perform this
skill.

Cue   As above.

Comment   Gradually decrease your help until the child
can do it herself.

Comment   Eventually increase the distance the child
must creep until she creeps down the stairs
from the top.

Comment   Always stay close to the child as she practices
this skill in case she slips as well as to provide
her with security.

	Behavioral Objectives	RM IV 10

RM IV 10	WALKS AS ADULT, NO LONGER STIFF LEGGED	Comment
General Objective	Enhance child's existing skill in walking.	
Specific Objective	When walking, the child will walk in an adult manner without stiff legs.	To be observed.

Activities		
RM IV 10.1	See the following series of practice activities: RM IV 3, 4, 5, 6, and 7.	Evaluation
Comment	Repetition of these activities will provide the child with ample practice until you observe him walking in an adult manner without stiff legs.	

	Behavioral Objectives	RM IV 11

RM IV 11	EFFORT TO JUMP	Comment
General Objective	Develop advanced locomotor skills.	
Specific Objective	The child will attempt to demonstrate the ability to jump.	

Activities		
RM IV 11.1	Place the child on a large wooden block (approximately the height of one step). Hold both her hands, tell her to jump, and gently tug her forward.	Evaluation
Cue	Jump down.	
Comment	Make this a fun game—use STP for the child's attempt.	
RM IV 11.2	Repeat 11.1, but only hold one hand.	Evaluation

Cue	As above.
Comment	As above.

RM IV 11.3	Repeat 11.2 until the child has gained in both skill and confidence.	Evaluation
	Now ask her to jump by herself (without your help).	
	Stand in a position where you can catch her if necessary.	

Cue	Jump all by yourself.
Comment	As above.
Comment	The child may land on her hands and feet.

Behavioral Objectives	RM IV 12

RM IV 12	EFFORT TO RUN	Comment
General Objective	Develop advanced locomotor skills.	
Specific Objective	The child will make an effort to run.	

Activities

RM IV 12.1	See RM IV 4 for practice activities.	Evaluation
RM IV 12.2	Stand at the top of a grassy slope.	Evaluation
	Roll a ball down the slope, take the child's hand, and run after the ball.	
Material	Ball.	
Cue	Let's run after the ball.	
Comment	Gradually reduce your help as the child becomes better at running.	
RM IV 12.3	Play games to stimulate running.	Evaluation
	Tell the child to hold his arms out sideways from his body and play airplane.	
	Play other running games.	

RM IV 13	PUSHES CHAIR ABOUT, CLIMBS ON IT	Comment
General Objective	Encourage development of advanced loco-motor skills.	
Specific Objective	The child will demonstrate the ability to climb into an adult chair.	

Activities

RM IV 13.1	See also RM IV 2 for practice activities.	Evaluation
RM IV 13.2	Take the child to an adult chair.	Evaluation
	Encourage her to climb into it, turn, and sit down.	
	Give her as much help as necessary. Repeat.	
Cue	Climb into the "big person's" chair.	
Comment	Gradually reduce your help until the child can accomplish this herself.	

RM IV 14	WALKS BACKWARD	Comment
General Objective	Encourage development of advanced loco-motor skills.	
Specific Objective	When asked to do so, the child will be able to take a few steps backwards.	

Activities

RM IV 14.1	Take the child into a large open area like the backyard.	Evaluation
	Take his arms and step forward, encouraging him to step backwards.	
Cue	Step back.	
Comment	Make this a game, if played indoors, play music; outdoors, sing songs, etc.	
Comment	Repeat this activity until the child gains skill at it—then gradually reduce the amount of	

help you give to the child by not holding his hands/arms.

Comment   You may still have to prompt child by touching first one foot and then the other as he steps backward.

	Behavioral Objectives	RM IV 15

RM IV 15	KICKS LARGE BALL (DEMONSTRATION)	Comment
General Objective	Develop new locomotor skills.	
Specific Objective	When a large ball is placed before the child, she will kick it after a demonstration.	

Activities

RM IV 15.1	Place a large stationary ball in front of the child.	Evaluation
	The child will start by just "walking into" the ball.	
	Praise her for this and then demonstrate kicking the ball.	
	Have the child imitate you; if necessary guide her foot in the act of kicking.	
Material	Large stationary ball.	
Cue	Kick the ball.	
Comment	At first hold the child's hand to help her maintain her balance.	
	Gradually fade your help.	

	Behavioral Objectives	RM IV 16

RM IV 16	SQUATS IN PLAY	Comment
General Objective	Enhance locomotor skills.	
Specific Objective	The child will demonstrate the ability to squat in play.	

Activities

RM IV 16.1	See RM IV 1 for practice activities.	Evaluation
RM IV 16.2	Tell the child you are going to play a game. Stand in front of him with hands on your hips and squat. Encourage the child to do the same.	Evaluation
Cue	Squat like me.	
Comment	Make this like a game; use RHYTHM PRO-CEDURE.	
Comment	Play games like "duck walk" in which child must walk like a duck, hands on hips in squatting position.	
Cue	As above.	
RM IV 16.3	If possible take the child to a sandpile. Give him a bucket and shovel. Squat in front of the pile; tell him to do the same. Play with the child in the sandpile in the squatting position.	Evaluation
Cue	As above.	
Comment	Use STP when the child is able to squat and play.	

Behavioral Objectives	RM IV 17

RM IV 17	THROWS BALL OVERHAND	Comment
General Objective	Development of throwing skills.	
Specific Objective	The child will be able to throw a ball over-hand.	

Activities

RM IV 17.1	Teach as in LIVING SKILLS PROCE-DURE, P/S/SH V 1.3.	Evaluation
RM IV 17.2	Let child observe other children playing ball.	Evaluation

RM IV 17.3	Let child throw ball into low basket, then higher and farther.	Evaluation
Material	Laundry basket.	
Comment	Keep the ball "games" successful for the child.	
	She does not have to compete—win or lose at this point in life, she only needs to learn and enjoy a skill.	

Behavioral Objectives   RM V 1

RM V 1	RUNS WELL (RARELY FALLS)	Comment
General Objective	Development of advanced locomotion skills.	
Specific Objective	The child will rarely fall when running.	

Activities

RM V 1.1	See RM IV 12 for practice activities.	Evaluation
RM V 1.2	Provide many opportunities for child to run on open ground, slopes, etc.	Evaluation
Comment	Children often fall but are not seriously injured. Adults should not overreact. This teaches fear. It's important that the child gain skills even at the risk of some bruises and scraped knees.	

Behavioral Objectives   RM V 2

RM V 2	CLIMBS AND STANDS ON CHAIR	Comment
General Objective	Encourage development of advanced locomotor skills.	
Specific Objective	The child will climb into a chair and stand on it.	

Activities

RM V 2.1	See RM IV 2 and RM IV 12 for practice activities.	Evaluation

RM V 2.2	Provide child with opportunities to climb on playground equipment, rocks, and other surfaces to generalize this skill.	Evaluation
Comment	Children often fall but are not seriously injured. Adults should be careful not to teach fear but rather general skills. Don't overreact to little scrapes and bruises.	

	Behavioral Objectives	RM V 3
RM V 3	WALKS UP AND DOWN STAIRS WITHOUT HELP, TWO FEET PER STEP	Comment
General Objective	Development of independence in climbing stairs.	
Specific Objective	The child will go up and down stairs placing both feet on each step.	

	Activities	
RM V 3.1	Observe and note child's way of going up and down stairs.	Evaluation
RM V 3.2	Teach child to use both feet by showing her. Teach as in LIVING SKILLS PROCEDURE, P/S/SH V 1.3.	Evaluation

	Behavioral Objectives	RM V 4
RM V 4	KICKS BALL FORWARD	Comment
General Objective	Development of locomotor skills.	
Specific Objective	When kicking a ball, the child will be able to make it go forward.	

	Activities	
RM V 4.1	Provide child with opportunity to kick balls.	Evaluation
Material	Ball.	

Cue	Kick the ball.	
	Kick it with your toe, etc.	
RM V 4.2	Teach as outlined in LIVING SKILLS PRO-CEDURE, P/S/SH V 1.3.	Evaluation

	Behavioral Objectives	RM V 5

RM V 5	WALKS ON TIPTOES	Comment
General Objective	Develops new locomotor skills.	
Specific Objective	The child will be able to walk on tiptoes.	

Activities		
RM V 5.1	Teach as in LIVING SKILLS PROCEDURE P/S/SH V 1.3.	Evaluation
RM V 5.2	Have child tiptoe over various textures.	Evaluation
Materials	Grass, rocks, fabrics, etc.	
Cue	As appropriate.	
RM V 5.3	Play "Quiet as a mouse" or "cat" games. Whisper and walk on tiptoe during these games.	Evaluation

	Behavioral Objectives	RM V 6

RM V 6	JUMPS DOWN WITH BOTH FEET	Comment
General Objective	Development of locomotor skills.	
Specific Objective	The child will jump down and land on both feet.	

Activities		
RM V 6.1	Adult supports child when he jumps.	Evaluation
RM V 6.2	Arranges low one inch by twelve inch boards. Child jumps off one.	Evaluation

	Child jumps off two, etc.	
	Adult increases height of objects for child to jump from.	
Materials	Boards, steps, blocks, etc.	
RM V 6.3	Adult responds to child's effort with smiles, touches, and pleasure.	Evaluation

	Behavioral Objectives	RM V 7

RM V 7	CAN CARRY BREAKABLE OBJECT	Comment
General Objective	Development of coordination	
Specific Objective	The child will be able to carry delicate objects without breaking them.	

Activities

RM V 7.1	Adult helps child learn how to place hands over a ball, pretending it is glass.	Evaluation
	Child holds ball over a pillow.	
	Child walks with ball.	
	Use STP for the child's efforts in this "pretend" game.	
Materials	Ball, pillow.	
RM V 7.2	Adult uses "magic tape" on floor or sidewalk.	Evaluation
	Child walks carefully on the magic tape line.	
	Child walks on line carrying a bell.	
	Object of the game is to walk so carefully the bell does not ring.	
Materials	Magic tape.	
	Bell.	
RM V 7.3	Child carries objects carefully on trays.	Evaluation
RM V 7.4	Child moves little pieces of furniture carefully, without bumping.	Evaluation
Comment	When the above activities are done well by the child, she may be permitted to carry delicate objects.	

	Behavioral Objectives	RM V 8

RM V 8	WALKS A BALANCE BEAM	Comment
General Objective	Improved balance and walking skills	
Specific Objective	The child will be able to walk without losing balance forward with alternating feet on a balance beam.	

Activities

RM V 8.1	Introduce the child to a balance beam that is flat on the floor.	Evaluation
	Show the child how to walk on the beam in an alternating fashion.	
	Have the child walk on the beam while you hold the child's hand if necessary.	
Material	An eight inch balance beam (eight inches wide by two inches by six to ten feet long)	
RM V 8.2	Encourage the child to walk without your help at his own pace.	Evaluation
Comment	The child may walk heel/toe at first; encourage the use of alternating steps.	
Comment	It may be helpful for the child to use a balance pole in both hands.	
RM V 8.3	Raise the board four inches on the floor. Repeat walking with alternating steps as above.	Evaluation
RM V 8.4	As the child becomes proficient, obstacles can be placed on the beam for the child to step over. Further, the child can carry small objects as he walks along.	Evaluation

	Behavioral Objectives	PFM I 1

PFM I 1	EYE CONTACT	Comment
General Objective	Development of eye contact with adult.	

Specific Objective	When adult's face is placed in infant's line of vision, the infant will demonstrate eye contact.	

Activities

PFM I 1.1	Adult places face close to infant's face. Smile and talk to child to maintain eye contact.	Evaluation
Cue	Look at me.	
PFM I 1.2	Adult holds bright object or round toy near the eye. Call infant's name.	Evaluation
Cue	Look at this.	
Comment	Talk animately to attract infant's attention.	
PFM I 1.3	Adult holds infant with head cupped in hands. Adult leans toward infant, smiles.	Evaluation
Cue	Look at me.	
Comment	Make exaggerated sounds to encourage infant to look at your face.	
Comment	Try to focus your attention on infant during feeding time.	
Comment	Use plenty of STP when infant establishes eye contact.	
PFM I 1.4	PROGRAMMING PROCEDURE.	Evaluation

	Behavioral Objectives	PFM I 2
PFM I 2	FOLLOWS HORIZONTAL MOVEMENT OR LIGHT TO MIDLINE	Comment
General Objective	Development of visual tracking.	

Specific Objective	When presented with an object or light source, the infant will visually follow the object or light source to the midline.	

Activities

PFM I 2.1	Place infant's crib in different positions to provide variable visual stimulation (both natural and artificial light) to both eyes.	Evaluation
PFM I 2.2	Adult attracts infant's attention to a pen light. Gradually move pen light to the right or to the left.	Evaluation
Material	Pen light.	
Cue	See the light.	
Comment	At first move the light short distances.	
Comment	When the infant can follow short distances, begin to move light farther distances to the left or right.	

Behavioral Objectives PFM I 3

PFM I 3	CRIES OR STARTLES IN RESPONSE TO LOUD NOISES	Comment
General Objective	Development of receptive language.	
Specific Objective	When a sudden loud noise is produced, the infant will cry or startle.	

Activities

PFM I 3.1	Adult produces a sudden loud noise, that is, slams a door.	Evaluation
Comment	Observe the infant's response, which should be:	

1. head drops backwards
2. neck extends
3. arms/legs fling outwards and back.

Behavioral Objectives	PFM I 4

PFM I 4	DIMINUATION OF ACTIVITY FOR LOUD OR UNUSUAL SOUNDS	Comment
General Objective	Encouragement of infant attending to loud or unusual sounds.	
Specific Objective	The infant will increase the degree of attending to loud or unusual sounds.	

Activities

PFM I 4.1	Adult makes sounds with object on either side of the infant's head eight-eighteen inches. Repeat on opposite side.	Evaluation
Materials	Bells, rattles, pans, etc.	
Cue	Just sound the object at first. Later, cue "listen." And later yet, "Listen to the bell."	
Comment	Eventually, move sounding object farther from infant's head.	
PFM I 4.2	Say infant's name eight-fifteen inches on either side of head. Shape infant to turn head to sounds of name.	Evaluation
Cue	Child's name.	

Behavioral Objectives	PFM I 5

PFM I 5	SHOWS INTEREST IN BLACK/WHITE FORMS	Comment
General Objective	Provide for encouraging infant's interest in black and white forms.	
Specific Objective	Infant will look at black and white forms with interest.	

Activities

PFM I 5.1	Lay infant on stomach in crib. Place black and white form cards on sides of crib—one or two on each side.	Evaluation

Name cards as placed.

Name frequently when infant is looking at them.

Replace daily.

Materials	Black/white "face" cards.
	Black/white "shape" cards.
	Black/white "numbers" cards.
	Black/white "phonetic symbols" cards.
	Black/white "felt dolls" and/or toys.
Cue	Name objects.

Behavioral Objectives   PFM I 6

PFM I 6	**FOLLOWS PAST MIDLINE**	Comment
General Objective	Develop ability of infant to follow the movement of an object past the midline.	
Specific Objective	Infant will usually follow the movement of an object past the midline.	

Activities

PFM I 6.1	Place infant on his back.	Evaluation
	Move brightly colored object within eight-twelve inches of infant's face.	
	Move it a little to each side of center at first. As infant's eyes follow the object, move it farther and farther to each side.	
Materials	Bright yarn, rattles, sound tins, etc.	
Cue	Look.	
	Look at the _____ .	

Behavioral Objectives   PFM I 7

PFM I 7	**RETAINS TOY BRIEFLY**	Comment
General Objective	Development of ability to grasp objects.	

Specific Objective	When an object is placed in the infant's hand, the object will be held briefly.	

Activities

PFM I 7.1	Adult places small object inside infant's hand and allows her fingers to close around it.	Evaluation
	Adult takes hands away.	
Material	Round clothespin, etc.	
Cue	Hold the object.	
Comment	Infant will involuntarily **drop** the object When she drops it, repeat the activity.	
Comment	Do not force infant to hold object.	
Comment	Vary the objects for this activity. Use Physical Stimulation Activities to vary texture of objects infant grasps.	

	Behavioral Objectives	PFM I 8

PFM I 8	RESPONDS TO HUMAN VOICE BY ATTENDING, STOPPING, OR CHANGING ACTIVITY	Comment
General Objective	Develop ability of infant to attend and respond to the human voice.	
Specific Objective	Infant will stop or change a behavior in response to the human voice.	

Activities

PFM I 8.1	Place infant where he can see your face—about 8–15 inches away.	Evaluation
	Talk to infant using large facial movements while making many interesting sounds.	
	Shape infant to follow your face as you move it.	
	Reward with STP.	
Cue	Interesting sounds.	
	Call infant's name.	
PFM I 8.2	PROGRAMMING PROCEDURE.	Evaluation

| *PFM I 8.3* | Observe to see if infant quiets when adult calls to him from a short distance. | Evaluation |
| | If not, repeat PFM I 8.1 and then move out from infant farther and farther as long as infant quiets at sound of adult voice. | |

| | Behavioral Objectives | PFM I 9 |

PFM I 9	HOLDS TOY ONE MINUTE	Comment
General Objective	Development of ability to grasp objects.	
Specific Objective	When an infant toy is placed in the infant's hand, the toy will be held for at least a minute.	

Activities

PFM I 9.1	Adult shows infant a colorful toy or squeeze toy.	Evaluation
	Place toy in infant's hand; retain hand over hers.	
	Adult causes toy to make noise.	
Materials	Rattle, squeeze toy.	
Cue	Hold the toy, rattle, etc.	
Comment	Gradually reduce help by reducing pressure on infant's hand.	
Comment	Use smiles, touches, and pleasure for success.	
PFM I 9.2	Repeat 9.1 using different types of toys with less adult assistance.	Evaluation

| | Behavioral Objectives | PFM I 10 |

PFM I 10	FOLLOWS OBJECT 180°	Comment
General Objective	Develop ability of infant to follow a moving object 180°.	
Specific Objective	The infant will follow a moving object 180°.	

Activities

PFM I 10.1	Move a pen light directly in front of infant's face–1 to 2 feet away.	Evaluation
	Move it a little to the right and then to the left of center until infant follows the light 180°.	
	Reward with smiles, touches, and pleasure.	
	Shape when necessary.	
Material	Pen light	
Cue	Look.	
	Look at the light.	

PFM I 10.2	Move bright colored objects directly in front of infant's face—8-12 inches.	Evaluation
	Move object a little to the right and then the left of center until infant follows it 180°.	
	Reward with smiles, touches, and pleasure.	
	Shape when necessary.	
Materials	Yarn balls, rattles, etc.	
Cue	Look.	
	Look at the _____ .	

PFM I 10.3	Hang a bright toy, such as a yarn ball over the crib about two feet above infant's face.	Evaluation
	Place infant so his face is under the toy.	
	Move the toy.	
	Infant's eyes will follow movement of the toy.	
Materials	Yarn balls, toys, etc.	
Cue	Look.	
	Look at the _____ .	

Behavioral Objectives   PFM I   11

PFM I 11	GLARES AT TOY PLACED IN HAND	Comment
General Objective	Encourage infant to look or glare at objects in hand.	

Specific Objective	Infant will look or glare at objects in hand.	

Activities		
PFM I 11.1	Place toy in infant's hand.	Evaluation
	Guide hand into infant's area of vision.	
	See if infant looks intensely at toy.	
	See if infant then looks at hand.	
	Repeat with new toy.	
Materials	Rattles, yarn balls, bell, etc.	
Cue	Look.	
	Look at the _____ .	

	Behavioral Objectives	PFM I 12

PFM I 12	HAND REGARD	Comment
General Objective	Development of the ability to look at hands.	
Specific Objective	The infant will demonstrate the ability to look at his hands.	

Activities		
PFM I 12.1	Adult moves infant's hands in front of his face.	Evaluation
Cue	Look at your hands.	
PFM I 12.2	Adult repeats 12.1, moving fingers for infant to watch.	Evaluation
Cue	Look at your hands.	
PFM I 12.3	Adult places red infant socks on infant's hands.	Evaluation
	Cut socks so thumb and fingers show.	
Cue	Look at your hands.	
Comment	Eliminate socks when infant consistently looks at hands.	
Comment	Use physical stimulation procedure to infant's hands.	

PFM I 12.4	PROGRAMMING PROCEDURE.	Evaluation
	Behavioral Objectives	PFM I 13

PFM I 13	DISAPPEARANCE OF PALMAR REFLEX	Comment
General Objective	Observation for absence of palmar reflex.	To be observed.
Specific Objective	Infant will not automatically grasp object in hand.	

Activities

PFM I 13.1	Place finger in infant's hand. See if she grasps finger.	Evaluation
Materials	Finger, toys.	
Cue	Here.	
	Take the _____ .	

	Behavioral Objectives	PFM I 14

PFM I 14	GRASPS RATTLE (THUMB PARTICIPATES)	Comment
General Objective	Development of ability to grasp objects.	To be observed.
Specific Objective	When a rattle is placed in the infant's hand, the infant will grasp the rattle using his thumb.	

Activities

PFM I 14.1	Repeat PFM I 9.1.	Evaluation
PFM I 14.2	Adult introduces smaller objects to be held by infant, such as cereal bits.	Evaluation
	Encourage the infant to grasp using his thumb and several fingers.	
Material	Cereal bits.	
Cue	Hold the object.	

Comment	Adult may aid child in using thumb during initial trials.
Comment	Repeat activity until infant consistently uses thumb in grasping.

	Behavioral Objectives	PFM I 15

PFM I 15	HANDS ENGAGE AT MIDLINE	Comment
General Objective	Development of ability to utilize both hands.	
Specific Objective	When placed in a sitting position, the infant will bring her hands together at the midline.	

Activities

PFM I 15.1	Place infant in a sitting position with support if necessary.	Evaluation
	Rub each palm briskly with fingertips; open her hands if necessary.	
	Place infant's hands together with your hands.	
	Rub her hands together.	
Comment	Talk or sing to infant during the activity. Always make it a game.	
PFM I 15.2	Place infant as above.	Evaluation
	Hold toy or bright object directly in front of her at midline.	
	Encourage her to reach for toy at midline with both hands.	
Materials	Sound toys.	
Cue	Reach for the toy, ball, etc.	
Comment	Encourage child to use both hands.	
Comment	Adult may use his hands over infant's hands to grasp for an object.	
Comment	Gradually reduce adult support on hands.	

| Comment | Use smiles, touches, and pleasure for success and always allow her to play with toy after a successful attempt. | |

| | Behavioral Objectives | PFM I   16 |

PFM I 16	HAND PLAY	Comment
General Objective	Encouragement of hand play.	To be observed.
Specific Objective	During periods of no adult attention, the infant will engage in hand play.	

Activities

PFM I 16.1	Repeat activities PFM I 12.1 to 12.3.	Evaluation
Comment	Reinforcement and practice of hand regard is essential if hand play is to occur.	
PFM I 16.2	Place infant in crib and position yourself out of his line of vision.	Evaluation
	Observe if he regards and plays with his hands.	

| | Behavioral Objectives | PFM I   17 |

PFM I 17	MOUTHS OBJECTS	Comment
General Objective	Develop infant's ability to bring objects to mouth.	
Specific Objective	Infant will develop ability to bring objects to mouth.	

Activities

PFM I 17.1	Clap infant's hands together.	Evaluation
	Place flavored object in infant's hand.	
	Direct object and hand to infant's mouth.	
	Repeat.	
Materials	Toys, spoon, cleaned fruits, flavorings— honey, milk, cereal.	

Cue	Taste it.
Comment	It may help to tape or wrap the object to the infant's hand.

<hr>

Behavioral Objectives   PFM I   18

<hr>

PFM I   18 **LOOKS WITH INTENT AT OBJECTS IN HAND**   Comment

General
Objective — Encouragement of infant's ability to look at objects in hand.

Specific
Objective — Infant will increase interest in objects held in hand.

<hr>

Activities

PFM I   18.1 — Give infant bright colored, textured, sound toys, keys, etc., one at a time.   Evaluation

Place one in infant's hand.

When infant begins to lose interest in one toy, give another.

Materials — Sound toys, textured toys, keys, etc.

Cue — Look.

Look at the _____ .

PFM I   18.2 — PROGRAMMING PROCEDURE.   Evaluation

Material — Food as desired.

<hr>

Behavioral Objectives   PFM I   19

<hr>

PFM I   19 **PAYS PARTICULAR ATTENTION TO *TONES* OF VOICES**   Comment

General
Objective — Development of receptive language.

Specific
Objective — When adult speaks to infant in different tones of voice, infant will demonstrate attention by bodily or facial action.

<hr>

Activities

PFM I 19.1	Adult speaks softly and soothingly to infant.	Evaluation
Comment	Observe if infant seems to quiet.	
PFM I 19.2	Adult adjusts tone of voice, even using an angry voice, but not directed at the infant.	Evaluation
Comment	Observe if infant becomes disturbed or frightened.	
Comment	Do not continue to use angry tone once you have observed infant's reaction.	
	Immediately attend to infant in a soothing, positive manner.	

	Behavioral Objectives	PFM I 20

PFM I 20	BEGINS TO LOCALIZE SOUND LATERALLY	Comment
General Objective	Develop ability of infant to localize sounds laterally.	
Specific Objective	Infant will begin to localize sounds laterally.	

Activities

PFM I 20.1	Sound to either side of infant's head.	Evaluation
	Infant turns to sound.	
	Then sound toy behind, in front of, and to the sides of infant.	
	Infant seeks source of sound.	
	As infant improves, move farther away when sounding toy.	
Materials	Bells, sound toys, etc.	
Cue	Listen.	
	Listen to the _____ .	
PFM I 20.2	PROGRAMMING PROCEDURE.	Evaluation
Material	Food as desired.	

| *PFM I 20.3* | General Listening Sensorial Activities. | Evaluation |
| | Behavioral Objectives | PFM II 1 |

PFM II 1	REACHES FOR OBJECT	Comment
General Objective	Develop eye-hand coordination.	
Specific Objective	When an object or toy is placed before the infant, she will reach for the object.	

Activities

PFM II 1.1	Adult holds rattle or squeeze toy a few inches in front of infant's face.	Evaluation
	Shake or squeeze it to encourage her to reach out.	
Materials	Rattle, squeeze toy.	
Cue	Get the rattle, toy.	
Comment	Initially give her the object even if she reaches out without grasping.	

| *PFM II 1.2* | Repeat 1.1 varying objects. | Evaluation |
| Materials | Blocks, plastic rings, dolls, etc. | |

PFM II 1.3	Hang a plastic ring on a string or elastic band from infant's crib.	Evaluation
	Encourage her to reach for it.	
Materials	String, elastic plastic ring.	
Cue	Get the ring.	
Comment	Use smiles, touches, and pleasure for successful reaching.	
Comment	Hanging objects should always be within the infant's reach.	

PFM II 1.4	Tie string or elastic across infant's crib.	Evaluation
	Place two or more objects on string that have different shape and texture.	
Materials	String, cardboard with different materials, bells, shapes, balls, etc.	

Comment   As above.

Comment   The position of the objects may be switched
                       and the objects varied.

                       Behavioral Objectives   PFM II   2

PFM II   2   GRASPS ONLY LARGE OBJECTS   Comment

General   Development of infant's ability to grasp ob-
Objective   jects.

Specific   When a large object is given to the infant, the
Objective   infant will grasp it with both hands.

Activities

PFM II   2.1   Adult places large object in infant's hand.   Evaluation
                       Close fingers around the object.

Materials   Infant toys; squeeze toys; ball, etc.

Cue   Hold the ball.

PFM II   2.2   Adult continues 2.1 but turns infant's hands   Evaluation
                       loose.
                       Repeat until infant is able to grasp the object.

Materials   As above.

Cue   Hold the ball.

Comment   Use smile, touches, and pleasure for suc-
                       cessful grasping.
                       Vary object infant is to grasp.
                       Gradually reduce adult aid until infant can
                       grasp object himself.

                       Behavioral Objectives   PFM II   3

PFM II   3   APPROACHES OBJECTS WITH TWO   Comment
                      HANDS

General   Develop ability to bring hands together at
Objective   midline and to develop voluntary grasp.

Specific Objective	When offered an object to grasp, the infant will approach the object with both hands.

Activities

PFM II 3.1	Adult places infant on side, bringing both arms forward in front of him.	Evaluation
	Rub palms briskly with fingertip.	
Comment	It may be necessary to open her hands.	

PFM II 3.2	Adult brings infant's hands together, patting or rubbing them.	Evaluation
Comment	The infant may resist so it may be necessary to sing, talk, or make some other sounds to get her to attend.	

PFM II 3.3	Place squares of different textured cloth or cardboard covered with cloth between infant's hands and rub her hands over them.	Evaluation
Cue	Rub your hands together.	
Material	Old squares of varied textured cloth, approximately three by three inches.	
Comment	Size and shape of cloth or squares may be mixed.	

PFM II 3.4	Place small ball, block, or brightly colored toy between her hands.	Evaluation
	Encourage her to grasp it.	
Cue	Touch the ball, block, etc.	
Materials	Block, ball, toy.	

	Behavioral Objectives	PFM II 4

PFM II 4	ATTENDS TO OBJECTS DROPPED FROM SIGHT	Comment
General Objective	Encouragement of infant's interest in looking for objects dropped from sight.	
Specific Objective	Infant will look for objects dropped from sight.	

Activities

PFM II 4.1	Seat infant.	Evaluation
	Give infant a sound toy to play with.	
	Guide infant to drop toy into a container.	
	Look with exaggerated interest for toy. Find it in container. Show infant.	
Materials	Sound toy. Bright objects, container.	
Cue	See the _____ .	
	Drop the _____ .	
	Where is the _____ ?	
	Here is the _____ .	

PFM II 4.2	Seat infant in high chair.	Evaluation
	Give toy to infant to drop.	
	Help infant drop toy.	
	Guide infant in looking for toy.	
	Exaggerated adult efforts to see.	
	Show excitement when infant sees toy.	
Materials	Nonbreakable toys, rag dolls, stuffed animals, color cards, phonetic symbols, etc.	
Cue	Here is your _____ .	
	Drop your _____ .	
	Where is the _____ ?	
	Here is the _____ . Wow!	

PFM II 4.3	PROGRAMMING PROCEDURE.	Evaluation
Material	Food as desired.	

	Behavioral Objectives	PFM II 5

PFM II 5	USES HANDS TO AFFECT OBJECTS (REACH, GRASP, SPLASH, BANG)	Comment
General Objective	Develop skill in reaching and grasping.	

Specific Objective	When presented with an object, the infant will use his hands to affect the object by reaching, grasping, banging, etc.	

Activities		
PFM II 5.1	Adult places child in a supported sitting position.	Evaluation
	Provide opportunities for her to grasp and handle a wide variety of objects.	
	Encourage her to explore and play with objects, that is, banging on floor or table, against other objects.	
Cue	Touch the _____ .	
Materials	Toys, rattles, balls, blocks.	
Comment	Vary the size, shape, texture, and color of objects.	
Comment	You may put your hands over infants' to demonstrate, but gradually fade assistance.	
PFM II 5.2	Place rubber squeeze toys in infant's bathtub.	Evaluation
	Encourage her to squeeze, splash, etc.	
Cue	Touch the _____ .	
Material	Squeeze toy.	

Activities		
PFM II 5.3	Homemade crib mobile as described in PFM II 1.4 (see illustration in Chapter 4).	

	Behavioral Objectives	PFM II 6

PFM II 6	SCOOPS TO GRASP OBJECTS	Comment
General Objective	Development of hand dexterity and eye-hand coordination.	
Specific Objective	When provided with a small pellet, the infant will make a scooping motion in grasping the object.	

Activities

PFM II 6.1	Adult places infant in infant seat or supported in high chair with a toy.	Evaluation
	Place sugar pellets, frosted breakfast food bits, etc. one at a time on tray for him to practice picking up.	
	Encourage the infant to pick up the pellet.	
Cue	Pick up the _____ .	
Materials	Sugar pellets, raisins, frosted breakfast food bits, small candies, etc.	
Comment	Adult may show child or even guide his hand toward pellet.	
Comment	Gradually fade assistance as he is able to complete task.	

Behavioral Objectives	PFM II 7

PFM II 7	RESECURES DROPPED OBJECT	Comment
General Objective	Develop hand dexterity and eye-hand coordination.	
Specific Objective	The infant will resecure an object that has been dropped.	To be observed.

Activities

PFM II 7.1	Adult places infant in infant's seat or in supported sitting position.	Evaluation
	Provide her with a wide variety of toys to explore and grasp one at a time.	
	Infant will release grasp on object to surface such as high chair tray.	
	Encourage her to pick the object up again.	
Cue	Pick up the _____ .	
Materials	Toys, blocks, balls, etc.	
Comment	Adult may show the infant by dropping and resecuring the object. In addition, adult may guide infant's hand.	
	Gradually fade assistance as infant becomes successful.	

| Comment | Vary the size, color, shape, and texture of the objects presented. | |

| | Behavioral Objectives | PFM II 8 |

PFM II 8	FIXATES WHERE OBJECT DISAPPEARS	Comment
General Objective	Encouragement of infant's ability to fixate where object disappears.	
Specific Objective	Infant will fixate where object disappears.	

Activities

PFM II 8.1	Seat infant. Hold sound toy in front of infant's face about eight–twelve inches.	Evaluation
	Once infant focuses on sound toy, move it slowly out of range of vision or behind a piece of paper.	
	Note if infant stares at last place object was seen.	
Materials	Sound toy. Piece of paper.	
Cue	Look.	

PFM II 8.2	Hold infant. Place bottle on table in view of infant.	Evaluation
	Turn around with infant; see if infant turns head to locate bottle.	
Material	Bottle.	

| | Behavioral Objectives | PFM II 9 |

PFM II 9	TRANSFERS OBJECTS FROM HAND TO HAND	Comment
General Objective	Develop eye-hand coordination and hand dexterity.	
Specific Objective	The infant will transfer an object from one hand to the other.	

Activities

| PFM II   9.1 | Adult places infant in high chair or in a supported sitting position. | Evaluation |

Place a toy or spoon in her left hand.

Put her right hand on the toy or spoon.

Encourage her to place it in her other hand.

Cue   Take it with your right (left) hand.

Materials   Rattle, toy, spoon, etc.

Comment   Adult may demonstrate how to do this activity. Fade assistance as infant does this herself.

Comment   Vary the objects used.

Comment   If the infant prefers to use one hand over the other, try placing toy in hand she uses less.

| | Behavioral Objectives | PFM II   10 |

| PFM II   10 | APPROACHES OBJECTS WITH ONE HAND | Comment |

General Objective   Develop eye-hand coordination and hand dexterity.

Specific Objective   When an object is placed before the infant, he will approach it with one hand or the other.

Activities

| PFM II   10.1 | Adult places infant in supported sitting position. | Evaluation |

Offer him a toy, rattle, etc.

Encourage the infant to grasp the object with one hand or the other.

Cue   Take it with your right (left) hand.

Materials   Rattle, toy, etc.

Comment   During earlier developmental level, the infant's approach is two handed. This may persist so it may be necessary to practice and repeat this activity until the infant begins a one-handed approach to objects.

Comment	Use smiles, touches, and pleasure when one hand is used.
Comment	An infant at this level is far from being ready to establish handedness. However, ample opportunity is given to learn to reach for and grasp an object with either hand.

Behavioral Objectives   PFM II   11

PFM II 11	SITS, TAKES TWO TOYS	Comment
General Objective	Develop reach and grasp, eye-hand coordination.	
Specific Objective	When infant is placed in a sitting position she will grasp two objects.	

Activities

PFM II 11.1	Place infant in a supported sitting position.	Evaluation
	Present toys that are easy to grasp two at a time.	
	Encourage her to grasp the dangling toys, take them from your hand, or pick them up from a high tray or table.	
Cue	Pick up both toys.	
Materials	Rattles, small blocks, etc.	
Comment	The infant may try to pick up one toy at a time. Encourage her to take both toys by placing one in each hand with your hands over hers.	
	Gradually fade assistance.	

Behavioral Objectives   PFM II   12

PFM II 12	DEFINITELY SHAKES RATTLE	Comment
General Objective	Develop ability to affect objects.	
Specific Objective	When a rattle is placed in the infant's hand, he will definitely shake it to make noise.	

Activities

PFM II 12.1	Adult places infant in supported sitting position.	Evaluation
	Present rattle for infant to grasp.	
	Place your hand over his and shake the rattle.	
Cue	Shake the rattle.	
Materials	Rattle, cereal or beans in a small can with lid.	
Comment	Make it a game and express exaggerated reaction to noise.	
PFM II 12.2	Repeat 12.1, but do not aid the infant in shaking the rattle.	Evaluation
	Encourage him to shake it himself by demonstrating a shaking motion and giving a verbal cue.	
	Repeat until he shakes rattle unaided.	
Cue	Shake the rattle.	
Materials	As above.	
Comment	Use STP for success.	

	Behavioral Objectives	PFM II 13

PFM II 13	**LOOKS FOR FALLEN OBJECTS**	Comment
General Objective	Develop infant's ability to look for fallen objects.	
Specific Objective	Infant will actively search for fallen objects.	

Activities

PFM II 13.1	Seat infant in high chair.	Evaluation
	Give infant favorite toy.	
	Help toy drop.	
	Observe if infant actively looks for toy.	
Materials	High chair.	
	Toys.	

Cue	Oh-oh _____ dropped.
	Oh-oh _____ fell.
	Where is _____ ?
	Here it is!

PFM II 13.2	PROGRAMMING PROCEDURE.	Evaluation
Material	Food as desired.	

	Behavioral Objectives	PFM II 14

PFM II 14	FINDS PARTIALLY HIDDEN OBJECTS	Comment
General Objective	Develop infant's ability to find partially hidden objects.	
Specific Objective	Infant will find partially hidden objects.	

Activities

PFM II 14.1	Seat infant in front of adult.	Evaluation
	Place toy in front of infant.	
	Cover a small part of toy with a cloth.	
	Infant will take toy.	
	Repeat, but cover more of the toy.	
Materials	Toys, Unit Materials, cloth.	
Cue	Here is a _____ .	
	Take the _____ .	
	Where is the _____ ?	

PFM II 14.2	Place toy partly hidden under pillow.	Evaluation
	Repeat as above.	
Materials	Toys, Unit Materials, pillow.	
Cue	As above.	
	It's *under* the pillow.	

PFM II 14.3	Seat infant. Place large toy in front of infant. Move slowly around adult until partially hidden behind adult.	Evaluation

Material	Large toy.
Cue	As above.

	Behavioral Objectives	PFM II 15

PFM II 15	LOCALIZES SOUNDS WELL	Comment
General Objective	Development of infant's ability to localize sounds well.	
Specific Objective	Infant will increase ability to localize sounds.	

Activities

PFM II 15.1	Time how long it takes infant to locate sounds in room using activities listed below.	Evaluation
Material	Stopwatch.	
PFM II 15.2	Adult sounds bell or rattle in area around head of infant. Infant looks for source of sound.	Evaluation
Materials	Bells, rattles, chimes, pots and spoon, etc.	
Cue	Listen, look.	
PFM II 15.3	Adult responds to infant's effort with smiles, touches, and pleasure.	Evaluation
PFM II 15.4	Adult moves farther from infant and sounds bell or rattles. Infant looks for source of sound.	Evaluation
Materials	Bells, rattles, chimes, pots and spoon, etc.	
Cue	Look, listen.	
PFM II 15.5	Adult moves and hides in and around room. Adult sounds toy. Infant looks for source of sound.	Evaluation
Materials	Bells, rattles, chimes, pots and spoons, etc.	
Cue	Look.	

Behavioral Objectives	PFM III 1

PFM III 1	RESPONDS TO "NO" AND NAME	Comment
General Objective	Develop infant's ability to stop activity when told "no" and to attend to her name.	
Specific Objective	When the infant is told "no" or her name is called, the infant will respond with understanding.	

Activities

PFM III 1.1	Adult says "no" with firm tone.	Evaluation
	Remove her hand or infant from object as "no" is said.	
Cue	No.	
Comment	Use smiles, touches, and pleasure when she responds to "no." Show her you are very pleased.	
PFM III 1.2	Adult should use infant's name when speaking to her: i.e, "Is _____ hungry?" "Does _____ want to go bye-bye?"	Evaluation
Cue	Infant's name.	
PFM III 1.3	Say the infant's name and observe whether she responds or attends by (1) looking at you, or (2) stopping activity.	Evaluation
Cue	Infant's name.	
Comment	Use smiles, touches, and pleasure when infant responds to her name.	

Behavioral Objectives	PFM III 2

PFM III 2	MAY USE ONE OBJECT TO MOVE ANOTHER	Comment
General Objective	To develop increased eye-hand control.	

Specific Objective	When presented with two objects, the infant will use one object to move the other.	

Activities

PFM III 2.1	Adult places infant in supported sitting position. Present him with two toys. Put one toy in the infant's hand and with your hand over his, move the other toy. Repeat.	Evaluation
Cue	See how they move.	
Materials	Blocks, balls, squeeze toys.	
Comment	Continue to demonstrate the task to see if the infant will imitate.	
PFM III 2.2	Repeat 2.1, but do not assist infant with your hand. Encourage him to do this himself. As above, repeat demonstration and continue.	Evaluation
Comment	Gradually fade assistance when infant is successful.	

	Behavioral Objectives	PFM III 3

PFM III 3	DROPS ONE OF TWO TOYS TO TAKE A THIRD OFFERED	Comment
General Objective	Encouragement of infant's ability to take a preferred object.	
Specific Objective	With a toy in each hand, the infant will drop one of the toys to take a third object offered to her.	

Activities

PFM III 3.1	Adult places infant in supported sitting position. Place a toy in each hand.	Evaluation

	Then offer her a third, favorite or preferred toy.
Cue	Take this one.
Materials	Two toys (blocks, dolls, rattles, etc.). A favorite toy or a bit of food (cereal, cookie, etc.).
Comment	Adult may help infant to release object in one hand and take new object if infant can't do it herself.
Comment	Use smiles, touches, and verbal encouragement to get infant to drop the toy to take the other toy or food.
Comment	Use smiles, touches, and pleasure when infant completes the task.

Behavioral Objectives   PFM III   4

PFM III 4	"RAKES" RADIALLY AND ATTAINS OBJECTS	Comment
General Objective	Develop eye-hand coordination.	
Specific Objective	When presented with a toy, the infant will rake radially to attain the toy.	To be observed.

Activities

PFM III 4.1	Place infant in supported sitting position. Present a sound toy within the infant's reach. Encourage him to get the toy.	Evaluation
Cue	Get the toy.	
Materials	Squeeze toy, shaker, etc.	
Comment	Note if the infant uses a radial raking motion to draw the toy within his grasp.	
Comment	Use smiles, touches, and pleasure for success.	
Comment	Allow infant to play with toy, once he receives it.	

PFM III 5	USES ONE OBJECT TO AFFECT ANOTHER	Comment
General Objective	Development of infant's ability to use one object to affect another.	
Specific Objective	The infant will increase in ability to use one object to affect another.	

Aotivition

PFM III 5.1	Adult places two objects in front of infant.	Evaluation
	Adult pounds one object with the other.	
	Adult helps infant imitate.	
	Infant imitates pounding.	
	Adult rewards infant's efforts.	
Materials	Blocks, sponge, pots, spoons, etc.	
Cue	Hit it.	
	Hit the _____ .	
PFM III 5.2	Adult places two objects in front of infant.	Evaluation
	Adult pushes one object with the other.	
	Adult helps infant imitate pushing.	
	Adult rewards infant's efforts.	
Materials	As above.	

PFM III 6	MANIPULATES STRING OR SMALL OBJECT	Comment
General Objective	Develop fine motor coordination and manipulative skills.	
Specific Objective	When presented with a small object, the child will manipulate it.	

Activities

PFM III 6.1	Present the infant with a small cube, peg, or block.	Evaluation
	Encourage him to turn it around and look at it without dropping it.	
	Talk about the object—color, shape, texture, etc.	
Materials	Cube, block, peg, etc.	
Cue	Play with or See the _____ . Turn it around with your fingers.	
Comment	Vary the shape, color, and texture of the objects used.	
PFM III 6.2	Substitute brightly colored yarn for the objects described in 2.1.	Evaluation
	Gently wrap the yarn around his wrist (or over his head or ear); tell him to pull it off.	

Behavioral Objectives	PFM III 7

PFM III 7	PINCER GRASP USED, THUMB AND FOREFINGER	Comment
General Objective	Develop fine motor skills.	
Specific Objective	When attempting to pick up objects, the infant will use the pincer grasp using thumb and forefinger.	

Activities

PFM III 7.1	Sit facing the infant. Hand her small objects; pennies, poker chips, bottle caps, etc. to see if she uses pincer grasp (finger against thumb).	Evaluation
	If she does not, place the object in her hand in the pincer position.	
Materials	Pennies, bottle caps, poker chips.	

Cue	Hold it with your thumb and finger.	
Comment	Repeat and practice until infant uses pincer grasp.	
PFM III 7.2	Put the same objects listed in 3.1 before the infant.	Evaluation
	Place a shoe box with a hole cut out in the top in front of her also.	
	Tell her to pick up the objects with her thumb and finger and put them in the hole.	
Materials	As above; shoe box—hole in top.	
Cue	Pick up the _____ with your thumb and finger and put them in here.	
Comment	Make it a game.	
Comment	Make sure infant uses pincer grasp.	

	Behavioral Objectives	PFM III 8

PFM III 8	UNCOVERS HIDDEN TOY	Comment
General Objective	Development of infant's ability to uncover hidden objects.	
Specific Objective	The infant will develop ability to uncover hidden objects.	

Activities		
PFM III 8.1	Place object in front of infant.	Evaluation
	Partially cover object with cloth.	
	Pull cloth off.	
	Be excited about finding object.	
	Repeat.	
	Let infant uncover object.	
	Repeat.	
Materials	Toys, jars, etc.	
Cue	Pull.	
	Pull the cloth.	

Look.

Look at the _____ .

Wow! Here is the _____ .

PFM III 8.2	Place object under a container.	Evaluation
	Lift container.	
	Be excited about finding the object.	
	Repeat.	
	Help infant lift container.	
	Be excited.	
Materials	Containers.	
	Toys.	
	Crumbs, raisins, etc.	
Cue	Lift the _____ .	
	Wow! Look at the _____ .	
PFM III 8.3	Place object in container.	Evaluation
	Cover with lid.	
	Raise lid.	
	Be excited about finding object in the container.	
	Repeat. Help infant put object in the container and then lift the lid.	
Materials	Many containers.	
	As above.	
Cue	Where's the _____ ?	
	Wow! Here is the _____ .	
Comment	Help infant generalize this concept by using many different containers and objects.	

	Behavioral Objectives	PFM III 9

PFM III 9	EXPLORES AND PROBES THE HOLES AND GROOVES IN TOYS	Comment
General Objective	Encourage continued development of hand dexterity and eye-hand coordination.	

Specific Objective	When provided with toys with holes or grooves, the infant will probe the holes or grooves with her finger.	

Activities		
PFM III 9.1	Provide the infant with a variety of doughnut-shaped stacking toys. Show her how to poke her finger through the hole.	Evaluation
	Make exaggerated actions and talk while you show her.	
	Encourage her to poke her finger through the hole.	
Materials	Doughnut-shaped stacking toys or rings.	
Cue	Poke your finger through the hole.	
PFM III 9.2	Give the baby some blocks or other plastic toys with finger holes.	Evaluation
	Again encourage her to play with and probe the holes in the toys.	
Materials	Blocks or toys with finger holes.	
Cue	As above.	

	Behavioral Objectives	PFM III 10

PFM III 10	BEGINS TO DELIBERATELY RELEASE OBJECTS	Comment
General Objective	Encourage development of reach-grasp-release pattern.	
Specific Objective	When provided with objects, the infant will pick them up and then release them deliberately.	

Activities		
PFM III 10.1	Place infant in high chair with a variety of toys in front of him.	Evaluation
	Tell him to pick objects up and guide his hand over to the side and help him release the object. Repeat.	

Materials	Toys.	
Cue	Drop the toy.	
Comment	Make this a fun game by making noise or big fuss as the toy hits the floor.	
Comment	Reduce your help as infant is able to drop the object himself.	
PFM III 10.2	Position infant as in 10.1. Place a cookie tin on the tray.	Evaluation
	Use wooden blocks or some other objects that will make noise and show the infant how to drop the objects in the tin.	
Materials	Blocks, bottle caps, etc. Cookie tin.	
Cue	As above.	
Comment	Make a fuss over the action and the noise so the infant is shown that *you* think it is fun.	

Behavioral Objectives   PFM III   11

PFM III 11	ATTENDS TO DETAIL	Comment
General Objective	Develop visual and tactile perceptual abilities.	
Specific Objective	When provided with interesting objects, the infant will attend to the details of the object by manipulating, looking intently, exploring, etc.	

Activities

PFM III 11.1	Place the infant in a high chair.	Evaluation
	Introduce a number of interesting objects one at a time.	
	Encourage the infant to manipulate, explore, and look at the object.	
Materials	Blocks, toys, cubes, rings, etc.	
Cue	See the _____ .	
	The _____ is (color) . This is a (name object) .	

	Behavioral Objectives	PFM III 12

PFM III 12	REMOVES OBJECT FROM CONTAINER	Comment
General Objective	Develop ability to remove objects from container.	
Specific Objective	When a container with an object is presented to the infant, he will remove it from container.	

Activities

PFM III 12.1	Hold a container with a bright object or toy in front of the infant.	Evaluation
	If necessary, guide his hand into the container so he can grasp the object.	
	Have him secure the object. Repeat.	
Materials	Container, toy.	
Cue	Pick up the _____ .	
Comment	Gradually withdraw your assistance as infant can do this himself.	
PFM III 12.2	Put some cereal bits in the container with the objects.	Evaluation
	Tell the infant to pick up the toy and give it to you.	
	When he has done this, tell him to get the cereal bits out of the container and let him eat them.	
Materials	Container, toy, cereal bits.	
Cue	Pick up the _____ and then you can have the cereal.	

	Behavioral Objectives	PFM III 13

PFM III 13	REACHES FOR IMAGE OF TOY IN MIRROR	Comment
General Objective	Encourage infant to reach for image of toy in mirror.	

Specific Objective	When infant sees an image of a toy in a mirror, she will reach out for it.	

Activities		

PFM III 13.1	See also P/S/SH II 21. Place an unbreakable infant mirror in front of infant.	Evaluation
	Stand behind child and present a favorite toy in a position where the image will be seen by the infant.	
	Encourage the infant to touch the image, guiding her hand if necessary.	
Materials	Unbreakable mirror, toy.	
Cue	Touch the _____ .	
Comment	Gradually fade your help.	
Comment	Make this like a game; show the infant you think it's fun.	

	Behavioral Objectives	PFM III 14

PFM III 14	TEARS PAPER	Comment
General Objective	Develop ability to tear paper.	
Specific Objective	When given appropriate paper substance, infant will tear and crumple the material.	

Activities		

PFM III 14.1	Place infant on sheet or in large basket, low box, or playpen. This will help adult contain and clean up mess. Give infant paper substance to tear and crumple.	Evaluation
	Show infant how to tear and crumple.	
	Use STP to reward infant's efforts.	
Materials	Toilet paper, tissue paper, cereal boxes, old newspaper or magazines.	
Cue	Tear it.	

PFM III 15	NEAT PINCER GRASP	Comment
General Objective	Develop neat pincer grasp.	
Specific Objective	When presented with small objects, the child will grasp them with a neat pincer grasp.	

Activities

PFM III 15.1	Practice PFM III 3 activities.	Evaluation
PFM III 15.2	Place child in a high chair.	Evaluation
	Present cereal bits, sugar cubes, raisins, etc. on the tray and allow her to practice picking them up with the pincer grasp.	
	Repeat until the child is proficient at using the pincer grasp.	
Materials	Raisins, sugar cubes, cereal bits.	
Cue	Pick them up with your thumb and finger.	
Comment	Allow the child to eat the cereal or whatever when she uses the pincer grasp to pick it up.	

PFM III 16	PLACES OBJECTS IN CONTAINER	Comment
General Objective	Develop ability to place object in a container.	
Specific Objective	When provided with an object and a container, the child will place the object into the container.	

Activities

PFM III 16.1	Place the child in a high chair.	Evaluation
	Present a metal container and some bottle caps on the tray.	
	Pick up a cap and drop it into the container, exaggeratedly talking about the fun.	

Tell the child to pick up a cap and put it into the container. Guide the child's hand with your hand if necessary. Repeat.

Materials	Metal container, bottle caps, buttons, etc.
Cue	Drop it in here.
Comment	Give only as much help as necessary; gradually fade your assistance.
Comment	Use much STP for success.
Comment	Vary the objects (color, size, shape, texture) that you have the child drop.

Behavioral Objectives	PFM III 17

PFM III 17	PALMAR GRASPS CRAYON—DOTS IMITATIVELY	Comment
General Objective	Develop child's ability to grasp writing instrument.	
Specific Objective	The child will use the Palmar grasp to hold a crayon and dot a piece of paper imitatively.	

Activities

PFM III 17.1	Place the child in a high chair.	Evaluation
	Present a thick crayon and a piece of plain, colored paper on the tray.	
	Place the crayon in the child's palm, your hand over hers, and "dot" the colored paper making exaggerated talk about how much fun it is.	
Materials	Crayon, colored paper.	
Cue	Let's put some dots on the paper.	
Comment	Make this a game, reciting a rhyme (RHYMING PROCEDURE) or singing a song.	
Comment	Give only as much help as is necessary.	
PFM III 17.2	Place child as in 17.1.	Evaluation
	This time, demonstrate to the child how to dot the paper without guiding her hand. Tell her to dot the paper as you do.	

Materials	Crayon, colored paper.	
Cue	Dot the paper like Mommy (Daddy).	
Comment	As above.	
PFM III 17.3	Place the child as in 17.1 and 17.2. This time present the crayon and paper and have her pick the crayon up herself. Again demonstrate dotting.	Evaluation
Materials	As above.	
Cue	As above.	

	Behavioral Objectives	PFM III 18

PFM III 18	IMITATES SOUND OF TOYS	Comment
General Objective	Develop child's ability to imitate sounds.	
Specific Objective	When presented with a sound toy, the child will mimic the sound.	

Activities		
PFM III 18.1	Place child in a high chair.	Evaluation
	Present a small drum (a closed, sturdy box will do) and show the child how to "bang the drum."	
	Imitate the sound the drum makes, that is, "boom, boom."	
	Encourage the child to make the same sound.	
Material	Drum.	
Cue	The drum goes "boom."	
Comment	Present a wide variety of sound toys or objects you make that make sound.	
	Each time imitate the sound and encourage the child to do the same.	
Comment	Use STP for child's attempt to mimic the sound.	

PFM III 19	PERCEIVES ROUNDNESS	Comment
General Objective	Development of cognitive perception of roundness in environment.	
Specific Objective	When shown round objects, child will respond with recognition.	

Activities

PFM III 19.1	Present child with many round objects. Use TOUCH PROCEDURE I.	Evaluation
Materials	Ball, spheres, geometric solid.	
Cue	It's round.	
PFM III 19.2	Use Unit Activities as outlined earlier.	Evaluation
Materials	Shapes Unit Materials.	
Cue	Circle. Round.	
PFM III 19.3	Note all objects in home and yard that are round or circular.	Evaluation
PFM III 19.4	Present child with shapes. See if child can match round or circular objects. Do only as a game.	Evaluation

PFM III 20	EASY RELEASE	Comment
General Objective	Develop child's voluntary release of objects.	
Specific Objective	The child will be able to release objects with ease.	

Activities

PFM III 20.1	See PFM III 10 for practice activities. Repeat.	Evaluation

| *PFM III 20.2* | Provide the child with many opportunities to drop objects—from high chair, into container, etc. | Evaluation |
| | Encourage easy release as this should be made into a fun activity. | |

Behavioral Objectives   PFM III 21

PFM III 21	BEGINS IMITATIVE SCRIBBLING	Comment
General Objective	Development of child's skills in imitating through use of materials in hand.	
Specific Objective	When given a crayon, the child will imitate adults in scribbling.	

Activities

PFM III 21.1	Place crayon in child's hand.	Evaluation
	Child will hold crayon with Palmar Grasp.	
	Adult demonstrates dotting and scribbling on a piece of paper.	
	Child imitates adult.	
Materials	Paper, thick crayon.	
Cue	Make a red dot.	
	Make blue lines, etc.	
Comment	Coordinate with Color Units.	
PFM III 21.2	Try this activity with a RHYTHM PROCEDURE.	Evaluation
	Observe if child attempts to imitate rhythm pattern.	

Behavioral Objectives   PFM III 22

| *PFM III 22* | BOOKS—PATS PICTURES | Comment |
| General Objective | Development of child's interest in pictures in books. | |

Specific Objective	The child will show interest in pictures by patting the book.	

Activities

PFM III *22.1*	Read to child from hard picture books. Point out pictures while reading and making appropriate sounds. Ask child to "show me the _____ ." Direct child's hand to pat the right picture. Repeat with other pages.	Evaluation
Material	Hard picture book.	
Cue	Show me the _____ .	
PFM III *22.2*	Use PROGRAMMING PROCEDURE when necessary.	Evaluation
Material	Food as desired.	

	Behavioral Objectives	PFM III 23

PFM III *23*	BUILDS TOWER WITH TWO CUBES	Comment
General Objective	Develop eye-hand coordination.	
Specific Objective	When presented with blocks, the child will build a tower of two cubes.	

Activities

PFM III *23.1*	Place the child in a high chair. Present some different colored large cubes (blocks) on the tray. Demonstrate to the child how to place one block on top of the other. Encourage the child to imitate; you may guide her hand to pick up one block and place it on top of the other.	Evaluation

Materials	Cubes, blocks approximately two inches or three inches square.
Cue	Build a tower like me; put this one on top of this one.
Comment	Give only as much help as necessary; gradually fade your help when child can accomplish the task.
Comment	Use STP for successful attempt and let child push blocks over as a reward.

Behavioral Objectives   PFM III   24

PFM III 24	FILLS BOX OR CUP WITH TOYS	Comment
General Objective	Develop child's ability to place objects in a container.	
Specific Objective	When presented with a number of objects and a container, the child will fill the container with the toys.	

Activities

PFM III 24.1	See also PFM III 16 for practice activities.	Evaluation
PFM III 24.2	Place child in a high chair.	Evaluation
	Present him with some toys and a box.	
	Demonstrate by picking up one toy and placing it in the box.	
	Encourage him to put the toys in the box.	
	Give help if necessary.	
Materials	Toys, box.	
Cue	Put the toys in the box.	
Comment	Give only as much help as necessary.	
Comment	Make this a game; use STP for successful attempts.	
Comment	Vary objects as to color, shape, texture, and size.	

Comment	Child may stop after dropping one object in box; encourage him to continue by praising him after each object and telling him to keep going until the box is filled.

	Behavioral Objectives	PFM III 25

PFM III 25	PLAYS APPROPRIATELY WITH NESTING CUPS	Comment
General Objective	Infant will develop fine motor and manipulative skills.	
Specific Objective	When given plastic nesting cups, the infant will be able to insert the cups in the correct order.	

Activities

PFM III 25.1	Provide the infant with a set of nesting cups. Allow infant to manipulate and randomly play with them. Then show the infant how to do this by first giving the infant the two largest cups. Continue until the infant has mastered placing one cup in the other.	Evaluation
Materials	Set of plastic nesting cups or measuring cups.	
PFM III 25.2	Gradually add smaller cups, one at a time, to the cups the infant has mastered. Continue until the entire set has been mastered.	Evaluation

	Behavioral Objectives	PFM III 26

PFM III 26	ASSISTS TURNING BOOK PAGES	Comment
General Objective	Develop ability to turn pages of a book.	
Specific Objective	When a book is presented to the child, he will help to turn the pages.	

Activities

PFM III 26.1	Seat the child in your lap with a picture book in your hands.	Evaluation
	Place the child's hand on the upper right hand corner of the page and guide his hand to turn the page.	
Material	Large, hard picture book.	
Cue	Help me turn the pages.	
Comment	Make this like a game. Use STP for child's successful attempt.	
Comment	Repeat this exercise many times to show the child that you like it and that books are fun.	
	Choose books that have interesting pictures.	

	Behavioral Objectives	PFM III 27

PFM III 27	TOYS THROWN IN PLAY	Comment
General Objective	Develop hand coordination.	
Specific Objective	The child will be able to throw toys during play.	

Activities

PFM III 27.1	Place child in a sitting position.	Evaluation
	Give him a toy.	
	Sit across from him holding out your hands.	
	Tell him to throw you the ball.	
	You may move back and help the child to throw the ball if he cannot do it himself.	
Material	Ball.	
Cue	Throw the ball to _____ .	
Comment	Give only as much help as necessary.	
Comment	Use STP for any attempt at throwing the ball.	

Comment   Repeat the activity until the child is able to throw the ball (not necessary to have it thrown directly to you).

	Behavioral Objectives	PFM III 28

PFM III 28	ENJOYS LOOKING OUT WINDOW AT MOVING CARS AND TREES	Comment
General Objective	Develop child's interest in looking at objects.	
Specific Objective	The child will demonstrate his enjoyment of looking out of windows.	

Activities

PFM III 28.1	Place the child's high chair or playpen near a window so he can see out.	Evaluation
	Sit next to him and point out the cars, people, animals, etc.	
Cue	Look at the _____ .	
Comment	Make this like a game. Show the child that you think it is fun and enjoy looking out the window.	
Comment	Place the child near the window daily, so that he may look out.	

	Behavioral Objectives	PFM III 29

PFM III 29	WORKS WITH FORM BOARDS	Comment
General Objective	Development of eye-hand coordination and spatial concepts.	
Specific Objective	The child will appropriately place forms in a board.	

Activities

PFM III 29.1	Familiarize the child with shapes by letting the child feel them, outline the edges, and identify them with eyes shut.	Evaluation

	Familiarize the child with the form board by tracing the outlines with the child's index finger.	
Cue	Circle, square, triangle, etc. Feel it.	
Materials	Simple large formboards with three shapes.	
PFM III 29.2	When the child is familiar with the shapes and board, demonstrate how to place the shapes appropriately. Use LIVING SKILLS PROCEDURE, Use STP.	Evaluation
Cue	Put it in. Put the _____ in. Take it out. Take the _____ out.	
Materials	As above.	
PFM III 29.3	Once the child succeeds in placing the objects correctly 80-85 percent of the time, begin moving the board in other positions for variety.	Evaluation
Cue	As above.	
Materials	As above.	
PFM III 29.4	Use materials with three or more forms.	Evaluation
Cue	As above.	
Materials	Any variety of such materials exist on the market.	
Comment	As such materials may be poorly made, work with the equipment until you know the child can succeed with it.	

	Behavioral Objectives	PFM IV 1
PFM IV 1	TWO OBJECTS HELD IN ONE HAND	Comment
General Objective	Development of child's fine motor control.	
Specific Objective	When given two small objects, the child can hold them in one hand.	

Activities

PFM IV 1.1	Open child's hand.	Evaluation
	Place two raisins or other small items in child's hand. Close hand.	
	Repeat with larger objects until child gains confidence in abilities.	
PFM IV 1.2	Adult responds to child's efforts with smiles, touches, and pleasure.	Evaluation

	Behavioral Objectives	PFM IV 2

PFM IV 2	BUILDS TOWER WITH THREE OR FOUR CUBES	Comment
General Objective	Development of eye-hand coordination.	
Specific Objective	When presented with blocks the child will build a tower of three to four cubes.	

Activities

PFM IV 2.1	Proceed as in PFM III 23.	Evaluation

	Behavioral Objectives	PFM IV 3

PFM IV 3	TURNS TWO OR THREE BOOK PAGES TOGETHER	Comment
General Objective	Development of ability to turn pages of a book.	
Specific Objective	When a book is presented to the child, she will help turn the pages two or three at a time.	

Activities

PFM IV 3.1	Adult responds to child's effort with smiles, touches, and pleasure.	Evaluation
PFM IV 3.2	Proceed as in PFM III 26.	Evaluation

	Behavioral Objectives	PFM IV 4
PFM IV 4	IMITATES ADULT ACTIVITIES	Comment
General Objective	Development of imitative learning process.	
Specific Objective	The child will increase imitative activities when with adults.	

	Activities	
PFM IV 4.1	Observe child. Note when child is imitating an adult behavior.	Evaluation
	Slow down.	
	Exaggerate adult actions.	
PFM IV 4.2	Adult responds to child's effort with smiles, touches, and pleasure.	Evaluation
PFM IV 4.3	Play games with child that involve simple actions the child can imitate.	Evaluation
	Use bodily parts.	
	Up and down, in and out, around, behind actions.	
	Use RHYTHM PROCEDURES whenever possible.	
Cue	Appropriate to game.	

	Behavioral Objectives	PFM IV 5
PFM IV 5	SPONTANEOUSLY SCRIBBLES	Comment
General Objective	Development of eye-hand coordination.	
Specific Objective	When given crayon and paper, the child will scribble spontaneously.	

	Activities	
PFM IV 5.1	Proceed as in SC IV 1.	Evaluation

	Behavioral Objectives	PFM IV 6

PFM IV 6	BUILDS TOWER WITH FIVE OR SIX CUBES	Comment
General Objective	Development of eye-hand coordination.	
Specific Objective	When presented with blocks, the child will build a tower of five or six cubes.	

Activities		
PFM IV 6.1	Teach as in PFM III 23.	Evaluation

	Behavioral Objectives	PFM IV 7

PFM IV 7	IMITATES PUSHING TRAIN OF CUBES	Comment
General Objective	Development of child's imitative learning process.	
Specific Objective	The child will imitate as adult pushes cubes as if they were a train.	

Activities		
PFM IV 7.1	Teach as in SC IV 5.	Evaluation

	Behavioral Objectives	PFM IV 8

PFM IV 8	STACKS RINGS ON PEG	Comment
General Objective	Development of eye-hand coordination.	
Specific Objective	The child will demonstrate the ability to stack rings on a peg.	

Activities

PFM IV 8.1	Place peg in front of child. Show how to put ring over peg. Guide child. Repeat. Let child do as much as possible alone.	Evaluation
Materials	Peg and rings.	
PFM IV 8.2	Adult responds to child's effort with smiles, touches, and pleasure.	Evaluation
PFM IV 8.3	Coordinate with words used in shapes and colors units.	Evaluation
Materials	Peg and rings.	
Cue	Try the red peg. Try the round blue ring.	
PFM IV 8.4	Use TOUCH PROCEDURE II.	Evaluation

	Behavioral Objectives	PFM V 1

PFM V 1	FITS TOYS TOGETHER	Comment
General Objective	Development of eye-hand coordination.	
Specific Objective	The child will be able to fit toys together.	

Activities

PFM V 1.1	Adult shows child how to fit parts of toys together. Adult guides child. Adult gives only as much help as is necessary. Child imitates.	Evaluation
Materials	Containers for toys. Tea sets. Wood puzzles, etc.	

Cue	Put the top on. Put it together, etc.	
PFM V 1.2	Adult responds to child's effort with touches, smiles, and pleasure.	Evaluation
PFM V 1.3	Use PROGRAMMING PROCEDURE if necessary.	Evaluation
Material	Reward.	

	Behavioral Objectives	PFM V 2

PFM V 2	PREFERENCE FOR HANDEDNESS	Comment
General Objective	Development of handedness.	To be observed.
Specific Objective	The child will begin showing a preference for the right or left hand.	

Activities

PFM V 2.1	Note and take data on	
	1. the number of times the child reaches for objects and which hand the child uses.	Evaluation
	2. the hand the child prefers to use for scribbling.	Evaluation
	3. the leg the child first puts into clothes or uses to step upon for kicking.	Evaluation
	4. the eye the child uses for looking into visual objects permitting only one eye.	Evaluation
Comment	There is no preferred side for handedness and the child should not be forced in either direction.	

	Behavioral Objectives	PFM V 3

PFM V 3	UNSCREWS LIDS	Comment
General Objective	Development of reasoning and eye-hand coordination.	
Specific Objective	The child will be able to unscrew lids.	

Activities

PFM V 3.1	Adult shows child how to unscrew film tin.	Evaluation
	Adult helps child.	
	Adult gives only the help necessary.	
	Child is given a small object (M & M, etc.) in the can when opened.	
	Child imitates adult.	
Materials	Film tin.	
	M and M's.	
	Raisins.	
Cue	Unscrew the lid.	
	Take it off.	
Comment	Apply to other situations.	
PFM V 3.2	Adult responds to child's effort with touches, smiles, and pleasure.	Evaluation

	Behavioral Objectives	PFM V 4
PFM V 4	TURNS DOORKNOB BACK	Comment
General Objective	Development of eye-hand coordination for self-help skill.	
Specific Objective	The child will be able to turn a doorknob.	

Activities

PFM V 4.1	Adult shows child to reach, turn, pull, and let go of doorknob in the air.	Evaluation
	Child imitates.	
Cue	Quiet at first.	
	Then reach, turn, pull, let go.	
PFM V 4.2	Adult places child on stool in front of door.	Evaluation
	Child practices on the real door.	

Materials	Door.	
	Stool.	
Cue	As before.	
PFM V 4.3	Adult responds to child's effort with touches, smiles, and pleasure.	Evaluation
PFM V 4.4	Use PROGRAMMING PROCEDURE if necessary.	Evaluation
Material	Reward.	

	Behavioral Objectives	PFM V 5
PFM V 5	TURNS BOOK PAGES ONE AT A TIME	Comment
General Objective	Development of eye-hand coordination.	
Specific Objective	The child will turn the pages of book one by one.	

Activities		
PFM V 5.1	Continue as in PFM III 26.	Evaluation
PFM V 5.2	Adult responds to child's efforts with touches, smiles, and pleasure.	

	Behavioral Objectives	PFM V 6
PFM V 6	RECALLS EVENTS OF PREVIOUS DAY	Comment
General Objective	Development of memory operations.	
Specific Objective	The child will be able to recall the events of the previous day.	

Activities		
PFM V 6.1	Teach as in SC V 7.	Evaluation

Behavioral Objectives	PFM V 7

PFM V 7	LISTENS TO STORIES	Comment
General Objective	Development of listening and reading abilities.	
Specific Objective	The child will sit and listen to stories.	

Activities		
PFM V 7.1	Teach as in SC V 8.	Evaluation

Behavioral Objectives	PFM V 8

PFM V 8	INCREASE VISUAL MEMORY SPAN— LOOKS FOR MISSING TOYS	Comment
General Objective	Development of cognition, memory, and related behavior.	
Specific Objective	The child will look for a missing toy when named.	

Activities		
PFM V 8.1	Teach as in SC V 6.	Evaluation

Behavioral Objectives	PFM V 9

PFM V 9	BUILDS TOWER OF SIX TO SEVEN CUBES	Comment
General Objective	Development of eye hand coordination.	
Specific Objective	When given cubes, the child will build a tower six to seven cubes high.	

Activities		
PFM V 9.1	Teach as in PFM III 23.	Evaluation

Behavioral Objectives	PFM V 10

PFM V 10	IMITATES VERTICAL STROKE	Comment
General Objective	Development of cognition, memory, and behavior.	
Specific Objective	The child will imitate adult' vertical lines.	

Activities		
PFM V 10.1	Teach as in SC V 3.	Evaluation

Behavioral Objectives	PFM V 11

PFM V 11	IMITATES CIRCULAR STROKE	Comment
General Objective	Development of eye-hand coordination.	
Specific Objective	The child will be able to imitate adult and make circular strokes.	

Activities		
PFM V 11.1	Teach as in SC V 4.	Evaluation

Behavioral Objectives	PFM V 12

PFM V 12	WORKS WITH PEGBOARD MATERIALS	Comment
General Objective	Development of eye-hand coordination.	
Specific Objective	The child will insert pegs in pegboard type materials.	

Activities		
PFM V 12.1	Demonstrate to the child how a stick or dowel can stand upright in a lump of clay. Demonstrate the removal of the stick from the clay. Repeat	Evaluation

	Guide the child's hand using Living Skills Procedure. Use STP.	
Cue	Hold it down. Put it in. Put the peg in the clay. Take it out. Pull it out.	
Materials	Lumps of Clay. Small dowels or sticks.	
PFM V 12.2	Demonstrate how to put a stick into and remove from a slab of styrofoam.	Evaluation
	Guide according to Living Skills Procedure permitting the child to perform more and more of the skill. Use STP.	
Cue	Put it in. Pull it out.	
Comment	Carefully prepare the materials so the pegs really do fit nicely in the holes. It is important that the child succeed.	
PFM V 12.3	As above but using smaller pegboard type materials.	Evaluation
Cue	As above.	
Materials	Commercially prepared pegboard materials.	
Comment	Many pegboard sets presently on the market are poorly cut. Work the pegs and boards until the materials are satisfactory. This will minimize the child's frustrations.	

	Behavioral Objectives	PFM V 13
PFM V 13	BUILDS TOWER OF EIGHT CUBES	Comment
General Objective	Development of eye-hand coordination.	
Specific Objective	When given cubes, the child will build a tower of eight cubes.	

Activities

PFM V 13.1	Teach as in PFM III 23.	Evaluation

	Behavioral Objectives	PFM V 14

PFM V 14	BUILDS TOWER OF NINE TO TEN CUBES	Comment
General Objective	Development of eye-hand coordination.	
Specific Objective	When given cubes, the child will build a tower of nine or ten cubes.	

Activities

PFM V 14.1	Teach as in PFM III 23.	Evaluation

	Behavioral Objectives	PFM V 15

PFM V 15	IMITATES BRIDGE	Comment
General Objective	Development of eye-hand coordination.	
Specific Objective	The child will be able to imitate adult and make "bridges."	

Activities

PFM V 15.1	Teach as in SC V 13.	Evaluation

	Behavioral Objectives	PFM V 16

PFM V 16	IMITATES CROSS	Comment
General Objective	Development of eye-hand coordination.	
Specific Objective	The child will be able to imitate adult and make "crosses."	

Activities

PFM V 16.1	Teach as in SC V 14.

PFM V 17	WORKS WITH PUZZLES	
General Objective	Development of eye-hand coordination, spatial concepts, and object identification.	
Specific Objective	The child will work with simple puzzles.	

Activities

PFM V 17.1	Continue as in PFM III 29 using simple puzzles.	Evaluation
Comment	Make sure the puzzles fit well and that a little child can succeed.	
PFM V 17.2	Increase difficulty of puzzle materials.	Evaluation

SC I 1	RESPONDS TO PHYSICAL STIMULATION	Comment
		The activities included are to be used throughout the period of sensorimotor development and applied whenever mentioned as sensorial materials or activities in the curriculum.
General Objective	Prepare parents to provide intense program to elicit basic physical responses.	
Specific Objective	Parents will provide an intense program to elicit basic physical responses.	

Activities

SENSORIAL ACTIVITIES
PROCEDURES

SC I   1.1

VISUAL SENSORIAL ACTIVITIES

Evaluation

Put old posters on the walls where the infant sleeps and move them around. Paint walls bright colors, strips, patterns, etc. Put pictures on ceiling; hang mobiles all over the ceiling.

Move the crib once a week to different areas of the room. Change sheets using different colors and patterns.

Make crib mobiles—tie string or mobile with string or cord attached to elastic around infant's wrist or ankles, then as the infant moves, so will the parts of the mobile.

Put colored cellophane in the windows so that as light comes through, the colors in the room will change.

At night, play flashing games with the light switch before the baby goes to sleep or if the baby is awake at night.

Use RHYTHM PROCEDURE and test to see if infant becomes upset when you occasionally change the pattern.

Permit infant to follow the pattern of a small flashlight. Use the light to help the infant reach the goals of phase she is in at the time.

Make simple black and white pictures of faces. Make many such faces and shapes of black and white construction paper.

Make numbers, shapes, and alphabet letters out of black and white paper; move them around the sides of the crib at the infant's eye level.

SC I   1.2

LISTENING SENSORIAL ACTIVITIES

Evaluation

Put a wind chime in the infant's room near an air source to catch the breeze.

Coo, talk, laugh, sing, and play soft music.

Make sounds that are loud and soft, high and low, laughing, crying.

Sing songs at bottle time. Use favorite songs, songs of your faith, happy songs, sad songs, etc. Have a little clock ticking in the infant's room.

Make sounds that go with words like happy, delicious, sad.

Teach nursery rhymes, poems, and scriptures. Say them over and over again to infant. This is good to do during feeding and the short time between feeding the infant and infant's sleep. Read simple, short stories. Use RHYTHM PROCEDURE whenever possible.

SC I 1.3

TOUCH AND SPATIAL SENSORIAL ACTIVITIES

Evaluation

Give the infant many things to touch and feel. Help move the infant's hands over them. This is TOUCH PROCEDURE I. Include warm and cold things.

Cuddle the infant's bare skin. Tickle infant, soothe her, and give her little pinches and backrubs. Brush infant's skin, head, spine and back, legs and arms, chest and tummy, fingers and toes. Begin with soft materials and then use rougher materials. Use sponges, brushes, scrubbers and scrapers, fabrics, etc.

When infant shows interest in hands, put bells on elastic or ribbons and make mittens from little stockings. Sew shapes and numbers or colors on the mittens. Talk, talk, talk with infant as she plays.

Activities

TEXTURE BLANKET

Sew old scraps of fabric together like a quilt. Sew elastic, buttons, and bells on it very carefully and strongly. Put lace, knitting, and cord on fabric, too. Place this *Texture Blanket* on the floor and put the infant on it. Apply perfume and/or other scents on the edges to make it more stimulating to the senses—vanilla, garlic oil, or extracts! Keep it safe!

BATHTIME PROCEDURE

Use food colors in bath water. Put perfumes, vanilla, extracts, and other scents in the water. After the infant is dry, wrap in old fabrics that feel different from the towel. Brush the infant's skin all over. Brush the bottoms of feet and hands, brush down the spine, etc. Use soft brushes, hair wigs, sponges, fabrics, etc. Brush between and around toes and fingers with a soft brush. Apply strokes with RHYTHM PROCEDURE whenever possible.

SC I 1.4   SMELL SENSORIAL ACTIVITIES   Evaluation

Take the infant outdoors and let her smell flowers, newly cut lawn, etc.

Take your infant to the kitchen and let her smell cooking materials. Example: Give infant a whiff of the vinegar, the garlic, the onions, and salad oil, and all the other smells that go into a salad.

Make smell bottles or just let infant smell spice bottles, perfume bottles, dusting powders, shaving lotions, etc.

Rub the infant with different smelling oils and powders at bath time. Always talk about the smells.

SC I 1.5   TASTE SENSORIAL ACTIVITIES   Evaluation

Provide opportunities for infant to mouth things that are too big to swallow. Use care. Different nipples, rubber tubes, etc. Put various flavors on tip of nipple or finger—honey, salt, vinegar, yogurt, mashed cottage cheese, juices, etc.

SC I 1.6   RHYTHM PROCEDURE   Evaluation

Do sensorial activity in one of many possible patterns. Choose any preferred pattern, but be consistent with one for a while, then add more.

Example: long-short-short-long. Short-short-long-short, etc.

SC I 1.7	ASSOCIATION PROCEDURE	Evaluation

Mix sensorial activities, but use the same rhythm pattern in both activities.

Example: sound a bell in the rhythm; then flash the room lights in the same rhythm.

Behavioral Objectives   SC I 2

SC I 2	ATTENDS TO CERTAIN SOUNDS OR SENSORY STIMULATIONS	Comment
General Objective	Encouragement of infant attending to certain sounds or sensory stimulations.	
Specific Objective	Infant will attend to stimulation and/or indicate changes of bodily movement in response.	

Activities

SC I 2.1	Use a visual, listening, touch, smell, or taste sensorial activity as described previously.	Evaluation
Materials	As in SC I 1.1–1.5.	
Cue	Look, listen, feel, smell, taste _____ .	
SC I 2.2	Use RHYTHM PROCEDURE when possible.	Evaluation
SC I 2.3	Use ASSOCIATION PROCEDURE when possible.	Evaluation

Behavioral Objectives   SC I 3

SC I 3	SHOWS INTEREST IN BLACK/WHITE FORMS	Comment
General Objective	Provide for and encourage infant's interest in black and white forms.	
Specific Objective	Infant will look at black and white forms with interest.	

Activities

SC I 3.1   Lay infant on stomach in crib.   Evaluation

Place black and white form cards on sides of crib—one or two on each side.

Name cards as placed.

Name frequently when infant is looking at them.

Replace daily.

Materials   Black/white "faces" cards

Black/white "shapes" cards.

Black/white "numbers" cards.

Black/white "phonetic symbols" cards.

Black and white felt dolls and toys.

Cue   Name objects.

Behavioral Objectives   SC I 4

SC I 4   FOLLOWS PAST MIDLINE   Comment

General
Objective   Develop ability of infant to follow the movement of an object past midline.

Specific
Objective   Infant will visually follow the movement of an object past the midline.

Activities

SC I 4.1   Place infant on his back.   Evaluation

Move brightly colored object within eight-twelve inches of infant's face.

Move it a little to each side of center at first.

As infant's eyes follow object, move it farther and farther to each side.

Materials   Bright yarn, rattles, sound tins, etc.

Cue   Look.

Look at the _____ .

SC I 5	RESPONDS TO HUMAN VOICE BY ATTENDING, STOPPING OR CHANGING ACTIVITY	Comment
General Objective	Develop ability of infant to attend and respond to the human voice.	
Specific Objective	Infant will stop or change a behavior in response to the human voice.	

Activities

SC I 5.1	Place infant where she can see your face—about eight-fifteen inches away.	Evaluation
	Talk to infant using large facial movements while making many interesting sounds.	
	Shape infant to follow your face as you move it.	
	Reward with STP.	
Cue	Interesting sounds.	
	Call infant's name.	
SC I 5.2	PROGRAMMING PROCEDURE.	Evaluation
SC I 5.3	Observe to see if infant quiets when adult calls to her from a short distance.	Evaluation
	If not, repeat SC I 5.1 and then move out from infant farther and farther as long as infant quiets at sound of adult voice.	

SC I 6	FOLLOWS OBJECT 180°	Comment
General Objective	Develop ability of infant to follow a moving object 180°.	
Specific Objective	The infant will follow a moving object 180°.	

Activities

SC I 6.1	Move a pen light directly in front of infant's face—one-two feet away.	Evaluation
	Move it a little to the right and then left of center until infant follows the light 180°.	
	Shape when necessary.	
	Reward with STP.	
Material	Pen light.	
Cue	Look.	
	Look at the light.	

SC I 6.2	Move bright colored objects directly in front of infant's face—eight-twelve inches.	Evaluation
	Move it a little to the right and then the left of center until infant follows it 180°.	
	Shape when necessary.	
	Reward with STP.	
Materials	Yarn balls, rattles, etc.	
Cue	Look.	
	Look at the _____ .	

SC I 6.3	Hang a bright toy, such as yarn ball over the crib about two feet above infant's face.	Evaluation
	Place infant so his face is under the toy.	
	Move the toy.	
	Infant's eyes will follow movement of the toy.	
Materials	Yarn balls, toys, etc.	
Cue	Look.	
	Look at the _____ .	

SC I 6.4	PROGRAMMING PROCEDURE.	Evaluation
Material	Food as desired.	

SC I 7	ATTENDS TO ADULT MOUTH	Comment
General Objective	Encouragement of infant's attention to adult mouth.	
Specific Objective	Infant will increase attentiveness to adult mouth when being spoken to.	

Activities

SC I 7.1	Adult talks to infant with faces eight–twelve inches apart.	Evaluation
	Adult slowly and clearly forms sounds of interest to infant.	
Cue	m, d, g, p, n, etc.	
	Name of infant.	
	Names of toys.	
	Names of family members.	
SC I 7.2	Adult responds to infant's effort with smiles, touches, and pleasure.	Evaluation
SC I 7.3	If infant does not attend well use PROGRAMMING PROCEDURE.	Evaluation
Material	Food as desired.	

SC I 8	VISUAL INTEREST BEGINS	Comment
General Objective	Encourage development of infant's period of visual interest.	
Specific Objective	Infant will become very interested in visual sensory activities.	

Activities

| *SC I 8.1* | Provide many of the activities described in SC I 1.1—VISUAL SENSORIAL ACTIVITIES. | Evaluation |
| Materials | As appropriate. | |

Cue	As appropriate.	
SC I 8.2	Place infant where he can follow activities going on around him.	Evaluation
	Include infant whenever possible.	
Cue	Talk about what infant is seeing.	
Comment	Sometimes infant may cry in the dark or cry when unable to see what is going on.	
	Turn on a small light and/or place infant where he is able to see.	

Behavioral Objectives   SC I   9

SC I 9	BEGINNING OF MEMORIZATION OF PATTERNS	Comment
General Objective	Encourage ability of infant to recognize patterns in the environment.	
Specific Objective	Infant will begin to recognize patterns in the environment.	

Activities	Use RHYTHM PROCEDURE.	
SC I 9.1	Flash room lights or pen light for infant.	Evaluation
	Flash lights in a definite pattern for several weeks.	
	Change pattern.	
	Note infant response.	
	Return to first pattern.	
Materials	Pen light.	
	Room lights.	
Cue	Look.	
	Count.	
SC I 9.2	Brush infant according to TOUCH SENSORIAL PROCEDURE using RHYTHM PROCEDURE.	
	Occasionally change pattern.	
	Note infant response.	
	Return to first pattern.	

SC I 10	LOOKS WITH INTENT AT OBJECT IN HAND	Comment
General Objective	Encouragement of infant's ability to look directly at object in hand.	
Specific Objective	Infant will increase interest in objects held in hand.	

Activities

SC I 10.1	Give infant bright colored, textured, sound toys, keys, etc.	Evaluation
	Place in infant's hand.	
	When infant begins to lose interest in one toy, give another.	
Materials	Sound toys, textured toys, keys, bells, etc.	
Cue	Look.	
	Look at the _____ .	
SC I 10.2	PROGRAMMING PROCEDURE.	Evaluation
Material	Food as desired.	

SC I 11	BEGINS TO LOCALIZE SOUNDS LATERALLY	Comment
General Objective	Develop ability of infant to localize sounds laterally.	
Specific Objective	Infant will begin to localize sounds laterally.	

Activities

SC I 11.1	Sound toy to either side of infant's head.	Evaluation
	Infant turns to sound.	
	Use RHYTHM PROCEDURE.	
	Then sound toy behind, in front of, and to the sides of infant.	

Infant seeks source of sound.

As infant improves, move farther away when making sound.

Materials	Bells, sound toys, keys, etc.
Cue	Listen.
	Listen to the _____ .

SC I 11.2   PROGRAMMING PROCEDURE.   Evaluation

Material   Food as desired.

SC I 11.3   General LISTENING SENSORIAL AC-   Evaluation
TIVITIES.

Behavioral Objectives   SC II 1

SC II 1   OBJECT PERMANENCE BEGINS   Comment

General
Objective   Encouragement of concept of object permanence.

Specific
Objective   Infant will begin to conceive of object permanence.

Activities

SC II 1.1   Seat infant. Face infant.   Evaluation

Hold bright sound toy in front of infant's face.

Move object slowly behind a piece of paper.

Shake the sound toy behind the paper.

Bring sound toy out where infant can see it again. Shake it.

Act surprised and enthusiastic.

Repeat.

Materials   Sound toys, necklaces, bells, etc. Piece of paper.

Cue   Look. See the _____ .
Where is the _____ ?
Here is the _____ .

SC II 1.2	Hide face behind paper. Call infant.	Evaluation
	Continue as in SC II 1.1.	
Materials	Piece of paper.	
Cue	Here's Mama. Where's Mama?	

| | Behavioral Objectives | SC II 2 |

SC II 2	TURNS HEAD TOWARD SPEAKING VOICE	Comment
General Objective	Encouragement of infant's ability to locate source of speech.	
Specific Objective	Infant will turn head toward speaking voice.	

Activities

SC II 2.1	Adult makes noises or calls infant's name eight-twelve inches from left, right, front, and back of infant's head.	Evaluation
	Infant turns head to see source of sound.	
Cue	Name.	
	Look, here I am.	

| SC II 2.2 | Use PROGRAMMING PROCEDURE. | Evaluation |
| Material | Food as desired. | |

SC II 2.3	Adult moves farther from infant and calls.	Evaluation
	Infant turns head to see source of sound.	
Cue	Name.	

| SC II 2.4 | Adult moves and hides in and around room. Adult calls infant and makes sound. Infant looks for source of sound. | Evaluation |
| Cue | Name. Look, here I am. | |

Behavioral Objectives   SC II 3

SC II 3	ATTENDS TO OBJECTS DROPPED FROM SIGHT	Comment
General Objective	Encouragement of infant's interest in looking for objects dropped from sight.	
Specific Objective	Infant will look for objects dropped from sight.	

Activities

SC II 3.1	Seat infant.	Evaluation
	Give infant a sound toy to play with.	
	Guide infant to drop toy into a container.	
	Look with exaggerated interest for toy. Find it in container. Show infant.	
Materials	Sound toy. Bright objects, container.	
Cue	See the _____ .	
	Drop the _____ .	
	Where is the _____ ?	
	Here is the _____ .	
SC II 3.2	Seat infant in high chair.	Evaluation
	Give toy to infant to drop.	
	Help infant drop toy.	
	Guide infant in looking for toy.	
	Exaggerated adult efforts to see.	
	Show excitement when infant sees toy.	
Materials	Nonbreakable toys, rag dolls, stuffed animals, color cards, phonetic symbols, etc.	
Cue	Here is your _____ .	
	Drop your _____ .	
	Where is the _____ ?	
	Here is the _____ . Wow!	
SC II 3.3	PROGRAMMING PROCEDURE.	Evaluation
Material	Food as desired.	

SC II 4	FIXATES WHERE OBJECT DISAPPEARS	Comment
General Objective	Encouragement of infant's ability to fixate where object disappears.	
Specific Objective	Infant will fixate where object disappears.	

Activities

SC II 4.1	Seat infant.	Evaluation
	Hold sound toy in front of infant's face about eight–twelve inches.	
	Once infant focuses on sound toy, move it slowly out of range of vision or behind a piece of paper.	
	Note if infant stares at last place object was seen.	
Materials	Sound toy. Piece of paper.	
Cue	Look.	
SC II 4.2	Hold infant. Place bottle on table in view of infant.	Evaluation
	Turn around with infant; see if infant turns head to locate bottle.	
Material	Bottle.	

SC II 5	TALKS AND GESTURES TO OBJECTS	Comment
General Objective	Provide infant with opportunities to talk and gesture to objects.	
Specific Objective	Infant will talk and gesture to objects.	

Activities

SC II 5.1	Give infant variety of toys and sensorial UNIT MATERIALS.	Evaluation

Change them frequently.

Observe infant during play.

Note if infant talks and gestures to the objects.

Materials   Toys in general. Sensory UNIT MATE-
RIALS.

Behavioral Objectives   SC II 6

SC II 6	USES HANDS TO AFFECT OBJECTS (REACH, GRASP, SPLASH, BANG)	Comment
General Objective	Develop skill in reaching and grasping.	
Specific Objective	When presented with an object, the infant will use his hands to affect the object by reaching, grasping, banging, etc.	

Activities

SC II 6.1	Adult places infant in a supported sitting position.	Evaluation

Provide opportunities for him to grasp and handle a wide variety of objects.

Encourage him to explore and play with objects, that is, banging on floor or table, against other objects.

Cue   Touch the _____ .

Materials   Toys, rattles, balls, blocks.

Comment   Vary the size, shape, texture, and color of objects.

Comment   You may put your hands over infant's to demonstrate, but gradually fade assistance.

SC II 6.2	Place rubber squeeze toys in infant's bathtub. Encourage him to squeeze, splash, etc.	Evaluation
Cue	Touch the _____ .	
Material	Squeeze toy.	

SC II 7	RESECURES DROPPED OBJECT	Comment
General Objective	Develop hand dexterity and eye-hand coordination.	
Specific Objective	The infant will resecure an object that has been dropped.	To be observed.

Activities

SC II 7.1	Adult places infant in infant's seat or in supported sitting position.	Evaluation
	Provide her with a wide variety of toys to explore and grasp one at a time.	
	Infant will release grasp on object to surface such as high chair tray.	
	Encourage her to pick the object up again.	
Cue	Pick up the _____ .	
Materials	Toys, blocks, balls, etc.	
Comment	Adult may show the infant by dropping and resecuring the object. In addition, adult may guide infant's hand.	
	Gradually fade assistance as infant becomes successful.	
Comment	Vary the size, color, shape, and texture of the objects presented.	

| SC II 8 | LOOKS FOR FALLEN OBJECTS | Comment |
| General Objective | Develop infant's ability to look for fallen objects. | |

Specific Objective	Infant will actively search for fallen objects.	

Activities

SC II 8.1	Seat infant in high chair.	Evaluation
	Give infant favorite toy.	
	Help toy drop.	
	Observe if infant actively looks for toy.	
Materials	High chair. Toys.	
Cue	Oh-oh _____ dropped.	
	Oh-oh _____ fell.	
	Where is _____ ?	
	Here it is!	

SC II 8.2	PROGRAMMING PROCEDURE.	Evaluation
Material	Food as desired.	

Behavioral Objectives   SC II 9

SC II 9	FINDS PARTIALLY HIDDEN OBJECTS	Comment
General Objective	Develop infant's ability to find partially hidden objects.	
Specific Objective	Infant will find partially hidden objects.	

Activities

SC II 9.1	Seat infant in front of adult.	Evaluation
	Place toy in front of infant.	
	Cover a small part of toy with a cloth.	
	Infant will take toy.	
	Repeat, but cover more of the toy.	
Materials	Toys, UNIT MATERIALS, cloth.	
Cue	Here is a _____ .	
	Take the _____ .	
	Where is the _____ ?	

SC II 9.2	Place toy partly hidden under pillow. Repeat as above.	Evaluation
Materials	Toys, UNIT MATERIALS, pillow.	
Cue	As above. It's *under* the pillow.	
SC II 9.3	Seat infant. Place large toy in front of infant. Move toy slowly around you until partially hidden behind you.	Evaluation
Material	Large toy.	
Cue	As above.	

	Behavioral Objectives	SC II 10

SC II 10	LOCALIZES SOUNDS WELL	Comment
General Objective	Development of infant's ability to localize sounds well.	
Specific Objective	Infant will increase ability to localize sounds.	

Activities

SC II 10.1	Time how long it takes infant to locate sounds in room using the following activities.	Evaluation
Material	Stopwatch.	
SC II 10.2	Adult sounds bell or rattle in areas around head of infant. Infant looks for source of sound.	Evaluation
Materials	Bells, rattles, chimes, pots, and spoons, etc.	
Cue	Listen, look.	
SC II 10.3	Adult responds to infant's effort with smiles, touches, and pleasure.	Evaluation
SC II 10.4	Adult moves farther from infant and sounds bell or rattles. Infant looks for source of sound.	Evaluation

Materials	Bells, rattles, chimes, pots, and spoons, etc.
Cue	Look, listen.
SC II 10.5	Adult moves and hides in and around room. Evaluation Adult sounds toy. Infant looks for source of sound.
Materials	Bells, rattles, chimes, pots, and spoons, etc.
Cue	Look.

Behavioral Objectives   SC II 11

SC II 11	RETAINS OBJECTS IN HANDS	Comment
General Objective	Development of infant's ability to retain objects in hands.	
Specific Objective	Infant will increase ability to hold objects in hands.	

Activities

SC II 11.1	Seat infant.	Evaluation
	Give infant toys, sensorial UNIT MATERIALS, and household objects of various sizes and different weights.	
	Help infant hold or grasp the various objects.	
	Permit infant to do as much as possible by herself.	
Materials	Toys, sensorial UNIT MATERIALS, household objects.	
Cue	Hold it. This is a _____ . Take the _____ . It's big. It's little. It's light.	
SC II 11.2	Use PROGRAMMING PROCEDURE to develop strength in skill.	Evaluation

SC II 12	ATTEMPTS TO ACQUIRE OBJECTS TO SELF	Comment
General Objective	Develop eye-hand coordination.	
Specific Objective	When presented with a toy, the infant will rake radially to attain the toy.	

Activities

SC II 12.1	Place infant in supported sitting position. Present a sound toy within the infant's reach. Encourage him to get the toy.	Evaluation
Cue	Get the toy.	
Materials	Squeeze toy, shaker, etc.	
Comment	Note if the infant uses a radial raking motion to draw the toy within his grasp.	
Comment	Use smiles, touches, and pleasure for success.	
Comment	Allow infant to play with toy, once he secures it.	

Behavioral Objectives   SC III   1

SC III 1	USES ONE OBJECT TO AFFECT ANOTHER	Comment
General Objective	Development of infant's ability to use one object to affect another.	
Specific Objective	The infant will increase in ability to use one object to affect another.	

Activities

SC III 1.1	Adult places two objects in front of infant. Adult pounds one object with the other. Adult helps infant imitate. Infant imitates pounding. Adult rewards infant's efforts.	Evaluation

Materials	Blocks, sponge, pots, and spoons, etc.
Cue	Hit it.
	Hit the _____ .

SC III 1.2	Adult places two objects in front of infant.	Evaluation
	Adult pushes one object with the other.	
	Adult helps infant imitate pushing.	
	Adult rewards infant's efforts.	
Materials	As above.	
Cue	Push it.	
	Push the _____ .	

SC III 1.3	Adult places two objects in front of infant.	Evaluation
	Adult ties objects together.	
	Adult pulls one object—the second follows.	
	Adult helps infant imitate activity.	
	Infant imitates.	
	Adult rewards infant's efforts.	
Materials	String.	
	As above.	
Cue	Pull.	
	Pull them.	

Behavioral Objectives	SC III 2

SC III 2	MANIPULATION WITH FOREFINGER AND THUMB TO AFFECT OBJECTS	Comment
General Objective	Development of infant's ability to manipulate with forefinger and thumb to affect objects.	
Specific Objective	The infant will begin to move and play with objects with his thumb and forefinger.	

Activities

SC III 2.1	Place infant in high chair.	Evaluation
	Give infant crumbs or liquids on tray.	

	Show infant how to push materials around on tray.	
	Reward efforts.	
Materials	Sand, liquid, crumbs, cooked rice, etc.	
Cue	Push. Push it.	
SC III 2.2	Place infant in high chair.	Evaluation
	Give infant crumbs or liquid on tray.	
	Show infant how to use thumb and forefinger to pick up and drop materials.	
Materials	As above.	
Cue	Pick it up.	
	Drop it.	
SC III 2.3	Infant may also be helped to raise foods to mouth using activities and materials above.	Evaluation

Behavioral Objectives		SC III 3

SC III 3	SYMBOLIC MEANING BEGINS	Comment
General Objective	Encouragement of infant's opportunities to associate symbolic meanings in environment.	
Specific Objective	Infant will perceive meaning in verbal and visual symbols.	

Activities		
SC III 3.1	Gesture come, wait, no, stop, bye-bye, and peek-a-boo when word is spoken.	Evaluation
Cue	Come, wait, no, stop, bye-bye.	
SC III 3.2	WORD COMMAND PROCEDURE: Play games for word commands like come, wait, no, stop, bye-bye, and peek-a-boo.	Evaluation
	Reward with smiles, touches, and pleasure.	
Cue	Come, wait, no, stop, bye-bye, peek-a-boo.	

SC III 3.3	PROGRAMMING PROCEDURE. Used with word games.	Evaluation

SC III 4	BEGINS TO MATCH TWO OBJECTS	Comment
General Objective	Development of infant's ability to match two objects.	
Specific Objective	The infant will begin to be able to match two objects.	

Activities

SC III 4.1	Present materials to infant from ACTIVI- TIES PROCEDURE. Present one at a time. Using wall, play and match materials. When infant seems sure of two or more ob- jects, see if infant can match them correctly.	Evaluation
Materials	Colors, shapes, numbers, or phonetic sym- bols.	
Cue	This is a _____ .	
SC III 4.2	When infant seems sure of two or more parts from the UNIT ACTIVITIES materials, pre- sent two to four for matching. Demonstrate. Infant matches.	Evaluation
Materials	As above.	
Cue	Match it.	

SC III 5	UNCOVERS HIDDEN TOY	Comment
General Objective	Development of infant's ability to uncover hidden objects.	

Specific Objective	The infant will develop ability to uncover hidden objects.	
Activities		
SC III 5.1	Place object in front of infant.	Evaluation
	Partially cover object with cloth.	
	Pull cloth off.	
	Be excited about finding object.	
	Repeat.	
	Let infant uncover object.	
	Repeat.	
Materials	Toys, jars, etc.	
Cue	Pull.	
	Pull the cloth.	
	Look.	
	Look at the _____ .	
	Wow! Here is the _____ .	
SC III 5.2	Place object under a container.	Evaluation
	Lift container.	
	Be excited about finding the object.	
	Repeat.	
	Help infant lift container.	
	Be excited.	
Materials	Containers.	
	Toys.	
	Crumbs, raisins, etc.	
Cue	Lift the _____ .	
	Wow! Look at the _____ .	
SC III 5.3	Place object in container.	Evaluation
	Cover with lid.	
	Raise lid.	
	Be excited about finding object in the container.	
	Repeat. Help infant put object in the container and then lift the lid.	

Materials	Many containers.
	As above.
Cue	Where's the _____ ?

SC III 6	BEGINNING OF SYMBOLIC MEANING	Comment
General Objective	Development of infant's ability to recognize symbolic meanings.	
Specific Objective	The infant will begin to recognize that language and symbols are being used in the environment to represent objects familiar to him.	

Activities

SC III 6.1	Adult begins use of UNIT ACTIVITIES early in Phase III. Color is good to begin with. Follow as outlined in Chapter 4.	Evaluation
Materials	As in UNITS for color, shapes, numbers, phonetics, words.	
Cue	As is appropriate.	
SC III 6.2	Use of the general language program as outlined earlier will provide many opportunities for the development of this important goal.	Evaluation

---

SC III 7	OVERPERMANENCE OF OBJECTS	Comment
General Objective	Encouragement of infant's tendency to demonstrate over permanence of objects.	

Specific Objective	The infant will show tendency to expect objects to remain where last seen.	

Activities		
SC III 7.1	Seat infant.	Evaluation
	Slowly move a toy behind a piece of cardboard in front of infant.	
	Infant will continue looking at place where object disappeared.	
	Continue pulling object until it comes out the other side of the cardboard.	
	Show infant.	
	Change toys and cardboard.	
	Repeat.	
Materials	Toys.	
	UNIT MATERIALS, etc.	
	Cardboard, construction paper, paper rolls, string.	
Cue	Here's a _____ .	
	Look at the _____ .	
	Where is the _____ ?	
	Here is the _____ .	

Behavioral Objectives   SC III   8

SC III 8	BEGINNING INDICATION OF CAUSALITY	Comment
General Objective	Development of causality concept.	
Specific Objective	The infant will begin to see cause and effect relationships.	

Activities		
SC III 8.1	Observe infant as he drops objects.	Evaluation
	When infant follows a dropped object and then deliberately drops another, the cause and effect concept is being developed.	

Also observe this activity in infant's practice at spilling drinks, dropping food to pets, etc.

SC III 8.2	Place infant in high chair.	Evaluation
	Give infant many unbreakable objects to drop.	
Materials	Unbreakable objects.	
Cue	Drop it.	
	Oh-Oh. You dropped it.	
Comment	Place sheet under high chair area.	
SC III 8.3	Seat infant in bathtub.	Evaluation
	Give infant cup and colored water to spill.	
	Clean tub and infant after play.	
Materials	Large container of colored water.	
	Cup.	
Cue	Here is some _____ .	
	Oh-Oh. It spilled.	
SC III 8.4	Use PROGRAMMING PROCEDURE if necessary.	Evaluation

---

Behavioral Objectives   SC III   9

SC III 9	RESPONDS TO "NO"	Comment
General Objective	Development of infant's ability to respond to "no."	
Specific Objective	The infant will respond to "no."	

Activities

SC III 9.1	Proceed as in L III 3.1 and L III 3.2 only.	Evaluation

Behavioral Objectives   SC III   10

SC III 10	RESPONDS TO NAME	Comment
General Objective	Development of infant's ability to respond to name.	
Specific Objective	The infant will respond to name.	

Activities

SC III 10.1	Adult uses infant's name continually when speaking to him.	Evaluation
Cue	Infant's name.	
	"Is _____ hungry?	
	"Does _____ want to go bye-bye?"	
SC III 10.2	Call infant's name from outside room and see if infant responds by:	Evaluation
	1. looking at adult or	
	2. stopping activity or	
	3. vocalization.	
Cue	Infant's name.	
Comment	Adult responds to infant's effort with smiles, touches, and pleasure.	
SC III 10.3	Enlarge a photograph of infant. Cover with clear contact paper. Paste on back of unbreakable infant's mirror. Point to picture or infant's face in mirror and name infant.	Evaluation
Materials	Nonbreakable infant mirror.	
	Picture.	
	Glue.	
Cue	Name infant.	
SC III 10.4	Use PHONETIC SYMBOL PROCEDURE for infant's name.	Evaluation
SC III 10.5	Use TOUCH PROCEDURE II to help teach infant to say his own name.	Evaluation
SC III 10.6	Use TAPE PROCEDURE.	Evaluation
Materials	Tape, recorder, microphone.	

SC III 10.7	Use PROGRAMMING PROCEDURE.	Evaluation
Materials	Food as desired.	

Behavioral Objectives	SC III 11

SC III 11	EXPLORES AND PROBES HOLES AND GROOVES IN TOYS	Comment
General Objective	Encourage continued development of hand dexterity and eye-hand coordination.	
Specific Objective	When provided with toys with holes or grooves, the infant will probe the holes or grooves with her finger.	

Activities

SC III 11.1	Provide the infant with a variety of doughnut-shaped stacking toys. Show her how to poke her finger through the hole.	Evaluation
	Make exaggerated actions and talk while you show her.	
	Encourage her to poke her finger through the hole.	
Material	Doughnut-shaped stacking toys or rings.	
Cue	Poke your finger through the hole.	
SC III 11.2	Give the baby some blocks or other plastic toys with finger holes.	Evaluation
	Again encourage her to play with and probe the holes in the toys.	
Materials	Blocks or toys with finger holes.	
Cue	As above.	

Behavioral Objectives	SC III 12

SC III 12	REMOVES OBJECT FROM CONTAINER	Comment
General Objective	Develop ability to remove objects from container.	

Specific Objective	When a container with an object is presented to the infant he will remove it from container.	

Activities		
SC III 12.1	Hold a container with a bright object or toy in front of the infant.	Evaluation
	If necessary, guide his hand into the container so he can grasp the object	
	Have him secure the object. Repeat.	
Materials	Container, toy.	
Cue	Pick up the _____ .	
Comment	Gradually withdraw your assistance as infant can do this himself.	
SC III 12.2	Put some cereal bits in the container with the objects.	Evaluation
	Tell the infant to pick up the toy and give it to you.	
	When he has done this, tell him to get the cereal bits out of the container and let him eat them.	
Materials	Container, toy, cereal bits.	
Cue	Pick up the _____ and then you can have the cereal.	

	Behavioral Objectives	SC III 13

SC III 13	SEQUENTIAL PLAY	Comment
General Objective	Development of sequential play patterns.	
Specific Objective	When provided with several toys, the infant will play with them sequentially.	

Activities		
SC III 13.1	Provide the infant with a toy.	Evaluation
	When infant plays with it for more than a minute or two, remove it from sight.	

Encourage infant to play with second toy.

Repeat with new toys.

Materials	Several toys.
Cue	Here is a _____ .
	The _____ is gone.
	Play with this _____ .

SC III 13.2	Provide infant with two toys.	Evaluation
	Use PROGRAMMING PROCEDURE to encourage infant to put one down and pick up the second.	
Materials	As above.	
Cue	As above.	

Behavioral Objectives   SC III   14

SC III 14	PLACES OBJECTS IN CONTAINER	Comment
General Objective	Develop ability to place object in a container.	
Specific Objective	When provided with an object and a container, the infant will place the object into the container.	

Activities

SC III 14.1	Place the infant in a high chair.	Evaluation
	Present a metal container and some bottle caps on the tray.	
	Pick up a cap and drop it into the container, exaggeratedly talking about the fun, etc.	
	Tell the infant to pick up a cap and put it into the container. Guide the infant's hand with your hand if necessary. Repeat.	
Materials	Metal container, bottle caps, buttons, etc.	
Cue	Drop it in here.	
Comment	Give only as much help as necessary; gradually fade assistance.	

Comment   Use STP for success.

Comment   Vary the objects (color, size, shape, texture)
                 that you have the infant drop.

Behavioral Objectives   SC III   15

SC III   15   SCRIBBLING IMITATIVELY WITH   Comment
                 CRAYON

General   Development of infant's skills in imitating
Objective   through use of materials in the hand.

Specific   When given a crayon, the infant will imitate
Objective   adults in scribbling.

Activities

SC III   15.1   Place crayon in infant's hand.   Evaluation

                 Infant will hold crayon with palmar grasp.

                 Adult demonstrates dotting and scribbling on
                 a piece of paper.

                 Infant imitates adult.

Materials   Paper.

                 Thick crayon.

Cue   Make a red dot.

                 Make blue lines, etc.

Comment   Coordinate with Color Units.

SC III   15.2   Try this activity with a RHYTHM PRO-   Evaluation
                 CEDURE.

                 Observe if infant attempts to imitate adult
                 rhythm pattern.

Behavioral Objectives   SC III   16

SC III   16   BEGINS OTHER IMITATIVE   Comment
                 BEHAVIORS

General   Development of intense imitative learning
Objective   procedures.

Specific Objective	When presented with human models, the infant will imitate behaviors and activities.	

Activities

SC III 16.1	Expose infant to many social and learning situations. Observe and note infant's efforts to imitate.	Evaluation
SC III 16.2	Use smiles, touches, and pleasure to encourage infant's efforts.	Evaluation
SC III 16.3	When infant shows particular interest in activity, slow down and move deliberately a few times.	Evaluation

	Behavioral Objectives	SC III 17

SC III 17	PERCEIVES ROUNDNESS	Comment
General Objective	Development of cognitive perception of roundness in environment.	
Specific Objective	When shown round objects, infant will respond with recognition.	

Activities

SC III 17.1	Present infant with many round objects. Use TOUCH PROCEDURE I.	Evaluation
Materials	Balls, spheres, geometric solids.	
Cue	It's round, etc.	
SC III 17.2	Use shapes UNIT ACTIVITIES as outlined in Chapter 4.	Evaluation
Materials	Shapes Unit materials.	
Cue	Circle. Round.	
SC III 17.3	Note all objects in home and yard that are round or circular.	Evaluation

SC III 17.4	Present infant with shapes. See if infant can match round or circular objects or place into one-piece puzzle. Do only as a game.	Evaluation

	Behavioral Objectives	SC III 18

SC III 18	REGARDS PICTURES IN BOOK	Comment
General Objective	Development of infant's interest in pictures in books.	
Specific Objective	The infant will show interest in pictures by patting the book or pointing in it.	

Activities

SC III 18.1	Read to infant from hard picture books. Point out pictures while reading and making appropriate sounds. Ask infant to "Show me the _____ ." Direct infant's hand to pat the right picture. Repeat with other pages.	Evaluation
Material	Hard picture book.	
Cue	Show me the _____ .	
SC III 18.2	Use PROGRAMMING PROCEDURE when necessary.	Evaluation
Material	Food as desired.	

	Behavioral Objectives	SC III 19

SC III 19	OVERPERMANENCE OF OBJECTS DISAPPEARS	Comment
General Objective		To be observed
Specific Objective		

Activities

SC III 19.1	Use activities outlined in SC III 7.	Evaluation
	Observe and note when child anticipates the object coming out at the other end of the cardboard or container.	
SC III 19.2	Draw object using RHYTHM PROCEDURE to add interest.	Evaluation
SC III 19.3	Use PROGRAMMING PROCEDURE to help shape child's attention to opposite end of cardboard.	Evaluation

---

Behavioral Objectives	SC III 20

SC III 20	SPACE PERCEPTION	Comment
General Objective	Development of child's sense of space perception and relationship.	
Specific Objective	The child will begin to perceive spatial relationships bodily and through placement of objects.	

Activities

SC III 20.1	Use spatial box (a small cardboard box with a slot in the top and an open bottom).	Evaluation
	Let child place toy in, on, under, etc.	
	Adult gives language.	
Materials	Spatial Box.	
	Toys.	
Cue	In, on, under, etc.	
SC III 20.2	During the bath, place wet wash cloth on all parts of child's body and name.	Evaluation
Materials	Bath.	
	Washcloth.	
Cue	As appropriate.	

SC III 20.3	During bath, move wash cloth over body parts saying "around," "between," "on," "off," etc.	Evaluation
Materials	Wash cloth.	
	Bath.	
Cue	As moving wash cloth.	
SC III 20.4	Cover big boxes with solid colors, i.e., contact paper or fabric. Cut holes on sides in various shapes.	Evaluation
	Encourage child to crawl in and out, on and off, etc.	
Materials	Cardboard boxes.	
	Contact paper.	
Cue	Name spatial position.	
SC III 20.5	Name child's location daily in general environment.	Evaluation
Cue	You are *under* the chair.	
	You are *in* the crib, etc.	

	Behavioral Objectives	SC III 21
SC III 21	TRIAL AND ERROR PROCESS BEGINS	Comment
General Objective	Development of child's ability to apply the process of trial and error to aspects of cognition.	
Specific Objective	When imitating rhythm or matching objects, the child will use the process of trial and error.	

Activities		
SC III 21.1	Provide matching opportunities through use of UNIT ACTIVITIES materials, or toys such as shapes dropped through matching holes into a box.	Evaluation
Materials	As in UNITS or toys requiring trial and error process.	
Cue	As appropriate.	

SC III 21.2	Use STP with enthusiasm for child's efforts. Stress successes. *Ignore* mistakes.	Evaluation
SC III 21.3	Bang on pan using RHYTHM PROCEDURE. Encourage child's efforts to imitate.	Evaluation
Materials	Pan and spoon. Drum.	
Cue	Do this. Sound out rhythm.	

Behavioral Objectives   SC III   22

SC III 22	CAUSALITY ESTABLISHED	Comment
General Objective	Establishment of causality concept.	
Specific Objective	When presented with opportunities to show cause and effect relationships, the child will anticipate result.	

Activities

| *SC III 22.1* | Observe child to see if he anticipates the result of spilling, dropping, or throwing objects. Note if child anticipates the result. | Evaluation |
| *SC III 22.2* | Provide opportunities through activities as outlined in SC III 8. | Evaluation |

Behavioral Objectives   SC III   23

SC III 23	COMPREHENDS A FEW OBJECTS BY NAME	Comment
General Objective	Development of child's ability to comprehend a few objects by name.	
Specific Objective	The child will increase in ability to comprehend a few objects by name.	

Activities

SC III 23.1	Place toy in front of child.	Evaluation
	Name toy repeatedly.	
	Play with child and toy.	
	Name toy carefully.	
	Repeat throughout the day for several days.	
	Repeat with another object of interest to the child.	
	Ask child for one of the two toys.	
Material	Toy.	
Cue	Name of toy.	
Comment	The name of the object may need to be spoken hundreds of times before understood by child.	
SC III 23.2	Use UNIT ACTIVITIES as outlined in Part I of this book.	Evaluation
SC III 23.3	Use TOUCH PROCEDURE II.	Evaluation
SC III 23.4	Use TAPE PROCEDURE.	Evaluation
Materials	Tape, recorder, microphone.	
SC III 23.5	Use PROGRAMMING PROCEDURE.	Evaluation
Material	Food as desired.	

	Behavioral Objectives	SC III 24

SC III 24	BUILDS TOWER WITH TWO CUBES	Comment
General Objective	Develop eye-hand coordination.	
Specific Objective	When presented with blocks, the child will build a tower of two cubes.	

Activities

SC III 24.1	Place the child in a high chair.	Evaluation
	Present some different colored large cubes (blocks) on the tray.	

Demonstrate to the child how to place one block on top of the other.

Encourage the child to imitate; you may guide his hand to pick up one block and place it on top of the other.

Material	Cubes, blocks approximately 2 inch or three inch square.
Cue	Build a tower like me; put this one on top of this one.
Comment	Give only as much help as necessary; gradually fade help when child can accomplish the task.
Comment	Use STP for successful attempt and let child push blocks over as a reward.

Behavioral Objectives   SC III   25

SC III 25	FILLS BOX OR CUP WITH TOYS	Comment
General Objective	Develop child's ability to place objects in a container.	
Specific Objective	When presented with a number of objects and a container, the child will fill the container with the toys.	

Activities

SC III 25.1	See also PFM III 16 for practice activities.	Evaluation
SC III 25.2	Place child in a high chair.	Evaluation
	Present her with some toys and a box.	
	Demonstrate by picking up one toy and placing it in the box.	
	Encourage her to put the toys in the box.	
	Give help if necessary.	
Materials	Toys, box.	
Cue	Put the toys in the box.	
Comment	Give only as much help as necessary.	

Comment	Make this a game; use STP for successful attempts.
Comment	Vary objects as to color, shape, texture, and size.
Comment	Child may stop after dropping one object in box; encourage her to continue by praising her after each object and telling her to keep going until the box is filled.

Behavioral Objectives	SC III 26

SC III 26	ENJOYS LOOKING OUT WINDOW AT MOVING CARS, TREES, ETC.	Comment
General Objective	Develop child's interest in looking at objects.	
Specific Objective	The child will demonstrate his enjoyment of looking out of windows.	

Activities

SC III 26.1	Place the child's high chair or playpen near a window so he can see out.	Evaluation
	Sit next to him and point out the cars, people, animals, etc.	
Cue	Look at the _____ .	
Comment	Make this a game. Show the child that you think it is fun and enjoy looking out the window.	
Comment	Place the child near the window daily, so that he may look out.	

Behavioral Objectives	SC IV 1

SC IV 1	SCRIBBLES SPONTANEOUSLY	Comment
General Objective	Development of spontaneity in child's conceptual-motoric abilities.	
Specific Objective	When given crayon and paper, the child will scribble spontaneously.	

Activities

SC IV 1.1	Provide child with large crayon, paper, or newsprint.	Evaluation
	Give child opportunities to begin scribbling spontaneously.	
Materials	Paper. Newsprint. Large Crayons.	
Cue	Colors.	
Comment	Coordinate with color units.	
SC IV 1.2	Continue as in SC III 15.	Evaluation

Behavioral Objectives   SC IV   2

SC IV 2	**BUILDS TOWER WITH THREE OR FOUR CUBES**	Comment
General Objective	Development of eye-hand coordination.	
Specific Objective	When presented with blocks, the child will build a tower of three-four cubes.	

Activities

SC IV 2.1	Teach as outlined in PFM III 23.	Evaluation

Behavioral Objectives   SC IV   3

SC IV 3	**TURNS TWO OR THREE BOOK PAGES TOGETHER**	Comment
General Objective	Development of ability to turn pages of a book.	
Specific Objective	When a book is presented to the child, she will be able to turn the pages two or three at a time.	

Activities

SC IV 3.1	Adult responds to child's effort with smiles, touches, and pleasure.	Evaluation

SC IV 3.2	Teach as in PFM III 26.	Evaluation

	Behavioral Objectives	SC IV 4

SC IV 4	BUILDS TOWER WITH FIVE OR SIX CUBES	Comment
General Objective	Development of eye-hand coordination.	
Specific Objective	When presented with blocks, the child will build a tower of five or six cubes.	

Activities

SC IV 4.1	Teach as outlined in PFM III 23.	Evaluation

	Behavioral Objectives	SC IV 5

SC IV 5	IMITATES PUSHING TRAIN OF CUBES	Comment
General Objective	Development of child's imitative learning processes.	
Specific Objective	The child will imitate an adult pushing cubes as a train.	

Activities

SC IV 5.1	Adult lines up cubes and pushes them saying choo-choo.	Evaluation
	Adult helps child push the cubes again saying choo-choo.	
	Repeat. Let child do as much as possible himself.	
Materials	Cubes.	
Cue	Choo-Choo.	
	Push the choo-choo.	
SC IV 5.2	Line up two sets of cubes.	Evaluation
	Adult pushes one.	

	Child pushes the other.	
	Race.	
Materials	As above.	
Cue	As above.	

SC IV 5.3	Push cubes over edge of boxes, tables, chairs, and other objects.	Evaluation
	Pick up and repeat.	
Materials	Cubes.	
Cue	Choo-choo.	
	Push the choo-choo.	

Behavioral Objectives   SC IV 6

SC IV 6	FORMULATES NEGATIVE JUDGMENT	Comment
General Objective	Development of evaluative cognitive operations.	
Specific Objective	When given an opportunity to evaluate or judge wants, the child will use "no."	

Activities

SC IV 6.1	Make up yes/no questions.	Evaluation
	Frequently use head shaking gesture.	
	Demonstrate the appropriate answer at first.	
	When child can either say yes/no or gesture with head do not demonstrate answers anymore.	
Cue	Is your hand red?	
	Do you like eggs?	
	Is this the ball?	
	Is this b?	
	Are you hungry?	
Comment	Child may deliberately give you the wrong answer during this period. Just accept his answer and go on as if it were a game.	

SC IV 7	OBJECT PERMANENCE	Comment
General Objective	Development of concept of permanence.	
Specific Objective	The child will understand that objects still exist even when out of sight.	

Activities

SC IV 7.1	Place child on floor.	Evaluation
	Place toys on floor in front of child.	
	Cover one toy at a time with a cloth.	
	Remove cloth.	
	Show child it's still there.	
Materials	Toys.	
Cue	Here is a _____ .	
	Where is the _____ ?	
	The _____ is still here.	
SC IV 7.2	Cover furniture items with cloth.	Evaluation
	Remove as above.	
	Show child items are still there.	
Cue	As above.	
SC IV 7.3	Put items in cupboard.	Evaluation
	Shut door.	
	Proceed as above.	
Cue	Here is a _____ .	
	Where is the _____ ?	
	The _____ is still here.	

Behavioral Objectives   SC IV   8

SC IV 8	SAYS "NO" WITH REASON	Comment
General Objective	Development of child's ability to make judgments.	

Specific Objective	The child will say "no" for a reason.	

Activities

SC IV 8.1	Use activities as outlined in SC IV 6.	Evaluation
SC IV 8.2	Observe that child gives "no" for a reason rather than as an exercise of will.	Evaluation

	Behavioral Objectives	SC IV 9

SC IV 9	GROWTH IN OBJECT IDENTIFICATION	Comment
General Objective	Development of child's ability to identify objects.	
Specific Objective	The child will show increased interest in numbers of objects she is able to identify.	

Activities

SC IV 9.1	Observe the number of objects the child is able to name, point to, or fetch correctly.	Evaluation
SC IV 9.2	Continue teaching UNIT ACTIVITIES for color, shape, numbers, and phonetics.	Evaluation
	Begin UNITS for body parts, animals, etc., if not already started.	
SC IV 9.3	When child shows interest in an object, write a card for the object's name. Give card to child while interest is shown.	Evaluation
	Tape card on object whenever possible.	
Materials	Paper or cards.	
Cue	Naming objects.	
Comment	Use a felt tip pen and make the words on the cards one-half inch to one inch when possible.	
Comment	Print small phonetic symbol above word with red ink when helpful.	
	Draw phonetic symbol to child's attention.	

	Behavioral Objectives	SC V 1

SC V 1	UNDERSTANDS SPATIAL CONCEPTS	Comment
General Objective	Development of cognitive relationships.	
Specific Objective	The child will understand the meaning of in, on, behind, etc.	

Activities		
SC V 1.1	Adult repeats spatial activities as in SC III 20.	Evaluation
SC V 1.2	See L V 17 for activities using word cards when possible.	Evaluation

	Behavioral Objectives	SC V 2

SC V 2	ANSWERS "WHAT DO YOU DO WITH _____ ?"	Comment
General Objective	Development of cognitive relationships.	
Specific Objective	The child will give simple answers to question of "What do you do with _____ ?"	

Activities		
SC V 2.1	Adult asks question during daily activities many times. Adult answers question.	Evaluation
Materials	Food, toys, clothing.	
Cue	What can we do with this? Eat it. What can we do with this? Wear it. What can we do with this? Throw it. Roll it.	
SC V 2.2	Adult asks question. Child answers.	Evaluation
Materials	As above.	
Cue	As above.	

Comment	Stress successes.	
	Ignore mistakes.	
	Repeat later with correct answer.	
SC V 2.3	Adult responds to child's effort with touches, smiles, and pleasure.	Evaluation
SC V 2.4	Use TAPE PROCEDURE.	Evaluation
Materials	Tape, recorder, microphone.	
SC V 2.5	Use PROGRAMMING PROCEDURE if necessary.	Evaluation
Material	Reward.	

Behavioral Objectives   SC V   3

SC V 3	IMITATES VERTICAL STROKE	Comment
General Objective	Development of cognitive and imitative behavior.	
Specific Objective	The child will be able to imitate an adult and make up and down lines.	

Activities

SC V 3.1	Show child how to make up and down lines on paper.	Evaluation
	Help guide child's hand.	
	Child will imitate adult.	
Materials	Crayon.	
	Paper.	
Cue	Up and down.	
	Write like this.	
Comment	Coordinate with color UNIT ACTIVITIES.	
SC V 3.2	Use PROGRAMMING PROCEDURE as necessary.	Evaluation
Material	Food as desired.	

SC V 4	IMITATES CIRCULAR STROKE	Comment
General Objective	Development of cognitive and imitative behavior.	
Specific Objective	The child will be able to imitate adult and make circular strokes.	

Activities

SC V 4.1	Show child how to make circles.	Evaluation
	Help guide child's hand over adult drawing and then guide child's own efforts.	
	Child will imitate adult.	
Materials	Crayons.	
	Paper.	
	Fabric or sandpaper form.	
Cue	Around and around.	
	Make a red circle.	
	It's round.	
Comment	Coordinate with shape, color, and number UNIT ACTIVITIES.	
SC V 4.2	Use PROGRAMMING PROCEDURE if necessary.	Evaluation
Material	Reward.	
SC V 4.3	Adult responds to child's effort with touches, smiles, and pleasure.	Evaluation

SC V 5	BUILDS TOWER OF SIX TO SEVEN CUBES	Comment
General Objective	Development of cognitive relationships.	
Specific Objective	When given cubes, the child will build a tower six to seven cubes high.	

Activities

SC V 5.1	Teach as in PFM III 23.	Evaluation

Behavioral Objectives	SC V 6

SC V 6	INCREASED SERIAL MEMORY SPAN— LOOKS FOR MISSING TOYS	Comment
General Objective	Development of cognition, memory, and related behavior.	
Specific Objective	The child will look for a missing toy when named.	

Activities

SC V 6.1	Adult names several toys.	Evaluation
	Adult covers toys with a cloth.	
	Adult asks child where the various toys are.	
	Child finds toys under cloth.	
Material	Toys.	
	Cloth.	
Cue	Where is the _____ ?	

SC V 6.2	Adult names several toys.	Evaluation
	Adult hides toys behind back.	
	Adult asks child where the various toys are.	
	Child finds toys.	
	Repeat hiding behind child's back.	

SC V 6.3	Adult names several toys.	Evaluation
	Adult hides toys in room.	
	Adult and child look for toys.	
Materials	As above.	
Cue	As above.	

SC V 6.4	Adult responds to child's effort with touches, smiles, and pleasure.	Evaluation

SC V 6.5	Adult and child look together for things around the home, at the store, etc.	Evaluation

SC V 6.6	Use PROGRAMMING PROCEDURE if necessary.	Evaluation

Behavioral Objectives	SC V 7

SC V 7	RECALLS EVENTS OF PREVIOUS DAY	Comment
General Objective	Development of memory operations.	
Specific Objective	The child will be able to recall the events of the previous day.	

Activities

SC V 7.1	Adult and child make an activities chart and book for a day with big event of interest for the child.	Evaluation
	Adult reads book to child.	
	Adult and child discuss day's activities.	
	Adult and child reread book noting that it happened "yesterday."	
	Adult and child look at activity chart noting that it happened "yesterday."	
SC V 7.2	Reward child's efforts at recall with smiles, touches, and pleasure.	Evaluation

Behavioral Objectives	SC V 8

SC V 8	LISTENS TO STORIES	Comment
General Objective	Development of listening abilities and reading readiness.	
Specific Objective	The child will sit and listen to stories.	

Activities

SC V 8.1	Read short stories of interest to the child daily.	Evaluation
	Coordinate with UNIT ACTIVITIES.	
	Include little books of child's experiences.	

Materials	Books.
	Little Experience Books.
	UNIT Books.
Cue	As is appropriate.
Comment	Read with enthusiasm.
SC V 8.2	Use PROGRAMMING PROCEDURE if it is Evaluation very difficult for child to sit.
Material	Food as appropriate.
Comment	Read as part of daily routine, perhaps at nap or bedtime.

Behavioral Objectives   SC V 9

SC V 9	POINTS OUT BIG AND LITTLE Comment
General Objective	Development of class products.
Specific Objective	When shown objects, the child will be able to point to big and/or little ones.

Activities	
SC V 9.1	Adult and child stand together. Evaluation
	Adult and child compare body parts for size—big and little.
Cue	My hand is big.
	Your hand is little.
	Who has the big foot? etc.
SC V 9.2	Adult places large and small kinds of food Evaluation before child.
	Adult and child sort food according to size.
Material	Food.
Cue	The raisins are small.
	The melon is big.

SC V 9.3	The adult will read to child from books that deal with big and little.	Evaluation
Materials	Picture books.	
SC V 9.4	The adult will help the child see big and little objects throughout the home and neighborhood.	Evaluation
SC V 9.5	Adult responds to child's effort with touches, smiles, and pleasure.	Evaluation
SC V 9.6	Use PROGRAMMING PROCEDURE if necessary.	Evaluation
Material	Reward.	

SC V 9.7	Adult shows child a small balloon and calls it "little." Adult blows up balloon and calls it "big." Adult lets out the air and calls it "little" again. Repeat.	Evaluation
Material	Balloon.	
Cue	Now it's big. Now it's little. Balloon.	

	Behavioral Objectives	SC V 10
SC V 10	TURNS BOOK PAGES ONE AT A TIME	Comment
General Objective	Development of eye-hand coordination.	
Specific Objective	The child will turn the pages of a book one by one.	

Activities		
SC V 10.1	Continue as in PFM III 26.	Evaluation
SC V 10.2	Adult responds to child's effort with touches, smiles, and pleasure.	Evaluation

Behavioral Objectives	SC V 11

SC V 11	BUILDS TOWER OF EIGHT CUBES	Comment
General Objective	Development of cognitive relationships.	
Specific Objective	When given cubes, the child will build a tower of eight cubes.	

Activities		
SC V 11.1	Teach as in PFM III 23.	Evaluation

Behavioral Objectives	SC V 12

SC V 12	BUILDS TOWER OF NINE TO TEN CUBES	Comment
General Objective	Development of cognitive relationships.	
Specific Objective	When given cubes, the child will build a tower of nine to ten cubes.	

Activities		
SC V 12.1	Teach as in PFM III 23.	Evaluation

Behavioral Objectives	SC V 13

SC V 13	IMITATES BRIDGE	Comment
General Objective	Development of cognitive and imitative behavior.	
Specific Objective	The child will be able to imitate adult and make "bridges."	

Activities		
SC V 13.1	Show child how to draw "bridges."	Evaluation
	Help guide child's hand on adult drawing and then for child's own efforts.	
	Child will imitate adult.	

Materials	Crayons.
	Paper.
	Fabric or sandpaper form.
Cue	This is a bridge.
	Feel the bridge.
	Make a bridge with your fingers.
Comment	Point out bridges or arches in general environment.

| SC V 13.2 | Use PROGRAMMING PROCEDURE if necessary. | Evaluation |

| Material | Reward. |

| SC V 13.3 | Adult responds to child's effort with touches, smiles, and pleasure. | Evaluation |

	Behavioral Objectives	SC V 14
SC V 14	IMITATES CROSS	Comment
General Objective	Development of cognitive and imitative behavior.	
Specific Objective	The child will be able to imitate adult and make "crosses."	

Activities

SC V 14.1	Show child how to draw "crosses."	Evaluation
	Help guide child's hand on adult drawing and child's efforts.	
	Child will imitate adult.	
Materials	Crayons.	
	Paper.	
	Fabric or sandpaper form.	
Cue	This is a cross.	
	Feel the cross.	
	Make a cross.	
Comment	Point out crosses in general environment.	

SC V 14.2	Use PROGRAMMING PROCEDURE if necessary.	Evaluation
Material	Reward.	
SC V 14.3	Adult responds to child's effort with touches, smiles, and pleasure.	Evaluation

Behavioral Objectives	SC V 15

SC V 15	FINDS BOOK BY NAME	Comment
General Objective	Development of memory operations.	
Specific Objective	The child will find her book by the name.	

Activities

SC V 15.1	Include books in naming games as in L III 22.	Evaluation
Materials	Books.	
Cue	This book is called _____ .	
	Go get _____ .	
Comment	Include books from UNITS ACTIVITIES.	

Behavioral Objectives	SC V 16

SC V 16	RECOGNIZES TEN SHAPES	Comment
General Objective	Development of more complex cognitive products through manipulation of figures and symbols.	
Specific Objective	The child will recognize ten shapes in his environment.	

Activities

| *SC V   16.1* | Teach as outlined in UNIT ACTIVITIES and as in SC V 27. | Evaluation |
| *SC V   16.2* | Encourage child to name the shapes when possible. | Evaluation |

| *SC V 16.3* | Adult responds to child's efforts with touches, smiles, and pleasure. | Evaluation |

| | Behavioral Objectives | SC V 17 |

SC V 17	RECOGNIZES ELEVEN COLORS	Comment
General Objective	Development of cognition, memory through figural and symbolic activities.	
Specific Objective	The child will recognize eleven colors in her environment.	

Activities

SC V 17.1	Teach as outlined in UNIT ACTIVITIES, and as in SC V 27.	Evaluation
SC V 17.2	Encourage child to name the colors when possible.	Evaluation
SC V 17.3	Adult responds to child's effort with touches, smiles, and pleasure.	Evaluation

| | Behavioral Objectives | SC V 18 |

SC V 18	RECOGNIZES NUMBERS ONE TO TEN	Comment
General Objective	Development of cognition memory through figural and symbolic activities.	
Specific Objective	The child will recognize numbers from zero through ten.	

Activities

SC V 18.1	Teach as outlined in UNIT ACTIVITIES and in SC V 27.	Evaluation
SC V 18.2	Encourage child to name the numbers when possible.	Evaluation
SC V 18.3	Adult responds to child's effort with touches, smiles, and pleasure.	Evaluation

SC V 19	RECOGNIZES PHONETIC SYMBOLS	Comment
General Objective	Development of cognition and memory through figural and symbolic activities.	
Specific Objective	The child will recognize phonetic symbols.	

Activities

SC V 19.1	Teach as outlined in UNIT ACTIVITIES and as in SC V 27.	Evaluation
SC V 19.2	Encourage child to name the symbols when able to do so.	Evaluation
SC V 19.3	Adult responds to child's effort with touches, smiles, and pleasure.	Evaluation

SC V 20	MATCHES SMELLS	Comment
General Objective	Development of cognition and classification through sensorial activities.	
Specific Objective	The child will be able to match smells.	

Activities

SC V 20.1	Adult pours small amount of spices in little piles on tray.	Evaluation
	Child tastes and smells the spices.	
	Adult names the spices.	
	Child smells and names.	
Materials	Spices, onions, vanilla, etc.	
Cue	This is _____ .	
SC V 20.2	Child smells spices through holes in film tins.	Evaluation
	Adult and child match smells.	
	Child matches smells alone.	

Materials	Spice bottles.	
	Film tins.	
	Scented sponges.	
	Scented candles.	
Cue	This is _____ .	
SC V 20.3	Adult responds to child's effort with touches, smiles, and pleasure.	Evaluation

Behavioral Objectives   SC V   21

SC V 21	MATCHES SOUNDS	Comment
General Objective	Development of cognition and classification through sensorial activities.	
Specific Objective	The child will be able to match sounds of objects.	

Activities		
SC V 21.1	Child listens to sounds of objects being shaken in container.	Evaluation
	Adult names sound; child shakes.	
	Child names sounds.	
Materials	Film tins, buttons, water, salt, BBs, etc.	
Cue	This sounds like _____ .	
SC V 21.2	Adult and child listen and then match sounds.	Evaluation
	Child matches sounds.	
Materials	As above.	
Cue	As above.	
SC V 21.3	Adult and child listen for sounds in the environment.	Evaluation
SC V 21.4	Adult responds to child's effort with touches, smiles, and pleasure.	Evaluation

SC V 22	MATCHES TEXTURES	Comment
General Objective	Development of cognition, evaluation, and classification through sensorial activities.	
Specific Objective	The child will be able to match textures.	

Activities

SC V 22.1	Adult shows child two objects of different textures. Child touches, shuts eyes, and touches again.	Evaluation
Materials	Wallpaper, fabrics, sandpaper.	
Cue	This is rough. This is smooth.	
SC V 22.2	Adult shows child several objects, two of each texture. Adult helps child sort. Child sorts alone.	Evaluation
Materials	As above.	
Cue	As above.	
Comment	Sorting sets may be made for general matching, textures, shapes, numbers, etc.	

SC V 23	COUNTS TO TEN	Comment
General Objective	Development of cognition and memory for units, classes, and relations products.	
Specific Objective	The child will be able to count to ten.	

Activities

SC V 23.1	Teach as outlined in UNIT ACTIVITIES and in SC V 27.	Evaluation
SC V 23.2	Encourage child to count objects in the environment whenever possible.	Evaluation
SC V 23.3	Adult responds to child's effort with touches, smiles, and pleasure.	Evaluation

| | Behavioral Objectives | SC V 24 |

SC V 24	NAMES PHONETIC SYMBOLS	Comment
General Objective	Development of cognition and memory through figural and symbolic activities.	
Specific Objective	The child will name phonetic symbols.	

Activities

SC V 24.1	Teach as outlined in UNIT ACTIVITIES and in SC V 27.	Evaluation
SC V 24.2	Encourage child to sound the symbols in books.	Evaluation
SC V 24.3	Adult responds to child's effort with touches, smiles, and pleasure.	Evaluation

| | Behavioral Objectives | SC V 25 |

SC V 25	RECOGNIZES ONE OR MORE PRINTED WORDS	Comment
General Objective	Development of cognition and memory through figural, symbolic, and semantic activities.	
Specific Objective	The child will recognize one or more printed words.	

Activities

SC V 25.1	Teach words as outlined in UNIT AC-TIVITIES and as in SC V 27.	Evaluation
SC V 25.2	Encourage child to name sounds and words found in general environment.	Evaluation
SC V 25.3	Adult responds to child's effort with touches, smiles, and pleasure.	Evaluation

	Behavioral Objectives	SC V 26

SC V 26	SORTS BY BIG/LITTLE, COLOR, SHAPE, OR TEXTURE	Comment
General Objective	Development of multiple operations for multiple products through manipulation of figures and symbols.	
Specific Objective	The child will be able to sort objects by size, color, shape, or texture.	

Activities

SC V 26.1	Teach as outlined in SC V 22.	Evaluation
Materials	Buttons, fabrics, nuts and bolts, objects; rick-rack, macaroni, beans, etc.	
Cue	As appropriate.	
Comment	Use as games.	
SC V 26.2	Adult responds to child's effort with touches, smiles, and pleasure.	Evaluation

	Behavioral Objectives	SC V 27

SC V 27	PARTICIPATES IN UNIT ACTIVITIES	Comment
General Objective	Development of child's knowledge of world around him.	
Specific Objective	The child will participate in various unit activities presented by parents.	

Activities

SC V 27.0   UNIT ACTIVITIES PROCEDURE.

Make paper objects for wall, mobile, and play.

Find toys that fit the units.

Find actual things that fit the units.

Find small stories and books about the unit (including flannel boards).

Find small objects and word cards for readers.

Find pictures (find in art, photos, calendars, magazines, etc.)

Find movies and filmstrips if available.

Arts and crafts.

Use games.

Use songs.

Use fingerplays.

Use poetry.

Use dramatizations.

Take the child to see the "real thing." Talk with the child while you look and learn.

Draw little pictures and write a little book for the child about what happened. It is great if you can take Polaroid pictures on the outing.

Remember these rules when you write the little book.

1. Keep it about the child's experience.
2. Don't start all the sentences with "the."
3. Make some sentences "long," some "short."
4. Make the sentences as different as you can.
5. Print the sentences in *big* letters—one half inch to an inch.

Comment   There is an example of a book for a "body" unit in the patterns section of this handbook.

Unit Ideas

Body	Toys
Shapes	Food
Colors	Health

Numbers	Transportation
Alphabet	Farm
Family	City
Clothing	Community Workers
Furniture	Holidays
Household Objects	Tools
House and Garden	Cowboys and Indians
Money	Shopping
Telling Time	Weather
Daddy's Work	Birds
Family Hobbies	Farm Animals
Plans	Zoo Animals
Insects	Sports
Sky-Universe	Stories and Nursery
Musical Instruments	Rhymes
	Geography

Favorite historical men or times

Favorite religious characters or stories

SC V 27.1 COLORS UNIT

Colors are easily taught through matching activities during the early years of life. Concentrate on one color for about a week. Put the big color on the walls, small ones on mobiles and toys. Combine with color books, toys, clothing, packages, paper, etc. This method is also applicable to older children.

When basic colors are well established in your child's mind and vocabulary, continue to teach noting light and dark, and various shades or degrees of colors. Paint cards are helpful.

Games may be made up such as special days for special colors. Or colors to wear on special days. Call children by colors; use matching sets for older children.

SC V 27.2 NUMERALS UNIT

Zero to twelve months: Poetry and songs at feeding time (One Little, Two Little, Three Little Indians; One Two, Buckle My Shoe; songs currently sung on educational TV programs), stuffed numbers, etc.

Activities

Six to twelve months: Use unit materials including large numbers on walls, small numbers on mobiles, in play, numbers books, blocks, etc. Introduce one at a time and then contrasting ones. Members of the family can wear numbers. *Outline with arms and finger* (including pencil position for fingers). Matching, blowing, fetching games may also be enjoyed now. Try stuffed number toys.

With older children just starting to learn numbers, begin in the same manner as outlined above. Coordinate with educational TV programs or with special occasions and interests.

Example: The fourth birthday: fours on
cakes, walls, favors, four bites
of cake, four cookies each,
etc.

Sandpaper numerals and other materials can be modified and made at home following the descriptions of Maria Montessori (1965) and Elizabeth Hainstock (1968).

NUMERICAL CONCEPTS

It is not enough for a child to recite her numerals or just recognize them. The child must also have some understanding of the meaning of the words and symbols. This process takes some time but can be used to make a lot of fun activities in the home and even can help with taking turns or other family squabbles.

Activities: count kisses, toys, bites, items grouped together, dice games for taking snacks, or taking turns helping mother cook. Special materials can be made as described in Montessori and Hainstock; ask questions continually, "How many boys are here? How many girls? How many children all together? How many crackers do you want?" Choose three numbers. (Pull a card and take what is says). Clapping games. Saying counting rhymes or listening to others count. Count real objects in nature, and count money. Grouping for games and noting things in pairs. Use ordinals as common vocabulary. Teach zero and use sets.

Addition, subtraction, multiplication, and division can all be taught through daily experiences, but especially through the use of thousands, hundreds, tens, and ones as outlined by Montessori.

SC V 27.3

READING

Reading readiness may be taught in the first phase of development. It is begun as mother reads to her infant at feeding time. Mother and father play babbling games and even give the baby phonetic symbols for the baby's sounds. Late in the first year, units may be begun or words put up on the wall. Remember black and white cards with phonetic symbols during the first months of life.

There are two approaches to teaching reading and both work for some people.

Phonetics—this is taught through the unit method and games.
Word Identification—may be taught easily. Just tell the child
the name of something she is interested in and give her a card
with the name printed on it. Read to the child and point out
words in books (best with large words) that she asks about.
Combine the approaches by putting the phonetic symbols just
above a word in books or on cards of interest to the child. They
will be absorbed and learned together. Teach the alphabet with
big letters, phonetics with the small letters.

1. Make consonants of blue paper, vowels of red paper; cover
   with clear contact paper.
2. Read books of interest and on level of child.
3. Write words on index cards for new toys, etc.
4. Make sandpaper letters for the baby to feel. These can be
   purchased.
5. Try "Button Button" games using symbols, scavenger hunts
   for sounds, words, numbers, and shapes.
6. Make word boxes with matching words on cards and little
   objects.
7. Play written instruction games.
8. Write experience books or unit books.
9. When child is reading, make "grammar" cards with nouns,
   verbs, etc. on different colors. Then let child make sentences
   and see how grammar works.

The general learning environment of your home will prepare the
child to read and special help is given by (1) reading to the child a
great deal, (2) enjoying poetry, (3) working on shapes units or
recognition of geometric solids, (4) constant naming and labeling
process including the continual use of language for the child in
the home, (5) answering child's questions about letters and words
just as you answer her other questions.

SC V 27.4   GEOMETRY

Shapes and geometric solids may be introduced as a unit during
the first year using the wall, mobile, and toys. Follow the same
procedure with the older child.

Begin with contrasting shapes and then move on to more and
more advanced shapes or solids. Always match with similar
shapes and solid objects found in the home and community.
Show enthusiasm for these discoveries. *This work is most helpful
for future reading skills.* Shapes may be ironed onto little "mitts"
for babies or clothes for older tots, quiet books, etc.

	Behavioral Objectives	LI I

LI 1	REFLEX VOCALIZATIONS	Comment
General Objective	Encouragement of reflex vocalizations.	
Specific Objective	Infant will increase the amount of reflex vocalizations.	

Activities		
LI 1.1	Adult responds to infant's effort with touches, smiles, and pleasure.	Evaluation
LI 1.2	Adult imitates infant's sounds.	Evaluation
Cue	Mostly vowels.	
Comment	If infant has sensorial impairment, use hands of infant and adult on mouth, jaw, and throat areas.	
LI 1.3	PROGRAMMING PROCEDURE.	Evaluation
Material	Food as desired.	

	Behavioral Objectives	LI 2

LI 2	THROATY NOISES	Comment
General Objective	Encourage the production of infant's throaty noises.	
Specific Objective	Infant will increase the amount of throaty noises.	

Activities		
LI 2.1	Adult responds to infant's effort with touches, smiles, and enthusiastic pleasure.	Evaluation
Comment	If infant has sensory impairment, touch hands of infant and adult on mouth, jaw, and throat areas of both being used in activity.	
LI 2.2	Adult imitates infant's sounds.	Evaluation

| LI 2.3 | Put slight pressure on infant's stomach to produce sound. Follow with PROGRAMMING PROCEDURE. | Evaluation |
| Material | Food as desired. | |

| | Behavioral Objectives | LI 3 |

LI 3	INDICATES BODILY DISCOMFORT BY CHANGE IN PITCH	Comment
General Objective	Encourage infant's effort to make change in pitch as a sign of bodily discomfort.	
Specific Objective	Infant will increase the use of change of pitch as an indication of bodily discomfort.	

Activities

LI 3.1	Adult immediately responds to infant's change of pitch. Give appropriate care quickly.	Evaluation
Cue	General talk while caring for infant, that is, "You want your diapers changed, don't you?" "You are hungry, aren't you?"	
Comment	During the early months of life, it is important to act upon an infant's cries for help as quickly as possible. This is especially important with a handicapped child. It will encourage her assertiveness and trust in her effect on her environment.	

| | Behavioral Objectives | LI 4 |

LI 4	DIMINUATION OF ACTIVITY FOR LOUD OR UNUSUAL SOUNDS	Comment
General Objective	Encouragement of infant attending to loud or unusual sounds.	
Specific Objective	The infant will increase the degree of attending to loud or unusual sounds.	

Activities

LI 4.1	Adult makes sounds with object on either side of the infant's head 8–18 inches.	Evaluation
	Repeat on opposite side.	
Materials	Bells, rattles, pans, etc.	
Cue	Just sound the object at first. Later, cue, "Listen."	
	And later yet, "Listen to the bell."	
Comment	Eventually, move sounding object farther from infant's head.	
LI 4.2	Say infant's name 8–15 inches on either side of head.	Evaluation
	"Shape" infant to turn head to sounds of name.	
Cue	Infant's name.	

Behavioral Objectives   L I   5

LI 5	BABBLING AND COOING EFFORTS BEGIN	Comment
General Objective	Encouragement of babbling and cooing efforts.	
Specific Objective	The infant will increase his production of babbling and cooing sounds.	

Activities

LI 5.1	Adult responds to infant's effort with smiles, touches, and pleasure.	Evaluation
LI 5.2	Adult imitates infant's sounds as a game.	Evaluation
Cue	Infant's sounds may include m, p, b.	
LI 5.3	Gently roll or bounce infant to help make sounds.	Evaluation
LI 5.4	Place hands of infant and adult on mouth, jaw, and throat areas of both while making sounds.	Evaluation

LI 5.5	Place one hand on infant's mouth area to help shape sound.	Evaluation
	Put slight, quick pressure on infant's ribs or stomach to help elicit sound.	
	Reward and repeat.	
LI 5.6	PROGRAMMING PROCEDURE.	Evaluation
Material	Food as preferred.	

Behavioral Objectives   L I   6

LI 6	REPETITION OF SOUNDS FOR STIMULATION AND PLEASURE	Comment
General Objective	Encouragement of infant's repetition of sounds for stimulation and pleasure.	
Specific Objective	Infant will increase the repetition of sounds made for self-stimulation and pleasure.	

Activities

LI 6.1	Adult responds to infant's effort with smiles, touches, and pleasure.	Evaluation
LI 6.2	Adult imitates infant's sounds as a game.	Evaluation
LI 6.3	Make tape of infant's own sounds and play back to infant.	Evaluation
	Record sounds of other infants in same general developmental range and play for infant.	
Materials	Tape recorder, tape, microphone.	

Behavioral Objectives   L I   7

LI 7	FACIAL AND/OR VOCAL CHANGE OF EXPRESSION WHEN SPOKEN TO	Comment
General Objective	Encouragement of change of facial expression and/or vocalization when spoken to.	
Specific Objective	Infant will increase the amount of facial expression and/or vocalization when spoken to.	

Activities

L I 7.1	Adult responds to infant's effort with smiles, touches, and pleasure.	Evaluation
L I 7.2	Adult imitates infant's sounds as a game.	Evaluation
L I 7.3	Place mirror eight to fifteen inches from infant's face.	Evaluation
	Infant observes her own features during vocalization.	
Material	Nonbreakable infant mirror.	

Behavioral Objectives   L I 8

L I 8	LAUGHS AND SQUEALS	Comment
General Objective	Encouragement of infant's laughter and squeals.	
Specific Objective	The infant will increase amount of laughter and squealing vocalizations.	

Activities

L I 8.1	Adult responds to infant's effort with smiles, touches, and pleasure.	Evaluation
L I 8.2	Adult imitates infant's sounds as a game.	Evaluation
L I 8.3	Play favorite games with infant to elicit laughter and squeals; that is, tickle, bounce on knees, etc.	Evaluation
Cue	Make traditional sounds for such games.	
	Adult laughs at appropriate time.	
L I 8.4	PROGRAMMING PROCEDURE.	Evaluation
Material	Food as desired.	

Behavioral Objectives   L I 9

L I 9	DIFFERENTIATED CRYING	Comment
General Objective	Encouragement of differentiated crying.	

Specific Objective	The infant will increase in the production of differentiated crying.	

Activities		
LI 9.1	Adult immediately responds to infant's change in cry sound.	Evaluation
	Give appropriate care quickly.	
Cue	General talk while caring for infant, that is, "You want your diapers changed, don't you?"	
	"You are hungry, aren't you?", etc.	
Comment	During the early months of life, it is important to act upon an infant's cries for help as quickly as possible. This is especially important with a handicapped child. It will encourage her assertiveness and trust in her effect on her environment.	

LI 9.2	PROGRAMMING PROCEDURE.	Evaluation
Material	Food as desired.	

	Behavioral Objectives	LI 10

LI 10	ATTENDS TO ADULT MOUTH	Comment
General Objective	Encouragement of infant's attention to adult mouth.	
Specific Objective	Infant will increase attentiveness to adult mouth when being spoken to.	

Activities		
LI 10.1	Adult talks to infant with faces eight to twelve inches apart.	Evaluation
	Adult slowly and clearly forms sounds of interest to infant.	
Cue	m, p, etc.	
	Name of infant.	
	Name of toy.	
	Names of family members.	

L I 10.2	Adult responds to infant's effort with smiles, touches, and pleasure.	Evaluation
L I 10.3	If infant does not attend well, use PRO-GRAMMING PROCEDURE.	Evaluation
Material	Food as desired.	

Behavioral Objectives   L I   11

L I 11	BABBLING, COOING, CHUCKLING	Comment
General Objective	Encouragement of infant's babbling, cooing, and chuckling.	
Specific Objective	Infant will increase the amount of babbling, cooing, and chuckling vocalizations.	

Activities

L I 11.1	Adult responds to infant's effort with smiles, touches, and pleasure.	Evaluation
L I 11.2	If infant has sensory impairment, touch hands of infant and adult on mouth, jaw, and throat areas of both being used in activity.	Evaluation
L I 11.3	PHONETIC SYMBOL PROCEDURE. 1. Imitate infant's sounds. 2. Adult imitates infant's sounds while placing infant's hand on adult source of sound during vocalization. 3. Place infant's hand on source of infant's sound during vocalization. 4. Give infant phonetic symbol for sound being made. Allow to play.	Evaluation
Materials	Phonetic symbols m, b, p (probable).	
Cue	"Here is your *b*." "Chew your b." "Where is your *b*?"	
Comment	Environmental use of symbols. 1. Introduce with grasping reflex. 2. Leave symbols in infant's crib or play area or general environment. 3. Put symbols on wall at eye level of infant.	

4. Hang symbols on mobile in view of infant's eyes.
5. Adult directs infant's hand over symbols.
6. Adult directs infant's limbs to make shapes of symbols.
7. Adult emphasizes symbol and sound in general daily environment in presence of the infant.

Behavioral Objectives   L I   12

L I 12	MAKES RESPONSIVE SOUNDS WHEN SPOKEN TO	Comment
General Objective	Encouragement of responsive vocalization when infant is spoken to.	
Specific Objective	Infant will increase the amount of responsive sounds when spoken to.	

Activities

L I 12.1	Adult spends more time talking to infant. Adult places face eight to fifteen inches in front of infant's face while talking.	Evaluation
L I 12.2	Adult responds to infant's effort with smiles, touches, and pleasure.	Evaluation
L I 12.3	Adult imitates infant's sounds as a game.	Evaluation
L I 12.4	Adult stresses infant's name while talking and playing with infant.	Evaluation

Behavioral Objectives   L I   13

L I 13	RECOGNIZE FAMILIAR HUMAN VOICE	Comment
General Objective	Encouragement of infant's recognition of the sound of a familiar human voice.	
Specific Objective	The infant will become alert when she hears a familiar human voice.	

Activities

L I 13.1	Adult calls infant by name when nearby.	Evaluation
	Adult responds to infant's effort with smiles, touches, and pleasure.	
Cue	Name. Funny sounds. General talk.	
L I 13.2	Adult calls infant by name or makes sounds farther away from infant.	Evaluation
	A second adult (nearby) rewards infant with smiles, touches, and pleasure when infant alerts.	
Cue	Name. Funny sounds. General talk.	
L I 13.3	PROGRAMMING PROCEDURE.	Evaluation
Material	Food as desired.	

	Behavioral Objectives	**L I 14**

L I 14	LOCALIZES SOUNDS	Comment
General Objective	Develop ability of infant to localize sounds in his environment.	If infant's impairment hinders response, a second adult should help by shaping.
Specific Objective	The infant will increase his ability to localize sounds in his environment.	

Activities

L I 14.1	Adult sounds bell or rattle in area around head of infant.	Evaluation
	Infant looks for source of sound.	
Materials	Bells, rattles, chimes, pots, and spoons, etc.	
Cue	Listen, look.	

LI 14.2	Adult responds to infant's effort with smiles, touches, and pleasure.	Evaluation
LI 14.3	Adult moves farther from infant and sounds bell or rattles.	Evaluation
	Infant looks for source of sound.	
Materials	Bells, rattles, chimes, pots, and spoons, etc.	
Cue	Look, listen.	
LI 14.4	Adult moves and hides in and around room. Adult sounds toy.	Evaluation
	Infant looks for source of sound.	
Materials	Bells, rattles, chimes, pots, and spoons, etc.	
Cues	Look.	

Behavioral Objectives	LI 15

LI 15	RESPONDS WITH LAUGHTER	Comment
General Objective	Encouragement of laughter in response to others.	
Specific Objective	The infant will show ability to laugh when entertained by others.	

Activities

LI 15.1	Adult responds to infant's effort with smiles, touches, and pleasure.	Evaluation
LI 15.2	Adult imitates infant's sounds as a game.	Evaluation
Cue	Laugh.	
LI 15.3	Play favorite games with infant to elicit laughter and squeals, that is, tickle, bounce on knees, "horsie" game, etc.	Evaluation
Cue	Make traditional sounds for such games.	
	Laugh aloud at appropriate time.	
	Say "laugh."	

LI 15.4	If infant has sensory impairment, touch hands of infant and adult on mouth, jaw, and throat areas of both being used in activity.	Evaluation
LI 15.5	PROGRAMMING PROCEDURE.	Evaluation
Material	Food as desired.	

Behavioral Objectives   L I 16

LI 16	BABBLES SEVERAL SOUNDS IN ONE BREATH	Comment
General Objective	Encouragement of infant's ability to babble several sounds in one breath.	
Specific Objective	The infant will increase in his ability to babble several sounds in one breath.	

Activities

LI 16.1	Adult responds to infant's effort with smiles, touches, and pleasure.	Evaluation
LI 16.2	Adult imitates infant's sounds as a game.	Evaluation
LI 16.3	PHONETIC SYMBOL PROCEDURE 1. Imitate infant's sounds. 2. Adult imitates infant's sounds while placing infant's hand on adult source of sound during vocalization. 3. Place infant's hand on source of infant's sound during vocalization. 4. Give infant phonetic symbol for sound being made. Allow to play.	Evaluation
Materials	Appropriate phonetic symbols.	

Behavioral Objectives   L I 17

LI 17	ATTENDS TO LANGUAGE ENRICHMENT ACTIVITIES	Comment
General Objective	Expose infant to lullabies, poems, nursery rhymes, and simple songs and stories.	

Specific Objective	The infant will attend to familiar lullabies, poems, nursery rhymes, and simple songs and stories.

Activities

L I 17.1	Sing favorite lullabies and songs at bedtime and throughout the day.
Materials	Children's songbooks. Traditional songs of childhood.
Comment	Repeat the same melodies so the infant may begin to become familiar with recognizable patterns of sound.
L I 17.2	Tape record favorite songs and lullabies. Play throughout the day near infant.
Materials	Portable cassette, 4 inch or 8 inch track tapes, and recorder.
L I 17.3	Repeat favorite nursery rhymes and poems for infant throughout the day.
Materials	Texts of traditional children's poems and nursery rhymes.
L I 17.4	Add favorite poems and nursery rhymes to tape as mentioned above. Play near infant throughout the day.
L I 17.5	Read very simple and short picture stories to infant. This may be done at feeding time. Hold the picture so infant can see if possible. Tools: Simple handboard or picture books. Note: A very positive association with books may be developed by reading at feeding times. Note: find very simple, durable, and short picture books. Include them as a part of the infant's life during the first three phases or periods of development.
Materials	Portable cassette, four inch or eight inch track tapes, and recorder.
Comment	It may be comforting to infant if tape recorder is softly turned on in room before infant begins to awaken from nap.

L II 1	TURNS HEAD TOWARD SPEAKING VOICE	Comment
General Objective	Encouragement of infant's ability to locate source of speech.	
Specific Objective	Infant will turn head toward speaking voice.	

Activities

L II 1.1	Adult makes noises or calls infant's name eight to twelve inches from left, right, front, and back of infant's head.	Evaluation
	Infant turns head to see source of sound.	
Cue	Name. Look, here I am.	

L II 1.2	Use PROGRAMMING PROCEDURE.	Evaluation
Material	Food as desired.	

L II 1.3	Adult moves farther from infant and calls.	Evaluation
	Infant turns head to see source of sound.	
Cue	Name. Look, here I am.	

L II 1.4	Adult moves and hides in and around room.	Evaluation
	Infant looks for source of sound.	
Cue	Name. Look, here I am.	

Behavioral Objectives   L II   2

L II 2	HIGH SQUEAL	Comment
General Objective	Encouragement of high squeal.	To be observed.
Specific Objective	Infant will sound a high squeal.	

Activities

| L II 2.1 | Play games with infant that generally cause high squeal sound. These games could include tickling, "I'm going to get you," hiding, etc. | Evaluation |

| | Behavioral Objectives | L II 3 |

L II 3	VOCAL PLAY	Comment
General Objective	Encouragement of vocal play.	
Specific Objective	Infant will increase amount of vocal play.	

Activities

L II 3.1	Make phonetic sounds with infant. Use two at a time (da-da, ma-ma, etc.) Follow PHONETIC SYMBOL PROCEDURE.	Evaluation
L II 3.2	Adult responds to infant's effort with smiles, touches, and pleasure.	Evaluation
L II 3.3	Adult imitates infant's sounds as a game.	Evaluation
L II 3.4	TAPE PROCEDURE. Make tape of infant's own sounds and play back to infant. Record sounds of other infants in same general developmental range and play for infant.	Evaluation
Materials	Tape recorder, tape, microphone.	

| | Behavioral Objectives | L II 4 |

| L II 4 | IMITATES COUGH | Comment |
| General Objective | Encouragement of infant's abilities to imitate cough. | |

Specific Objective	Infant will increase ability to imitate cough.	"Cough Game" can begin as early as two months.

Activities

L II 4.1	Adult coughs. Infant imitates cough. Repeat.	Evaluation
Comment	Treat as a game.	
L II 4.2	Adult responds to infant's effort with smiles, touches, and pleasure.	Evaluation
L II 4.3	PROGRAMMING PROCEDURE if necessary to encourage Cough Games.	Evaluation
Material	Food as desired.	

	Behavioral Objectives	L II 5

L II 5	IMITATES PROTRUSION OF TONGUE	Comment
General Objective	Encouragement of infant's abilities to imitate protrusion of tongue.	
Specific Objective	Infant will imitate protrusion of tongue.	

Activities

L II 5.1	Adult faces infant—eight to twelve inches away. Adult sticks out tongue. Infant imitates. TONGUE GAME.	Evaluation
Comment	Treat as a game.	
L II 5.2	Adult responds to infant's effort with smiles, touches, and pleasure.	Evaluation
L II 5.3	Wash adult hands. Use fingers to touch infant's tongue. Guide tongue to "stick out."	Evaluation

L II 5.4	Place a drop of corn syrup on tip of infant's tongue when it comes out from mouth.	Evaluation
L II 5.5	PROGRAMMING PROCEDURE.	Evaluation
Materials	Corn syrup, favorite foods as desired.	

Behavioral Objectives		L II 6

L II 6	COMBINES SOUNDS AS MAMA AND DADA	Comment
General Objective	Encouragement of infant's ability to combine vowel and consonant sounds.	
Specific Objective	Infant will increase in ability to combine vowel and consonant sounds.	

Activities

L II 6.1	Adult responds to infant's effort with smiles, touches, and pleasure.	Evaluation
L II 6.2	Adult imitates infant's sounds as in a game.	Evaluation
L II 6.3	Adult makes sounds combining consonants and vowels that infant is observed to make.	Evaluation
	Adult combines these sounds in new ways as a game.	
L II 6.4	Use PHONETIC SYMBOL PROCEDURE.	Evaluation
L II 6.5	Use TOUCH PROCEDURE.	Evaluation
L II 6.6	Use PROGRAMMING PROCEDURE.	Evaluation
Material	Food as desired.	
L II 6.6	TAPE PROCEDURE. Make tape of infant's own sounds and play back to infant.	Evaluation
	Record sounds of other infants in same general developmental range and play for infant.	
Materials	Tape recorder, tape, microphone.	

Behavioral Objectives	L II 7

L II 7	GESTURES AND BABBLES TO OBJECTS	Comment
General Objective	Provide infant with opportunities to talk and gesture to objects.	To be observed.
Specific Objective	Infant will talk and gesture to objects.	

Activltles		
L II 7.1	Give infant variety of toys and sensorial UNIT MATERIALS.	Evaluation
	Change them frequently.	
	Observe infant during play.	
	Note if infant talks and gestures to the objects.	
Materials	Toys in general. Sensory UNIT MATERIALS.	

Behavioral Objectives	L II 8

L II 8	CRIES WITH "MUM-MUM-MUM"	Comment
General Objective	Encouragement of infant's ability to say "mum-mum-mum," especially when crying.	
Specific Objective	Infant will increase use of "mum-mum-mum" when crying.	

Activities		
L II 8.1	Adult responds to infant's effort with smiles, touches, and pleasure.	Evaluation
L II 8.2	Adult imitates infant's sounds as in a game.	Evaluation
L II 8.3	TOUCH PROCEDURE.	Evaluation
	If infant has sensory impairment, touch hands of infant and adult on mouth, jaw, and throat area of both being used in activity.	

L II .8.4	TAPE PROCEDURE.	Evaluation
	Make tape of infant's own sounds and play back to infant.	
	Record sounds of other infants in same general developmental range and play for infant.	
Materials	Tape recorder, tape, microphone.	

Behavioral Objectives

L II 9

L II 9	LISTENS TO SELF	Comment
General Objective	Encouragement of infant's ability to listen to himself.	To be observed.
Specific Objective	Infant will increase attention to his own vocalizations.	

Activities		
L II 9.1	Adult responds to infant's effort with smiles, touches, and pleasure.	Evaluation
L II 9.2	Adult imitates infant's sounds as in a game.	Evaluation
L II 9.3	TAPE PROCEDURE—tape infant's own sound and play back to infant.	Evaluation
	Record sounds of other infants in same general developmental range and play for infant.	
Materials	Tape recorder, tape, microphone.	

Behavioral Objectives

L II 10

L II 10	MAKES SERIAL VOWEL SOUNDS	Comment
General Objective	Encouragement of infant's abilities to make vowel sounds in a series.	
Specific Objective	Infant will increase in ability to make vowel sounds in a series.	

Activities

L II 10.1	Adult responds to infant's effort with smiles, touches, and pleasure.	Evaluation
L II 10.2	Adult imitates infant's sounds as in a game.	Evaluation
L II 10.3	Adult makes variations of infant's vowel patterns. See if infant imitates adult patterns.	Evaluation
L II 10.4	Use PHONETIC SYMBOL PROCEDURE.	Evaluation
Materials	Vowels.	
Cue	Vowels being sounded.	
L II 10.5	TAPE PROCEDURE—tape infant's own sounds and play back to infant.	Evaluation
	Record sounds of other infants in same general developmental range and play for infant.	
Materials	Tape recorder, tape, microphone.	

Behavioral Objectives	L II 11

L II 11	SINGLE SYLLABLE DA, MA	Comment
General Objective	Encouragement of infant's ability to make single syllable da, ma.	
Specific Objective	Infant will increase in ability to make single syllable da, ma.	

Activities

L II 11.1	Adult responds to infant's effort with smiles, touches, and pleasure.	Evaluation
L II 11.2	Adult imitates infant's sounds as in a game.	Evaluation
L II 11.3	Adult makes sounds in various patterns using RHYTHM PROCEDURE.	Evaluation
	See if infant imitates adult.	
L II 11.4	Use PHONETIC SYMBOL PROCEDURE.	Evaluation
L II 11.5	TOUCH PROCEDURE II.	Evaluation

L II 11.6	PROGRAMMING PROCEDURE.	Evaluation
Material	Food as desired.	

L II 11.7	TAPE PROCEDURE.	Evaluation

	Behavioral Objectives	*L II 12*

L II 12	GUMS OBJECTS	Comment
General Objective		To be observed.
Specific Objective		

Activities

L II 12.1	Provide opportunity for infant to bite and chew toys.	Evaluation
	Apply corn syrup on toys.	
Materials	Soft rubber toys, tasty substances.	
Cue	Bite the _____ .	

	Behavioral Objectives	*L II 13*

L II 13	TONGUE PLAY	Comment
General Objective	Encouragement of infant's ability to play with tongue.	
Specific Objective	Infant will increase in ability to play with tongue.	

Activities

L II 13.1	Adult responds to infant's effort with touches, smiles, and pleasure.	Evaluation
L II 13.2	Adult imitates infant's sounds as in a game.	Evaluation
L II 13.3	Adult moves tongue in a variety of ways. See if infant can imitate.	Evaluation

L II 13.4	Use TOUCH PROCEDURE II.	Evaluation
L II 13.5	Use PROGRAMMING PROCEDURE.	Evaluation
Material	Food as desired.	

	Behavioral Objectives	L III 1

L III 1	NONSPECIFIC DADA, MAMA	Comment
General Objective	Encouragement of infant's efforts to use sounds in nonspecific situations.	
Specific Objective	The infant will use DADA and MAMA in nonspecific situations.	

Activities

L III 1.1	Adult responds to infant's effort with smiles, touches, and pleasure.	Evaluation
L III 1.2	Adult imitates infant's sounds as in a game.	Evaluation
L III 1.3	Adult makes sounds in various patterns using RHYTHM PROCEDURE.	Evaluation
	Infant imitates adult.	
L III 1.4	Use PHONETIC SYMBOL PROCEDURE.	Evaluation
L III 1.5	TOUCH PROCEDURE II.	Evaluation
L III 1.6	PROGRAMMING PROCEDURE.	Evaluation
Material	Food as desired.	
L III 1.7	TAPE PROCEDURE.	Evaluation
Materials	Tape, recorder, microphone.	

	Behavioral Objectives	L III 2

L III 2	IMITATES SOUNDS	Comment
General Objective	Encouragement of infant's ability to imitate sounds.	
Specific Objective	The infant will increase in ability to imitate sounds.	

Activities

L III 2.1	Adult responds to infant's effort with smiles, touches, and pleasure.	Evaluation
L III 2.2	If infant has sensory impairment, touch hands of infant and adult on mouth, jaw, and throat areas of both being used in activity.	Evaluation
L III 2.3	Move from sounds adult imitates to sounds and combinations of sounds easy for infant to imitate.	Evaluation

L III 2.3 (continued):
Adult makes variety of sound patterns.

Use RHYTHM PROCEDURE.

Infant imitates adult.

L III 2.4	Use PHONETIC SYMBOL PROCEDURE.	Evaluation
L III 2.5	TOUCH PROCEDURE II.	Evaluation
L III 2.6	PROGRAMMING PROCEDURE.	Evaluation
Materials	Food as desired.	
L III 2.7	TAPE PROCEDURE.	Evaluation
Materials	Recorder, tape, microphone.	
L II 2.8	Sing simple melody based upon sound used by infant.	Evaluation

L II 2.8 (continued):
Repeat song at least 10 times a day. Sing with different syllables.

As infant's language increases, sing melody using infant vocabulary *or* words being encouraged for expressive language.

Comment   See the following suggested melody and its use.

Sing on sounds, m, n, b, p, g, d, t. Then sing words like mama, dada, hi, bye-bye, etc.

	Behavioral Objectives	L III 3

L III 3	RESPONDS TO "BYE-BYE" AND "NO"	Comment
General Objective	Develop infant's ability to respond to bye-bye and no.	
Specific Objective	The infant will respond with understanding when told bye-bye or no.	

Activities		
L III 3.1	Adult says no with firm tone. Remove infant's hands or infant from object as no is spoken.	Evaluation
Cue	"No!"	
Comment	Reward quickly with STP. Be very pleased when infant obeys.	
L III 3.2	Use WORD COMMAND PROCEDURE. Make a game of "no." Use same tone of voice each time infant reaches for something. Make the game fun. Repeat frequently.	Evaluation
Cue	"No!"	
L III 3.3	Provide many opportunities for infant to: 1. hear "let's go bye-bye," 2. gesture bye-bye, 3. talk about "bye-bye."	Evaluation
Cue	Bye-bye.	
L III 3.4	Help infant make bye-bye gesture whenever appropriate.	Evaluation
Cue	Bye-bye.	
L III 3.5	Adult responds to infant's effort with smiles, touches, and pleasure.	Evaluation
L III 3.6	Use PROGRAMMING PROCEDURE to help skill.	Evaluation
Material	Food as desired.	

| *L III 3.7* | TAPE PROCEDURE for name, no, and bye-bye. | Evaluation |
| Materials | Tape, recorder, microphone. | |

Behavioral Objectives L III 4

L III 4	RESPONDS TO OWN NAME	Comment
General Objective	Encouragement of infant's ability to respond to own name.	
Specific Objective	The infant will respond to the sound of his own name.	

Activities

| *L III 4.1* | Adult uses infant's name continually when speaking to him. | Evaluation |
| Cue | Infant's name. | |

Is _____ hungry?

Does _____ want to go bye-bye?

| *L III 4.2* | Call infant's name from outside room and see if infant responds by: | Evaluation |

1. looking at adult or
2. stopping activity or
3. vocalization.

| Cue | Infant's name. | |
| Comment | Adult responds to infant's effort with smiles, touches, and pleasure. | |

| *L III 4.3* | Enlarge a photograph of infant. Cover with clear contact paper. Paste on back of unbreakable infant's mirror. Point to picture or infant's face in mirror and name infant. | Evaluation |

| Materials | Nonbreakable infant mirror. | |

Picture.

Glue.

| Cue | Name infant. | |

L III 4.4	Use PHONETIC SYMBOL PROCEDURE for infant's name.	Evaluation
L III 4.5	Use TOUCH PROCEDURE II to help teach infant to say his own name.	Evaluation
L III 4.6	Use TAPE PROCEDURE.	Evaluation
Materials	Tape, recorder, microphone.	
L III 4.7	Use PROGRAMMING PROCEDURE.	Evaluation
Material	Food as desired.	

	Behavioral Objectives	L III 5

L III 5 General Objective	COMBINES SYLLABLES Encouragement of infant's ability to combine syllables.	Comment
Specific Objective	The infant will increase in ability to combine syllables.	

Activities

L III 5.1	Adult responds to infant's effort with smiles, touches, and pleasure.	Evaluation
L III 5.2	If infant has sensorial impairment, touch hands of infant and adult on mouth, jaw, and throat areas of both being used in activity.	Evaluation
L III 5.3	Adult makes combined phonetic syllables in various patterns using RHYTHM PROCEDURE. Infant imitates adult.	Evaluation
L III 5.4	Use PHONETIC SYMBOL PROCEDURE.	Evaluation
L III 5.5	Use TOUCH PROCEDURE II.	Evaluation
L III 5.6	Use PROGRAMMING PROCEDURE.	Evaluation
Materials	Food as desired.	
L III 5.7	Use TAPE PROCEDURE.	Evaluation
Materials	Tape, recorder, microphone.	

Behavioral Objectives	L III 6

L III 6	VOCABULARY OF ONE OR TWO WORDS	Comment
General Objective	Encouragement of vocabulary of one or two words.	
Specific Objective	The infant will demonstrate a vocabulary of one or two words.	

Activities

L III 6.1	Adult responds to infant's effort with smiles, touches, and pleasure.	Evaluation
L III 6.2	Adult frequently and clearly uses words of interest to infant: name of infant mama, daddy, favorite toys, pet, bottle.	Evaluation
L III 6.3	Adult gives infant phonetic symbols for beginning sounds of words above or adult may make words. Use PHONETIC SYMBOL PROCEDURE.	Evaluation
L III 6.4	Use TOUCH PROCEDURE II.	Evaluation
L III 6.5	Use TAPE PROCEDURE.	Evaluation
Materials	Tape, recorder, microphone.	

Behavioral Objectives	L III 7

L III 7	VARIATIONS IN VOLUME	Comment
General Objective	Encouragement of variation in infant's volume.	To be observed.
Specific Objective	The infant will be able to vary the volume of her vocalizations.	

Activities

L III 7.1	Observe variations in infant's volume of vocalization.	Evaluation
L III 7.2	Should there be problems in this area, use PROGRAMMING PROCEDURE and TOUCH PROCEDURE II.	Evaluation
Material	Food as desired.	

Behavioral Objectives   L III   8

L III 8	WAVES BYE-BYE	Comment
General Objective	Development of ability to wave bye-bye.	
Specific Objective	The infant will wave bye-bye appropriately.	

Activities

L III 8.1	Provide many opportunities for infant to 1. hear "lets's go bye-bye," 2. gesture bye-bye, 3. talk about "bye-bye."	Evaluation
Cue	Bye-bye.	
L III 8.2	Help infant make "bye-bye" gesture whenever appropriate.	Evaluation
Cue	Bye-bye.	
L III 8.3	Adult responds to infant's effort with smiles, touches, and pleasure.	Evaluation
L III 8.4	Use PROGRAMMING PROCEDURE to help skill.	Evaluation
Material	Food as desired.	
L III 8.5	TAPE PROCEDURE for name, no, and bye-bye.	Evaluation
Materials	Tape, recorder, microphone.	
Comment	For additional activities see P/S/SH III.	

L III 9	SYMBOLIC USE OF VOICE TONE	Comment
General Objective	Encouragement of infant's ability to use one voice tone symbolically.	
Specific Objective	The infant will use one voice tone symbolically.	

Activities		
L III 9.1	Adult responds to infant's effort with smiles, touches, and pleasure.	Evaluation
L III 9.2	Adult imitates infant's sounds as in a game.	Evaluation
L III 9.3	Use TOUCH PROCEDURE II.	Evaluation
L III 9.4	Use TAPE PROCEDURE.	Evaluation
Materials	Tape, recorder, microphone.	
L III 9.5	Use PROGRAMMING PROCEDURE.	Evaluation
Material	Food as desired.	

L III 10	"MAMA, "DADA" SPOKEN WITH MEANING	Comment
General Objective	Development of infant's ability to use "Mama" and "Dada" with meaning.	
Specific Objective	The infant will use "Mama" and "Dada" appropriately.	

Activities		
L III 10.1	Adult frequently and clearly uses "Mama" and "Dada" in presence of infant.	Evaluation
L III 10.2	Adult responds to infant's effort with smiles, touches, and pleasure.	Evaluation
Cue	Mama Dada	

L III 10.3	Adult gives infant phonetic symbols for beginning sounds of words or adult may make words.	Evaluation
	Use PHONETIC SYMBOL PROCEDURE.	
L III 10.4	Use TOUCH PROCEDURE II.	Evaluation
L III 10.5	Use TAPE PROCEDURE.	Evaluation
Materials	Tape, recorder, microphone.	
L III 10.6	Use PROGRAMMING PROCEDURE.	Evaluation
Material	Food as desired.	

Behavioral Objectives	L III 11

L III 11	ONE WORD BESIDES MAMA AND DADA	Comment
General Objective	Development of infant's ability to use one word besides mama and dada.	
Specific Objective	The infant will be able to use one word besides mama and dada.	

Activities

L III 11.1	Adult responds to infant's effort with smiles, touches, and pleasure.	Evaluation
L III 11.2	Adult frequently uses word of great interest to infant (family pet, favorite toy, etc.).	Evaluation
L III 11.3	Adult gives infant phonetic symbols for the beginning sounds of word or prints the word.	Evaluation
	Use PHONETIC SYMBOL PROCEDURE.	
L III 11.4	Use TOUCH PROCEDURE II.	Evaluation
L III 11.5	Use TAPE PROCEDURE.	Evaluation
Materials	Tape, recorder, microphone.	
L III 11.6	Use PROGRAMMING PROCEDURE.	Evaluation
Material	Food as desired.	

Behavioral Objectives	L III 12

L III 12	CAREFULLY LISTENS TO WORDS	Comment
General Objective	Development of infant's ability to listen to words carefully.	
Specific Objective	The infant will increase interest in listening to words carefully.	

Activities		
L III 12.1	If infant does not show interest in listening carefully to words, begin PROGRAMMING PROCEDURE for practice in attending.	Evaluation
Material	Food as desired.	
Comment	Use words of special interest to infant when using PROGRAMMING PROCEDURE.	
Comment	Use language with adult enthusiasm.	
Comment	Make funny sounds. Exaggerate facial expressions.	
L III 12.2	Use TOUCH PROCEDURE II.	Evaluation

Behavioral Objectives	L III 13

L III 13	UNDERSTANDS WHOLE WORDS AND PHRASES	Comment
General Objective	Development of infant's ability to understand phrases and wholes.	
Specific Objective	Phrases and whole sentences will become understandable to the infant.	

Activities		
L III 13.1	Adult definitely decides how to say certain things consistently one way—"Key Sentences."	Evaluation
	Adult says sentences or phrases with consistent intonation and enthusiasm.	
	Adult uses "Key Sentences" repeatedly at appropriate time.	

Cue	Let's go.	
	Bath time.	
	It's time to eat.	
	It's time to sleep.	
	Where's the doggie? etc.	
L III 13.2	Use TAPE PROCEDURE.	Evaluation
Materials	Tape, recorder, microphone.	

	Behavioral Objectives	L III 14

L III 14	RESPONDS CONSISTENTLY TO NAME	Comment
General Objective	Encouragement of infant's ability to respond consistently to name.	
Specific Objective	The infant will consistently attend or cease activity or come when name is called.	

Activities		
L III 14.1	Adult calls infant's name.	Evaluation
	Observe to see if infant attends, decreases, or ceases activity to listen, or comes.	
L III 14.2	If infant does not respond to own name, use activities outlined on L III 4.	Evaluation

	Behavioral Objectives	L III 15

L III 15	TWO OTHER WORDS BESIDES MAMA AND DADA	Comment
General Objective	Encouragement of infant's use of language.	
Specific Objective	The infant will use two words besides Mama and Dada.	

Activities		
L III 15.1	Adult listens carefully to infant's speech efforts.	Evaluation
	Adult observes whether or not infant has two words other than Mama and Dada.	

L III 15.2	If infant does not indicate use of two words, repeat activities of L III 11 intensely.	Evaluation
L III 15.3	Add the two new words to MAMA and DADA and infant's name on wall.	Evaluation
	Use as in PHONETIC SYMBOL PROCEDURE.	

Behavioral Objectives   L III   16

L III 16	COMPREHENDS "GIVE IT TO ME" WITH GESTURE	Comment
General Objective	Encouragement of infant's ability to comprehend "give it to me" with gesture.	
Specific Objective	The infant will understand and comply to the meaning of "give it to me" with gesture.	

Activities	NAMING PROCEDURE	
L III 16.1	Place infant in front of adult.	Evaluation
	Place a toy in front of infant.	
	Use language and gesture appropriately. Change toy. Repeat.	
Cue	Look, this is a _____ .	
	Now, give me the _____ .	
	Wait for response.	
	Great! That's the _____ .	
	Use with gesture.	
L III 16.2	Make infant quiet book.	Evaluation
	Point to object. Identify.	
	Use language and gesture appropriately. Change page. Repeat.	
Cue	Look, this is a _____ .	
	Now, give me the _____ .	
	Wait for response.	
	Great! That's the _____ .	
L III 16.3	Use PROGRAMMING PROCEDURE.	Evaluation
Material	Food as desired.	

L III 17	IMITATES SOUNDS AND WORDS	Comment
General Objective	Encouragement of infant's language development through the imitation of sounds and words.	
Specific Objective	The infant will show effort to imitate sounds and words.	

Activities

L III 17.1	Adult frequently repeats words of interest to infant before infant says them, after infant attempts to imitate adult speech and in games.	Evaluation
Cue	Pets, toys, bottle, siblings, etc.	
L III 17.2	Adult "reads" simple hard picture books to infant. Adult makes sounds of objects, animals, etc. Infant imitates.	Evaluation
Materials	Hard picture books of animals, machines, etc.	
Cue	Appropriate sounds.	
L III 17.3	Adult responds to infant's effort with smiles, touches, and pleasure.	Evaluation
L III 17.4	Use TAPE PROCEDURE for sounds and infant's efforts.	Evaluation
Materials	Tape, recorder, microphone.	
L III 17.5	Use PROGRAMMING PROCEDURE.	Evaluation
Material	Food as desired.	

L III 18	UNDERSTANDS GESTURES	Comment
General Objective	Development of infant's ability to understand gestures.	
Specific Objective	The infant will demonstrate the ability to comprehend gestures.	

Activities

L III 18.1	Use WORD COMMAND PROCEDURE with gestures.	Evaluation
	Begin very near infant.	
	Use same gesture each time word is used. When infant makes an effort, reward immediately.	
	As infant succeeds and understands move farther away.	
	Present as a game.	
	Present in a happy fashion many times a day.	
Cue	With gesture—	
	Come, wait, stop, no.	

L III 19	FOLLOWS ONE-STEP DIRECTIONS	Comment
General Objective	Development of child's ability to follow one-step directions.	
Specific Objective	The child will increase in ability to follow one-step directions.	

Activities

L III 19.1	Use WORD COMMAND PROCEDURE as outlined in L III 18.	Evaluation

L III *19.2*	Apply to other directions.	Evaluation
Cue	Put it down.	
	Put it here.	
	Find the _____ .	
	Don't touch, etc.	

Behavioral Objectives   L III   20

L III 20	COMPREHENDS A FEW OBJECTS BY NAME	Comment
General Objective	Development of child's ability to comprehend a few objects by name.	
Specific Objective	The child will increase in ability to comprehend a few objects by name.	

Activities

L III *20.1*	Place toy in front of child.	Evaluation
	Name toy repeatedly.	
	Play with child and toy.	
	Name toy carefully.	
	Repeat throughout the day for several days.	
	Repeat with another object of interest to the child.	
	Ask child for one of the two toys.	
Material	Toy.	
Cue	Name of toy.	
Comment	The name of the object may need to be spoken hundreds of times before understood by child.	
L III *20.2*	Use UNIT ACTIVITIES materials as outlined in Part I of this text.	Evaluation
L III *20.3*	Use TOUCH PROCEDURE II.	Evaluation
L III *20.4*	Use TAPE PROCEDURE.	Evaluation
Materials	Tape, recorder, microphone.	

L III 20.5	Use PROGRAMMING PROCEDURE.	Evaluation
Material	Food as desired.	

Behavioral Objectives   L III   21

L III 21	VOCALIZES THREE TO FOUR WORDS	Comment
General Objective	Development of child's ability to vocalize three to four words.	
Specific Objective	The child will vocalize three to four words.	

Activities

L III 21.1	Adult responds to child's effort with smiles, touches, and pleasure.	Evaluation
L III 21.2	Choose words child is attempting to vocalize and apply procedures outlined in L III 20 to these words.	Evaluation

Behavioral Objectives   L III   22

L III 22	COMMUNICATION BY GESTURE	Comment
General Objective	Development of child's ability to communicate by gesture.	
Specific Objective	The child will increase his ability to communicate by gesture.	

Activities

L III 22.1	Watch carefully for child's early efforts to communicate by gesture. Respond quickly.	Evaluation
L III 22.2	Adult responds to child's effort with smiles, touches, and pleasure.	Evaluation
L III 22.3	Continue teaching basic gestures in L III 18.	Evaluation
L III 22.4	Use PROGRAMMING PROCEDURE as necessary.	Evaluation
Material	Food as desired.	

Behavioral Objectives	L III 23

L III 23	INDICATES NEEDS BY POINTING OR VOCALIZING	Comment
General Objective	Development of child's ability to indicate needs by pointing or vocalizing.	
Specific Objective	The child will increase ability to indicate needs by pointing or vocalizing.	

Activities

L III 23.1	Watch carefully for child's early efforts to indicate needs by pointing or vocalizing. Respond quickly.	Evaluation
L III 23.2	Adult responds to child's effort with smiles, touches, and pleasure.	Evaluation
L III 23.3	Continue by teaching as in L III 18.	Evaluation
L III 23.4	Use PROGRAMMING PROCEDURE as necessary.	
Material	Food as desired.	

Behavioral Objectives	L III 24

L III 24	USES "JARGON"	Comment
General Objective	Development of child's ability to use "jargon."	
Specific Objective	The child will demonstrate the ability to use "jargon."	

Activities

L III 24.1	Listen carefully for child's early efforts to vocalize in his own language form. Respond quickly.	Evaluation
L III 24.2	Adult responds to child's effort with smiles, touches, and pleasure.	Evaluation
L III 24.3	Use TAPE PROCEDURE.	Evaluation

L III 24.4	Use PROGRAMMING PROCEDURE to encourage when necessary.	Evaluation
Material	Food as desired.	

	Behavioral Objectives	L IV 1

L IV 1	UNDERSTANDS SOME COMMANDS	Comment
General Objective	Development of child's ability to understand commands.	
Specific Objective	When given a command, the child will show increased understanding.	

Activities

L IV 1.1	Use WORD COMMAND PROCEDURE as outlined in L III 18 and L III 19.	Evaluation
Cue	Suggestions.	

Go ahead.	Come.
It's OK.	Stop.
Do it.	No.
Careful—be gentle, etc.	
Wait.	

	Behavioral Objectives	L IV 2

L IV 2	UNDERSTANDS SIMPLE QUESTIONS	Comment
General Objective	Development of child's ability to understand simple questions.	
Specific Objective	The child will show the ability to begin to understand the meaning of questions.	

Activities

L IV 2.1	Present questions in the form of games. Begin during Phase III.	Evaluation
L IV 2.2	Games of Identification. 1. Show child objects around the house and yard. Example: furniture.	Evaluation

2. Name them again and again.

3. Ask child, "Where is the TV?" etc.

4. Child crawls, walks, etc. to object.

5. Adult responds with enthusiasm.

6. If child is wrong, say nothing. Teach again. Stress successes.

L IV 2.3	Games of Wanting.	Evaluation

1. Name food and toys continually.

2. Present one to child.

3. Ask child, "Do you want the cookie?"

4. When child shows yes or no response, speak for child. Example: "Yes, Sally wants the cookie."

5. Present two or more objects. Ask child, "Do you want the cookie or the teddy bear?"

6. When child shows preference, speak for him. Example: "Tommy, you want the teddy bear."

L IV 2.4	Use PROGRAMMING PROCEDURE to help if necessary.	Evaluation
Material	Food as desired.	

Behavioral Objectives	L IV 3

L IV 3	TEN WORD VOCABULARY	Comment
General Objective	Development of child's expressive vocabulary.	
Specific Objective	The child will be able to express himself with ten words appropriately.	

Activities

L IV 3.1	Adult responds to child's effort with smiles, touches, and pleasure.	Evaluation
L IV 3.2	Choose words child shows interest in and intensify effort to help child learn them. Use	

procedures as outlined in L III 20 for these additional words.

Behavioral Objectives	L IV 4

L IV 4	IDENTIFIES FIVE NAMED OBJECTS BY POINTING	Comment
General Objective	Development of receptive language.	
Specific Objective	When asked to identify objects, the child responds by pointing to five named objects.	

Activities

L IV 4.1	Place five familiar objects in front of child.	Evaluation
	Name an object.	
	Point to object named.	
	Name an object.	
	Help child point to object named.	
	Reward successes with STP.	
	Merely rename objects child identifies incorrectly.	
	Repeat.	
Materials	Five objects well known to child.	
Cue	Appropriate name of object.	
	Show me the _____ .	
L IV 4.2	Frequently name five objects or animals in simple child's book.	
	When familiar to child, ask child to show you the _____ .	
	Reward with STP.	
Materials	Simple child's picture book.	
Cue	Look, this is a _____ .	
	Now, show me the _____ .	
	Wait for response.	
	Good. That's a _____ .	

L IV 5	NAMES ONE PICTURE	Comment
General Objective	Development of the child's meaningful expressive language.	
Specific Objective	The child will be able to name one picture.	

Activities		
L IV 5.1	Show child a picture in a book.	Evaluation
Cue	What is this? What does this animal say?	
L IV 5.2	Adult responds to child's effort with smiles, touches, and pleasure.	Evaluation
L IV 5.3	If child has difficulty, follow general language procedures.	Evaluation
L IV 5.4	If teaching animal names, use ANIMAL UNIT and take child to see the animals being named whenever possible.	Evaluation
L IV 5.5	Tape a picture of an object to the object. May also use a photograph. Encourage association of both.	Evaluation
Materials	Objects. Pictures. Photographs.	

L IV 6	RECOGNIZES PICTURES WITHOUT NAMING	Comment
General Objective	Development of receptive language.	
Specific Objective	The child will recognize many pictures he cannot name.	

Activities

L IV 6.1	Continue as in L IV 5.	Evaluation
Cue	Look, this is a _____ .	
	Now, show me the _____ .	
	Wait for response.	
	Yes, that's the _____ .	
L IV 6.2	Adult responds to child's effort with smiles, touches, and pleasure.	

Behavioral Objectives		L IV 7

L IV 7	PULLS FOR COMMUNICATION	Comment
General Objective	Development of child's ability to indicate wants.	
Specific Objective	When the child wants something, she will communicate by pulling at adult.	

Activities

L IV 7.1	Immediately pay attention to the child's pulls. Bend down to look at child's face. Try to understand and help child.	Evaluation
Cue	What do you want?	
	Show me what you need?	
	What is it?	
	Oh, you want some _____ .	
L IV 7.2	If necessary, use PROGRAMMING PROCE-DURE.	Evaluation
Material	Food as desired.	

Behavioral Objectives		L IV 8

L IV 8	IMITATES ANIMAL AND TOY SOUNDS	Comment
General Objective	Development of child's expressive language.	

Specific Objective	The child will be able to imitate animal and toy sounds.	

Activities		
L IV 8.1	Adult responds to child's effort with smiles, touches, and pleasure.	Evaluation
L IV 8.2	Encourage child's efforts as outlined in L III 17.	Evaluation

	Behavioral Objectives	*L IV 9*

L IV 9	VOCABULARY OF 20 WORDS	Comment
General Objective	Development of child's expressive vocabulary.	
Specific Objective	The child will be able to express herself appropriately using 20 words.	

Activities		
L IV 9.1	Adult responds to child's effort with smiles, touches, and pleasure.	Evaluation
L IV 9.2	Choose words child shows interest in. Intensify effort to help the child learn them. Use procedures as outlined in L IV 3 for these additional words.	Evaluation

	Behavioral Objectives	*L IV 10*

L IV 10	SPONTANEOUS COMBINATIONS OF TWO OR THREE WORDS	Comment
General Objective	Development of child's expressive language.	
Specific Objective	The child will spontaneously combine two or three words.	

Activities		
L IV 10.1	Adult responds to child's effort with smiles, touches, and pleasure.	Evaluation

L IV 10.2	List words child says.	
	Begin combining those words and use frequently for child.	
	Use with objects or symbols wherever possible.	
Cue	Doggie—bow-wow. Repeat. The doggie says bow-wow.	
Comment	The child may be very frustrated and difficult to live with until he has succeeded at this skill.	
L IV 10.3	Use TAPE PROCEDURE.	Evaluation
Materials	Tape, recorder, microphone.	
L IV 10.4	Use PROGRAMMING PROCEDURE if necessary.	Evaluation
Material	Food as desired.	

Behavioral Objectives   L V 1

L V 1	POINTS TO ONE NAMED BODY PART	Comment
General Objective	Development of child's self-concept.	
Specific Objective	When pointed to, the child will be able to name one body part.	

Activities

L V 1.1	Continue Spatial Games during bath time.	Evaluation
	Name with emphasis the body parts being washed.	
	Have child move or raise the body parts while being dried.	
Cue	Show me your arm. Wiggle your fingers. Give me your foot. The washcloth is between your legs.	
L V 1.2	Body UNIT ACTIVITIES as outlined in Part 1.	Evaluation

L V 1.3	Use PROGRAMMING PROCEDURE if necessary.	Evaluation
Material	Reward.	

	Behavioral Objectives	**L V 2**

L V 2	RECOGNIZES 120–275 WORDS	Comment
General Objective	Development of receptive language.	
Specific Objective	The child will recognize and respond to 120–275 words.	

Activities

L V 2.1	Use WORD LEARNING PROCEDURE as outlined in L III 20.	Evaluation
L V 2.2	Observe and list words responded to by child.	Evaluation

	Behavioral Objectives	**L V 3**

L V 3	POINTS TO TEN PICTURES	Comment
General Objective	Development of receptive and expressive language.	
Specific Objective	When named, the child will point to ten pictures correctly.	

Activities

L V 3.1	Teach child names of objects on ten pictures. Teach one by one. Use as a game. Help child point to correct picture when named. Do not help child any longer than necessary.	Evaluation
Materials	Ten pictures.	

Cue	Look, this is a _____ .	
	Now, show me the _____ .	
	Wait for response.	
	Good. This is a _____ .	
L V 3.2	Adult responds to child's effort with touches, smiles, and pleasure.	Evaluation
L V 3.3	Use PROGRAMMING PROCEDURE if necessary.	Evaluation

	Behavioral Objectives	L V 4
L V 4	USES TWO-WORD SENTENCE	Comment
General Objective	Development of expressive language.	
Specific Objective	The child will speak in a two-word sentence.	

Activities		
L V 4.1	Teach as in L V 11.	Evaluation

	Behavioral Objectives	L V 5
L V 5	NAMES EIGHT PICTURES	Comment
General Objective	Development of expressive language.	
Specific Objective	The child will name eight pictures when asked to identify them.	

Activities		
L V 5.1	Continue naming pictures as outlined in L IV 5.	Evaluation
L V 5.2	Coordinate with UNIT ACTIVITIES.	Evaluation
L V 5.3	Continue as outlined in L IV 5.	Evaluation

Behavioral Objectives	L V 6

L V 6	USES SOME PREPOSITIONS, PRONOUNS, AND ADJECTIVES	Comment
General Objective	Development of expressive language.	
Specific Objective	The child will begin to use adjectives, prepositions, and pronouns in his speech.	

Activities		
L V 6.1	Emphasize adjectives, prepositions, and pronouns in adult speech.	Evaluation
Cue	Adjectives—colors, big/little, fat/thin, good/bad, etc.	
	Prepositions—with, to, under, behind, on, in, etc.	
	Pronouns—I, me, mine; him, his; her, hers; we, our; you, your; they, them, theirs.	
L V 6.2	Adult responds to child's effort with touches, smiles, and pleasure.	Evaluation
L V 6.3	Play simple lotto or other games using these words.	Evaluation
L V 6.4	Use TAPE PROCEDURE.	Evaluation
Materials	Tape, recorder, microphone.	
L V 6.5	Use PROGRAMMING PROCEDURE if necessary.	Evaluation
Material	Reward.	

Behavioral Objectives	L V 7

L V 7	VOCABULARY OF 20–300 WORDS	Comment
General Objective	Development of receptive-expressive language.	
Specific Objective	The child will respond to and/or express herself with 20 to 300 words.	

Activities

L V 7.1	Continue enlarging child's vocabulary as outlined in WORD LEARNING PROCEDURE, L III 20.	Evaluation
L V 7.2	Coordinate with UNIT ACTIVITIES.	Evaluation

Behavioral Objectives	L V 8

L V 8	IDENTIFIES USES OF MANY OBJECTS	Comment
General Objective	Development of semantic relations.	
Specific Objective	When shown objects, the child can identify by usage.	

Activities

L V 8.1	During the general routine of a day, adult will feed, dress, toilet, bathe, and play with the child.	Evaluation
	For a week, carefully and briefly tell child the use of everything being used.	
Cue	This is the dress you wear. This is the cup you drink from. This is the ball you play with, etc.	
L V 8.2	Play this game.	Evaluation
	Place several objects in front of the child.	
	Ask child to show you or point to the objects according to their use.	
Materials	Cup, stocking, toy, etc.	
Cue	Show me the one you wear. Show me the one you drink from, etc.	
L V 8.3	Use pictures and continue as in L V 8.1 and in L V 8.2.	Evaluation
Cue	As above.	
L V 8.4	As a game, show child pictures or objects. Ask child to tell you what to do with each.	Evaluation

Materials	Pictures of objects. Objects.
Cue	What do you do with this?

L V 8.5	Show child pictures of object or objects. Act out the use of the object. Child imitates the action or, when possible, acts without imitation.	Evaluation

Materials	Pictures of objects. Objects.
Cue	Show me what we do with the cup. Show me what we do with the towel.

L V 8.6	Adult responds to child's effort with touches, smiles, and pleasure.	Evaluation

Behavioral Objectives   L V 9

L V 9	TALKS ABOUT FEELINGS AND ACTIVITIES	Comment
General Objective	Development of ability to verbalize feelings and experiences.	
Specific Objective	The child will recognize and express emotions and experiences appropriately.	

Activities

L V 9.1	Adult tells child the name of his feelings at various times.	Evaluation
Cue	You feel angry. You feel happy. You feel sad.	

L V 9.2	Adult describes own feelings and exaggerates a little the facial features and body gestures involved.	Evaluation
Cue	I feel very angry. I feel sad today. I am so happy.	

LV 9.3	Adult shows child pictures of faces with different emotions.	Evaluation
	Discuss with child.	
	Make faces and gestures that also indicate the same emotions.	
	Child imitates.	
Materials	Pictures of different emotional states.	
Cue	The man is sad.	
	The little boy is happy.	
LV 9.4	Adult demonstrates emotions.	Evaluation
	Adult asks child to identify.	
Cue	How do I feel?	
LV 9.5	Child demonstrates emotion as asked for by adult.	Evaluation
Cue	Show me a happy face.	
	Show me how you feel angry.	
LV 9.6	Child demonstrates an emotion.	Evaluation
	Adult guesses the emotion.	
Cue	I think you feel happy.	
	I think you feel angry.	
Comment	Apply the above procedures to experiences of child.	Evaluation

Behavioral Objectives	LV 10

LV 10	SPEECH WITH POINTING	Comment
General Objective	Development of semantic and figural relationships.	
Specific Objective	The child will point to things he talks about.	

Activities		
LV 10.1	Adult points to things while talking to child.	Evaluation
	Child imitates.	

Cue	Look at this _____ .	
	There is the _____ .	
L V 10.2	Child points to things while talking about them.	Evaluation
L V 10.3	Adult really listens to child.	Evaluation
	Adult responds to child's effort with touches, smiles, and pleasure.	
Comment	Adult should get down on child's level whenever possible.	
L V 10.4	Adult points to pictures while talking about them.	Evaluation
	Child imitates.	
Materials	Pictures.	
Cue	Look at the _____ .	

	Behavioral Objectives	L V 11
L V 11	USES THREE-WORD SENTENCES	Comment
General Objective	Development of expressive language.	
Specific Objective	The child will speak in three-word sentences.	

Activities

L V 11.1	Observe and note child's three-word sentence pattern.	Evaluation
L V 11.2	Adult responds to child's effort with touches, smiles, and pleasure.	Evaluation
L V 11.3	Carefully make three- or four-word sentences when talking to child.	Evaluation
	Use when sharing an interest with the child.	
Comment	Get down on child's level where child can see adult's face.	

L V 11.4	Use TAPE PROCEDURE for child's efforts and adult sentences too.	Evaluation
Materials	Tape, recorder, microphone.	
L V 11.5	Use PROGRAMMING PROCEDURE if necessary.	Evaluation
Material	Reward.	

Behavioral Objectives   L V   12

L V 12	USES I, ME, MINE, AND YOU.	Comment
General Objective	Development of expressive language.	
Specific Objective	The child will use I, me, mine, and you appropriately in speech.	

Activities

L V 12.1	Adult emphasizes above pronouns in daily speech.	Evaluation
L V 12.2	Adult responds to child's effort with touches, smiles, and pleasure.	Evaluation
L V 12.3	Play simple lotto or other games using these words.	Evaluation
L V 12.4	Use TAPE PROCEDURE.	Evaluation
Materials	Tape, recorder, microphone.	
L V 12.5	Use PROGRAMMING PROCEDURE if necessary.	Evaluation
Material	Reward.	

Behavioral Objectives   L V   13

L V 13	COMPREHENDS TIME WORDS	Comment
General Objective	Development of advanced language concepts.	

Specific Objective	The child will comprehend that time is being referred to in relation to activities.	

Activities

L V 13.1	Adult refers to "time" for activities in daily routine.	Evaluation
Cue	It's time to go. It's time to eat.	
L V 13.2	Adult sings a little "time" song during daily routine.	Evaluation
Cue	It's time to play. It's time to play, cheer up. It's time to play, etc.	
L V 13.3	Adult coordinates child's routine with a large wall clock. Adult and child check with clock for daily activities.	Evaluation
Materials	Posterboard. Brad. Pictures. Felt tip pens.	

Behavioral Objectives	L V 14

L V 14	USES PLURALS	Comment
General Objective	Development of ability to express language units and classes.	
Specific Objective	The child will begin using plurals in his expressive language.	

Activities

L V 14.1	Adult stresses s at end of words during general speech.	Evaluation
L V 14.2	Adult plays games with child involving two or more of the same objects.	Evaluation

Materials	Balls, dolls, containers, shoes, hats, etc.	
Cue	As appropriate.	
L V 14.3	Adult uses PHONETIC SYMBOL PROCEDURE in general environment. Adult adds *s* to words on wall and other parts of the procedure.	Evaluation
L V 14.4	Adult plays "body game" using plural parts of the body.	Evaluation
Cue	Arms, legs, hands, etc.	

Behavioral Objectives	L V 15

L V 15	QUESTIONS BEGIN	Comment
General Objective	Development of ability to seek information through use of language.	
Specific Objective	The child will begin asking questions.	

Activities

L V 15.1	Adult asks many questions very simply when around child.	Evaluation
Cue	What's this? Where is the doll? etc.	
L V 15.2	Adult responds to child's effort with touches, smiles, and pleasure.	Evaluation
L V 15.3	Adult really listens to child's questions. Adult answers quickly and simply. Adult shows child other examples of answer when possible. Generalize in environment.	Evaluation
L V 15.4	Use TAPE PROCEDURE.	Evaluation
Materials	Tape, recorder, microphone.	
L V 15.5	Use PROGRAMMING PROCEDURE if necessary.	Evaluation
Material	Reward.	

Behavioral Objectives	L V 16

L V 16	USES COMPOUND AND COMPLEX SENTENCES	Comment
General Objective	Development of complex expressive language.	
Specific Objective	Child uses simple compound and complex sentences.	

Activities		
L V 16.1	Adult uses simple compound sentences when talking to child.	Evaluation
Cue	Let's go and see. We will walk and we will play on the way.	
L V 16.2	Adult responds to child's effort with touches, smiles, and pleasure.	Evaluation
L V 16.3	Adult really listens to child's efforts. Restates child's efforts occasionally but not critically.	Evaluation
L V 16.4	Use TAPE PROCEDURE.	Evaluation
Materials	Tape, recorder, microphone.	
L V 16.5	Use PROGRAMMING PROCEDURE if necessary.	Evaluation
Material	Reward.	

Behavioral Objectives	L V 17

L V 17	ACTS OUT IN, ON, RUN, WALK	Comment
General Objective	Development of behavioral response to semantic stimuli.	
Specific Objective	The child will act out words of action and spatial position.	

Activities

L V 17.1	Adult repeats spatial activities outlined in SC III 20.	Evaluation
L V 17.2	Adult gives child word cards for spatial positions while repeating L V 17.1 (Give cards one at a time).	Evaluation
Materials	Word cards as appropriate.	
Cue	As appropriate.	
L V 17.3	Adult plays with child using actions and naming them.	Evaluation
Cue	Run, walk, crawl, sing, etc.	
L V 17.4	Adult responds to child's effort with touches, smiles, and pleasure.	Evaluation
L V 17.5	Adult gives child word cards for action games.	Evaluation
Materials	Word cards.	
Cue	As above.	
L V 17.6	If child succeeds easily in all of above activities, make sentences for action games using word cards the child knows well.	Evaluation
Materials	Toys, boxes, word cards, sentence cards.	
Cue	Write on cards: Put doll in the box. Walk with the doll. Run to the box, etc.	
Comment	Print should be one-half to one inch, basically lower case, and small red phonetic symbols should be placed above difficult sounds.	

Behavioral Objectives   L V 18

L V 18	KNOWS FIRST AND LAST NAME	Comment
General Objective	Development of cognition and memory.	

Specific Objective	The child will identify himself by first and last name.	
Activities		
L V 18.1	Adult calls child by first and last name.	Evaluation
Cue	First and last name of child.	
L V 18.2	Adult takes pictures of child.	Evaluation
	Adult and child talk about pictures.	
	Adult uses child's first and last name at all times while talking.	
Materials	Pictures of child.	
Cue	First and last name of child.	
L V 18.3	Adult puts pictures on wall.	Evaluation
	Adult prints child's full name and places under pictures.	
	Follow as in PHONETIC SYMBOL PROCEDURE.	
L V 18.4	Use TAPE PROCEDURE.	Evaluation
Materials	Tape, recorder, microphone.	
L V 18.5	Use PROGRAMMING PROCEDURE if necessary.	Evaluation
Material	Reward.	

	Behavioral Objectives	P/S/SH I 1
P/S/SH I 1	REGARDS FACE—ACTIVITY DIMINISHES	Comment
General Objective	Development of ability to attend to human face.	
Specific Objective	When infant looks at adult face, activity decreases.	

Activities

P/S/SH I 1.1	Adult gets in position where infant can see face.	Evaluation
	Call to her.	
	If infant does not respond, grasp her chin and move face toward adult.	
P/S/SH I 1.2	Adult puts head down close to infant's face.	Evaluation
	Move away quickly from line of vision.	
	Then move close again.	
	Repeat until infant starts to look.	
	Stay in sight and smile.	
Cue	Hello, peek-a-boo.	
Comment	Talk soothingly to her attempting to have her look at your face and decrease her activity.	

	Behavioral Objectives	P/S/SH I 2
P/S/SH I 2	QUIETS WHEN PICKED UP	Comment
General Objective	Development of sensitivity to body contact.	
Specific Objective	When infant is picked up, the infant will quiet.	

Activities

P/S/SH I 2.1	When infant cries, cuddle and hold him firmly.	Evaluation
Comment	Talk soothingly.	
P/S/SH I 2.2	Walk around room, gently rocking infant in your arms.	Evaluation
Comment	As above.	
P/S/SH I 2.3	Gently rub infant's head while doing 2.1 or 2.2 above.	Evaluation

Comment	As above.
Comment	It may not always be necessary to pick him up; try gently stroking his back or turning while talking soothingly.

	Behavioral Objectives	P/S/SH I 3

P/S/SH I 3	EYE CONTACT	Comment
General Objective	Development of eye contact with adult.	
Specific Objective	When adult face is placed in infant's line of vision, the infant will demonstrate eye contact.	

Activities

P/S/SH I 3.1	Adult places face close to infant's face. Smile and talk to child to maintain eye contact.	Evaluation
Cue	Look at me.	
P/S/SH I 3.2	Adult holds bright object or round toy near the eye. Call infant's name.	Evaluation
Cue	Look at this.	
Comment	Talk animately to attract infant's attention.	
P/S/SH I 3.3	Adult holds infant with head cupped in hands. Adult leans toward infant, smiles.	Evaluation
Cue	Look at me.	
Comment	Make exaggerated sounds to encourage infant to look at your face.	
Comment	Try to focus your attention on infant during feeding time.	
Comment	Use plenty of smiles, touches, and pleasure when infant establishes eye contact.	
P/S/SH I 3.4	PROGRAMMING PROCEDURE.	Evaluation

Behavioral Objectives	P/S/SH I 4

P/S/SH I 4	EMOTIONAL RESPONSE TO DISTRESS	Comment
General Objective	Develop parent's ability to discern distress in the infant.	To be observed.
Specific Objective	When the infant displays distress, the parents will respond appropriately.	

Activities

P/S/SH I 4.1	When infant displays emotional distress, the adult should check the cause of the distress.	Evaluation
Comment	Adult should check for open diaper pin, room temperature, feeding schedule, gas, wet or soiled diaper, etc.	
Comment	Adult should not respond to *Unnecessary* crying or distress.	
Comment	See also P/S/SH I 2.	

Behavioral Objectives	P/S/SH I 5

P/S/SH I 5	SMILES RESPONSIVELY TO MOTHER	Comment
General Objective	Development of awareness to mother.	
Specific Objective	The infant will smile in response to her mother.	

Activities

P/S/SH I 5.1	Mother places her face directly in front of infant's face.	Evaluation
	Smile at the infant.	
	Give infant time to smile back.	
P/S/SH I 5.2	Mother smiles and talks soothingly to infant when attending to her needs.	Evaluation
Comment	Smile at infant and encourage her to smile back.	
	Repeat and use smiles, touches, and pleasure for successes.	

P/S/SH I 5.3	PROGRAMMING PROCEDURE.	Evaluation
	Behavioral Objectives	P/S/SH I 6

P/S/SH I 6	RECOGNIZES MOTHER (VISUALLY)	Comment
		Observe infant's reaction to strangers and/or mother.
General Objective	Development of awareness of mother.	
Specific Objective	When mother is in infant's line of vision, the infant will demonstrate recognition by attending, getting excited, showing greater interest, etc.	

Activities

P/S/SH I 6.1	See basic P/S/SH Phase I activities.	Evaluation
	Behavioral Objectives	P/S/SH I 7

P/S/SH I 7	FOLLOWS MOVING PERSON (VISUALLY)	Comment
General Objective	Development of visual tracking.	
Specific Objective	When adult moves in infant's line of vision, the infant will usually follow the movement.	

Activities

P/S/SH I 7.1	Adult talks to baby from different places in room.	Evaluation
	Observe if she follows with her eyes.	
Cue	Look at me.	

P/S/SH I 7.2	Place infant in infant seat. Walk across line of vision and observe if child follows movement.	Evaluation
Cue	Look at me.	
P/S/SH I 7.3	Repeat 7.2 using a noisemaker to encourage following behavior.	Evaluation
Materials	Sound toy, noisemaker.	
Cue	Look at me.	
Comment	Repeat the activity gradually reducing the use of a noisemaker.	
Comment	Use smiles, touches, and pleasure for successful behavior.	
Comment	Gradually move farther away from her as she gains proficiency at following movement.	
P/S/SH I 7.4	PROGRAMMING PROCEDURE. Use second adult to shape desired behavior.	Evaluation

Behavioral Objectives		P/S/SH I 8
P/S/SH I 8	RESPONDS EMOTIONALLY TO DELIGHT	Comment
General Objective	Development of responses to pleasurable activities.	
Specific Objective	When provided with a pleasurable activity, the infant will respond by smiling, cooing, etc.	

Activities		
P/S/SH I 8.1	Adult smiles, talks, and gently strokes infant.	Evaluation
Comment	Observe if baby smiles, coos, etc.	
Comment	Adult encourages infant by showing delight.	
P/S/SH I 8.2	After diapering or feeding, adult cuddles, coos to, smiles, and strokes infant.	Evaluation
Comment	As above.	

P/S/SH I 8.3   During bath time, use BATHTIME PRO-   Evaluation
                    CEDURE.

Comment   Encourage infant to respond to these
                    pleasurable activities.

	Behavioral Objectives	P/S/SH I 9

P/S/SH I 9   SQUEALS WITH PLEASURE   Comment

General   Development of vocal response to pleasurable
Objective   activities.

Specific   When provided with a pleasurable activity,
Objective   the infant will respond by cooing, gurgling, or
                    squealing.

Activities

P/S/SH I 9.1   After feeding or diapering, adult coos or talks   Evaluation
                    to the infant.

Comment   Talk constantly to child.

Comment   Use plenty of smiles, touches, and pleasure
                    when infant vocalizes by cooing or making
                    sounds.

P/S/SH I 9.2   Use BATH TIME PROCEDURE.   Evaluation

Comment   As above.

	Behavioral Objectives	P/S/SH I 10

P/S/SH I 10   HAND REGARD   Comment

General   Development of the ability to look at hands.
Objective

Specific   The infant will demonstrate the ability to look
Objective   at his hands.

Activities

P/S/SH I	*10.1*	Adult moves infant's hands in front of his face.	Evaluation
Cue		Look at your hands.	
P/S/SH I	*10.2*	Adult repeats 10.1, moving fingers for infant to watch.	Evaluation
Cue		Look at your hands.	
P/S/SH I	*10.3*	Adult places red infant socks on infant's hands. Cut sock so thumb and fingers show.	Evaluation
Cue		Look at your hands.	
Comment		Eliminate socks when infant consistently looks at hands.	
Comment		Use TOUCH SENSORIAL PROCEDURE to infant's hands.	
P/S/SH I	*10.4*	PROGRAMMING PROCEDURE.	Evaluation

Behavioral Objectives	P/S/SH I 11

P/S/SH I	*11*	SMILES AT MIRROR IMAGE	Comment
General Objective		Development of positive response to infant's own face.	
Specific Objective		When a mirror is placed before infant's face, the infant will respond by smiling.	

Activities

P/S/SH I	*11.1*	Adult places a stainless flexible infant mirror or shiny cookie sheet in a position where infant can see her image. Encourage baby to smile by talking soothingly or tickling her chin.

Material	Unbreakable infant mirror.
Cue	Look at your face.
Comment	Repeat this activity until infant smiles at her face.
Comment	Gradually reduce the touching of infant's chin when her smile is spontaneous.
Comment	Adult may use tapping on mirror surface, or blinking a flashlight in the mirror to draw attention to the mirror.

	Behavioral Objectives	P/S/SH I 12
P/S/SH I 12	MAY SOBER AT SIGHT OF STRANGERS	Comment
General Objective Specific Objective		To be observed.

Activities		
P/S/SH I 12.1	Provide opportunities for infant to see strangers.	Evaluation
Comment	Not all infants will sober at seeing strangers.	

	Behavioral Objectives	P/S/SH I 13
P/S/SH I 13	ENJOYS EVENING PLAY WITH FATHER	Comment
General Objective	Development of positive exposure to father.	
Specific Objective	When father plays with infant, infant will respond in a positive manner by smiling, squealing, cooing, etc.	

Activities

P/S/SH I 13.1	Infant's father repeats activities P/S/SH 8.1 to 8.3.	Evaluation
P/S/SH I 13.2	Father repeats HOPE PROCEDURE.	Evaluation
Comment	Infant's father is encouraged to play with the baby in a variety of ways.	

Behavioral Objectives	P/S/SH I 14

P/S/SH I 14	SPONTANEOUS SOCIAL SMILE	Comment
General Objective	Development of infant's ability to smile spontaneously in a variety of environmental situations.	
Specific Objective	When provided with adult attention the infant will spontaneously smile.	To be observed.

Activities

P/S/SH I 14.1	Adult provides infant with many activities that are pleasurable to the infant.	Evaluation
	These activities and procedures are presented throughout the curriculum.	
Comment	Adult should observe the infant to note the frequency of spontaneous smiling.	
Comment	Encourage the infant to smile by the use of smiles, touches, and pleasure.	
P/S/SH I 14.2	PROGRAMMING PROCEDURE.	Evaluation

Behavioral Objectives	P/S/SH I 15

P/S/SH I 15	HAND PLAY	Comment
General Objective	Encouragement of hand play.	To be observed.
Specific Objective	During periods of no adult attention, the infant will engage in hand play.	

Activities

P/S/SH I 15.1	Repeat activities P/S/SH 10.1 to 10.3.	Evaluation
Comment	Reinforcement and practice of hand regard is essential if hand play is to occur.	
P/S/SH I 15.2	Place infant in crib and position yourself out of her line of vision.	Evaluation
	Observe if she regards and plays with her hands.	

	Behavioral Objectives	P/S/SH I 16

P/S/SH I 16	CRIES IF ADULT STOPS PLAYING WITH HIM	Comment
General Objective	To develop infant's ability to play alone.	To be observed.
Specific Objective	During periods of no adult attention, the infant will engage in quiet play after a period of crying.	

Activities

P/S/SH I 16.1	Infants may cry when adult stops playing with them.	Evaluation
	Usually the infant will stop crying after a short period of time and go back to playing by himself.	
Comment	If crying persists or infant appears to be in great distress, adult should employ P/S/SH I 4.1.	
Comment	See also P/S/SH I 2.1 to 2.3.	

	Behavioral Objectives	P/S/SH I 17

P/S/SH I 17	LAUGHS OUT LOUD, SMILES, SOBERS	Comment
General Objective	Development of spontaneous response to pleasure, and encouragement of vocal response to same.	

Specific Objective	The infant will laugh aloud in response to a variety of stimulus situations and/or environments.	

Activities

P/S/SH I 17.1	Place infant on back. Place your mouth on stomach and make "motorboat" sound. Repeat to encourage child to laugh.	Evaluation
Comment	Immediately use smiles, touches, and pleasure when infant laughs.	
P/S/SH I 17.2	Place infant on back. Babble or make exaggerated sounds.	Evaluation
Comment	As above.	
P/S/SH I 17.3	GENTLY tickle infant all over her body.	Evaluation
Comment	As above.	

Behavioral Objectives   P/S/SH I   18

P/S/SH I 18	ANTICIPATES ON SIGHT OF FOOD*	Comment
General Objective	To encourage infant's positive response to food or feeding time.	To be observed.
Specific Objective	When provided with the opportunity to see food, the infant will anticipate feeding by opening his mouth, getting excited, etc.	

Activities

P/S/SH I 18.1	Place infant in a position where he can see and hear his food being prepared. Bring spoon to infant's mouth so he can see it.	Evaluation
Cue	Open wide, here it comes, etc. Name the food.	
Comment	Use plenty of smiles, touches, and pleasure if infant opens mouth.	
Comment	If child doesn't open mouth in anticipation, physically open the mouth, place the food in.	
Comment	Praise child immediately.	

Comment	Gradually reduce assistance as infant opens his own mouth.	
Comment	Do not rush feeding time. This is a great opportunity to practice many of the skills in the curriculum.	
Comment	If infant anticipates food inconsistently, wait for him to open his mouth instead of shoveling food in.	
P/S/SH I 18.2	PROGRAMMING PROCEDURE. Use second adult to shape looking behavior.	Evaluation

*Denotes self-help skill

	Behavioral Objectives	P/S/SH II 1
P/S/SH II 1	CRIES WHEN IGNORED BY ADULT	Comment
General Objective	Development of awareness of others.	
Specific Objective		To be observed.
Activities		
P/S/SH II 1.1	Adult enters room and ignores infant. Observe whether or not infant cries.	Evaluation

	Behavioral Objectives	P/S/SH II 2
P/S/SH II 2	CRIES WHEN LEFT BY ADULT	Comment
General Objective	Development of awareness of others.	
Specific Objective		To be observed.
Activities		
P/S/SH II 2.1	Adult puts infant down and leaves the room. Observe whether or not infant cries.	Evaluation

Behavioral Objectives	P/S/SH II 3

P/S/SH II 3	STRETCHES ARMS TO BE TAKEN	Comment
General Objective	Development of ability to indicate wants.	
Specific Objective	The infant will stretch out his arms to be taken with others.	

Activities

P/S/SH II 3.1	Approach infant with arms outstretched, smiling face.	Evaluation
	Approach infant in this manner all the time when planning to pick infant up.	
	Infant will imitate this gesture.	
Cue	Come. Up we go. Let's go.	

Behavioral Objectives	P/S/SH II 4

P/S/SH II 4	EMOTIONAL RESPONSE APPRO-PRIATE TO SPECIFIC SITUATIONS	Comment
General Objective	Development of emotional responses in specific situations.	
Specific Objective	The infant will increase his emotional responses to specific situations.	

Activities

P/S/SH II 4.1	Adult notes situations that are normally emotional for infants.	Evaluation
	Adult exaggerates normal behaviors.	
	Infant imitates, that is, smiles and laughs at happy situations, cries or pouts when disappointed.	
P/S/SH II 4.2	Adult imitates infant's emotional responses in exaggerated way.	Evaluation

P/S/SH II 4.3	When infant cries, smiles, laughs, etc., place nonbreakable infant mirror eight to twelve inches in front of infant's face. Infant observes.	Evaluation
Material	Nonbreakable mirror.	
Cue	Look. See the baby smile, etc.	

Behavioral Objectives	P/S/SH II 5

P/S/SH II 5	FEEDING, PATS BOTTLE*	Comment
General Objective	Development of hand involvement in feeding process.	
Specific Objective	The infant will pat the bottle during feeding.	

Activities

P/S/SH II 5.1	During bottle feeding, place infant's hand on bottle. Guide hand to pat the bottle.	Evaluation
Material	Bottle of milk or juice.	
Cue	Pat it. Pat the bottle.	
P/S/SH II 5.2	PROGRAMMING PROCEDURE.	Evaluation
Material	Bottle of milk or juice.	

---

*Denotes self-help skill.

Behavioral Objectives	P/S/SH II 6

P/S/SH II 6	PLAYS WITH FOOT	Comment
General Objective	Development of body image.	

Specific Objective	The infant will become aware of feet through play.	

Activities

P/S/SH II 6.1	Hang mobile with sound toys across crib.	Evaluation
	Place infant so that feet can kick and sound the toys.	
	Guide infant's feet to success at sounding the toys.	
Materials	Bells, beads, rattles hung from mobile.	
Cue	Kick the _____ .	
	Push the _____ .	
	Get it with your feet.	

P/S/SH 6.2	Hang mobile with sound toys above infant's crib.	Evaluation
	Attach a cord to mobile.	
	Place infant in crib.	
	Attach cord to infant's feet or wrist.	
	Alternate. As infant moves, mobile moves and sounds are made.	
Materials	Mobile, cord, elastic, sound toys.	
Cue	Move your leg.	
	Move your hand.	
	Listen.	

P/S/SH II 6.3	Make mitts of infant's stocking with hole for thumb. Just leave as stockings for feet.	Evaluation
	Sew bells or objects from UNIT ACTIVITIES onto mitts and stockings for feet.	
	Help infant reach for objects when wearing mitts and stockings.	
Materials	Stockings, bells, UNIT ACTIVITIES MATERIALS.	
Cue	Get the _____ .	
	Grab the _____ .	

	Behavioral Objectives	P/S/SH II 7

P/S/SH II 7	DISCRIMINATES STRANGERS	Comment
General Objective		To be observed.
Specific Objective		

Activities

P/S/SH II 7.1	Provide opportunities for infant to see strangers.	Evaluation
Comment	Not all infants will react to the same degree.	

	Behavioral Objectives	P/S/SH II 8

P/S/SH II 8	SMILES AND VOCALIZES AT MIRROR IMAGE	Comment
General Objective	Development of positive response to infant's own face.	
Specific Objective	When a mirror is placed before infant's face, the infant will respond by smiling.	

Activities

P/S/SH II 8.1	Adult places a stainless flexible infant mirror or shiny cookie sheet in a position where infant can see his image.	Evaluation
	Encourage baby to smile by talking soothingly or tickling his chin.	
Material	Unbreakable infant mirror.	
Cue	Look at your face.	
Comment	Repeat this activity until infant smiles at his face.	
Comment	Gradually reduce the touching of infant's chin when his smile is spontaneous.	
Comment	Adult may use tapping on mirror surface, or blinking a flashlight in the mirror to draw attention to the mirror.	

Behavioral Objectives	P/S/SH II 9

P/S/SH II 9	RESPONDS WITH FEAR TO LOSS OF SUPPORT OR TO SUDDEN LOUD NOISES	Comment
General Objective	Development of responsiveness to environment.	To be observed
Specific Objective	The infant will be afraid of sudden loud noises and loss of support.	

Activities

P/S/SH II 9.1	Note infant's reaction to sudden loud noises.	Evaluation
Materials	Cymbal, bang pans, thunder, vacuum.	
Cue	Bang! That's loud. You're OK.	
Comment	The intensity of reaction is not the same in all infants.	
P/S/SH II 9.2	Hold infant over bed, about 12 inches above. Hold infant out straight with one hand under head and neck, the other under hips and legs.	Evaluation
	Lower adult hands about three inches quickly.	
	Note infant's reaction.	
Cue	Ooops. It's okay.	

Behavioral Objectives	P/S/SH II 10

P/S/SH II 10	HOLDS BOTTLE*	Comment
General Objective	Development of infant's feeding skills.	
Specific Objective	The infant will develop ability to hold the bottle.	

Activities

P/S/SH II 10.1	Place both of infant's hands on bottle during feeding.	Evaluation

*Denotes self-help skill.

	Release adult support of bottle gradually.	
Material	Bottle.	
Cue	Hold it. Hold the bottle.	

P/S/SH II 10.2	PROGRAMMING PROCEDURE	Evaluation
Materials	Bottle.	
Comment	Adult holds bottle as infant grows full and tired.	
Comment	String, fabric, or rope wound around bottle may help grasping.	

Behavioral Objectives	P/S/SH II 11

P/S/SH II 11	STRAINED FOOD TAKEN WELL*	Comment
General Objective	Development of eating skills.	
Specific Objective	The infant will develop the ability to eat strained foods well.	

Activities

P/S/SH II 11.1	Present strained foods in very liquid form. Gradually thicken as infant learns to eat.	Evaluation
Materials	Liquified cereals and strained foods, spoon.	
P/S/SH II 11.2	Add tiny bits of crushed ice to the food. Place far back on tongue. Ice will encourage infant to use tongue.	Evaluation
Materials	As above. Bits of ice.	
Comment	If a small spoon is not available, use popsicle stick or tongue depressor.	
Comment	Touch infant's tongue in several places with depressor or stick for awareness.	

_____

*Denotes self-help skill.

P/S/SH II 12	BEGINS SHOWING FEAR OF STRANGERS	Comment
General Objective	Diminish infant's fear reaction to strangers.	
Specific Objective	When strangers approach the child, the infant's degree of fear will be minimal.	

Activities

P/S/SH II 12.1	Adult should suggest that people do not rush to touch or grab baby.	Evaluation
	Allow opportunities for him to see strangers.	
Cue	Don't be afraid.	
Comment	If "strangers" are friends or relatives, adult should make an exaggerated positive response to them to encourage infant not to be afraid.	

P/S/SH II 13	PATS IMAGE OF SELF IN MIRROR	Comment
General Objective	Encourage development of body image.	
Specific Objective	When presented with his image in a mirror, the infant will respond by patting it.	

Activities

P/S/SH II 13.1	Hold mirror in front of infant.	Evaluation
	Encourage the infant to reach for and touch the image.	
Materials	Unbreakable mirror, cookie sheet.	
Cue	Where's the baby? Where's _____ ? (infant's name)	
Comment	If infant does not try to touch the image, take her hand and place it on her image. Make it a game.	

Comment	Use smiles, touches, and pleasure for success.	

	Behavioral Objectives	P/S/SH II 14
P/S/SH II 14	GOES TO FAMILIAR PERSON FOR COMPANIONSHIP	Comment
General Objective	Development of social interaction skills.	
Specific Objective	The infant will go to familiar people for companionship.	

Activities

P/S/SH II 14.1	Allow friends or relatives to play with infant. In addition, it is helpful if other people can provide care for the infant (i.e., feed, diaper, etc.) sometimes. Show the infant that you like these people by exaggerated actions or speech.	Evaluation
Cue	See how Aunt _____ loves you. Grandma is feeding you.	

	Behavioral Objectives	P/S/SH II 15
P/S/SH II 15	UNHAPPINESS IS SPECIFICALLY FEAR OR DISGUST, ETC.	Comment
General Objective	Develop social response repertoire.	
Specific Objective	Given a stressful situation, the infant will respond with specific expressions, that is, fear, disgust.	To be observed.

Activities

P/S/SH II 15.1	See activities described for P/S/SH II 4. Observe the infant's reactions to stress and note whether she responds differently to anger, frustration, etc.	Evaluation
Material	Unbreakable infant mirror.	

Cue　　　　　　Is ＿＿＿＿＿scared? (name)
　　　　　　　Is ＿＿＿＿＿＿ angry?
　　　　　　　Is ＿＿＿＿＿＿ sad?

	Behavioral Objectives	P/S/SH II　16

P/S/SH II　16	HAPPINESS IS SPECIFICALLY ELATION OR AFFECTION	Comment
General Objective	Develop social response repertoire.	
Specific Objective	Given a delightful situation, the infant will respond with specific expressions of happiness, affection, etc.	To be observed.

Activities		
P/S/SH II　16.1	See also P/S/SH II 4 and P/S/SH II 15.	Evaluation
	Encourage the infant to respond in a differentiated manner to happy times.	
	The adult should respond in an exaggerated fashion and encourage the infant to imitate.	
	If the situation calls for affection, the adult should hold out his arms and hug infant.	
	Encourage infant to hug back.	
Material	Unbreakable mirror.	
Cue	Is ＿＿＿＿＿＿ happy? (name) I love (name).＿	

	Behavioral Objectives	P/S/Sh II　17

P/S/SH II　17	AMUSES SELF BRIEFLY	Comment
General Objective	Develop infant's ability to play by herself.	To be observed.
Specific Objective	When infant is provided with periods of non-adult attention, child will be able to amuse self.	

Activities

P/S/SH II   17.1   Place the infant in a playpen within sight of   Evaluation
an adult.

Present a variety of toys or objects near the
baby.

Put a mobile where the baby can see it.

Place designs around the playpen where she
can see them.

Play a radio with soft music in the
background.

Materials   Toys, dolls, spoons, plastic cups, rattles,
mobiles, geometric shapes, numbers.

Comment   Periodically change the position of the toys or
hanging objects.

Comment   Move her playpen near a window where she
may see the activity outside.

Comment   Use smiles, touches, and pleasure for periods
of self-amusement—gradually increase longer
periods of play.

	Behavioral Objectives	P/S/Sh II 18

P/S/SH II 18	FEEDS SELF COOKIE*	Comment
General Objective	Develop infant's self-feeding skill.	
Specific Objective	When a biscuit is placed in the infant's hand, he will feed himself the biscuit.	

Activities

P/S/SH II   18.1   Place infant in supported sitting position in a   Evaluation
high chair at mealtime.

Put several bite-size biscuits, cookies, crackers, banana slices, etc. on the high chair tray.

Encourage the infant to pick up the food and
eat it.

---

*Denotes self-help skill.

Material	Bite-sized food.
Cue	Pick up and eat your _____ .
Comment	If the infant does not pick up the food, place it in his hands and guide his hand.
Comment	Use smiles, touches, and pleasure for success.
Comment	Gradually fade assistance as he learns to feed himself.

Behavioral Objectives   P/S/SH II   19

P/S/SH II 19	CHEWS FOOD*	Comment
General Objective	Develop ability to eat solid food.	
Specific Objective	When provided with semisolid food, the infant will chew the food.	

Activities

P/S/SH II 19.1	Place infant in a high chair.	Evaluation
	Offer her some soft foods that she enjoys, that is, bananas, peaches, etc. near the back of her mouth.	
	Encourage her to chew and swallow the food.	
Material	Semisolid food.	
Cue	(Infant's name) is chewing and swallowing all by herself.	
Comment	If she cannot chew by herself, place your fingers around her mouth and gently move her jaws up and down.	
Comment	At first only use food the infant likes. Then introduce other semisolid foods.	
Comment	Gradually fade any assistance as she is able to chew and swallow well.	

---

*Denotes self-help skill.

	Behavioral Objectives	P/S/SH II 20

P/S/SH II 20	PULLS TOY AWAY FROM ADULT	Comment
General Objective	Encourage infant to imitate social action.	
Specific Objective	When a toy is held out to the infant, he will pull the toy away from the adult.	

Activities

P/S/SH II 20.1	Place infant in a supported sitting position.	Evaluation
	Hold a favorite toy in your hand within his reach.	
	Talk exaggeratedly about the toy.	
Material	Infant's favorite toy.	
Cue	What a fun toy this is.	
Comment	Do not tell the infant to take the toy, rather see if he will imitate the action to take the toy away.	
Comment	Offer VERY SLIGHT resistance to see if he will actually pull toy away.	

	Behavioral Objectives	P/S/SH II 21

P/S/SH II 21	REACHES PERSISTENTLY FOR TOYS	Comment
General Objective	Develop social response repertoire.	
Specific Objective	When presented with a toy, the infant will reach for it persistently.	

Activities

P/S/SH II 21.1	Place child in supported sitting position.	Evaluation
	Present a favorite toy just out of her reach.	
	Encourage her to reach for the toy, but do not let her have it on her first attempt.	
Material	Infant's favorite toy.	

Cue	Get your toy.
Comment	Do not frustrate the infant by prolonging this activity. If she keeps reaching for the toy after her initial unsuccessful attempt, allow her to touch, grasp, and play with toy.
	Repeat the activity.

	Behavioral Objectives	P/S/SH III 1

P/S/SH III 1	WORKS FOR TOY OUT OF REACH	Comment
General Objective	Develop goal-directed behavior.	
Specific Objective	When toy is presented out of reach, the infant will work to secure the toy.	

Activities

P/S/SH III 1.1	Place infant in a sitting position.	Evaluation
	Present her favorite toy in her line of vision. Then place the toy under a table or chair or in a place where she must show some effort to get the toy. Encourage her to get the toy.	
Material	Toy.	
Cue	See your _____ . It's under the chair. Get it.	
Comment	Really praise the infant with STP when she attempts to get the toy, even if her attempt is unsuccessful.	

P/S/SH III 1.2	Repeat 1.1, but place the toy in a different location.	Evaluation
Material	Toy.	
Cue	See your _____ . It's under the _____ . Get it.	
Comment	Vary the toy and the location, making this activity a game. The object is to develop the infant's perseverance in acquiring a desired object.	

P/S/SH III　2	PLAYS PEEK-A-BOO	Comment
General Objective	Encourage infant to play games for fun.	
Specific Objective	The infant will play peek-a-boo.	

Activities

P/S/SH III　2.1	Place the infant in a sitting position.	Evaluation
	Place your hands over your face, drop your hands and say "peek-a-boo" with exaggeration.	
Cue	Peek-a-boo.	
P/S/SH III　2.2	Place the infant's hands over his face, pull them down and say "peek-a-boo."	Evaluation
Cue	Peek-a-boo.	
P/S/SH III　2.3	Hide behind a chair or table and say "peek-a-boo." Hide again and encourage infant to peek out for you.	Evaluation
Cue	Peek-a-boo.	
P/S/SH III　2.4	Place the infant behind an object. Encourage him to say "peek-a-boo."	Evaluation

P/S/SH III　3	RESPONDS TO OWN NAME	Comment
General Objective	Encouragement of infant's ability to respond to own name.	
Specific Objective	The infant will respond to the sound of her own name.	

Activities

P/S/SH III 3.1	Adult uses infant's name continually when speaking to her.	Evaluation
Cue	Infant's name.	

"Is _____ hungry?"

"Does _____ want to go bye-bye?"

P/S/SH III 3.2	Call infant's name from outside room and see if infant responds by:	Evaluation

1. looking at adult or
2. stopping activity or
3. vocalization.

Cue	Infant's name.
Comment	Adult responds to infant's effort with smiles, touches, and pleasure.

P/S/SH III 3.3	Enlarge a photograph of infant. Cover with clear contact paper. Paste on back of unbreakable infant's mirror. Point to picture or infant's face in mirror and name infant.	Evaluation
Material	Nonbreakable infant mirror.	
	Picture.	
	Glue.	
Cue	Name Infant.	

P/S/SH III 3.4	Use PHONETIC SYMBOL PROCEDURE for infant's name.	Evaluation

P/S/SH III 3.5	Use TOUCH PROCEDURE II to help teach infant to say her own name.	Evaluation

P/S/SH III 3.6	Use TAPE PROCEDURE.	Evaluation
Materials	Tape, recorder, microphone.	

P/S/SH III 3.7	Use PROGRAMMING PROCEDURE.	Evaluation
Materials	Food as desired.	

Behavioral Objectives	P/S/SH III 4

P/S/SH III 4	RESPONDS TO PICK-UP GESTURE WITH UNDERSTANDING	Comment
General Objective	Develop meaningful response to pick-up gesture.	
Specific Objective	When an adult makes the pick-up gesture to the infant, he will respond with understanding.	

Activities

P/S/SH III 4.1	Place infant in a sitting position.	Evaluation
	Hold out your arms toward him.	
	Encourage him to hold out his arms to be picked up.	
Cue	I'll pick you up.	
Comment	If infant does not hold his arms out, pull them out toward you before you pick him up.	
Comment	Give only as much help as necessary, but *do not* pick the infant up until he holds his arms out.	

Behavioral Objectives	P/S/SH III 5

P/S/SH III 5	FEEDS SELF BOTTLE*—PUTS IN AND REMOVES FROM MOUTH	Comment
General Objective	Develop skill and independence in self-feeding.	
Specific Objective	When presented with a bottle, the infant will be able to feed herself by placing bottle in mouth and removing.	

Activities

P/S/SH III 5.1	Place infant's hands around the bottle.	Evaluation
	Gently move the bottle toward her mouth.	

*Denotes self-help skill.

Allow the infant to hold her own bottle during feeding.

After feeding, guide her hands to remove the bottle.

Cue   See how <u>(infant's name)</u> feeds herself.

Comment   Help the infant only as much as necessary, gradually reducing your aid as she becomes better at this activity.

	Behavioral Objectives	P/S/SH III 6

P/S/SH III 6	STRONG ANXIETY REGARDING STRANGERS	Comment
General Objective	Encourage infant not to be anxious regarding strangers.	
Specific Objective	Reduce infant's anxiety toward strangers.	

Activities

P/S/SH III 6.1	Request that strangers not approach infant rapidly or attempt to touch or grab him quickly.	Evaluation
	Allow him to see strangers in a variety of situations.	
	Be fairly nonchalant toward strangers by talking soothingly to the infant.	

	Behavioral Objectives	P/S/SH III 7

P/S/SH III 7	REMAINS DRY ONE TO TWO HOURS*	Comment
General Objective		To be observed.
Specific Objective		

---

*Denotes self-help skill.

Activities

P/S/SH III   7.1   After putting a dry diaper on infant, check   Evaluation
the diaper every ten minutes for wetness.

Write down how long the infant is dry.

	Behavioral Objectives	P/S/SH III 8

P/S/SH III   8   ABLE TO PLAY ALONE FOR ABOUT   Comment
AN HOUR—BUT PREFERS COMPANY

General   Develop infant's ability to play alone.
Objective

Specific   When left alone, the infant will be able to play
Objective   for approximately one hour.

Activities

P/S/SH III   8.1   Place the infant's high chair or playpen near   Evaluation
an area of activity, that is, kitchen, living
room.

Present him with a wide variety of toys or interesting objects.

Then do some other activity and allow him to
play alone.

Materials   Toys.

Comment   Use STP to reinforce the infant for playing
alone. If possible place his playpen or chair
near a window. Place a radio or stereo in the
background.

Comment   At first he may play for periods shorter than
an hour.

Gradually increase the amount of time he
plays alone, occasionally talking to him to let
him know you are there.

Comment   Gradually move farther away from him until
you are only in his sight.

Behavioral Objectives   P/S/SH III   9

| P/S/SH III   9 | ACCEPTS NEW SOLID FOOD* | Comment |

| *P/S/SH III   9* | | |

General
Objective

Develop acceptance of new solid foods.

Specific
Objective

When presented with new solid foods, the infant will accept them.

Activities

| *P/S/SH III   9.1* | During feeding time introduce a new solid food to the infant (one she hasn't eaten before). | Evaluation |

Encourage her to eat the food by praising her and talking exaggeratedly about how tasty it is.

Material

New solid food.

Cue

Oh how good these _____ are.

Comment

Introduce new foods one at a time.

Use STP if the infant accepts the food, but do not force the food on the child.

---

*Denotes self-help skill.

Behavioral Objectives   P/S/SH III   10

| *P/S/SH III   10* | FINGER FEEDS* | Comment |

General
Objective

Develop infant's skill in finger feeding.

Specific
Objective

When presented with finger foods, the infant will be able to finger feed himself.

---

*Denotes self-help skill.

Activities

P/S/SH III	*10.1*	Place several bite-size pieces of infant's favorite food on the tray of his high chair at mealtime.	Evaluation
		Encourage him to pick up the food with his fingers and feed himself.	
		If the infant is unable, place your hands over his and gently guide the food to his mouth, but only give as much help as necessary.	
Material		Bits of food.	
Cue		Feed yourself some _____ all by yourself.	
Comment		Gradually fade your help as he is able to feed himself.	
		Use STP for successful attempts.	

Behavioral Objectives	P/S/SH III 11

P/S/SH III	*11*	EATS MASHED FOODS*	Comment
General Objective		Develop infant's ability to eat mashed table foods.	
Specific Objective		When presented with mashed table foods, the infant will eat them.	

Activities

P/S/SH III	*11.1*	Place the infant in high chair at mealtime.	Evaluation
		Present her with some mashed food, that is, potatoes, bananas, macaroni, etc.	
		Talk exaggeratedly about how good the food is.	
Cue		Oh how good these _____ are.	
Comment		In between spoonfuls give her liquid to help in swallowing.	
Comment		Be cheerful and use STP when she accepts the food.	

*Denotes self-help skill.

Behavioral Objectives	P/S/SH III 12

P/S/SH III 12	WAVES BYE-BYE RESPONSIVELY	Comment
General Objective	Encourage infant to wave bye-bye.	
Specific Objective	The infant will wave bye-bye in response to an adult.	

Activities

P/S/SH III 12.1	Raise the infant's hand and have him wave bye-bye to an adult leaving the room.	Evaluation
Cue	Bye-bye.	
P/S/SH III 12.2	Repeat 12.1 but have the infant touch fabric or soft sandpaper to get feel of bye-bye motion.	Evaluation
P/S/SH III 12.3	Repeat these activities with different people leaving the room as a game.	Evaluation
Comment	Reward with STP.	
Comment	Gradually reduce your help as the infant improves his ability to wave bye-bye.	
Comment	See also L III 8.	

Behavioral Objectives	P/S/SH III 13

P/S/SH III 13	PLAYS PAT-A-CAKE RESPONSIVELY	Comment
General Objective	Encourage infant to play pat-a-cake.	
Specific Objective	The infant will play pat-a-cake in response to an adult.	

Activities

P/S/SH III 13.1	Place your hands over the infant's and bring them together as a game.	Evaluation
Cue	Play pat-a-cake.	

Comment	You may wish to use the children's nursery rhyme as follows:	

Pat-a-cake, pat-a-cake, baker's man,
Bake me a cake as fast as you can,
Pat it, roll it, mark it with a "b,"
Put it in the oven for baby and me.

P/S/SH III 13.2	Hang some dangling objects in front of the infant and encourage her to bring her hands to midline.	Evaluation
Materials	Fabric, sponges, nylon balls, bells and so on.	
Comment	Allow infant to do this herself by gradually reducing your help.	

	Behavioral Objectives	P/S/SH III 14

P/S/SH III 14	OFFERS TOYS TO ADULT, BUT DOES NOT WANT TO GIVE THEM UP	Comment
General Objective	Encourage infant to give toys to adult (sharing).	
Specific Objective	The infant will offer a toy to an adult, but may not want to release it.	

Activities

P/S/SH III 14.1	Place a toy in the infant's hand	Evaluation
	Ask him to give you the toy by extending your hand.	
	If necessary guide his hand toward yours.	
	Encourage him to release the toy, but give it back to him IMMEDIATELY.	
Material	Toy.	
Cue	Let me hold the _____ for awhile.	
Comment	Repeat this activity many times, making it a game but always return the toy so he is aware that he will get it back.	

Behavioral Objectives   P/S/SH III 15

P/S/SH III 15	ENJOYS DROPPING TOYS FROM PLAYPEN OR CHAIR TO BE RETRIEVED BY ADULT	Comment
General Objective	Discourage child from dropping toys to manipulate adults.	
Specific Objective	Observe that the infant can drop toys from playpen or chair to be picked up by adult, then extinguish this behavior.	To be observed.

Activities

P/S/SH III 15.1	Infant is in playpen or high chair.	Evaluation
	The infant will throw toys on the floor with the expectation that the adult will retrieve them.	
	If you play this game with the infant and reinforce the behavior, she will think you should give her service. When she throws toys, do not scold her, just take the toys away for a few minutes.	
Comment	The infant should spend time on the floor with her toys so she can practice throwing objects and can retrieve them herself.	

Behavioral Objectives   P/S/SH III 16

P/S/SH III 16	INCREASED AFFECTION AND INTEREST IN FAMILY GROUP	Comment
General Objective	Develop infant's affection and interest in family.	
Specific Objective	The infant will demonstrate an increase in affection and interest in the family group.	

Activities

P/S/SH III 16.1	Place the infant's playpen, or let him play on the floor, near family living or activity areas.	Evaluation
	Talk to him soothingly and tell him what you are doing.	

P/S/SH III 16.2	Use physical affection (hugs and kisses) as a reward (the STP procedure).	Evaluation
	Respond to his attempts to gain affection by showing affection.	
	Encourage him to hug and kiss you in return.	
Cue	Give Mommy (Daddy) a hug and kiss.	

Behavioral Objectives	P/S/SH III 17

P/S/SH III 17	RELEASES OBJECT TO ANOTHER UPON REQUEST	Comment
General Objective	Encourage child to release object to another upon request.	
Specific Objective	When an adult requests an object, the child will release it to the adult.	

Activities

P/S/SH III 17.1	See P/S/SH III 14 for practice activities.	Evaluation
P/S/SH III 17.2	Give the child a toy to hold.	Evaluation
	Hold out your hand and ask the child to give it to you.	
Material	Toy.	
Cue	Give me the _____ .	
Comment	Use STP when the child releases the toy to you.	
Comment	Make it like a game by saying a poem or singing a song.	

Behavioral Objectives	P/S/SH III 18

P/S/SH III 18	DISTINGUISHES BETWEEN YOU AND ME	Comment
General Objective	Develop child's ability to distinguish between you and me.	
Specific Objective	The child will demonstrate the ability to distinguish between you and me.	

Activities

P/S/SH III	18.1	Give the child a toy to play with.	Evaluation
		Then ask the child to "Give the toy to *me*."	
		Hold the toy out to the child and say "Now *you* take it."	
		Repeat this activity.	
Material		Toy.	
Cue		Use "me" and "you."	
P/S/SH III	18.2	Take a number of toys and place them before the child.	Evaluation
		Play a game where you divide the toys between "you" and "me" by saying—"This one belongs to you and this one is for me."	
Materials		Toys.	
Cue		Use "me" and "you."	
Comment		Use "you" and "me" exaggeratedly.	
P/S/SH III	18.3	Repeat the activity in 18.2 but encourage the child to answer the question "Who does this belong to?" with the words "you" and "me."	Evaluation
Comment		Use STP for correct response.	

	Behavioral Objectives	P/S/SH III 19

P/S/SH III	19	SHOWS FEAR, AFFECTION, ANGER, JEALOUSY, SYMPATHY, AND ANXI-ETY	Comment
General Objective		Develop child's emotional response reper-toire.	
Specific Objective		When presented with varying situations, the child will respond with fear, anger, etc.	

Activities

P/S/SH III	19.1	When the child shows an emotion, talk to her about it; label it.	Evaluation
Cue		Is <u>(child's name)</u> scared?	

Does (child's name) love me?

Are you angry? Sad?, etc.

P/S/SH III 19.2   Use an unbreakable mirror so the child is able   Evaluation
to see her face when she displays emotion.

Cue   Is (child's name) scared?

Does (child's name) love me?

Are you angry? Sad?, etc.

	Behavioral Objectives	P/S/SH III 20

P/S/SH III 20	DRY AFTER NAP*	Comment
General Objective	Encourage dryness after a nap.	
Specific Objective	When the child wakes up from a nap, he will be dry.	To be observed.

Activities

P/S/SH III 20.1	Limit the child's liquid intake before naps.	Evaluation
Comment	After the child wakes up from a nap, he should be dry.	
	Praise him and reward him if he wakes up dry.	

———

*Denotes self-help skill.

	Behavioral Objectives	P/S/SH III 21

P/S/SH III 21	FUSSES UNTIL CHANGED*	Comment
General Objective		
Specific Objective		To be observed.

———

*Denotes self-help skill.

Activities

P/S/SH III   21.1

Comment	Children at this age are often intolerant of wetness.	Evaluation
	Change the child as soon as possible, but do not encourage fussing during changing.	
	Do not encourage or reward this behavior.	

	Behavioral Objectives	P/S/SH III 22

P/S/SH III 22	BEGINS TO COOPERATE IN DRESSING*	Comment
General Objective	Encourage child to cooperate in dressing.	
Specific Objective	When dressing the child, he will begin to cooperate in the dressing.	

Activities

P/S/SH III 22.1	When dressing the child, encourage him to hold his arms out toward the sleeve.	Evaluation
	If necessary help the child to raise his arms, but only give as much help as needed.	
Cue	Raise your arm.	
Comment	Use STP when the child attempts to raise his arm.	
P/S/SH III 22.2	Repeat 22.1 for putting on socks, pants, shoes, etc.	Evaluation
Cue	Raise your leg.	
Comment	Use STP when the child attempts to raise his leg.	

---

*Denotes self-help skill.

	Behavioral Objectives	P/S/SH III 23

P/S/SH III 23	MANIPULATES STRING OR SMALL OBJECT	Comment
General Objective	Develop fine motor coordination and manipulative skills.	
Specific Objective	When presented with a small object, the child will manipulate it.	

P/S/SH III 23.1	Present the child with a small cube, peg, or block.	Evaluation
	Encourage her to turn it around and look at it without dropping it.	
	Talk about the object—color, shape, texture, etc.	
Materials	Cube, block, peg, etc.	
Cue	Play with or See the _____ . Turn it around with your fingers.	
Comment	Vary the shape, color, and texture of the objects used.	

P/S/SH III 23.2	Substitute brightly colored yarn for the objects described in 23.1.	Evaluation
	Gently wrap the yarn around her wrist (or over her head or ear). Tell her to pull it off.	

	Behavioral Objectives	P/S/SH III 24

P/S/SH III 24	SHOWS SHOE, EYE, NOSE, ETC. RESPONSIVELY	Comment
General Objective	Develop body image.	
Specific Objective	When asked to point to eye, nose, etc. the child will be able to respond correctly.	

Activities

P/S/SH III 24.1 Place the child in a sitting position.   Evaluation

Sit directly in front of him and ask him to point to his nose, eye, etc.

If the child is unable to respond to your verbal command, place your hand over his and guide his finger to his nose.

Repeat.

Cue   Show me your _____ .

Comment   Give only as much help as needed, gradually fading your assistance.

Comment   Make this a game by singing or saying a poem.

	Behavioral Objectives	P/S/SH III 25

P/S/SH III 25   HUGS AND SHOWS AFFECTION   Comment
                  TOWARD DOLL OR TEDDY BEAR

General   Encourage child to hug and show affection
Objective   to doll or teddy bear.

Specific   The child will demonstrate affection toward
Objective   a doll or teddy bear by hugging it.

Activities

P/S/SH III 25.1 Show the child how to hug and kiss a doll   Evaluation
                   or teddy bear.

Give the doll to the child and encourage her to do the same.

Materials   Doll, teddy bear.

Cue   Hug dolly (teddy); give him a kiss.

P/S/SH III 25.2 Give the doll to the child and ask her to take   Evaluation
                   care of it, that is, rock it to sleep, talk to it, etc.

Materials   As above.

Cue   Talk to dolly (teddy).
                  Sing to dolly (teddy).

P/S/SH III 26	PLAYS NEAR OTHER CHILDREN	Comment
General Objective	Encourage child to play near other children.	
Specific Objective	When placed near other children, the child will play.	

Activities

P/S/SH III 26.1	Take the child to a playground or other area where children are playing.	Evaluation
	Take along some of his favorite toys.	
	Place him near the other children and encourage him to play with his toys.	
Materials	Toys.	
Cue	Play with your _____ .	
Comment	Use smiles, touches, and pleasure when the child plays with his toys.	

P/S/SH III 27	VARIES BEHAVIOR ACCORDING TO EMOTIONAL REACTION OF OTHERS	Comment
General Objective	Develop child's awareness of other's emotional reaction.	
Specific Objective	When others present emotional reaction to child, she will vary her behavior according to that reaction.	

Activities

P/S/SH III 27.1	When the child does a cute action applaud, laugh, and make a big fuss over it.	Evaluation
Cue	Oh my, how well you do that, etc.	
Comment	Use smiles, touches, and pleasure to reinforce child.	

P/S/SH III	*27.2*	Ask the child to repeat the action for someone else.	Evaluation
		Make a fuss over her action.	
P/S/SH III	*27.3*	Use positive reactions to child when she does something cute or funny.	Evaluation
P/S/SH III	*27.3*	If the child does something wrong, show the child your displeasure with a stern face and tell the child that it makes you unhappy.	Evaluation
		See if child stops the behavior.	
Cue		I feel sad when you don't listen to me, etc.	

Behavioral Objectives	P/S/SH III 28

P/S/SH III	*28*	INDICATES WANTS WITHOUT CRYING	Comment
General Objective		Encourage child to indicate his wants without crying.	
Specific Objective		When the child wants something, he will indicate his want without crying.	

Activities

P/S/SH III	*28.1*	If the child wants something (drink of water, a toy, etc.) and crys to obtain it, ignore his crying; ask him if he wants a drink, a toy, etc.	Evaluation
		Encourage him to say yes, shake his head, point, etc. Reinforce this behavior.	
Cue		Do you want a _____ ?	
Comment		Use smiles, touches, and pleasure when child indicates a want without crying.	
P/S/SH III	*28.2*	Encourage the child to indicate his wants by asking, pointing, etc.	Evaluation
		Immediately reinforce this behavior and tell the child how good he is for asking for something without crying and how happy it makes you.	

	Behavioral Objectives	P/S/SH III 29

P/S/SH III 29	ATTEMPTS TO PLAY BALL WITH ADULT	Comment
General Objective	Develop motor and social skills.	
Specific Objective	When a ball is rolled to the infant, she will attempt to roll it back in a playful fashion.	

Activities

P/S/SH III 29.1	Sit on floor with infant between your outstretched legs. Pass a ball back and forth, beginning at a few inches distance. Gradually increase distance.	Evaluation
Materials	Soft sponge, nylon, or rubber ball.	
Cue	Catch the ball. Give me the ball.	

P/S/SH III 29.2	Keeping infant between your legs, increase the distance and roll the ball. Encourage the infant to roll it back. Help infant as necessary.	Evaluation
Materials	As before.	
Cue	Catch the ball. Roll the ball.	
Comment	STP.	

	Behavioral Objectives	P/S/SH III 30

P/S/SH III 30	HOLDS SPOON AND PUTS INTO DISH*	Comment
General Objective	Encourage child in his early attempts at self-feeding with a spoon.	
Specific Objective	When the child is presented with a spoon, he will grasp the spoon and insert it into a dish.	

*Denotes self-help skill.

Activities

P/S/SH III   *30.1*   Place child in high chair at mealtimes.   Evaluation

Put a dish of food in front of him and hand him spoon.

Encourage him to put the spoon into the dish of food.

If the child does not respond, guide his hand toward the dish, fill with food, and guide spoon to his mouth.

Materials   Dish, spoon.

Cue   Put the spoon in the dish.

Comment   Give only as much help as necessary to get the child to put the spoon in the dish. Remember you will want him to simply place the spoon in the dish at this time; you will help him to get the spoon to his mouth.

Comment   Use smiles, touches, and pleasure for a successful attempt in putting the spoon in the dish.

Behavioral Objectives	P/S/SH III 31

P/S/SH III *31* GRASPS CUP WITH FINGERS, BUT LIKELY TO TIP CUP TOO QUICKLY*	Comment
General Objective Encourage child to hold cup to prepare for self-drinking.	
Specific Objective When child is presented with a cup, she will hold it with a finger grasp.	

Activities

P/S/SH III   *31.1*   Place child in high chair at mealtimes.   Evaluation

Present her with a plastic cup half full of milk, juice, etc.

---

*Denotes self-help skill.

	Encourage her to grasp the cup; if she does not respond, place her fingers around the cup and gently assist her in raising it toward her mouth.
Material	Plastic cup.
Cue	Hold your cup.
Comment	Give only as much help as necessary to get the child to hold her own cup; remember you will still have to help her get it to her mouth.
Comment	Use smiles, touches, and pleasure for successful attempt at holding the cup.

	Behavioral Objectives	P/S/SH III 32
P/S/SH III 32	INDICATES WET PANTS BUT NOT TOILET NEEDS*	Comment
General Objective	Encourage child to indicate wet pants.	
Specific Objective	When the child has wet pants, he will indicate this to an adult.	To be observed.

Activities

P/S/SH III 32.1	Observe the child when you suspect he has wet pants.	Evaluation
	He may appear fidgety, uncomfortable, or pull at the front of his pants.	
	This may be a sign he is wet.	
	Encourage the child to tell you he is wet or indicate it to you in some way.	
Cue	Are you wet?	
Comment	The goal here is to have the child *indicate* he is wet to you.	
	Reinforce him for telling you or showing you he is wet.	

---

*Denotes self-help skill.

Behavioral Objectives   P/S/SH III 33

P/S/SH III 33	TRIES TO PUT ON CLOTHING*	Comment
General Objective	Encourage child to attempt to put on clothes.	
Specific Objective	The child will attempt to put on clothes in an effort to dress herself.	

Activities

P/S/SH III 33.1	When you are dressing the child, encourage her to attempt to dress herself.	Evaluation
	She will attempt (unsuccessfully) to put on the clothes; assist her and praise her for trying to dress herself.	
Cue	Try to put on your _____ .	
Comment	Complete self-dressing occurs at a later period. At this point we simply want to encourage attempts at dressing.	

---

*Denotes self-help skill.

Behavioral Objectives   P/S/SH III 34

P/S/SH III 34	EXTENDS ARM OR LEG COOPERATIVELY WHEN BEING DRESSED*	Comment
General Objective	Encourage the child to cooperate fully in dressing by extending his arm or leg.	
Specific Objective	When dressing the child, he will cooperate by extending his arm or leg.	

Activities

P/S/SH III 34.1	See P/S/SH III 22 for practice activities.	Evaluation
P/S/SH III 34.2	Repeat activities in P/S/SH III 22 until child extends arm or leg on request and cooperates fully.	Evaluation

---

*Denotes self-help skill

| Cue | Put out your arm, leg, etc. |
| Comment | Use smiles, touches, and pleasure when child cooperates. |

	Behavioral Objectives	P/S/SH IV 1

P/S/SH IV 1	IMITATES OBSERVED ACTIVITIES	Comment
General Objective	Encouragement of child's efforts to imitate others.	
Specific Objective	The child will imitate adult activities.	

Activities

P/S/SH IV 1.1	Observe and note child's efforts to imitate with STP.	Evaluation
P/S/SH IV 1.2	Encourage child's efforts to imitate with STP.	Evaluation
P/S/SH IV 1.3	Utilize child's interest in imitation to teach many practical life skills.	Evaluation

	Behavioral Objectives	P/S/SH IV 2

P/S/SH IV 2	PULLS A TOY	Comment
General Objective	Development of child's ability to pull objects.	
Specific Objective	The child will pull toys during play.	

Activities

P/S/SH IV 2.1	Provide child with toy that can be pulled behind.	Evaluation
	Place string or handle in child's hand.	
	Help child pull object.	
	Let child pull alone as soon as possible.	

Materials	Pull toys.
	Plastic water container, partly filled with colored water and toys to slosh. String and ring to pull with.
	Seal top of container with tape.
Cue	Pull!
	Pull the _____ .
Comment	Children in this period also love to carry objects. It's a good time for a "pick up box" for toys.

	Behavioral Objectives	P/S/SH IV 3

P/S/SH IV 3	SHORT ATTENTION SPAN	Comment
General Objective	Development of attention span.	
Specific Objective	The child will show a short attention span.	

Activities

P/S/SH IV 3.1	Observe and note length of time child stays at any one activity.	Evaluation
P/S/SH IV 3.2	Use PROGRAMMING PROCEDURE to increase attention span if absolutely necessary.	Evaluation
Materials	Food as desired.	
Comment	The child will require more toys and time during this period than most adults are prepared for, which is normal.	

	Behavioral Objectives	P/S/SH IV 4

P/S/SH IV 4	NEGATIVISM—OPPOSES MOST REQUESTS	Comment
General Objective		To be observed.

Specific
Objective

Activities		
P/S/SH IV 4.1	Note and observe occurrence of negativism.	Evaluation
P/S/SH IV 4.2	Use a lot of STP when child does occasionally try to please adults.	Evaluation
Comment	Adult attitude must be one of patience and humor.	
Comment	Do not take all this negativism personally.	
Comment	Firmly but kindly direct child when necessary.	
P/S/SH IV 4.3	Help child have many happy and successful experiences each day.	Evaluation
Comment	This is more important than punishing!	
Comment	This is a very critical period in the development of self-concept.	
	Child must come through with a sense of worth.	

	Behavioral Objectives	P/S/SH IV 5
P/S/SH IV 5	TRIES TO PUT ON SHOES*	Comment
General Objective	Development of self-help skills.	
Specific Objective	When presented with a pair of her own shoes, the child will attempt to put them on.	

Activities		
P/S/SH IV 5.1	Observe and note when child tries to put on shoes.	Evaluation
Comment	Use STP and encourage efforts although the task is too difficult.	

*Denotes self-help skill.

P/S/SH IV 5.2	Adult provides little knit slippers that fit either foot.	Evaluation
	Adult shows child how to pull on knit slippers.	
	Adult helps child until child can care for herself.	
Materials	Knit slippers.	
Cue	Toes in.	
	Pull!	

	Behavioral Objectives	P/S/SH IV 6

P/S/SH IV 6	CAN TAKE OFF SMALL ITEMS OF CLOTHING*	Comment
General Objective	Development of dressing skills.	
Specific Objective	The child will be able to take off small items of clothing.	

Activities

P/S/SH IV 6.1	Adult practices alone on simple way to remove mittens, hats, socks, and shoes.	Evaluation
	Adult shows child.	
	Adult helps child until no longer needed.	
Materials	Mittens, hats, socks, and shoes.	
Cue	Pull! Off! Push!	
P/S/SH IV 6.2	Use STP to encourage child.	Evaluation
P/S/SH IV 6.3	Use PROGRAMMING PROCEDURE if necessary.	Evaluation
Material	Reward.	

*Denotes self-help skill.

	Behavioral Objectives	P/S/SH IV 7

P/S/SH IV 7	CAN UNZIP ZIPPERS*	Comment
General Objective	Development of dressing skills.	
Specific Objective	The child can unzip zippers.	

Activities

P/S/SH IV 7.1	Adult helps child unzip child's jacket.	Evaluation
	Adult places one of child's hands to hold clothing at the top of zipper.	
	Adult guides child's other hand to pull zipper down.	
	Adult helps child only as long as necessary.	
Materials	Jacket with zipper. Formboard with zipper. Doll clothing with a zipper.	
Cue	Hold here. Pull down.	
Comment	The secret of this skill is to hold the zipper firmly.	

*Denotes self-help skill.

	Behavioral Objectives	P/S/SH IV 8

P/S/SH IV 8	FILLS SPOON, BUT SPILLS MUCH WHILE ATTEMPTING TO FEED SELF*	Comment
General Objective	Development of eating skills.	
Specific Objective	The child will fill spoon and feed himself a little.	

*Denotes self-help skill.

Activities

P/S/SH IV 8.1	See P/S/SH III 30 for practice activities.	Evaluation
P/S/SH IV 8.2	Place child in high chair at mealtime.	Evaluation
	Provide him with a dish of food that has some consistency and will stick to spoon (mashed potatoes, pudding, mashed bananas, etc).	
	Stand behind him and encourage him to fill the spoon and bring it to his mouth.	
	Assist him to guide the spoon to his mouth if necessary.	
Material	Mashed food.	
Cue	Eat all by yourself.	
Comment	Gradually fade your assistance as child demstrates more skill.	
Comment	The child will spill a great deal at first; be prepared for this—use a plastic drop cloth under his chair.	

Behavioral Objectives	P/S/SH IV 9

P/S/SH IV 9	TURNS SPOON IN MOUTH*	Comment
General Objective	Develop independent feeding skills.	
Specific Objective	When attempting to feed herself, the child will turn the spoon in her mouth.	

Activities

P/S/SH IV 9.1	See P/S/SH III 20 and P/S/SH IV 8 for practice activities.	Evaluation
P/S/SH IV 9.2	Once child is placing spoon in mouth fairly well, the next step is to get her to turn the spoon to tip the food in her mouth and scoop it off with her top lip.	Evaluation
	Assist the child to turn the spoon and use her lip with your finger.	

---

*Denotes self-help skill.

Material	Mashed food.
Cue	Turn the spoon; scoop off the food with your lip.
Comment	Gradually reduce your help as the child becomes more proficient at this skill.
Comment	Use STP for successful attempts.

	Behavioral Objectives	P/S/SH IV 10

P/S/SH IV 10	CUP LIFTED TO MOUTH, DRINKS WELL*	Comment
General Objective	Development and refinement of independent feeding skills.	
Specific Objective	When attempting to drink liquid, the child will lift the cup to his mouth and drink without spilling.	

Activities

P/S/SH IV 10.1	See P/S/SH III 31 for practice activities.	Evaluation
P/S/SH IV 10.2	Present child with one-handled plastic cup filled about one-third of the way.	Evaluation
	Teach as outlined in P/S/SH V 1.3 for LIVING SKILLS PROCEDURE.	

*Denotes self-help skill.

	Behavioral Objectives	P/S/SH IV 11

P/S/SH IV 11	HANDS EMPTY CUP TO ADULT*	Comment
General Objective	Development of social and eating skills.	

*Denotes self-help skill.

Specific Objective	The child will hand an empty cup to an adult.	

Activities

P/S/SH IV 11.1	See P/S/SH III 31 for practice activities.	Evaluation
P/S/SH IV 11.2	Respond to child's gesture with appropriate language and smiles.	Evaluation
Material	Cup.	
Cue	All done? All gone? Do you want more?	
P/S/SH IV 11.3	"Handing" things may be practiced as a skill or refined through use of PROGRAMMING PROCEDURE.	Evaluation
Material	Reward.	

	Behavioral Objectives	P/S/SH IV 12

P/S/SH IV 12	HOLD GLASS WITH BOTH HANDS*	Comment
General Objective	Development of eating skills.	
Specific Objective	The child will hold a glass with two hands.	

Activities

P/S/SH IV 12.1	Teach as outlined for other skills in P/S/SH III 31.	Evaluation
P/S/SH IV 12.2	Adult responds to child's effort with smiles, touches, and pleasure.	Evaluation
P/S/SH IV 12.3	Use LIVING SKILLS PROCEDURE as outlined in P/S/SH V 1.3.	Evaluation

*Denotes self-help skill.

Behavioral Objectives   P/S/SH IV 13

P/S/SH IV 13	BOWEL AND BLADDER MAY BE REGULATED IN DAYTIME*	Comment
General Objective	Development of toileting skills.	
Specific Objective	Some days, the child will be able to regulate toileting in the daytime.	

Activities

P/S/SH IV 13.1	Choose words to be used in potty training. Use them consistently.	Evaluation
P/S/SH IV 13.2	Let child watch family members use the toilet. Use language chosen.	Evaluation
P/S/SH IV 13.3	Let child sit on potty. Use PROGRAMMING PROCEDURE to encourage child to sit up to maximum of five minutes.	Evaluation
Materials	Potty. Rewards.	
Cue	As appropriate.	
Comment	These activities are preparatory. The child is not expected to master toileting at this time.	
P/S/SH IV 13.4	Seat child on potty at times of day when she is likely to urinate or defecate normally. Reward child if this occurs.	Evaluation
Comment	If child becomes fussy or discouraged, drop it for a few days, and then start again.	
Comment	Don't make this skill a negative problem.	
Comment	Try giving the child a little orange juice ten minutes or so before you hope she will urinate.	
Comment	Running water from the tap often helps child urinate.	
Comment	Child's hand can be held in warm water to help child urinate.	
Comment	See also Chapter 4.	

---

*Denotes self-help skill.

Behavioral Objectives P/S/SH IV 14

P/S/SH IV 14 IDENTIFIES PARTS OF OWN BODY Comment

General
Objective Development of child's self-concept.

Specific
Objective The child will be able to identify parts of his own body.

Activities

P/S/SH IV 14.1 See BODY UNIT ACTIVITIES as outlined in Evaluation
Part I.

P/S/SH IV 14.2 Teach using NAMING PROCEDURE and Evaluation
TOUCH PROCEDURE I.

Behavioral Objectives P/S/SH IV 15

P/S/SH IV 15 EATING AND DRINKING SKILLS Comment
WELL ESTABLISHED*

General
Objective Development of eating and drinking skills.

Specific
Objective The child will be able to eat and drink with some skill.

Activities

P/S/SH IV 15.1 Continue as outlined in P/S/SH IV 8, 9, Evaluation
10, 11, and 12.

P/S/SH IV 15.2 Observe and note successes and mistakes. Evaluation

P/S/SH IV 15.3 Use STP to encourage child's efforts. Evaluation

P/S/SH IV 15.4 Use PROGRAMMING PROCEDURE if nec- Evaluation
essary.

Material Reward.

---

*Denotes self-help skill.

Behavioral Objectives   P/S/SH IV 16

P/S/SH IV 16	ASKS FOR FOOD, TOILET, AND DRINK BY GESTURE OR WORD*	Comment
General Objective	Development of expressive language.	
Specific Objective	The child will use gestures to indicate need for food, drink, or toileting.	

Activities

P/S/SH IV 16.1	Reward child's efforts to indicate needs by gesture. Respond quickly to help.	Evaluation
	Use STP to further encourage the gestures.	
P/S/SH IV 16.2	Use PROGRAMMING PROCEDURES to teach gestures if necessary.	Evaluation
Material	Reward.	

*Denotes self-help skill.

Behavioral Objectives   P/S/SH V 1

P/S/SH V 1	HELPS IN HOUSE IN SIMPLE TASKS	Comment
General Objective	Development of practical life skills.	
Specific Objective	The child will try to help in simple household tasks.	

Activities

P/S/SH V 1.1	Adult helps child find simple tasks to help with around the house.	Evaluation
	Adult helps set the task up in such a way that the child can succeed.	
	Suggested tasks:	
	Carrying silverware to table on a tray, Carrying small sacks, Carrying clothes to the laundry, etc.	

Helping pick up house and yard,
Simple pouring,
Wiping and dusting,
Sorting of laundry, etc.

P/S/SH V 1.2	Adult uses child's love of imitation to teach practical life skills when possible.	Evaluation
P/S/SH V 1.3	LIVING SKILLS PROCEDURE.	Evaluation

    1. Adult thinks through actions involved and writes them in order.

    2. Adult speaks very little while teaching a skill.

    3. Show skills. Let child learn last step first.

    4. Adult does everything up to last step.

    5. Child does last step successfully.

    6. Reward is in the success.

    7. Adult lets child do last two steps.

    8. Adult lets child do last three steps, etc.

    9. Use STP for child's efforts.

Behavioral Objectives	P/S/SH V 2

P/S/SH V 2	PLAYS WITH TOY TELEPHONE, "READS" NEWSPAPER	Comment
General Objective	Development of social skills through play and imitation.	
Specific Objective	The child will enjoy pretending to read newspapers and talk on the telephone.	

Activities

P/S/SH V 2.1	Show child how to talk and dial toy telephone. Use LIVING SKILLS PROCEDURE as outlined in P/S/SH V 1.3.	Evaluation
Material	Toy phone.	

P/S/SH V 2.2	Teach child skills involved in "reading" the newspaper as outlined in LIVING SKILLS PROCEDURE; P/S/SH V 1.3.	Evaluation
Material	Newspaper (small section can be cut from divided center of old paper).	
Cue	Turn the page. Read.	

	Behavioral Objectives	P/S/SH V 3

P/S/SH V 3	CURIOUS AND BUSY	Comment
General Objective	Development of child's concept of the world around him.	
Specific Objective	The child will seem endlessly curious and busy.	

Activities

P/S/SH V 3.1	Exploit the child's curiousity and love of learning. Use the principles of DISCOVERY and MANIPULATION outlined in Part I.	Evaluation
P/S/SH V 3.2	Adult responds to child's effort with smiles, touches, and pleasure.	Evaluation

	Behavioral Objectives	P/S/SH V 4

P/S/SH V 4	USES ME, YOU, I, MINE	Comment
General Objective	Development of child's expressive language and sense of possession.	
Specific Objective	The child will use me, you, I, and mine.	

Activities

P/S/SH V 4.1	Teach as in L V 12.	Evaluation

Behavioral Objectives	P/S/SH V 5

P/S/SH V 5	CALLS SELF BY NAME	Comment
General Objective	The child will know who she is by calling herself by her name.	
Specific Objective	When asked what her name is, the child will respond by saying her own name.	

Activities

P/S/SH V 5.1	When child asks for items, adult says, (child's name) wants _____ .	Evaluation
Cue	Child's name.	
P/S/SH V 5.2	Adult asks "who wants a _____" in response to child's questions.	Evaluation
P/S/SH V 5.3	When referring to things belonging to child, adult says, "This is '(child's name)'s ball, toys," etc.	Evaluation
P/S/SH V 5.4	Adult puts child's name in a variety of places with different size letters, repeats child's name.	Evaluation
P/S/SH V 5.5	Adult uses puppets to play with child. Adult has puppet talk to child, repeat her name, ask her her name, etc.	Evaluation

Behavioral Objectives	P/S/SH V 6

P/S/SH V 6	TEMPER TANTRUMS	Comment
General Objective		To be observed.
Specific Objective		

Activities

P/S/SH V 6.1	Note and observe occurrence of temper tantrums.	Evaluation

P/S/SH V 6.2	Suggestions for extinguishing temper tantrums:	Evaluation

1. Walk away if at all possible.
2. Totally ignore as if it is not going on.
3. Do *not* give child what he wants when he has a temper tantrum.
4. Child will probably not hurt himself seriously.
5. Reward child for better behavior patterns at other times.

Comment	Some parents have shocked little children out of temper tantrums by getting on the floor and kicking and screaming themselves.
Comment	Some parents have shocked little children out of temper tantrums by putting an icy cold wet cloth over child's face or pouring ice water on child.
Comment	Tired or discouraged children often cry or have temper tantrums. Talking, scolding, pleading, or threatening won't help. Try distraction. Plan to endure. Don't become emotionally involved.

	Behavioral Objectives	P/S/SH V 7

P/S/SH V 7	HAS MOTHER-BABY RELATIONSHIP WITH DOLLS	Comment
General Objective	Development of social relations and responsibility through play and imitation.	
Specific Objective	The child will play with baby dolls.	

Activities

P/S/SH V 7.1	Teach child to play with baby dolls. Adult plays with the baby doll. Child imitates.	Evaluation

| *P/S/SH V 7.2* | For teaching specific skills involved see P/S/SH V 1.3. | Evaluation |

| | Behavioral Objectives | P/S/SH V 8 |

P/S/SH V 8	SELF-CENTERED PLAY	Comment
General Objective	Development of play skills.	
Specific Objective	The child will play rough and tumble games, notice other children, but play alone or on parallel level only.	

Activities

P/S/SH V 8.1	Observe and note child's play pattern.	Evaluation
P/S/SH V 8.2	Provide child with opportunities to be near other children.	Evaluation
	Do not force child to play.	
	Child will begin cooperative play at a later phase of development.	

| | Behavioral Objectives | P/S/SH V 9 |

P/S/SH V 9	SEPARATES READILY FROM MOTHER WHEN WELL HANDLED	Comment
General Objective	Development of social trust.	
Specific Objective	The child will separate readily from his mother when well handled.	

Activities

P/S/SH V 9.1	Expose child to situations with many people seen frequently.	Evaluation
P/S/SH V 9.2	If child is still a little afraid of leaving mother, ask friends to come frequently and spend a minute or two with child alone.	Evaluation
	Increase length of time for separation.	
P/S/SH V 9.3	Adult responds to child's effort with smiles, touches, and pleasure.	Evaluation

	Behavioral Objectives	P/S/SH V 10

P/S/SH V 10	NEEDS HELP IN FEEDING, NO LONGER TURNS SPOON BEFORE IT REACHES MOUTH*	Comment
General Objective	Development of feeding skills.	
Specific Objective	The child will stop turning the spoon before it gets to his mouth, but he will still need help in feeding.	

Activities

P/S/SH V 10.1	Help child straighten spoon by adjusting hand position. Reward efforts with STP.	Evaluation
P/S/SH V 10.2	Use LIVING SKILLS PROCEDURE as outlined in P/S/SH V 1.3.	Evaluation
P/S/SH V 10.3	Use PROGRAMMING PROCEDURE if necessary.	Evaluation
Material.	Reward.	

*Denotes self-help skill.

	Behavioral Objectives	P/S/SH V 11

P/S/SH V 11	DRINKS HOLDING SMALL GLASS ONE-HANDED*	Comment
General Objective	Development of feeding skills.	
Specific Objective	The child will be able to hold a small glass in one hand as she drinks.	

Activities

P/S/SH V 11.1	See P/S/SH III 31.	Evaluation
P/S/SH V 11.2	Increase weight and size of cup as child's skill improves.	Evaluation

*Denotes self-help skill.

P/S/SH V 11.3	See P/S/SH V 1.3 for LIVING SKILLS PROCEDURE.	Evaluation
P/S/SH V 11.4	Adult responds to child's effort with smiles, touches, and pleasure.	Evaluation

Behavioral Objectives	P/S/SH V 12

P/S/SH V 12	PULLS ON SIMPLE CLOTHES*	Comment
General Objective	Development of dressing skills.	
Specific Objective	The child will be able to pull on simple garments, find large armholes and put arms into them.	

Activities

P/S/SH V 12.1	Use LIVING SKILLS PROCEDURE as outlined in P/S/SH V 1.3.	Evaluation
Materials	Clothing.	
Cue	As appropriate.	
P/S/SH V 12.2	Jacket may be laid on the floor, arms out, front open.	Evaluation
	Child lays down on jacket, puts in arms, stands up and pulls the jacket on.	

*Denotes self-help skill.

Behavioral Objectives	P/S/SH V 13

P/S/SH V 13	REMOVES UNLACED SHOES*	Comment
General Objective	Development of dressing skills.	
Specific Objective	The child can remove shoes if laces are untied.	

*Denotes self-help skill.

Activities

P/S/SH V 13.1	Use LIVING SKILLS PROCEDURE as out-lined in P/S/SH V 1.3.	Evaluation
Materials	Unlaced shoes.	
Cue	Push.	
	Push it off.	

	Behavioral Objectives	P/S/SH V 14

P/S/SH V 14	REMOVES COAT*	Comment
General Objective	Development of dressing skills.	
Specific Objective	The child can remove his coat.	

Activities

P/S/SH V 14.1	Use LIVING SKILLS PROCEDURE as out-lined in P/S/SH V 1.3.	Evaluation
Materials	Coat, jacket, etc.	
Cue	Take it off.	

*Denotes self-help skill.

	Behavioral Objectives	P/S/SH V 15

P/S/SH V 15	OFTEN DRY DURING NAPS*	Comment
General Objective	Development of toileting skills.	
Specific Objective	The child is often able to stay dry during naps.	

Activities

P/S/SH V 15.1	Do not give child liquids to drink before she goes to sleep.	Evaluation

*Denotes self-help skill.

P/S/SH V	15.2	If child is awakening take her to the potty right away to prevent urinating in pants.	Evaluation
P/S/SH V	15.3	Remain positive even when accidents occur.	Evaluation
P/S/SH V	15.4	Adult responds to child's effort with smiles, touches, and pleasure.	Evaluation
Comment		See also Chapter 4.	

Behavioral Objectives	P/S/SH V 16

P/S/SH V 16		VERBALIZES OR SIGNS TOILET NEEDS CONSISTENTLY*	Comment
General Objective		Development of toileting skills.	
Specific Objective		The child will consistently verbalize or sign when he needs to use the toilet.	

Activities

P/S/SH V	16.1	Reward child's efforts to indicate needs by gesturing. Help him quickly.	Evaluation
P/S/SH V	16.2	Use STP to further encourage the gestures.	Evaluation
P/S/SH V	16.3	Use PROGRAMMING PROCEDURE to teach gestures if necessary.	Evaluation
Material		Reward.	
Comment		See also Chapter 4.	

*Denotes self-help skills.

Behavioral Objectives	P/S/SH V 17

P/S/SH V 17	NOTICES DIFFERENT FACIAL EXPRESSIONS	Comment
General Objective	Development of social awareness.	
Specific Objective	The child will recognize anger, sorrow, and joy by the expressions on faces.	

Activities

P/S/SH V 17.1   See activities to develop this skill as outlined   Evaluation
in L V 9.

	Behavioral Objectives	P/S/SH V 18

P/S/SH V 18	POSSESSIVE WITH TOYS	Comment
General Objective	Development of self-concept.	
Specific Objective	The child does not willingly share his toys.	

Activities

P/S/SH V 18.1	Note and observe this behavior.	Evaluation
Comment	It is normal for children this age to refuse to share.	
	It is not a moral issue now. Ignore it.	
Comment	It is impossible to learn to share until we have learned to possess.	
P/S/SH V 18.2	Let the child learn to share other than by sharing his possessions. Let him carry a tray with refreshments to others.	Evaluation
	Let him help others when he asks.	
P/S/SH V 18.3	Adult responds to child's effort with smiles, touches, and pleasure.	Evaluation

	Behavioral Objectives	P/S/SH V 19

P/S/SH V 19	INSISTS ON SAME ROUTINE	Comment
General Objective	Development of sense of order in the universe.	

Specific Objective	The child will rigidly insist upon routine.	

Activities

P/S/SH V 19.1	Observe and note this behavior.	Evaluation
P/S/SH V 19.2	Use this behavior to help child learn habits of picking up, going to bed, etc.	Evaluation
P/S/SH V 19.3	Use this behavior to have a certain time for stories, unit activities, prayers, etc.	Evaluation
Comment	This behavior can complicate life for adults but is very useful in training children.	

	Behavioral Objectives	*P/S/SH* V 20

P/S/SH V 20	HELPS PUT THINGS AWAY	Comment
General Objective	Development of child's sense of order.	
Specific Objective	The child will help put things away.	

Activities

P/S/SH V 20.1	Have a place for everything.	Evaluation
	Mark shelves or drawers with color codes or pictures so child can match objects to their places.	
P/S/SH V 20.2	Adult responds to child's effort with smiles, touches, and pleasure.	Evaluation
Comment	This is another aspect of a rigid sense of routine and the child may be quite rigid about this sense of order.	

	Behavioral Objectives	*P/S/SH* V 21

P/S/SH V 21	PUSHES TOY—GOOD STEERING	Comment
General Objective	Development of skills in pushing and steering.	

Specific Objective	The child will be able to push and steer toys.	

Activities

P/S/SH V 21.1	See RM IV 7 for practice activities.	Evaluation
P/S/SH V 21.2	Provide the child with ample opportunities to push toys around the home.	Evaluation
	Set up a small obstacle course and encourage child to steer around the objects without touching them.	
Materials	Push toy.	
	Obstacle course.	
Cue	Push the toy—don't touch it against the box, etc.	

	Behavioral Objectives	P/S/SH V 22

P/S/SH V 22	BEGINNING EFFORTS TOWARD COOPERATIVE PLAY	Comment
General Objective	Development of play and social skills.	
Specific Objective	The child will make beginning efforts to play cooperatively with other children.	

Activities

P/S/SH V 22.1	Observe and note child's play pattern.	Evaluation
P/S/SH V 22.2	Provide child with many opportunities to be near other children. Do not force child to play.	Evaluation
P/S/SH V 22.3	When child wants to play, give him a toy or something to bring into the game. This will warm his reception by the other children.	Evaluation
Materials	Toys.	
	Refreshments, etc.	

Behavioral Objectives   P/S/SH V   23

P/S/SH V 23	SELF-FEEDS WITH LITTLE SPILLING*	Comment
General Objective	Development of feeding skills.	
Specific Objective	The child will spill less often when feeding herself.	

Activities

P/S/SH V 23.1	Continue rewarding child's efforts with STP.	Evaluation
P/S/SH V 23.2	Continue using P/S/SH V 1.3 for LIVING SKILLS PROCEDURE	Evaluation
P/S/SH V 23.3	Use PROGRAMMING PROCEDURE for special areas of trouble.	Evaluation
Material	Reward.	
P/S/SH V 23.4	Make charts with stars if child responds to this sort of reward system. Hang chart in obvious place. Invite comments.	Evaluation
P/S/SH V 23.5	During initial training, use foods that will stick to the spoon or fork (mashed potatoes, applesauce, etc.)	Evaluation

---

*Denotes self-help skill.

Behavioral Objectives   P/S/SH V   24

P/S/SH V 24	ATTEMPTS TO BUTTON AND UNBUTTON*	Comment
General Objective	Development of dressing skills.	
Specific Objective	The child will try to button and unbutton buttons that are within reach.	

---

*Denotes self-help skill.

Activities

P/S/SH V	*24.1*	Observe and note child's efforts.	Evaluation
P/S/SH V	*24.2*	Give child opportunities to play with large buttons.	Evaluation
		Be patient with his efforts.	
P/S/SH V	*24.3*	Teach as outlined in LIVING SKILLS PROCEDURE, P/S/SH V 1.3.	Evaluation
P/S/SH V	*24.4*	Give child button frames to work on, encouraging his efforts and guiding his hands to button or rebutton.	Evaluation
Materials		Button frames.	
Comment		Use STP for success, give only as much help as necessary.	

	Behavioral Objectives	P/S/SH V 25

P/S/SH V 25	PUTS ON UNTIED SHOES—OFTEN ON WRONG FEET*	Comment
General Objective	Development of dressing skills.	
Specific Objective	The child will put on untied shoes, but they may be on the wrong feet.	

Activities

P/S/SH V	*25.1*	Adult sits behind child and shows her how to pull on shoe.	Evaluation
Comment		Adult may place shoes almost all the way on the child's foot and allow her to complete the task.	
Comment		Give only as much help as is necessary.	
Comment		Red tape on one foot and on shoe to match can help child with problems of reversed shoes.	

---

*Denotes self-help skill.

Behavioral Objectives	P/S/SH V 26

P/S/SH V 26	TRIES TO BRUSH TEETH*	Comment
General Objective	Development of self-care skills.	
Specific Objective	The child will try to brush his own teeth.	

Activities

P/S/SH V 26.1	Child may first be taught to rub salt and soda on teeth with index finger.	Evaluation
	Show child how to put paste on.brush.	
	Next demonstrate brushing motion while encouraging child to do the same.	
	Continue to demonstrate to child—encourage him.	
Materials	Tray, small toothbrush, paste.	
Cue	Brush your teeth.	
Comment	Reward success with STP.	
P/S/SH V 26.2	Adult provides tray of materials for child to brush with.	Evaluation
	Materials should be small.	

*Denotes self-help skill.

Behavioral Objectives	P/S/SH V 27

P/S/SH V 27	WASHES AND DRIES HANDS*	Comment
General Objective	Development of self-care and hygiene skills.	
Specific Objective	The child will wash and dry her hands.	

*Denotes self-help skill.

Activities

P/S/SH V 27.1	Adult arranges wash area so child can physically succeed at the skill.	Evaluation
	A stool may be necessary, towel and rack within reach.	

P/S/SH V 27.2	Place stool in front of sink.	Evaluation
	Place soap in child's wet hands and move her hands back and forth.	
	Place child's hands under water until all soap is removed.	

Materials   Basin, sink, soap, towel, small stool.

Cue   Wash your hands.
                   Get the soap off, etc.

Comment   Give only as much assistance as necessary.

P/S/SH V 27.3	Repeat 27.2, but let child assume more responsibility for herself.	Evaluation

Comment   Use STP for successful attempts.

Comment   Encourage, praise, and assist child when necessary.

P/S/SH V 27.4	Place towel over child's hands and help her to dry them thoroughly.	Evaluation

Cue   Dry your hands.

Comment   Repeat until child understands the activity. Give only as much help as necessary.

P/S/SH V 27.5	Continue practice until child can do this unassisted.	Evaluation

Behavioral Objectives	P/S/SH V 28

P/S/SH V 28	DRY AT NIGHT IF TAKEN UP AT LEAST ONCE*	Comment
General Objective	Development of toileting skills.	

---

*Denotes self-help skill.

Specific Objective	The child will often be dry all night if taken to the bathroom during the night.

Activities

P/S/SH V 28.1	Adult takes child to bathroom at intervals during the night.	Evaluation
	As time passes, the intervals will be longer.	
Comment	This needs to be done consistently.	
P/S/SH V 28.2	If problem persists, check child at hourly intervals through the night and chart when child is wet.	Evaluation
	Continue for several nights.	
	After pattern emerges, get child up at appropriate time.	
Comment	See also Chapter 4.	

Glossary

INTRODUCTION TO GLOSSARY

The following simple glossary is presented for parent readers who often find the professional jargon confusing and overwhelming. The key words that appear frequently in the textbook have been defined in laymen's terms. Professional and paraprofessional readers may find the glossary useful during parent training sessions.

Attend—to pay attention
Cognition—refers to thinking or using the mind in a purposeful manner
Concept—an idea or thought
Control of Error—try not to make a mistake in the game
Cue—certain words or actions always used to help teach a child
Developmental—process of growing step by step
Environment—the world around us
Expressive Language—being able to express what you want other people to understand
Fine Motor Skills—using the hands and fingers
Gestures—movements of the body that have meaning
Gross Motor Skills—moving large parts of the body
Handicap—a problem that results from an impairment
Impairment—a problem with the body or the senses that makes it hard to learn
Infant—a baby from birth to 15 months
Manipulation—using the hands and fingers to handle objects or materials
Midline—the middle of the body
Mobiles—a form that moves materials hanging from it

Motor—moving parts of the body

Perceptual—activities involving the senses

Procedure—teaching steps

Prone—on the stomach or face down

Receptive Language—understanding what other people communicate to you

Reflexes—an involuntary action

Reinforcement—a reward

Self-Help—learning to take care of yourself, that is, feeding, toileting, etc.

Sensory—using sight, hearing, touch, smell, and taste

Shaping—rewarding the baby when he makes good efforts to do what you are teaching him until, finally, he is able to do the entire thing

Spatial Relationships—the distance between one person and other people and things

Stabiles—a form that doesn't move. Infant's learning materials hang from it.

Supine—on the back or face up

Bibliography

Apgar, V. Perinatal problems and the central nervous system. In U.S. Department of Health, Education, and Welfare, Children's Bureau, *The child with central nervous system deficit.* Washington, D.C.: U. S. Government Printing Office, 1965.

Apgar, V., & Beck, J. *Is my baby all right?* New York: Pocket Books, 1973.

Armstrong, G. T. *The plain truth about child rearing.* Pasadena, California: Ambassador College Press, 1970.

Bayley, N. *Bayley scales of infant development.* New York: Psychological Corporation, 1969.

Beck, J. *How to raise a brighter child.* New York: Trident Press, 1967.

Bender, M., & Valletutti, P. J. *Teaching the moderately and severely handicapped* (Volume I). Baltimore: University Park Press, 1976.

Bloom, B. S. *Stability and change in human characteristics.* New York: Wiley, 1964.

Bluma, S. M., Shearer, M. S., Frohman, A. H., & Hilliard, J. M. *Portage guide to early education.* Portage, Wisconsin: Cooperative Educational Service Agency 12, 1976.

Boyd, R. D. *The Boyd developmental progress scale.* San Bernadino: Inland Counties Regional Center, 1974.

Brazelton, T. B. *Neonatal assessment scale.* Philadelphia: J. B. Lippincott, 1973.

Caldwell, B. M. The importance of beginning early. In J. B. Jordan & R. F. Dailey (Eds.), *Not all little wagons are red.* Arlington, Virginia: Council for Exceptional Children, 1973.

Capute, A. J., Accardo, P. J., Vining, E. P., Rubenstein, J. E., & Harryman, S. *Primitive reflex profile.* Baltimore: University Park Press, 1978.

Cattell, P. *The measurement of intelligence of infants and young children.* New York: Psychological Corporation, 1940.

Connelly, K. *Parental and classroom speech helps for children.* Magnolia, Arkansas: Magnolia School District.

Denenberg, V. H. The effects of early experience. In E. S. Hafez (Ed.), *The behavior of domestic animals* (2nd ed.). London: Baltimore, Tindall, and Cox, 1969.

DeWeerd, J. Introduction. In J. B. Jordan, A. H. Hayden, M. B. Karnes, & M. M. Wood (Eds.), *Early childhood education for exceptional children.* Reston, Virginia: The Council for Exceptional Children, 1977.

Dodson, F. *How to parent.* Los Angeles: Nash, 1970.

Dreikurs, R. *Children the challenge.* New York: Harper and Row, 1967.

Dyer, W. W. *Your erroneous zones.* New York: Avon, 1976.

Erickson, M. T., Johnson, N., & Campbell, F. Relationships among scores on infant tests for children with developmental problems. *American Journal of Mental Deficiency,* 1970, *75,* 102–104.

Fallen, N. H., & McGovern, J. E. *Young children with special needs.* Columbus, Ohio: Charles E. Merrill, 1978.

Final report on evaluation of Handicapped Children's Early Education Program. Columbus, Ohio: Battelle Center for Improved Education, 1976.

Finnie, N. R. *Handling the young cerebral palsied child at home.* 2nd Edition. New York: E. P. Dutton, 1975.

Foxx, R. M., & Azrin, N. H. *Toilet training the retarded.* Champaign: Research Press, 1973.

Frankenburg, W., Camp, B., VanNatta, P. A., & Demersseman, J. A. Reliability and stability of the Denver Developmental Screening Test. *Child Development,* 1971, *42,* 1315–1325.

Frankenburg, W. K., Dodds, J. B., & Fandal, A. *The Denver Developmental Screening Test.* Denver: The University of Colorado Medical Center, 1970.

Fredericks, H. D., Riggs, C., Furey, T., Grove, D., Moore, W., McDonnell, J., Jordan, E., Hanson, W., Baldwin, V., and Wadlow, M. *The teaching research curriculum for moderately and severely handicapped.* Springfield: Charles C Thomas, 1976.

French, J. L. *Pictorial test of intelligence.* Boston: Houghton Mifflin, 1964.

Frost, J. L., & Kissenger, J. B. *The young child and the educative process.* New York: Holt, Rinehart, and Winston, 1976.

Giannini, M., Amler, A., Chused, E., Cohen, H., deLeo, J., Gallerzzo, L., Greenspan, H., Kaessler, H., Haas, M., Michall-Smith, H., O-Hare, D., Swallow, K., Taft, L., Winick, M., & Goodman, L. *The rapid developmental screening checklist.* New York: American Academy of Pediatrics, 1972.

Gillete, H. E. *Systems of therapy in cerebral palsy.* Springfield, Illinois: Charles C Thomas, 1969.

Gorham, K. A. A lost generation of parents. *Exceptional Children,* 1975, *41,* 521–525.

Haeussermann, E. *The developmental potential of preschool children.* New York: Grune and Stratton, 1958.

Hainstock, E. *Teaching Montessori in the home.* New York: Random House, 1968.

Hart, V. *Beginning with the handicapped.* Springfield: Charles C Thomas, 1974.

Hayden, A. H., & Edgar, E. B. Identification, screening, and assessment. In J. B. Jordan, A. H. Hayden, M. B. Karnes, & M. M. Wood (Eds.), *Early childhood education for exceptional children.* Reston, Virginia: The Council for Exceptional Children, 1977.

Hayes, C. *The ape in our house.* New York: Harper, 1951.

Haynes, U. *A developmental approach to casefinding with special reference to cerebral palsy, mental retardation, and related disorders.* Washington, D.C.: U.S. Government Printing Office, 1967.

Hill, N. *Think and grow rich.* New York: Fawcett Crest, 1960.

Hill, P. *Working with parents: A resource guide for family involvement.* New Brunswick, N. J.: Rutgers University Center for Infancy and Early Childhood.

Howell, K. W., Kaplan, J. S., & O'Connell, C. Y. *Evaluating exceptional children: A task analysis approach.* Columbus, Ohio: Charles E. Merrill, 1979.

Hunt, J. McV. *Intelligence and experience.* New York: The Ronald Press, 1961.

Kakalik, J., Brewer, G., Dougharty, L., Fleischauer, P., Genensky, S., & Wallen, L. *Improving services to handicapped children.* Santa Monica, California: The Rand Corporation, 1974.

Kaufman, B. N. *To love is to be happy with.* New York: Fawcett Crest, 1977.

Kazdin, A. E. Assessment of retardation. In J. T. Neisworth & R. M. Smith, (Eds). *Retardation: Issues, assessment, and intervention.* New York: McGraw-Hill, 1978, pp. 271–295.

Kent, L. R. *Language acquisition program for the retarded or multiply impaired.* Champaign: Research Press, 1974.

Kirk, S. A. *Early education of the mentally retarded.* Urbana: University of Illinois Press, 1958.

Knobloch, H., & Pasamanick, B. *Gesell and Amatruda's developmental diagnosis.* Hagerstown, Maryland: Harper and Row, 1974.

Knoblock, H., Pasamanick, B., & Sherard, G. A developmental screening inventory for infants. *Pediatrics,* 1966, *38,* 1095–1108.

Kubler-Ross, E. *On death and dying.* New York: MacMillan, 1969.

Lazarus, R. S. *Psychological stress and the coping process.* New York: McGraw-Hill, 1966.

Leboyer, F. *Loving hands.* New York: Alfred A. Knopf, 1979.

Lerry, J. *The baby exercise book for the first fifteen months.* New York: Pantheon Books, 1973.

Lipton, M. A. Early experience and plasticity in the central system. In T. D. Tjossem (Ed.), *Intervention strategies for high risk infants and young children.* Baltimore: University Park Press, 1976.

Lynch, L., Rieke, J., Soltman, S., Hardman, D., & O'Conor, M. *Preschool profile, model preschool center for handicapped children.* Seattle: University of Washington, 1974.

Mardell, C. D., & Goldenberg, D. S. *Developmental indicators for the assessment of learning.* Highland Park, Illinois: DIAL, Inc., 1975.

Meade, D. E. *Six approaches to child rearing.* Provo: Brigham Young University Press, 1976.

Meier, J. H. Screening, assessment, and intervention for young children at developmental risk. In T. D. Tjossem (Ed.), *Intervention strategies for high risk infants and young children.* Baltimore: University Park Press, 1976.

McCarthy, D. *The McCarthy scales of children's abilities.* New York: Psychological Corporation, 1973.

Montessori, M. *Dr. Montessori's own handbook.* New York: Schocken, 1965.

———— . *The absorbent mind.* New York: Dell, 1967.

Moore, R. S., & Moore, D. N. *School can wait.* Provo: Brigham Young University Press, 1979.

Mori, A. A., & Masters, L. F. *Teaching the severely mentally retarded: Adaptive skills training.* Germantown, Maryland: Aspen Systems Corporation, 1980.

Orem, R. C. *Montessori and the special child.* New York: G. P. Putnam & Sons, 1969.

Painter, G. *Teach your baby.* New York: Simon and Schuster, 1971.

Parad, H. J. Principles of crisis intervention. In H. J. Parad, *Emergency psychiatric care.* Bowie, Maryland: Charles Press, 1975.

Pasanella, A. L., & Volkmor, C. B. *Coming back . . . or never leaving.* Columbus, Ohio: Charles E. Merrill, 1977.

Piaget, J. *The origins of intelligence in children.* New York: International Universities Press, 1952.

Piaget, J., & Inhelder, B. *The psychology of the child.* (Translation by H. Weaver). New York: Basic Books, 1969.

Pickens, C. *Tips for teachers on school parent communication.* Magnolia, Arkansas: Magnolia School District.

Quick, A. D., & Campbell, A. A. *Project Memphis: Lesson plans for enhancing preschool developmental progress.* Dubuque: Kendall/Hunt, 1976.

Rakourtz, E., & Rubin, G. S. *Living with your new baby.* New York: Franklin Watts, 1978.

Sanford, A. R. *Learning accomplishment profile.* Chapel Hill, N.C.: Training Outreach Project, 1973.

Sanford, A. R., with Bailey, D., Johnson, W. C., Leonard, J., & O'Connor, P. D. *A manual for use of the learning accomplishment profile.* Winston-Salem, N.C.: Kaplan School Supply Corp., 1974.

Skeels, H. M., & Dye, H. B. A study of the effects of differential stimulation on mentally retarded children. *Convention proceedings American association on mental deficiency.* 1939, *44,* 114-136.

Steadman, D. J. Early childhood intervention programs. In B. M. Caldwell & D. J. Steadman (Eds.), *Infant education: A guide for helping handicapped children in the first three years.* New York: Walker and Company, 1977.

Terman, L. M., & Merrill, M. A. *Stanford-Binet intelligence scale.* Boston: Houghton Mifflin, 1960.

Thompson, W. R., & Heron, W. The effects of restricting early experience on the problem-solving capacity of dogs. *Canadian Journal of Psychology.* 1954, *8,* 17-31.

Tjossem, T. D. Early intervention: Issues and approaches. In T. D. Tjossem (Ed.), *Intervention strategies for high risk infants and young children.* Baltimore: University Park Press, 1976.

Wabash guide to early developmental training. Boston: Allyn and Bacon, 1977.

Wadsworth, B. J. *Piaget's theory of cognitive development.* New York: David McKay, 1971.

Wechsler, D. *Wechsler preschool and primary scale of intelligence.* New York: Psychological Corp., 1967.

White, B. L. *The first three years of life.* Englewood Cliffs, New Jersey: Prentice-Hall, 1975.

Wolfensberger, W. *The principle of normalization in human services.* Toronto: National Institute on Mental Retardation, 1972.

Index

A

Ability to learn, 4
Absent corneal reflexes, 25
Accardo, P.J., 166
Acceptance
  of others, 96
  as state of grief, 82, 89, 144,
    149-150
Accidents, 9
Accommodation, 15, 16, 18
Actions vs. feelings, 98
Activities
  See also Procedures
  fine motor development, 132
  gross motor development, 131-132
  language enrichment, 378
  life enrichment, 142-144
  listening sensorial, 123, 303, 313
  motor skills, 127, 131-133
  numbered, 38-39
  perceptual, 127, 131-133, 132
  programmed, 39-40
  sensorial, 122-124

smell sensorial, 124, 305
spatial concept, 131
spatial sensorial, 123-124, 304
taste sensorial, 124, 305
timed, 38
touch sensorial, 123-124, 304
visual sensorial, 122, 303
ACTIVITIES PROCEDURE, 325
Administrators, 64, 66
Aesthetics, 150
Age, developmental, 151
Airborne toxins, 8
Alcohol, 8
Anecdotal record, 32
Anger, 82, 85, 87, 106
Animal research, 4-5
Anoxia, 9
Apgar Scale, 25
Arm movement, 11
Assessment, 28-62
  criterion-referenced approach to,
    31-33
  defined, 28
  educational, 29-31

About the Authors

Dr. Allen A. Mori is currently an associate professor of special education at the University of Nevada, Las Vegas. He received his B.A. in government at Franklin and Marshall College, his M.Ed. in special education at Bloomsburg State College, and his Ph.D. in special education at the University of Pittsburgh. Dr. Mori has had extensive experience working with young handicapped children and has consulted with numerous programs providing direct service to young children with special needs. He has also published extensively in the area of special education including a text (with L.F. Masters, Ed.D.) published by Aspen Systems Corporation entitled *Teaching the Severely Mentally Retarded: Adaptive Skills Training.*

Ms. Jane Ellsworth Olive is currently a Child Development Specialist for Southern Nevada Mental Retardation Services providing early intervention for children with special needs. She received her B.A. degree in world religions and philosophy at Mills College. Her training as an educator was acquired at Brigham Young University where she became certified in general education and music. She is a trained Montessori preschool teacher and early childhood special educator. She holds a M.A. degree in anthropology and a M.Ed. in special education from the University of Nevada, Las Vegas. Ms. Olive has been a preschool teacher of the deaf, a parent educator, a developmental specialist, and an active sponsor of programs in parent training in the southwest. Ms. Olive has also authored articles, parent training materials, and other literature in the area of early childhood special education.